MODERN PRUSSIAN HISTORY 1830–1947

We work with leading authors to develop the
strongest educational materials in history,
bringing cutting-edge thinking and best
learning practice to a global market.

Under a range of well-known imprints, including
Longman, we craft high-quality print and electronic
publications which help readers to understand and
apply their content, whether studying or at work.

To find out more about the complete range of our
publishing please visit us on the World Wide Web at:
www.pearsoneduc.com

MODERN PRUSSIAN HISTORY 1830–1947

Edited by

PHILIP G. DWYER

An imprint of **Pearson Education**

Harlow, England · London · New York · Reading, Massachusetts · San Francisco
Toronto · Don Mills, Ontario · Sydney · Tokyo · Singapore · Hong Kong · Seoul
Taipei · Cape Town · Madrid · Mexico City · Amsterdam · Munich · Paris · Milan

Pearson Education Limited
Edinburgh Gate
Harlow
Essex CM20 2JE
England

and Associated Companies around the world.

Visit us on the World Wide Web at:
www.pearsoneduc.com

First published 2001

© Pearson Education Limited 2001

All rights reserved; no part of this publication may be reproduced, stored in a retrieval system, or transmitted in any form or by any means, electronic, mechanical, photocopying, recording, or otherwise without either the prior written permission of the Publishers or a licence permitting restricted copying in the United Kingdom issued by the Copyright Licensing Agency Ltd., 90 Tottenham Court Road, London, W1P 0LP.

ISBN 0-582-29271-9

British Library Cataloguing-in-Publication Data
A catalogue record for this book can be obtained from the British Library

Library of Congress Cataloging-in-Publication Data
Modern Prussian history, 1830–1947 / edited by Philip G. Dwyer.
   p. cm.
   Includes bibliographical references and index.
   ISBN 0-582-29271-9 (pbk.)
   1. Prussia (Germany)--History--1815-1870. 2. Prussia (Germany)--History--1870-3. Conservatism--Germany--Prussia--History. 4. Militarism--Germany--Prussia---History. 5. Prussia (Germany)--History, Military. I. Dwyer, Philip G.

DD424.M64 2000
943'.07--dc21   00-057559

10 9 8 7 6 5 4 3 2 1
04 03 02 01 00

Set by 7 in 11/13 New Baskerville
Produced by Pearson Education Asia Pte Ltd.
Printed in Singapore

CONTENTS

List of maps viii
List of figures ix
List of tables x
List of Prussian monarchs xi
List of Prussian heads of state xii
Preface xiii
About the contributors xvi

Introduction: Modern Prussia – continuity and change
Philip G. Dwyer 1
    Conservatives and the monarchy 4
    The urban and rural environments 8
    Religion in state and society 12
    The state, the army and Prussianism 16

1. Prussia in history and historiography from the nineteenth to the twentieth centuries
Stefan Berger 21
    Modifying and transforming Prussianism in the Kaiserreich 22
    Prussian historiography in the Weimar Republic 24
    Symbiosis or resistance? Prussian historiography under National Socialism ... 27
    The history of Prussia after the end of Prussia: The GDR 29
    The history of Prussia after the end of Prussia: The FRG 33
    Prussian history in the reunified Germany since 1990 38

PART ONE: CONSERVATIVES AND THE MONARCHY

2. Restoration Prussia
Thomas Stamm-Kuhlmann 43
    Defining 'Restoration' 43
    Restoration as the programme of a 'party' 46
    Early anti-revolutionary proclamations 48
    A moderate king, the reform ministers and their adversaries 50
    Romanticism and Restoration ideology 53
    The Restoration Party gains ground 56
    Hunting down the *Zeitgeist* 59

CONTENTS

    Transforming the military into an instrument of royal prerogative 61
    Conclusion 62

3. Revolution and counter-revolution in Prussia, 1840–50
   David E. Barclay 66
       The coming of revolution, 1840–48 67
       The liberal and democratic revolutions, spring – autumn 1848 73
       Counter-revolution and compromise, spring 1848 – January 1850 79
       Aftershocks, 1849–50 83

4. The changing concerns of Prussian conservatism, 1830–1914
   Hermann Beck 86
       The theoretical foundations of Prussian conservatism 88
       The search for a new identity 93
       The development of conservatism in the empire 97

PART TWO: THE URBAN AND RURAL ENVIRONMENTS

5. The Prussian Zollverein and the bid for economic superiority
   Hans-Joachim Voth 109
       Launchpad for take-off or precursor of unification? 110
       German economic development 113
       Prussia's political influence 118
       Prussia's economic power 120
       Conclusion 124

6. The Prussian labour movement, 1871–1914
   Dick Geary 126
       The national context 126
       Varieties of Prussian labour 129
       Epilogue: Prussian labour in the Weimar Republic 143

7. Agrarian transformation and right radicalism: Economics and politics in rural Prussia, 1830–1947
   Shelley Baranowski 146
       Agricultural change and political mobilization, 1830–1914 147
       War-making, urban priorities and the decline of agrarian influence, 1914–33 156
       Unkept promises: Prussian agriculture from the Third Reich to the occupation, 1933–47 163

PART THREE: RELIGION IN STATE AND SOCIETY

8. Religious conflicts and German national identity in Prussia, 1866–1914
   Marjorie Lamberti 169
       Protestant liberals and Catholics in the era of national unification 170
       The *Kulturkampf* 174
       Religious cleavages and antagonisms in public life 178
       The historical consequences 186

9. Prussian Protestantism
   Nicholas Hope 188
      A search for identity and establishment 190
      A fragile new constitutional ('synodal') church order 195
      War and peace 199

PART FOUR: PRUSSIA, THE STATE AND PRUSSIANISM

10. Democratic Prussia in Weimar Germany, 1919–33
    Hagen Schulze 211
       The transformation of the pillars of monarchical authority 214
       The demise of the Prussian state 225

11. Prussia's military legacy in Empire, Republic and Reich, 1871–1945
    Dennis Showalter 230
       A Prussian army or a German one? The imperial years 232
       The Great War: From spiked helmets to steel helmets 238
       Weimar and the Prussian military heritage 240
       The Nazi years: Old wine in a new bottle? 244
       Conclusion 251

12. Prussia, Prussianism and National Socialism, 1933–47
    Brendan Simms 253
       National Socialism and Prussianism 254
       The National Socialist regime and Prussia 261
       Prussia, Prussianism, resistance and the Allies 266

Suggestions for further reading 274
Further research possibilities 295
Index 309

LIST OF MAPS

1. The kingdom of Prussia in 1815 — 306
2. The kingdom of Prussia, 1871–1918 — 307

LIST OF FIGURES

Figure 5.1	Measures of economic performance: Population growth and GDP growth per annum, 1840–60	115
Figure 5.2	Development of export volumes: Change in volume of exports in per cent, 1840–60	117
Figure 5.3	Contribution of customs duties: Percentage of total government revenue	120
Figure 5.4	Composition of investment in Prussia, 1816–40: Annual net investment in millions of 1913 marks	123

LIST OF TABLES

Table 6.1	Participation of workers in strikes	127
Table 6.2	Participation of workers in unions	127
Table 6.3	Expansion of German towns	128
Table 6.4	Population growth in towns of the Ruhr	136

LIST OF PRUSSIAN MONARCHS

Monarchs	*Ruled*
King Frederick William III (1770–1840)	1797–1840
King Frederick William IV (1795–1861)	1840–61
King William I, Emperor William I from 1871 (1797–1888)	1861–88
Emperor Frederick III (1831–88)	1888
Emperor William II (1859–1941)	1888–1918

LIST OF PRUSSIAN HEADS OF STATE

Minister-Presidents | *Governed*

Prince Otto von Bismarck — 23 September/8 October 1862–1 January 1873
Count Albrecht von Roon — 1 January 1873–9 November 1873
Prince Otto von Bismarck — 9 November 1873–20 March 1890
Count Georg Leo von Caprivi — 20 March 1890–22 March 1892
Count Botho zu Eulenburg — 23 March 1892–26 October 1894
Prince Chlodwig zu Hohenlohe-Schillingsfürst — 29 October 1894–15 October 1900
Prince Bernhard von Bülow — 17 October 1900–14 July 1909
Theobald von Bethman-Hollweg — 14 July 1909–13 July 1917
Georg Michaelis — 14 July 1917–1 November 1917
Count Georg von Hertling — 1 November 1917–30 September 1918

Vacancy — From 3 October 1918–11 November 1918

Paul Hirsch (SPD)/Heinrich Ströble (USPD) — 12 November 1918–3 January 1919
Paul Hirsch (SPD) — 3 January 1919–25 March 1919
Paul Hirsch (SPD) — 25 March 1919–26 March 1920
Otto Braun (SPD) — 27 March 1920–10 March 1921
Adam Stegerwald (Centre) — 21 April 1921–5 November 1921
Otto Braun (SPD) — 7 November 1921–23 January 1925
Wilhelm Marx (Centre) — 18 February 1925–20 February 1925
Otto Braun (SPD) — 6 April 1925–24 May 1932

Commissaries

Franz von Papen — 20 July 1932–3 December 1932
Kurt von Schleicher — 3 December 1932–28 January 1933
Franz von Papen — 30 January 1933–7 April 1933
Hermann Göring (NSDAP) — 11 April 1933–23 April 1945

PREFACE

Today most Europeans have forgotten what Prussia once stood for, and certainly many may not even know that it was once a country, and one of the most powerful, in Europe. There are very few symbols left, with the notable exception of the Brandenburg Gate and the Siegesäule in Berlin, to remind people what Prussia represented in the past. A few were deliberately destroyed after the war, notably the royal palace in (significantly East) Berlin, in an attempt to eradicate the last vestiges of the Hohenzollern monarchy. If Prussia is at all conjured up in the popular imagination, then it is likely to be in the image of an officer with a pointed helmet wearing a monocle, and a duelling scar down his face. In Germany, Prussian history is no longer taught as an independent discipline in schools and universities, as it once was (one is more likely to find university courses on Prussia outside of Germany), although this may have more to do with the inability of German historians to come to grips with their past and of the association of Prussia with authoritarianism. In the general public, on the other hand, there seems to be an inherent interest in, if not a certain fascination with, things Prussian. One testimony of this is the resurgence in publications dealing with Prussia that began in the 1970s and which reached a peak in the 1980s. During this time, as Tim Blanning has observed, German publishing companies were printing just about anything that had the magic word 'Prussia' in its title.[1] The resurgence in interest in Prussia was also evident on the occasion of an exhibition in Berlin in 1981 to mark the 750th anniversary of that city's founding. More than 500,000 visitors passed through the doors of the *Kunstgewerbemuseum* where the exhibition was housed; the ghost of Prussia loomed very much in the background.

The interest is understandable. The rise of Prussia to a position of preeminence in the German world at the end of the nineteenth century and the unification of the German states under Prussian hegemony was, without a doubt, one of the most important events in the history of modern Europe:

---

1 See Tim Blanning, 'The Death and Transfiguration of Prussia', *Historical Journal* 29 (1986), 433–59, for a review of the outpouring of works generated by the resurgence in interest in Prussia.

it signified a transfer of power from the periphery (France and Britain) eastwards to the centre where it was to remain until the rise of Stalinist Russia. However, the fact that unification was brought about by the Prussian military led to misconceptions about the nature of the Prussian state that have persisted, even among historians, to the present day.

One of the objectives of this collection of essays is to correct some of those misconceptions. It starts where the preceding volume, *The Rise of Prussia 1700–1830*, leaves off and ends with the official dissolution of the state of Prussia by the Allies in 1947. Just as there is a debate about when Prussia began, so, too, is there one about when it actually came to an end. There is a choice of dates – 1871, 1918, 1932, 1933 or 1947. The working assumption in this collection is that Prussia did not cease to exist as a state after the unification of Germany in 1871 and that, indeed, it continued to exert an influence, even if not always preponderant, for many decades to come. It seemed appropriate, then, to choose the date on which its death was officially pronounced, even though the body had long since expired.

This collection, like its predecessor, sets out to examine a number of major themes in the light of recent research. Once again, while not neglecting traditional political concerns, a deliberate effort has been made to broaden the approach by including chapters dealing with economics, religion, the transformation of the rural and urban environments, and the labour movement. The essays are preceded by a survey of the historical literature that will help the student place Prussian history in perspective. The essays presented here do not, of course, represent the full range of current opinion on Prussian history; each author has a distinctive viewpoint. However, they give some idea where historians of Prussia now stand and where they still might go. It is hoped that the following contributions will lead to a greater understanding of how Prussia evolved during the nineteenth and the first half of the twentieth centuries and how its evolution may have had an impact on the development of Germany during that same period. One has to be careful not to confuse the history of Prussia with the history of Germany, but it is impossible to consider the one without the other, and it is impossible to escape the question of the continuity of Prussia in the evolution of German history.

I am deeply indebted to all the contributors, not only for their unfailing co-operation, but for their generous support for the project. I am particularly grateful to Hamish Scott for his expert guidance during the early stages of planning for this and its companion volume, and especially to Andrew MacLennan, formerly of Addison Wesley Longman, for his unfailing enthusiasm and energy. This project has seen the light of day largely as a result of their faith in it. Thanks also to Heather McCallum for taking up

PREFACE

the project midstream. I should also like to thank Dennis Showalter, John Moses and Narelle Parkinson for their generous help and advice. Renate Oakley helped me with the translations from German into English. I am also happy to acknowledge, at a time when research money is difficult to come by, the support of the Research Management Committee at the University of Newcastle, Australia, and the Deutsche Akademische Austauschdienst for providing financial assistance towards the completion of this and its companion volume. Their generous support has made the project possible.

Philip G. Dwyer

The publishers are grateful to the following for permission to reproduce material in this book:

Figures 5.1 and 5.2: data from tables B1, A5 and F1 from Maddison A., *Dynamic Forces in Capitalist Development: a long-run comparative view*, © Angus Maddison 1991, by permission of Oxford University Press.

Figure 5.3 from *German Industry & German Industrialization: Essays in German Economic & Business History in the 19th and 20th Centuries*, Lee, W.R. (ed.), Routledge, 1991.

Maps 1 and 2 adapted from maps 6 and 7 of *A History of Prussia*, Koch, H.W., Longman, 1996 reproduced with permission of Pearson Education Limited.

ABOUT THE CONTRIBUTORS

Shelley Baranowski is Professor of History at the University of Akron, Ohio and is the author of two books – *The Confessing Church, Conservative Elites and the Nazi State* (Lewiston and Queenstown, 1986), and *The Sanctity of Rural Life. Nobility, Protestantism and Nazism in Weimar Prussia* (New York and Oxford, 1995) – as well as a number of articles on German Protestantism and the Prussian nobility.

David Barclay is Professor of History and Director of the Center for Western European Studies at Kalamazoo College, Michigan. His recent works include *Frederick William IV and the Prussian Monarchy 1840–1861* (Oxford, 1995); and *Anarchie und guter Wille. Friedrich Wilhelm IV und die preußische Monarchie* (Berlin, 1995). He is also the editor (with Elisabeth Glaser-Schmidt) of *Transatlantic Images and Perceptions: Germany and America since 1776* (New York and Cambridge, 1997); and (with Eric D. Weitz) *Between Reform and Revolution: German Socialism and Communism from 1840 to 1990* (New York and Oxford, 1998). He is currently writing a biography of Ernst Reuter and a history of the European revolutions of 1848–50.

Hermann Beck is Associate Professor of History at the University of Miami in Coral Gables, Florida. He has been a Fellow at the Berliner Historische Kommission (1993) and the Institute for Advanced Studies at Princeton (1997–98). He is the author of a number of articles on Prussian history as well as *The Origins of the Authoritarian Welfare State in Prussia: Conservatives, Bureaucracy and the Social Question, 1815–1870* (Ann Arbor, 1995). He is currently preparing a study on the relationship between the German educated elites, the *Bildungsbürgertum* and National Socialism.

Stefan Berger is Professor of History at the University of Glamorgan, Wales. He is the author of *The British Labour Party and the German Social Democrats, 1900–1931* (Oxford, 1994), *The Search for Normality: National Identity and Historical Consciousness in Germany since 1800* (Oxford, 1997) and *Social Democracy and the Working Class in the Nineteenth and Twentieth Century Germany* (London, 1999). He is currently working on a cultural history of German nationalism for Edward Arnold.

ABOUT THE CONTRIBUTORS

Philip Dwyer is Lecturer in Modern European History at the University of Newcastle, Australia. He is the editor of *The Rise of Prussia, 1700–1830* (Harlow, 2000), and author of a number of articles on Prussian foreign policy during the Napoleonic era. He is currently working on a study of Charles-Maurice de Talleyrand for Longman's 'Profiles in Power' series, as well as editing a collection of essays entitled *Napoleon, France and Europe: A Reassessment*.

Dick Geary is Professor of Modern History at the University of Nottingham, co-editor of Contemporary European History, a Fellow of the Alexander von Humboldt Foundation and a Research Associate at the Institute for Research on the European Labour Movement at the Ruhr University (Bochum). He has written several books on the European labour movement as well as *Hitler and Nazism* (London, 1993), and edited with Richard J. Evans, *The German Unemployed: Experiences and Consequences of Mass Unemployment from the Weimar Republic to the Third Reich* (London, 1987). He is currently writing *Hope and Impotence: Aspects of German Labour, 1871–1933* and *Unemployment and the Collapse of the Weimar Republic, 1923–33*.

Nicholas Hope is Reader in History at the University of Glasgow. In 1997–98, he was substitute for the Chair of Contemporary Church History at the University of Heidelberg. He is the author of *German and Scandinavian Protestantism 1700–1918* (Oxford, 1995).

Marjorie Lamberti is the Charles A. Dana Professor of History at Middlebury College, Vermont. She was a fellow at the Institute for Advanced Study in Princeton, NJ, in 1992–93; and at the Woodrow Wilson Center in Washington, DC, in 1997–98. She is the author of *Jewish Activism in Imperial Germany: the Struggle for Civil Equality* (New Haven, 1978), *State, Society, and the Elementary School in Imperial Germany* (New York and Oxford, 1989) and numerous articles on the Jewish community, education and school politics in Germany. Her current research project focuses on educational reform and the politics of culture in Weimar Germany.

Hagen Schulze is Chair of Modern German and European History at the Friedrich Meinecke Institute, at the Freie University of Berlin. His previous books include *Nation-Building in Central Europe* (New York, 1987), *The Course of German Nationalism: From Frederick the Great to Bismarck, 1763–1867* (Cambridge, 1991), *States, Nations and Nationalism: From the Middle Ages to the Present* (Oxford, 1996) and *Germany: A New History* (Cambridge, Mass., 1998).

Dennis Showalter is Professor of History at The Colorado College, Colorado Springs. He is the author of *Railroads and Rifles: Soldiers, Technology and the Unification of Germany* (London, 1975), *What Now? Der Stürmer in the Weimar Republic* (Hamden, Conn., 1982), *Tannenberg: Clash of Empires*

(Hamden, Conn., 1991), and *The Wars of Frederick the Great* (London, 1996), as well as of numerous articles and chapters on war and the German army.

Brendan Simms is College Lecturer and Admissions Tutor at Peterhouse, Cambridge and Newton Sheehy Teaching Fellow in International Relations at the Centre of International Studies, University of Cambridge. He is the author of *The Impact of Napoleon: Prussian High Politics and the Crisis of the Executive, 1797–1806* (Cambridge, 1997), *The Struggle for Mastery in Germany* (London, 1998), and of articles on Weimar Germany and the Third Reich.

Thomas Stamm-Kuhlmann, is Professor of History at the Ernst Moritz Arndt University in Greifswald. He is the author of numerous articles on Prussian history as well as of *König in Preussens großer Zeit, Friedrich Wilhelm III. Der Melancholiker auf dem thron* (Berlin, 1992) and *Die Hohenzollern* (Berlin, 1995), and is editor of the Hardenberg papers, *Tagebücher und autobiographische Aufzeichnungen des Staatskanzlers Karl August von Hardenberg, 1750–1822* (Munich, 1999).

Hans-Joachim Voth is currently an Assistant Professor in the Department of Economics, Universitat Pompeu Fabra, Barcelona, and Associate Director, Centre for History and Economics, King's College, Cambridge. He has held appointments as a research fellow at Clare College, Cambridge and a visiting appointment at Stanford University. His main work is on labour input during the Industrial Revolution. He has also published on the economic history of the Weimar Republic. His two latest contributions are 'German Banking and the Impact of the First World War', in C. Wrigley, ed., *The Impact of the First World War* (London, 1999), and 'Did High Wages or High Interest Rates Bring Down the Weimar Republic?' *Journal of Economic History* 55 (1995).

Introduction: Modern Prussia – continuity and change

PHILIP G. DWYER

The defeat of Germany in the Second World War saw not only the end of the Third Reich, but also the end of Prussia. On 25 February 1947, the Allied Control Council passed Law 46 formally dissolving the state of Prussia and striking it from the map.[1] The elimination of Prussia was part of a conscious effort by the Allies to eradicate from the German collective mind everything that might give rise to a resurgence of militarism and hence to an aggressive, expansionist Germany. The Allies were working on the assumption that Prussia had exerted a preponderant and an insidious influence over Germany and that the link between the two political-cultural entities – the cause of all of Europe's problems and which had led to two world wars – was Prussian militarism. Even before the First World War, Europe's statesmen in Paris, St Petersburg and especially in London believed that, just as Prussia had striven to become a great power in the eighteenth century, so Germany aspired to become a world power in the late nineteenth century. British observers regarded the kaiser's peculiar brand of foreign policy (*Weltpolitik*) to be nothing more than 'a variation on an aggressive basic theme' of Prussian-German foreign policy.[2] This view was reiterated in 1907 by the foreign office official, Sir Eyre Crowe, in a

---

1 Tim Blanning, 'The Death and Transfiguration of Prussia', *Historical Journal* 29 (1986), 442, has pointed out that Prussia is perhaps the only state, ever, to have been abolished 'on the moral grounds that it was a menace to humanity'. My thanks to Christopher Clark, Dick Geary and Wayne Reynolds for their comments on various drafts of this chapter.
2 Cited in Gregor Schöllgen, 'Germany's foreign policy in the age of imperialism', in Gregor Schöllgen (ed.), *Escape into War? The Foreign Policy of Imperial Germany* (Oxford, 1990), pp. 130–1. As Klaus Hildebrand, *German Foreign Policy from Bismarck to Adenauer: The Limits of Statecraft* (London, 1989), p. 22, has pointed out, however, the tendency of British statesmen to view

famous memorandum in which he argued that Germany was the heir of Prussia whose rise to power was based on 'systematic territorial aggrandisement achieved mainly at the point of the sword, the most important and decisive conquests being deliberately embarked upon by ambitious rulers or statesmen [...]'.[3] At the start of the First World War, the British government under Asquith declared the elimination of Prussian militarism to be an important war aim.[4] This type of thinking among European statesmen persisted right up to the 1940s. Prussian virtues, which were still assessed positively in Germany between the wars, had very much assumed negative qualities in the West where they became synonymous with unthinking obedience, contempt for human life, humourlessness, militarism and inhuman severity. During the Second World War, the Allies mistakenly believed that Prussianism, German militarism and Nazism were one and the same thing. Hence the decision to eradicate Germany's 'Prussian roots' in the post-war settlement.

The Allies could have saved themselves the trouble. Not only was Prussia long since dead in the minds of many Germans, but their views were based upon popular misconceptions still prevalent today, even among some modern German historians. The Prussian state may have been preponderant in the German Reich in terms of land mass and population, but its political and cultural influence had diminished considerably by the time the nineteenth century had drawn to a close. Nevertheless, it is important to determine the extent to which Prussia continued to influence the course of German and, by extension, European history after 1871. Any effort to do so, however, immediately runs into all sorts of problems, not the least of which is defining limits: what was Prussia and what was it to be 'Prussian'?

The former is much easier to answer than the latter; a state, after all, is defined by its political boundaries. This, however, does not help determine who within those boundaries identified with the state. At certain stages of its history, Prussia acquired, not always through expansion, substantial ethnic and religious minorities who felt no particular emotional or political attachment to the state. After the annexation of Polish territory in the eighteenth century, for example, one in four 'Prussians' was Polish. After the

---

Prussia and Germany negatively has to be seen within the context of colonial, naval and international tensions.
3   Imaneul Geis, *German Foreign Policy, 1871–1914* (London, 1976), pp. 194–5.
4   Hans Mommsen, 'The Prussian conception of the state and the German idea of Empire: Prussia and the German Empire in recent German history', in Mommsen, *Imperial Germany 1867–1918. Politics, Culture, and Society in an Authoritarian State* (London, 1995), pp. 41–56 (here p. 44).

Seven Days' War against Austria in 1866, Prussia annexed the North German States – Hanover, Hessen-Cassel, Hessen-Nassau, Schleswig-Holstein and Frankfurt – that had taken Austria's side. Following German unification in 1871, Prussia absorbed two new provinces – Mecklenburg-Schwerin and Strelitz – thereby becoming the largest single state in the new German Empire with two-thirds of the territory and about two-thirds of the population. In some instances, there was a transfer of formal allegiance to the Prussian monarchy. The majority of people who went to the polls in Hanover, for example, voted in favour of annexation in 1867 (although some, like the Catholic statesman Ludwig Windthorst, believed Prussia's annexation to be an unlawful act of force). However, there was certainly never any cultural identification with the new state and many of Prussia's new inhabitants, both Germans and non-Germans (Poles, Danes, Lithuanians), felt distinctly hostile towards Berlin and everything they associated with the 'Prussian system' – duty, justice, order, discipline, obedience, punctuality and unconditional loyalty to the throne. This hostility was sometimes of a confessional nature – the minority of Catholics in Prussia felt no particular liking towards the Protestant Hohenzollerns – but it was more often than not based upon regional-cultural differences.

The other side to this coin was that the ruling elite in Prussia had always been fearful that their country would somehow be swamped by the absorption of new lands and people and that it would thereby lose its inherent 'Prussian-ness'. At the end of the eighteenth century, for example, the problem of how to assimilate the Polish minorities over which Prussia ruled was a major preoccupation. The same problem reappeared after the wars of German unification. One of the reasons why Bismarck did not annex Austria after the war of 1866 was the fear that Prussia and its traditions would be swallowed up in a greater Germany.[5] King William I hesitated to adopt the imperial mantle in 1871 because he was afraid that Prussia would lose its integrity. He was heard to remark on the eve of his coronation at Versailles: 'Tomorrow will be the unhappiest day of my life. For we will be carrying the kingdom of Prussia to its grave.'[6] If he acquiesced, it was to save Prussia's essence, not to transform it into a united Germany. The ceremony marking the foundation of the Reich was, moreover, a purely Prussian military and aristocratic act: the date chosen, 18 January 1871, was the anniversary of the crowning of the first Prussian

---

5 This is suggested in David Calleo, *The German Problem Reconsidered: Germany and the World Order, 1870 to the Present* (Cambridge, 1978), p. 10. One also has to take into consideration the fear that such a state would most likely be ungovernable and that it would oblige the rest of Europe to act against it.

6 Cited in Sebastian Hoffner, *The Rise and Fall of Prussia* (London, 1980), p. 137.

king in 1701. During the Kaiserreich, the court of Berlin remained essentially a Prussian court, with Prussian rituals and ceremonies, often of a military nature. Prussian symbols were never transformed into national symbols.[7] Kaiser William II later diverged somewhat from this pattern and was as a result criticized by conservatives for playing too much the emperor and for neglecting his role as King of Prussia.[8]

All of this is to say that 'Prussia' was a composite, artificial construct which contained a wide variety of social and political formations and which was constantly being reshaped and redefined. Consequently, any attempt to determine what elements of the 'Prussian system' continued to influence the development of the German Reich after 1871, and what elements fell by the wayside, is problematic. In the context of a volume of essays that examines a number of important themes in Prussian history over long periods of time, it is nevertheless worth attempting a few generalizations. What seems clear is that many of the problems which burdened the German Empire were due to the social and political tensions which it inherited from Prussia.[9]

The following essays focus on a number of those social, religious and political tensions which helped define the course of Prussian and, by extension, German history: the evolving relationship between the nobility and the monarchy; the struggle between liberal reformers (both political and economic) and conservatives; the confessional tensions between the state, Catholics and Protestants; the question of the predominance of the Prussian military; and the continued influence of 'Prussianism' in the German Reich.

Conservatives and the monarchy

An area that has recently become the focus of attention in German history is the nature of conservatism and how it reacted to the various challenges it faced throughout the nineteenth and the first half of the twentieth centuries.[10]

---

7 Isabel V. Hull, 'Prussian Dynastic Ritual and the End of the Monarchy', in Carole Fink, Isabel V. Hull and MacGregor Knox, eds, *German Nationalism and the European Response, 1890–1945* (Norman, Okla., 1985), pp. 18–19.
8 Ibid., pp. 28–29 and 40; Gordon Craig, *The End of Prussia* (Madison, Wis., 1984), pp. 65–7.
9 This, in any event, is the argument first put forward by Hans-Ulrich Wehler, *The German Empire 1870–1914* (Leamington Spa, 1985).
10 See the collection of essays in Larry Eugene Jones and James N. Retallack, eds, *Between Reform, Reaction and Resistance. Studies in the History of German Conservatism from 1789 to 1945* (Providence and Oxford, 1993).

The first three essays in this collection reflect that growing interest and deal with: the development of a conservative ideology that was specifically Prussian; the manner in which the nobility reacted to and dealt with the reform impetus of the Prussian state; and the changing nature of the relationship of the nobility to the monarchy. As Thomas Stamm-Kuhlmann reminds us, conservative ideology, in Prussia as in the rest of Europe, was initially born out of a reaction to the French Revolution. Throughout the eighteenth century, the centralizing initiatives of the Prussian state had always had to contend with elements of the Prussian nobility and, to a lesser extent, the traditional middle classes, who made a self-conscious effort to maintain their old privileges and to preserve their social position.[11] This was also the case during the period between 1807 and 1822 when the Prussian monarchy, responding to the defeat of its army at the hands of Napoleon in 1807, introduced widespread changes, not only to the army, but also to agriculture and the state administrative apparatus. The state and those conservatives in favour of reform had to fight an uphill battle against the majority of the nobility who, more often than not, resisted these changes every step of the way. By 1822, with the death of one of the key reformers – Prussia's state chancellor, Karl August von Hardenberg – the Reform Movement had for all intents and purposes lost its impetus.

Even from this brief overview, one can see that the Prussian nobility by no means represented a monolithic bloc, and that there were different strands of conservatism in Prussia which constantly jostled with each other, and with the monarchy, for political influence. In short, it is misleading to speak of conservatives in a generic sense. As a general rule, the Junker estate owners in East Elbia were attached to traditional, local or provincial institutions and expressed a deep aversion to monarchical centralism in all its forms. They were never fully reconciled with the 'governmental' conservatives who increasingly occupied a number of key positions in the Prussian state after the 1820s and who wanted to introduce change gradually.[12] In the post-Napoleonic period, traditional conservatives formed what Stamm-Kuhlmann calls the 'Restoration Party', opposed to the 'Party of Movement' made up of liberals, democrats and radical reformers. The eventual ascendancy of the 'Restoration Party' at the court of Berlin was one of the reasons why the Reform Movement failed, or at least why

---

11 Robert Berdahl, *The Politics of the Prussian Nobility: The Development of a Conservative Ideology 1770–1848* (Princeton, NJ, 1988), esp. chs 6 and 7. For details of the Reform Movement, see Matthew Levinger, 'The Prussian reform movement and the rise of enlightened nationalism', in Philip G. Dwyer (ed.), *The Rise of Prussia, 1700–1830* (Harlow, 2000), pp. 259–77.
12 David Barclay, *Frederick William IV and the Prussian Monarchy 1840–1861* (Oxford, 1995), pp. 20–1.

many of the reforms were prevented from being successfully carried through.

In the face of threats to their privileges, conservatives began to think about their position in state and society and began to express their ideas in political pamphlets and newspapers. They also began to meet in small discussion groups that were precursors to later nineteenth-century conservative political parties. This is the subject of both Hermann Beck and David Barclay's contributions. One such group was founded by a number of pious young noble officers who, at the end of the Napoleonic wars, began to meet once a week at the tavern of an innkeeper named Mai. The group thus became known as the *Maikäferei* (which can very loosely be translated as the Maybug Society). Their discussions on Romantic Christian poetry were interspersed with anti-revolutionary politics. Although the group was fairly short-lived, many of its members went on to occupy powerful and influential positions in the government of Frederick William IV. Some of its members, like the brothers Leopold and Ernst Ludwig von Gerlach and Joseph Maria von Radowitz, went on to found the first conservative weekly, the *Berliner Politisches Wochenblatt*, which was to have such an important influence on the development of Prussian conservative attitudes towards the monarchy and the emerging modern bureaucratic state.[13] It also promoted a continuity in conservative thought that really reached full momentum only during the Kaiserreich. Conservatives in the 1830s and 1840s, in other words, were doing exactly the same thing as liberals, radicals and democrats; they were organizing themselves into associations, clubs and societies and using modern forms of media – political pamphlets, brochures and newspapers – to formulate and express their ideas. They had gone on the offensive in an attempt to articulate an ideology that would lead to the 'restoration' of traditional structures of authority in the state and which served as the theoretical basis for Prussian conservatism.

If the Prussian landed nobility traditionally resisted and rejected the centralizing initiatives of the state in favour of their own regional and local privileges, the Revolution of 1848 changed all that. There is no need to go into the details of the 1848 Revolution – the subject of David Barclay's chapter – except to say that in the wake of the dramatic series of events which culminated in a constitutional monarchy, conservatives had to rethink the place of the king in Prussian society and their relationship to the monarchy (both David Barclay and Hermann Beck underline this point).

---

13 Berdahl, *The Politics of the Prussian Nobility*, pp. 258–63; Hermann Beck, 'Conservatives and the Social Question in Nineteenth-Century Prussia', in Jones and Retallack (eds), *Between Reform, Reaction and Resistance*, pp. 67–74.

INTRODUCTION: MODERN PRUSSIA

The Prussian nobility as a whole became more conscious of its own class interests and began to look upon the institution of the monarchy as indispensable for the maintenance of authority (so, too, did many members of the middle class). Conservative ideology began to associate itself with the defence of the status quo. A new newspaper came on the scene, the *Neue Preußische Zeitung* – nicknamed the *Kreuzzeitung* because an iron cross was the centrepiece of its masthead – which became an energetic defender of the conservative cause (discussed in Hermann Beck's contribution). Conservatives also formed societies and associations, such as the Society for King and Fatherland (*Verein für König und Vaterland*), in an effort to organize themselves throughout the monarchy. By 1849, these societies had attracted as many as 60,000 members.[14] More importantly, perhaps, the constitution obliged conservatives to organize parliamentary groupings which were the forerunners of conservative political parties and which dominated the Prussian *Landtag* until about 1858, when a moderate liberal government was appointed by William I.

If some conservatives had come to terms with constitutional monarchy, they were thrown back onto the defensive when Bismarck came on the scene in 1862 and started actively pursuing liberal/nationalist policies. Conservatives were ultimately opposed to any kind of German national unification, or even to Prussian aggrandizement for that matter, on the grounds that Prussia would lose its identity and that they would lose their regional privileges. Very few conservative deputies in the Prussian *Landtag*, along with Bismarck, realized the potential of appealing to the people for mass support against the liberal majority in parliament. Deputies like Hermann Wagener, editor of the *Kreuzzeitung*, were the exception. Convinced that the masses were essentially loyal to the monarchy, he even went so far as to advocate the introduction of universal manhood suffrage, something that not even liberals had seriously contemplated before then.

The policies pursued by Bismarck were, then, both before and after the unification of Germany, profoundly anti-conservative. Conservatives were, after all, opposed to any extension of state power and this is exactly what Bismarck was attempting to do. Many conservatives were not even in favour of the *Kulturkampf*, since they saw no reason why the state should get involved in disputes about religion and public education. As a result of their inability to come to terms with the new forces in Prussian-German society, conservatives were well on their way to becoming a spent force in politics. It took some time before they regrouped and found a new identity and they did so largely through the creation of the German Conservative Party

---

14 Barclay, *Frederick William IV*, pp. 172–3.

(*Deutsch-Konservative Partei*) in 1876 that gave new life to their cause and enabled conservatives, taking advantage of the three-tiered electoral system introduced by Bismarck, to be overrepresented in both the German *Reichstag* and the Prussian *Landtag*.[15] The other conservative party that dominated Imperial Germany was the Free Conservative Party (*Freikonservative Partei*, renamed the *Reichspartei* after 1871). They were not mass parties in the modern sense, but were essentially made up of notables. They did, however, have close ties to other mass-based associations like the Agrarian League and the Navy League. It was only with the outbreak of revolution in 1918 that the conservative parties lost their power base, and were replaced by a genuinely modern mass party, the German National People's Party (DNVP).

The urban and rural environments

If conservative political thought evolved during the course of the nineteenth century, it nevertheless had difficulty keeping pace with the tremendous changes taking place in both the urban and rural landscapes. The groundwork for an industrial revolution was laid in the 1840s and is no better illustrated than by the increase in the length of railway laid: in 1840, there were 185 kilometres of railway in Prussia; by 1847, there were 1,424.[16] There were, of course, similar patterns of growth in the industries needed to support this industrial infrastructure. For example, the number of people employed in coal mines in the Ruhr valley between 1850 and 1860 doubled during that period, while coal production rose by 183 per cent.[17] Also, the population of Berlin increased from 200,000 in 1816 to 408,000 in 1846,[18] supplying a source of labour to the city's booming machine-building industry.

These growth patterns are relatively well known and any number of textbooks cite figures to show the amount of iron and wheat produced by Prussia, usually in comparison with the amounts produced by the Austrian Empire, in order to demonstrate Prussia's clear economic and industrial ascendancy. Until very recently, it was thought that the industrialization of Prussia was one of the key factors that helped determine the outcome of the

---

15 The three-class electoral law was an element of the Prussian constitution of 1850. It grouped voters by the amount of direct taxes they paid so that those who paid one third of Prussia's direct taxes elected as many deputies as those who paid the second and those who paid the last third.
16 Berdahl, *The Politics of the Prussian Nobility*, pp. 306–8.
17 James J. Sheehan, *German History, 1770–1866* (Oxford, 1989), p. 740.
18 Barclay, *Frederick William IV*, p. 102.

struggle between Prussia and Austria for the mastery of Germany. This view is based on the assumption that industrial might can be transferred into military might. However, Joachim Voth, in his chapter on the Prussian Customs Union, or Zollverein, has a very different interpretation.

There are a number of factors in this argument, Voth maintains, which need reassessing. He points out that, in the thirty or so years in which it existed, the Zollverein did not come even close to creating a unified economy – there were still different weights and measures and currencies in operation, and economic co-operation was sometimes more common with non-member states than between some member states. Even if there had been economic union, there was no guarantee that political union would automatically follow. It should be remembered that most member states of the Zollverein fought not with Prussia but against it on the side of Austria during the war of 1866. Even more importantly for the manner in which historians view the unification process, Voth argues that the Customs Union not only did not have a positive impact on the economic development of Germany, but that it did not bring any significant overall benefits to the economy of Prussia (even if individual provinces and industries did gain). In other words, there is no causal connection between the Zollverein and the founding of the Reich in 1871. Voth even throws doubt on the argument that the wars of German unification were decided by the manner in which the Prussian army harnessed the new technologies at its disposal (railway transportation, the telegraph, heavy artillery, modern explosives, the rifle).[19] The battle of Königgrätz was fought and won, he points out, before the Prussian supply trains could catch up with the troops.

The implications of Voth's findings are clear. If economic preponderance, industrial might and even logistics did not play a significant role in the struggle between Austria and Prussia for the mastery of Germany, then the focus of attention must shift from economics back to politics and statecraft, away from the rise of a national market and back to the person of Bismarck and the performance of the Prussian military in the field.

If historians have had a tendency to downplay the importance of the Zollverein in recent times, there can be no doubt that Prussia's rapid industrialization transformed the country from a predominantly rural to an increasingly urban society. The labour movement in Prussia – the subject of Dick Geary's contribution – was an important and significant part of this urbanization and industrialization process. In Berlin, the movement became

---

19 Dennis Showalter, *Railroads and Rifles. Soldiers, Technology and the Unification of Germany* (London, 1975), best explains how this was done.

one of the largest in Germany. In part, it was a consequence of the rapid rise in population; Berlin increased from about 800,000 in 1871 to over 2 million in 1919. The increase in population brought with it an appalling housing situation (perhaps worse in Germany than any other advanced European country) and all the social consequences that resulted from promiscuous living in tenement buildings. This kind of living had important implications, as Dick Geary demonstrates, for the socialization of the Berlin worker. Since civic buildings were not available to working-class associations in the urban centres, meetings often took place in the only public spaces that were available to them – the pub. There was, then, a close link between drinking and the development of a working-class consciousness. But it was above all the repressive and discriminatory nature of the Prussian state which incited workers to organize. Anti-socialist laws, for example, tended to be implemented more severely in Prussia than elsewhere, creating a reaction of solidarity among workers that had the opposite effect to what the German government intended. It is well known that during the Kaiserreich, despite or rather because of repressive measures against it, the German Social Democratic Party (SPD), the first mass political organization in history, grew into the largest socialist party in the world with over 1 million members by 1914.

Berlin, however, was only one of many Prussian towns. The labour movement in Prussia, as Geary's contribution shows, was incredibly diversified with regional, confessional and ethnic differences that reflected the eclectic make-up of the Prussian state. In the Ruhr, essentially a coal mining area around which developed a steel industry, levels of industrialization were particularly high, but the penetration of free trade unions and the SPD were weak. There are a number of factors that help explain this development, but the strength of Catholicism in this region is perhaps the most important. Unlike Protestants in Berlin, Prussian Catholics developed their own workers' associations (sports clubs, for example) which had almost as many members as their SPD counterparts (500,000 and 600,000 respectively). They also developed 'Christian Unions' which were remarkably successful in recruiting Catholics, not only in the Ruhr, but also in other Catholic regions like the Rhineland and Silesia.

Confessional differences within the labour movement were exacerbated by ethnic differences. During the Kaiserreich, more than 300,000 Poles migrated to the Ruhr. On the whole, relations between Germans and Poles were tense, not only in the Ruhr but also in Silesia, although there were occasions when the two groups united in actions against their employers. There is also the question of the female workforce, which was often unskilled, where wages were even lower and where hours were longer than those of their male counterparts. The official rhetoric of the SPD embraced the equality of the sexes, but in reality, as Dick Geary points out, many of its male members saw women in the workforce as a threat to their jobs. Before the First World War, the Prussian and German labour movements were overwhelmingly male, Protestant and urban.

As industry expanded, and Prussia underwent a population explosion that drifted towards the cities, the agrarian elites faced increasing challenges to their political prominence. The agricultural depression of the 1870s and 1880s exacerbated the situation in spite of tariffs put in place to act as a protective barrier to privilege the Prussian landed elite of East Elbia. It was this very agricultural protectionism that was long considered responsible for sustaining authoritarianism in Germany after 1871 (since protectionism was thought to have impeded agrarian modernization) by keeping in power a landlord class that ultimately played a substantial part in the downfall of the Weimar Republic and the installation of Adolf Hitler. However, and this is partly the object of Shelley Baranowski's essay, as a result of recent research, a much more complex picture has emerged in which patterns of authority and subordination between Prussian Junkers and their peasants, and between Junkers and the state, were more differentiated than was previously believed.

We now know, for example, that estate owners in Prussia were finding it increasingly difficult to maintain their position under the empire. Their influence was further diminished by the consequences of the First World War, which had the effect of weakening the rural economy. As well, a considerable amount of Prussia's agricultural land was transferred to Poland as a result of the Treaty of Versailles, a factor that helps account for the steep decline in grain production from pre-war levels during the Weimar period. Furthermore, during that same period, estate owners were simply unable to maintain their domination of the countryside in the face of the rise of the Nazis.

The Nazis proved remarkably successful in attracting votes in rural areas, but they were, in fact, sowing seeds on fertile ground. Both the landed elite and the peasantry had been represented in Imperial Germany by a powerful right-wing association, the Agrarian League, which had drawn Protestant estate owners into mass politics for the first time. The Agrarian League also attracted mass peasant membership who campaigned for the tariff protection so crucial for Junker survival. Prussian (and German) peasants did so simply because they, too, benefited on the whole from tariff protection. Although the League's influence waned after the First World War, it was replaced by other associations with similar political agendas, like the Rural League, which forged strong links with the right-wing German National People's Party (DNVP).

All of this means that there was already a tradition of right-wing radical politics in Prussian rural areas, especially in the Protestant east, long before the Nazis made their appearance. The land-owning elite had a visceral dislike of the Republic, while the peasants blamed successive Weimar governments for the economic difficulties they experienced in post-war Germany (Baranowski makes a distinction between elite and populist anti-republicanism). The end result was that the Protestant countryside became increasingly politically radicalized during the course of the 1920s and 1930s, something which benefited principally the Nazis.[20] The Nazis, of course, did not come to power because of support in the countryside, but, as Shelley Baranowski points out, the support of conservative groups remained essential in their rise to power.

Religion in state and society

One of the bulwarks of conservative politics in Prussia, as elsewhere in Europe, was religion. Christopher Clark has pointed elsewhere to the importance of the Pietist movement in the eighteenth century to an understanding of Prussian government and society.[21] The kings of Prussia had always exercised a great deal of authority in church affairs, and there had always been a strong tie between the monarchy and not only established churches, but revivalist movements. Without having the status of the monarchs of England, who were also heads of the Church of England, the Prussian kings were nevertheless considered to be supreme bishops of the Protestant churches in their domains. It was during the Reform Era, under Frederick William III's aegis, that the Prussian monarchy attempted to gain an even greater say in the workings of the Protestant churches by organizing them into a state church.

This is part of the material covered in the chapter on Prussian Protestantism by Nicholas Hope. At the king's behest, and despite a certain amount of friction, Lutheran and Reformed – that is, Calvinist – denominations joined together in 1817 to form a single Evangelical state church (*Landeskirche*), which was brought under the authority of the newly created Ministry of Religious Affairs (*Kultusministerium*).

---

20 See also Shelley Baranowski, 'Convergence on the right: agrarian elite radicalism and Nazi populism in Pomerania, 1923–33', in Jones and Retallack (eds), *Between Reform, Reaction and Resistance*, pp. 407–32.
21 See Christopher Clark, 'Piety, politics and society: Pietism in eighteenth-century Prussia', in Dwyer (ed.), *The Rise of Prussia, 1700–1830*, pp. 68–88.

It was the Prussian United Church of 1817 that dominated Protestant Germany after 1867, although there was never anything like a national German Protestant church. Protestant Prussia after 1871 remained a loose association of provincial churches with no clearly defined relations with the Reich; Bismarck made no attempt to absorb the various Protestant churches into the Old Prussian Union. The Prussian Protestant church leadership was, nevertheless, totally committed to the monarchy and even to the nation and was one of the mainstays of the war effort between 1914 and 1918. Nicholas Hope goes so far as to say that the German Protestant churches, but especially Prussia's, became the mouthpiece of the German High Command.

The close-knit relationship between the Church and the monarchy was necessarily called into question with Kaiser William II's abdication in 1918; it obliged the Protestant church in Prussia to redefine itself. Prussia-Germany had lost the war (God was obviously not on its side), it had lost its king, and it had lost much of its eastern Lutheran territories through the Treaty of Versailles in 1919. Under these conditions, the Protestant church was hardly likely to look kindly upon the new Republic. Moreover, the loss of its eastern territories introduced a new element into its thinking, that of the danger of atheist Bolshevism that conservative Germans associated with the barbaric Russian hordes. This may in part help explain why the Protestant church, which had never worked well with the Republic, found it in its heart to bless the opening of the Nazi parliament in March 1933. The Nazi message, after all, was essentially anti-Bolshevik.

If the Protestant churches and the Prussian state, on the whole, maintained a close relationship throughout the nineteenth and into the twentieth centuries, one cannot say the same for other religious minorities in Prussia, especially Catholics. Catholics had traditionally been tolerated in Prussia. After the annexation of Silesia (1740) and Poland (1772, 1793, 1795) under Frederick II and Frederick William II, Catholics became the largest religious minority in the Prussian state. With the annexation of Westphalia and the Rhineland at the end of the Napoleonic wars, Prussia became more than one-third Catholic. Although the Protestant nature of the state was never modified (the Prussian administration, even in the Rhineland, was exclusively Protestant), care was taken not to slight or antagonize Catholics; it would have been politically foolish to do so. Moreover, Prussian kings encouraged immigration, which included religious minorities, as a means of filling Prussia's sparsely populated lands. The Prussian kings practised religious toleration, then, but more out of political necessity than out of some sort of enlightened principle.

Despite this, tensions between Catholics and Protestants existed and began to appear as early as the 1820s in disputes about rearing children, mixed marriages and education in a way that foreshadowed the *Kulturkampf* (which literally means the 'struggle of civilizations') of the 1870s. Sometimes, as both David Barclay and Nicholas Hope point out in their chapters, regional tensions at the beginning of the nineteenth century arising between predominantly Protestant Prussia and the largely Catholic Rhineland were subsequently transformed into confessional tensions.[22] Religious frictions were also tinged with issues of race and nationality since, according to Nicholas Hope, Prussian Protestants usually associated Catholicism with the country's Polish minority. During the 1840s, however, largely as a result of Frederick William IV's efforts to sink religious differences and to recognize Catholic self-government, the position of Catholics in Prussia was greatly improved.

The unification of Germany under Prussian domination drastically altered the political balance of the confessions. Catholics suddenly found themselves relegated to the periphery of the new German Empire – in the west, south and east – while Protestants remained dominant in the north and centre. Unification also raised questions about what it was to be a 'normal' German citizen. The answer came back resoundingly from conservatives like Bismarck: one had to be Protestant and Prussian, otherwise one was suspected of being an 'enemy' of the Reich. The defeat of Catholic France and Austria in the wars of unification was widely hailed in Germany as the victory of Protestantism over Catholicism. A German-Protestant continuity was set up in contradistinction to the Catholic tradition of the old Holy Roman Empire.[23] Protestantism, in other words, became associated with German nationalism, while the Catholic Church was seen as being partly the representative of a foreign power – that is, the Vatican – and partly the representative of regional and national minorities (Poles, Alsatians, and even Bavarians) who were reluctant to admit the legitimacy of the new state.[24] Catholics, both in Prussia and in Germany, were largely opposed to any form of unification brought about by war.

This was just one of the many reasons outlined by Marjorie Lamberti, in her chapter on religious conflict and national identity in Prussia, that led Protestant liberals and nationalists to believe Catholics were opposed to national unification. Catholics thus became marginalized in the new Reich. Cultural uniformity was the prerequisite, she argues, for the building of a

---

22 See also Simon Hyde, 'Roman Catholicism and the Prussian State in the early 1850s', *Central European History* 24 (1991), 111–19.
23 Elisabeth Fehrenbach, 'Images of Kaiserdom: German Attitudes to Kaiser Wilhelm II', in John C. G. Röhl and Nicholas Sombart (eds), *Kaiser Wilhelm II: New Interpretations* (Cambridge, 1982), pp. 271–4.
24 Richard J. Evans, 'Religion and Society in Modern Germany', *European Studies Review* 3 (1982), 277–8.

modern nation state. Religion, then, became one of the key issues at stake in the struggle between two very different conceptions of the nation state – one based on cultural diversity, the other based on cultural conformity. During the 1870s, laws were passed abolishing the church supervision of schools, and dissolving the Jesuit order and expelling its members from the country, initiating a conflict between Church and state in Prussia that had, in fact, started in the southern German states (like Baden) some years before. Prussia in this instance followed the lead of the south and did not, as is sometimes argued, persuade the south to follow the Prussian example.[25] From 1874, the Prussian government began to imprison and expel bishops and priests who resisted these laws. By 1876, over 1,400 parishes in Prussia were without priests, while the church refused to fill vacant bishoprics. The situation did not return to normal until the *Kulturkampf* came to an end in the late 1870s and early 1880s, but by then the damage had been done, poisoning relations between Catholics and Protestants well into the twentieth century.

Persecuted Catholics quickly developed a complex network of social and political institutions to defend their particular interests and preserve their identity. These included social clubs, peasant leagues, and workers' associations like the Christian Trade Union (see Dick Geary's contribution). Probably the two most important institutions, however, which are discussed at length in Lamberti's chapter, were the Catholic Centre Party (*Zentrum*) and the People's Association for Catholic Germany (*Volksverein für das katholische Deutschland*). The Centre Party, which was formed well before the *Kulturkampf* got under way, rapidly gained widespread support so that, by the end of the 1870s, it was the largest single party in the Reichstag, a position it held until 1912 when it was superseded by the Social Democrats.[26] The People's Association for Catholic Germany, founded in 1890, had no less than 800,000 members by the eve of the First World War. Catholics had succeeded in creating a subculture that was distinct and separate from the main institutions of German society but that nevertheless played a pivotal role in the shaping of both Prussian and Imperial German society. However, the creation of what eventually became a confessional party inadvertently

---

25 Ellen Lovell Evans, *The German Center Party, 1870–1933. A Study in Political Catholicism* (Carbondale and Edwardsville, 1981), p. 38. For an overview of the *Kulturkampf* in Germany and Prussia, see chs 3, 4 and 5. For the cultural/intellectual background, see David Blackbourn, 'Progress and Piety: Liberals, Catholics and the State in Bismarck's Germany', in Blackbourn (ed.), *Populists and Patricians: Essays in Modern German History* (London, 1987), pp. 144–55.

26 Evans, *The German Center Party*, p. 95. See also Blackbourn, 'Catholics and Politics in Imperial Germany: The Centre Party and its Constituency', in Blackbourn (ed.), *Populists and Patricians*, pp. 188–214.

contributed to a political party system based on single social groupings and subcultures. This was an enormous hindrance to the development of parliamentary democracy in Germany, which may well have been Bismarck's primary intention in promoting the *Kulturkampf* – that is, to divert liberals from their constitutional goals.

The state, the army and Prussianism

At the beginning of November 1918, revolutionary uprisings in Berlin led to the collapse of the Hohenzollern monarchy: William II fled to Holland, a republic was proclaimed, and an armistice was signed that was eventually to bring about the end of the First World War. Military defeat led to a new political order based upon the principles of parliamentary government. The predominance of Prussian conservatives came to an end. The grossly unjust three-class electoral system, which had assured estate owners a disproportionate share of influence and condemned 82 per cent of eligible voters to political impotence, was finally abolished. Prussia as a state continued to exist (although it had lost the greater part of the provinces of West Prussia and Posen, as well as parts of East Prussia, Pomerania and eventually Upper Silesia), but there was a profound shift in the political balance of power in Prussia. Forces that had until then been considered political opponents of the state and excluded from the decision-making process – Catholics, Liberals, Social Democrats – assumed control and kept it until they were ousted by the Nazis in 1933.

The last three chapters in this collection all deal with the Prussian state after 1914 and the extent to which aspects of the 'Prussian system' continued on into the Weimar and Nazi eras. In the period immediately following the collapse of the Prussian monarchy, liberals began to debate the shape of the new German Republic. Hugo Preuss, co-founder of the pro-republican *Deutsche Demokratische Partei* (German Democratic Party) and Reich minister of the interior, prepared a draft constitution. He was so concerned about the hegemony of Prussia in Germany that he wanted to destroy the old federal system altogether and break up Prussia into several *Länder* (states) while at the same time gathering some of the smaller states into larger units. His plan was not adopted, however, and among its most effective adversaries were the Social Democrats unwilling to give up the power they had just acquired in Prussia. Like their monarchical predecessors, the new leaders considered Prussia's 'territorial integrity and political stability as the cornerstone of German national unity and the viability of its political system'.²⁷ A compromise kept the old German states intact and preserved Prussian dominance, at least in terms of population and land mass. The 'leap into the unitary state', as the socialist editor and politician Friedrich Stampfer later conceded, 'was not taken'.²⁸

If the Weimar constitution consequently retained the federal structure of the Reich, there was, nevertheless, a shift in relations old Prussia and Germany.²⁹ This is essentially the object of Hagen Schulze's contribution. Although it no longer had as much constitutional clout as it once did, the Prussian administration still dominated. The German civil service, despite the fact that it grew quite rapidly under Weimar, remained small compared to the territorial administrations of the federal states, notably Prussia's. Indeed, many of the German ministries, like the post, customs and finance, were unable to function effectively without Prussian co-operation. The continued preponderance of Prussia created an unbalanced federal structure.

This seems like a continuation of the situation that existed under Imperial Germany – Prussia's political influence was far greater than those of the other states. There were, however, two significant changes that are all too often ignored in the history textbooks. First, republican leaders in Weimar Prussia did not want to dominate Germany. Second, Weimar Prussia was in many respects more democratic, and certainly more liberal, than other German states. Indeed, it was one of the pillars of Germany's nascent democracy.³⁰ Not only was it a bastion of democratic political parties, there was at least a conscious, although admittedly half-hearted and ultimately unsuccessful effort to republicanize key institutions like the police, the civil service and the judiciary (these attempts are discussed at length in Hagen Schulze's chapter). This was far more than was attempted at a national level.

Moreover, Prussia showed that responsible democratic government could be achieved with a clearly defined and consistently pursued coalition policy. If Germany achieved relative stabilization after 1923, it was largely because Prussia, which still comprised about three-fifths of the total area and population of Germany, was ruled by a stable, effective, SPD-led coalition government until 20 July 1932.³¹ The fall of the Prussian government on

---

27 Dietrich Orlow, *Weimar Prussia, 1918–1925: The Unlikely Rock of Democracy* (Pittsburgh, Pa., 1986), p. 44.
28 Cited in Peter Gay, *Weimar Culture: The Outsider as Insider* (Harmondsworth, 1968), p. 19.
29 See also Orlow, *Weimar Prussia, 1918–1925*, pp. 92–114, and Orlow, *Weimar Prussia, 1925–1933: The Illusion of Strength* (Pittsburgh, Pa., 1991), pp. 109–29.
30 Orlow, *Weimar Prussia, 1918–1925*, p. 8.
31 Eberhard Kolb, *The Weimar Republic* (London, 1988), pp. 68–9. The Social Democratic minister-president, Otto Braun, formed a coalition made up of SPD, Centre, DDP and, for a time, DVP, which governed until July 1932.

that day was, in many respects, a prelude to the Nazi seizure of power six months later. All of this clearly indicates, and this is the crux of Hagen Schulze's argument, that views of Weimar Prussia as a state steeped in the traditions of militarism, or dominated by a reactionary rural-industrial oligarchy, are simply not accurate. Prussia was a shining example of democracy: it functioned better at the state level than Germany as a whole (despite the fact that it faced the same problems), and did so largely because all the major political parties in Prussia were convinced that, as a state and an idea, Prussia was destined to play a decisive role in German politics. If it failed, it is probably because, as Dietrich Orlow suggests in his detailed analysis of Weimar political parties, Prussia's leaders were convinced that 'fortress Prussia' would always be able to withstand attacks from any quarter.[32] In other words, it failed at the high political level, and not because democracy did not take root in Weimar Germany.

This brings us to the problem of Prussia's old elite pulling strings behind the scenes in order to prevent policies being implemented that they found inimical to their interests. The Nazi takeover of power, as Shelley Baranowski, Hagen Schulze and Brendan Simms remind us, was also the result of a Prussian intrigue, carried out by the old Prussian elite, in the name of narrow Prussian interests. Prussian Junkers contributed enormously to the political crisis which saw the dismissal of a series of chancellors – Brüning, von Papen, Schleicher – and which eventually led to the appointment of Hitler in January 1933. In other words, there are some ideological connections between Prussianism and National Socialism.

There is also the complex problem of Prussia's military legacy, central to any discussion of Prussian history, and which Dennis Showalter grapples with in his essay. The German army created after 1871 was new and lacked traditions similar to those found in, for example, the French and British armies. Like so many new institutions created in the nineteenth century, it had to create its own traditions. One way it did this was to foster an increased emphasis on 'Prussianism' through codes of behaviour, and through the adoption of certain values and attitudes that were considered to be inherently 'Prussian'.[33] Officers were, consequently, almost always conservative if not politically reactionary, partly because they were carefully screened, but also because social aspirations made them anxious to be

---

32 Dietrich Orlow, *Weimar Prussia, 1925–1933*, pp. 6 and 10.
33 Werner Mosse, 'Nobility and Bourgeoisie in Nineteenth Century Europe: A Comparative View', in Jürgen Kocka and Allan Mitchell, eds, *Bourgeois Society in Nineteenth-Century Europe* (Oxford and Providence, 1993), p. 91; Dennis E. Showalter, 'German Grand Strategy: A Contradiction in Terms?,' *Militaergeschichtliche Mitteilungen* 48 (1990), 76.

accepted by the Prussian nobility. This occurred to such an extent that bourgeois officers 'aped and exaggerated the modes of thought, the manners, and even the vices of their aristocratic brothers in arms'.[34]

This view has dominated the historical tradition and it has been assumed that the influence of Prussianism on the army, and indeed militarism on the domestic constitution of Prussia-Germany, was negative, even insidious. Hans-Jürgen Puhle, for example, describes Prussianism as something which 'demanded, and increasingly sought to achieve, often in an inhuman and repulsive way, the subordination to itself of all other purposes and expressions of life'.[35] This is strong language, which is perhaps more revealing of what some historians assume to be the legacy of Prussia rather than an objective analysis of its consequences. In doing so, Puhle is holding Prussian values responsible for the atrocities committed during the Second World War. So, too, does Hans-Ulrich Wehler, who believes that the Wehrmacht, 'moulded by Prussia' (*die preußisch geprägte Wehrmacht*), participated in the crimes of the National Socialists.[36]

There is no denying that there was a convergence of interests between the Nazis and the army even before Hitler came to power,[37] and that the Wehrmacht participated enthusiastically in the genocidal atrocities committed on the Eastern Front.[38] But, from there to conclude that the attitudes which prevailed in the army must somehow be rooted in a Prussian tradition is a very long bow to pull. Dennis Showalter argues that the atrocities committed by the German army during the Second World War had absolutely nothing to do with the 'Prussian spirit'. The Prussian army disappeared in 1919, even though 'Prussian' virtues and traditions eventually came to take on a nostalgic value. The new German army, the Reichswehr, developed its own traditions and its own behaviours: it was an

---

34 Craig, *The Politics of the Prussian Army 1640–1945*, (Oxford, 1955) p. 238. Much the same process, it should be noted, took place in the agrarian sphere. New recruits into the landowning class were rapidly assimilated to the cultural and political world of the Junker aristocracy. Some historians consequently speak of the 'feudalization of the bourgeoisie' – that is, the adherence of the middle classes to traditional, even feudal standards of behaviour (Lysbeth, Muncy, *The Junker in the Prussian Administration under William II, 1888–1914* (NY, 1970), esp. pp. 192–6).
35 Hans-Jürgen Puhle, 'Preussen: Entwicklung und Fehlentwicklung', in Hans-Jürgen Puhle and Hans-Ulrich Wehler, *Preussen im Rückblick* (Göttingen, 1980), p. 14.
36 Hans-Ulrich Wehler, *Preussen ist wieder chic...Politik und Polemik in zwanzig Essays* (Frankfurt am Main, 1983), p. 70.
37 See Manfred Messerschmidt, 'The Wehrmacht and the *Volksgemeinschaft*', *Journal of Contemporary History* 18 (1983), pp. 719–44; here p. 721.
38 See, for example, Omer Bartov, 'Operation Barbarossa and the origins of the final solution', in David Cesarani (ed.), *The Final Solution: Origins and Implementation* (London and New York, 1994), pp. 120–22.

army based on professionalism; it was a people's army with its own civic virtues; it was also anti-democratic and anti-republican. But it was not Prussian.

It was, nevertheless, the Prussian spirit that the Nazis hoped to capitalize on when they came to power. Stefan Berger, Hagen Schulze, Dennis Showalter and Brendan Simms all point to the fact that 'Prussianism' was an important weapon in the armoury of National Socialist propaganda.[39] A gigantic effort was made to associate National Socialist ideology with specifically Prussian virtues for two reasons: the first was to win over the conservatives, especially those in the army and the civil service; the second was to mobilize the population for war. Hence the unprecedented use of Prussian themes in film and popular literature. Prussian military heroes like Frederick the Great, Blücher (the victor of Waterloo) and Bismarck were touted on the screen defending Prussia (read the Third Reich) against the foreign enemies of the state. Prussian values were meant to become part of the foundation on which the new National Socialist character would be formed.

There is another side to this coin, however. In fact, relations between the Prussian nobility, whether urban or rural, and the Nazis were often strained, despite helping prepare the way for the Nazi seizure of power. Both Dennis Showalter and Brendan Simms point to the prominent part played by 'Prussian' officers in opposition to Hitler during the war. The only military attempt to overthrow Hitler, the disastrous bomb plot of 20 July 1944, was essentially Prussian. Indeed, many resisters justified themselves with references to traditional Prussian virtues. This signifies that Prussian virtues were not Nazi virtues and that 'Prussianism' was a much more complex, heterogeneous phenomenon than the stereotypical portrait of the monocled officer in jackboots goosestepping across Europe. Who, indeed, to paraphrase Brendan Simms, was the more Prussian? Those who carried out their orders to the bitter end, or those who plotted to kill Hitler? It was this last act which goes some way towards rehabilitating old Prussia.

---

39 On the use of Prussian symbols and values in Nazi propaganda, see Manfred Schlenke, 'Das "preußische Beispiel" in Propaganda und Politik des Nationalsozialismus', *Aus Politik und Zeitgeschichte* 27 (1968), pp. 16-23.

CHAPTER ONE

Prussia in history and historiography from the nineteenth to the twentieth centuries

STEFAN BERGER

When the German nation state was founded in 1871, most Prussian historians felt that Prussia had at long last fulfilled its historic mission of creating a unified Germany. In a euphoric letter to his friend Hermann Baumgarten (1825–93), Heinrich von Sybel (1817–95) gave expression to this feeling: 'At my age, where is one to find a new purpose in life?'[1] For Sybel, such a new purpose was quickly found: to defend the new Reich against both its external and internal 'enemies' – that is, notably the French, the Catholics and the Social Democrats. Yet, as the nineteenth century neared its conclusion, there was an increasing feeling among historians that the all too obvious politicization of historical writing that accompanied Prussianism[2] should give way to more 'objective' analysis. The time when historians had to contribute to the 'great struggle' for national unity was over. The nation state was a reality. Now, historians such as Max Lenz (1850–1932) argued, was the time for more sober reflection and analysis. However, as we shall see in this chapter, some of the main trajectories of Prussianism remained alive well into the twentieth century, albeit in a somewhat modified and toned-down version. Only after the end of the Second World War did the historiography of the German Democratic Republic reinterpret Prussian history along the lines set by the nineteenth-century socialist critique of Karl Marx (1818–83), Friedrich Engels (1820–95)

---

1 Sybel to Baumgarten, 27 January 1871, in Julius Heyderhoff and Paul Wentzke (eds), *Deutscher Liberalismus im Zeitalter Bismarcks. Eine politische Briefsammlung* (Bonn, 1925), p. 494.
2 On nineteenth-century Prussianism, see my chapter in Philip Dwyer (ed.), *The Rise of Prussia, 1700–1830* (Harlow, 2000), pp. 27–44.

and especially Franz Mehring (1846–1919).[3] In the Federal Republic of Germany, the demystification of Prussian history was undertaken by a new generation of social historians who had consciously broken with the nationalist tradition in German historiography. A much more critical view of Prussia was now being established in both parts of Germany, although, as we shall see, by no means all Prussian myths ended up in historiography's dustbin.

Modifying and transforming Prussianism in the Kaiserreich

The *Forschungen zur Brandenburgischen und Preußischen Geschichte* (1888–1944) quickly became the central journal for historical research on Prussia and it was dominated by the Prussians. However, this did not automatically mean that it published only political apologias. In fact, in the 1880s and 1890s, when the journal rose to prominence under the guidance of Gustav Schmoller (1838–1917), Otto Hintze (1861–1940) and Friedrich Meinecke (1862–1954), a new generation of historians significantly modified the belligerent Prussianism of the Droysens and Sybels. Historians such as Hintze, Hans Prutz (1843–1929), Reinhold Koser (1852–1914) and Bernhard Erdmannsdörffer (1833–1901) criticised the all too politically motivated analyses of the Prussian historians and attempted to come to a more balanced, sober assessment. This new generation of post-reunification historians concentrated on laying the foundations of archivally-based 'scientific' studies on Prussian history, lambasting 'popular history-writing' for its tendency to revel in the fantasies of yesteryear's facile Prussianism. Major editions of sources on Prussian history became the training ground for a whole new generation of historians of Prussia. Anyone who wanted to become a professional historian had to demonstrate his craft by contributing to one of the major editions of documents such as the *Acta Borussica* (from 1892), the *Urkunden und Aktenstücke zur Geschichte des Kurfürsten Friedrich Wilhelm von Brandenburg* (1864–1930), the *Publikationen aus den preußischen Staatsarchiven* (1878–1938) and the *Politische Korrespondenz Friedrichs des Großen* (1879–1939).

Otto Hintze's studies in Prussian administrative history were especially path-breaking. While Hintze recognized the character of Prussia as an authoritarian 'police state' (*Polizeistaat*), his major work *Die Hohenzollern und*

---

3   On the Marxist critics of Prussianism, see my chapter in *The Rise of Prussia*, pp. 40–44.

ihr Werk (1915) was still steeped in Prussianism, with the apologetic passages most obvious in the sections about the more immediate past. Nineteenth-century capitalism and the emergence of mass politics were, to a certain extent, beyond the comprehension of Hintze. Prussia, in his view, had politically regenerated Germany. It had been able to rise to its status of major European power only because it combined a progressive outlook with a strong monarchy. The latter held complete control over the civil service and the military, which allowed it to pursue a ruthless power policy and to overcome Prussia's vulnerable position in the middle of the European continent (the *Mittellage* theory). Hintze adhered to John Robert Seeley's (1834–95) dictum that the degree of internal liberty of any state was inversely proportional to the external military and political pressure exerted on that state. Hence, Prussia's militarism and its Machiavellian power politics were historically justified. The state bureaucracy's 'revolution from above', a term Hintze used for the first time, paved the way for Prussia's continued rise to prominence since the seventeenth century. Prussia's state-building process brought about a new idea and reality of the state in Europe, in which the head of the state ruled supreme and the standing army became the powerful means of internal despotism and external expansionism. The modern state had become a reality for the first time in Prussia. The Protestant-bourgeois ethos with its sober reasoning, its rational organization and its efficient economy was personified by the Prussian state. In brief, Prussia stood for an exemplary modernity.

Between 1905 and 1915, Hintze, and to a lesser extent Schmoller, set the major research agenda in Prussian history. Never before or since were so many source books edited and so many important dissertations on Prussian history written and published as in this decade. Even if some of these works were, as Adolf von Harnack (1851–1930) once remarked, 'counting the pebbles on the battlefield of Leuthen', the groundwork on which all future historiography of Prussia came to rest was laid in the decade before the outbreak of the First World War. In 1914, about 20 professional historians whose main research focus was on Prussian history occupied chairs at German universities. Most of them were characterized by ambiguities similar to those that we have noticed in Hintze: they stood between the desire for a more sober historiography and their continued commitment to the Prussian-German cause. So, for example, Koser, who became general director of the Prussian state archives in 1913, was one of the favourite historians of Wilhelm II. In his biography of Frederick the Great as well as in his *History of Brandenburg-Prussian Politics*, there were more than a few glimpses of the old Prussianism.

One of the key debates in Prussian history has been on the question of whether Prussian history actually came to an end in 1871. Had Prussia become a part of the new Reich and were the specific Prussian traditions infused with other values and traditions (*Verreichlichung Preußens*), or was it exactly the other way round: was Prussia such a dominant part of the new Reich that the new Germany was Prussianized (*Verpreußung Deutschlands*)? In 1871, a number of Prussian conservatives lamented the foundation of the German Reich, arguing that their prime loyalty was to Prussia not to Germany. This was not a prominent view, however, among mainstream German historians. Hence, at least within the historical profession, there was little sense that Prussia or Prussian history had come to an end. Prussia had fulfilled its national mission, and its traditions and values were to have an important place in the make-up of the new Germany. And yet the new nation state was to set its own agenda. True, the old Prussianism played its part in preventing the breakthrough of parliamentary forms of government, in contributing to the militarization of German society and in fostering the spirit of total submission (*Untertanengeist*) immortalized by Heinrich Mann's novel *Der Untertan*. But the links between Prussianism and modern racism or excessive nationalism were far more tenuous. The idea of the new Reich and the idea of the Prussian state coexisted rather uneasily. The dualism between Prussia and the Reich, however, was not only a constitutional problem; the historiography of Prussia now became increasingly entangled with the historiography of Germany. Prussia's distinct features increasingly dissolved into the picture of a larger German nation state.

Prussian historiography in the Weimar Republic

Historical writing during the First World War was characterized by an outburst of nationalism. In line with all other European historiographies, Prussian historians historically justified whatever political line their country and their rulers wanted to adopt. They described the war in terms of a defensive war against the barbarism of Russian Tsarism and the shallowness of 'Western civilization'. The war was a struggle of an allegedly besieged Prussian-German idealism and culture against its enemies. In particular, 'perfidious Albion', the British 'nation of shopkeepers' was planning to destroy the young Germany as its main rival for world power. The military prowess of Prussia was invoked to glorify the experience of war. Erich Marcks wrote in 1914: 'In human terms there is nothing greater than war, nothing more manly but also nothing more inspiring for the inner soul'.[4]

---

4   Erich Marcks, *Wo stehen wir? Die politischen, sittlichen und kulturellen Zusammenhänge unseres Krieges* (Stuttgart, 1914), p. 23. Note the use of the term 'our war' in the title of this booklet.

When the unimaginable happened; when the war was lost and the revolution swept away the ruling houses and dynasties in Germany; when the republic was declared, most historians felt as though the world they had known and cherished was gone forever. There was an acute sense of loss: loss of cherished traditions and values, loss of world-views which one had once taken for granted among the Protestant educated middle classes. In such an intellectual climate, the defence of Prussian-German traditions against the new forces of parliamentary democracy, republicanism and socialism became natural to most historians.

Moreover, Prussian historians, steeped in the lost world of the empire, continued to command the research agendas of Prussian history. Paul Fridolin Kehr (1860–1944) and Albert Brackmann (1871–1952) headed the Prussian state archive whose work was supported generously, even by the socialist prime minister of Prussia, Otto Braun (1872–1955). The 'Association for the History of the Mark Brandenburg' continued to play a vital role. And the Historical Commission for Research on East and West Prussia (*Historische Kommission für ost- und westpreußische Landesforschung*), founded in 1923, served as an umbrella organization for the many local historical associations and was a powerful promoter of research on Prussia. Furthermore, the University of Königsberg and the state archives and libraries in Königsberg and Danzig were important centres for the study of Prussian history. Dietrich Schäfer (1845–1929), Rudolf Kötzschke (1867–1949) and Willy Hoppe (1884–1960) were typical representatives of nationalist historians of Prussia in the Weimar period. Enmity to the unloved republic was a matter of fact for most historians. Among the history teachers at secondary schools, Prussianism continued to rule supreme. The socialists might have become the champions of the Weimar Republic, but their more critical view of Prussia and Prussian history continued to be ignored – both at school and at university level. The history of Prussia served as a counterfoil against which the republic was measured and found wanting. The bickering of political parties, the pluralism of social interests all clamouring for representation and the very idea of parliamentary democracy were regarded as alien phenomena forced onto Germany by the Western Allies. The Prussian myths, by contrast, served as a strong basis for the anti-parliamentarism and anti-republicanism of the political right during the Weimar Republic.

Historians working on foreign policy were directed towards two particular areas. First of all, many were all too willing to provide subsequent German governments with arguments allegedly proving Germany's innocence in the outbreak of the First World War. Several semi-official propaganda organizations employing and co-operating with some of the most well-known German historians aimed at influencing public consciousness. The so-called Department for Questions Relating to German War Guilt in the foreign office (*Kriegsschuldreferat*) was set up with the explicit task of winning the propaganda fight against the Treaty of Versailles. The major edition of sources entitled *Great Politics of the European Cabinets 1871–1914*, published in forty volumes between 1922 and 1927, remained clouded by such apologetic tendencies. Prussian militarism was almost never cited as one of the reasons behind the outbreak of the First World War. Instead, towards the end of the 1920s, conspiracy theories laying the blame firmly at the door of the Allies had very wide currency.

Next to the question of German war guilt, nothing preoccupied historians of Prussia in the inter-war period as much as the re-foundation of Poland. Prussian local history (*Landesgeschichte*) now became a highly politicized battlefield for both German and Polish historians about the legitimacy of the Polish state and the 'Germanness' or 'Polishness' of specific regions that had become part of Poland in 1918–19. Prusso-German historians invariably stressed the superiority of Prusso-German culture over Slav influences and countered Polish myths such as the concept of the 'ancient Polish land' of *Pomorze* (the notion of an all-embracing Pomeranian-Baltic history in which the very different histories of West and East Prussia were often united under the ahistorical term 'Eastern Pomerania').

While the majority of Prussian historians remained committed to the Prussian-German nation state created in 1871, a minority of established historians, most prominently Meinecke, converted from monarchism to a kind of pragmatic republicanism (*Vernunftrepublikaner*) after 1918. They attempted a limited reinterpretation of Prussian history, so as to accommodate the changes of 1918. Meinecke, for example, criticized the Prussian state for its rigorous pursuit of power politics which stood above everything else.[5] Yet even a modest supporter of the republic such as Fritz Hartung (1883–1967) could write in 1930 that the true importance and meaning of the Prussian state lay in its function for the 'renaissance of Germany'. 'Following the Thirty Years' War', he wrote, 'Prussia drummed into a depraved people a sense of firm state discipline and a serious and thorough work ethic; in its external relations it restored a sense of honour to the German name.'[6] A more critical view of Prussian history was developed only on the margins of the profession – among the small group of convinced republicans (*Herzensrepublikaner*) such as Eckart Kehr (1902–33). In

---

5   This is one of the key conclusions of Friedrich Meinecke's *Die Idee der Staatsräson in der neueren Geschichte* (1924).
6   Fritz Hartung, *Deutsche Geschichte vom Frankfurter Frieden bis zum Vertrag von Versailles, 1871–1919*, 3rd edn (Bonn, 1930), p. 3.

his work, Kehr castigated the pre-war Prussian-German imperialism and lambasted the methodological conservatism of the historical profession. Integrating economic, social and political history, his work and his politics remained extremely controversial and aroused much animosity from mainstream historians. For example, Gerhard Ritter (1888–1967) wrote about Kehr in 1931: 'This person should, it seems to me, preferably write his Habilitation in Russia rather than Königsberg. That is where he naturally belongs: for our historiography he is one of the most dangerous "aristocratic Bolshevists"' (*Edelboschewist*).[7]

Symbiosis or resistance? Prussian historiography under National Socialism

There is no shortage of embarrassing eulogies by historians of Prussia on the Nazis when political power was finally handed over to Hitler in 1933. As convinced republicans and Jews were forced out of the universities and into emigration, most German historians greeted the 'national revolution' of the Nazis with rapturous applause. The Nazis did not have to interfere massively into research agendas and the institutional autonomy of professional historians of Prussia because the conservatism of Prussian-German historians for the most part chimed in well with the aims of the Nazis. Some prominent historians such as Hermann Oncken (1869–1945) and Hintze were forced out of prominent positions or resigned. Meinecke had to give up the editorship of the *Historische Zeitschrift*, but on the whole continuity of personnel and research agendas prevailed. As far as Prussian history was concerned, it is noteworthy that Johannes Schultze (1881–1976), who edited the *Forschungen*, was an opponent of National Socialism and managed to keep the journal relatively free from Nazi propaganda or anti-Semitism – something which cannot be said of the *Historische Zeitschrift* after 1935. In fact, research on Prussian history continued its arch-conservative agenda and was probably least affected by explicit Nazi methodologies and politics. Yet the elimination of all Jewish historians registered no official protest, and many historians continued to support the Nazi state even when it had dawned on all but the most fanatic Nazis that their game was up. So, for example, Hoppe, who headed Berlin University between 1936 and 1942,

---

7 Cited in Hans-Ulrich Wehler, 'Eckart Kehr', in Wehler, *Deutsche Historiker* (Göttingen, 1973), p. 100. The Habilitation is the second doctorate needed to qualify for a professorship in Germany.

issued appeals to his fellow Germans as late as 1944 to hold out and fight for Germany's 'final victory' (*Endsieg*).

Historians engaged in *Ostforschung* who, as we have seen above, had already been doing battle with their Polish counterparts in the 1920s, rose to prominence under the Nazis, who bestowed official honours on them and used their work to achieve and realize their racist policies in Eastern Europe. Most historians were desperate to be of use. In the 1930s, their analysis of the historical records invariably lent support to revisionist claims of border changes in the East. For Hermann Aubin (1885–1969), the presupposed cultural superiority of the Germans over the Slavs was an important argument in favour of Charlemagne's attempt to bring civilisation to 'the sub-Germanic zone'. The widespread belief in the inferiority of the 'Slav race' also led German historians such as Aubin, Theodor Schieder (1908–84) and Werner Conze (1910–86) to become involved more actively with Nazi race policies during the Second World War. Brackmann's reputation as 'the worthy Führer of Ostforschung' brought him an *Adlerschild* (a high National Socialist decoration) of the German Reich presented by the Führer in person.

That even those historians who cannot possibly be construed as Nazis wrote to the ideological tune of the Nazis is visible, for example, in an article published by Carl Hinrichs (1900–62) in 1938 entitled 'The Ancestral Heritage [*Ahnenerbe*] of Frederick William I'. Hinrichs attempted to demonstrate that certain character traits of the Prussian king could be explained by reference to the 'composition of his blood'. He set about determining the percentage of German, Slav and Romance blood in the veins of various Prussian kings and came to the conclusion: 'King Frederick I and Frederick William I mark the highpoint of the German proportion of blood [in Prussian kings]; both have 54 per cent German blood, Frederick I has 28 per cent and Frederick William has 24 per cent Romance blood, Frederick I has 19 per cent and Frederick William has 12 per cent Slav blood'. Overall, Hinrichs concluded, 'the personality of Frederick William I is testimony for the truth of the sentence that the unity of ancestors [*Ahneneinheitlichkeit*] is synonymous with the effective realisation of specific hereditary traits [*Erbmassen*]'.[8]

While the Nazis did not generously finance university research projects on Prussian history, they did use the Prussian myths to great effect in their propaganda. Next to the Nazis' fight against the Versailles Treaty, the

---

8 Carl Hinrichs, 'Das Ahnenerbe Friedrich Wilhelms I.', in Hinrichs, *Preußen als historisches Problem. Gesammelte Abhandlungen* (Berlin, 1964), pp. 75, 90. Interestingly the article was reprinted in 1964!

espousal of Prussianism was probably the most effective propaganda tool of the NSDAP. Leading Nazis such as Joseph Goebbels liked to proclaim that National Socialism was the true heir to nineteenth-century Prussianism. For that reason, they initiated the so-called 'Day of Potsdam' on 21 March 1933 as a public demonstration of the unity of Prussian spirit and National Socialism. In particular, Frederick II, the so-called Wars of Liberation and the Bismarckian era served as reference points for the Nazis' own nationalism and their aggressive foreign policies. Frederick's birthday, the 24 January, was declared 'Frederick's Day', and the 150th anniversary of his death in 1936 was declared 'Frederick's Year'. Prominent historians like Ritter willingly helped the Nazis to make the connection. Ritter's biography of Frederick II, first published in 1936, explicitly makes the comparison of Frederick with Hitler. Among the so-called Prussian virtues, the Nazis chose to highlight the following: commitment to one's duty, service, discipline, obedience, loyalty and, above all, soldierly bravery. The army and the schools now propagated these values, especially towards the end of the Second World War. Frederick II's hopeless situation in the Seven Years' War and the 'miracle of the House of Brandenburg' were endlessly invoked by Nazi propaganda to underline their calls to hold out and wait for the 'miracle weapon' to turn the tides of war once again.

The history of Prussia after the end of Prussia: The GDR

In line with the allied perception of Prussia as the evil spirit of modern German history, some GDR historians in the late 1940s and early 1950s tended to emphasize the 'reactionary' character of Prussia. The GDR saw itself as consciously breaking with the Prussian tradition whereas, as GDR historians never tired of pointing out, those traditions continued in the FRG. Prussian history, Alexander Abusch (1902–82) argued, was an 'aberration' from the normal developmental path of modern nation states as described by Marx and Engels.[9] The transition from a feudal agrarian state to a capitalist industrial state was unusual in that its main promoter

---

9   Alexander Abusch, *Der Irrweg einer Nation* (Berlin, 1946).

was not the bourgeoisie, but the monarchical state. By the time the bourgeoisie became an important factor in its own right, it had already been feudalized and hence could not fulfil its historic mission of overthrowing Junker rule and the feudal order. Prussia, in this view, remained the state of the Junkers whose class rule was detrimental to the interests of the great majority of Prussian subjects. Furthermore, Prussian dominance over the unified German nation state after 1871 meant that the Junkers could ruin the whole of Germany by being responsible for the outbreak of the First World War and by bringing Hitler to power in 1933. Such rigorous condemnation of Prussia also served a specific political function: it legitimated the first stage of the land reform in the Soviet zone of occupation in which the big landowners were expropriated without any compensation.

In the 1950s, Prussia continued to be portrayed as a militaristic, reactionary and oppressive regime, a judgement which received quasi-official sanctioning by an official statement of the Sozialistishe Einheitspartei Deutschlands (SED) in 1955. In 1959, one of the most widely read textbooks on German history portrayed Prussian absolutism as the most brutal and open form of dictatorship by the Junker class, which was unparalleled in any of the other European feudal societies.[10] However, already in the 1960s, many GDR historians, in particular those working on economic and social history, rejected Abusch's one-sidedly negative interpretation of Prussian history. Dubbing it 'misery theory' (*Miseretheorie*), GDR historians now attempted to come to a more complex assessment of Prussian history. Agrarian historians, for example, emphasized the progressive features of East Elbian agriculture and the Prussian civil service was credited for the first time with achieving a 'revolution from above' that aimed at preserving Prussia's feudal system by adapting to economic and social change.

From the early 1970s, the GDR invested more money and resources to investigate Prussian and Berlin history. Under the chairwomanship of Evamaria Engel, much important work on *Landesgeschichte* was done in a special section of the Institute for History at the Academy of Sciences in East Berlin. Whereas earlier GDR research on Prussia focused on the forms of class rule and on class relationships, on the role of the Junkers and the state, and especially on the labour movement, new themes were now being investigated. Hartmut Harnisch's (*1934) work on Prussian agrarian history, Helga Schultz's (*1941) history of Berlin, or Ingrid Mittenzwei's (*1929) work on the emerging bourgeoisie in early modern Prussia are examples of

---

10 Gerhard Schilfert, *Deutschland von 1648–1789* (Berlin, 1959).

important milestones on the road towards a social and socio-economic history of Prussia.[11]

Most GDR historians, even where they did not one-sidedly condemn Prussia lock, stock and barrel, continued to distinguish between 'progressive' parts and 'reactionary' parts of Prussian history. GDR historians tended to differentiate between the Prussia of the General Legal Code of 1794, the Berlin Enlightenment, the world-famous university system, religious toleration, modern bureaucracy and efficient industrialization on the one hand and the militarism, expansionism, authoritarianism, illiberalism and anti-socialism on the other. In a famous article published in 1978, Ingrid Mittenzwei argued that Prussia was a Janus-faced phenomenon and pleaded for more such careful differentiation.[12] In her biography of Frederick II, she stresses that his economic policy ruthlessly squeezed the Prussian bourgeoisie, which was too feeble to do much about it, but she also gives due consideration to differing, conflicting interests within the economic bourgeoisie.[13] Her plea has to be seen in the context of the 'Inheritance and Tradition' debate that took place in the late 1970s and early 1980s. Leading GDR historians began to argue that the GDR inherited the 'positive' traditions, but that it was the task of professional historians to deal with the whole of the historical tradition. This was in line with attempts of the GDR leadership to propagate the GDR as a socialist German nation with its own national consciousness. An identity discourse was begun that aimed at invoking the whole of German history as the background against which the evolution of the socialist nation could be described. As a result, GDR historical research on Prussia was characterized by greater diversity of topics and methods in the 1980s. Even the 'arch-reactionary' Bismarck was now the topic of a much celebrated biography by Ernst Engelberg (*1909) who showed more than a little sympathy for the 'Iron Chancellor'.[14]

In certain areas, the old Prussianism was adapted for specific GDR needs. This was most obvious in relation to the historical judgement passed on Prussian military reformers and theorists such as Scharnhorst and Clausewitz. The GDR's home-made militarism frequently invoked the

---

11 Hartmut Harnisch, *Kapitalistische Agrarreform und Industrielle Revolution. Agrarhistorische Untersuchungen über das ostelbische Preussen zwischen Spätfeudalismus und bürgerlich-demokratischer Revolution von 1848/49 unter besonderer Berücksichtigung der Provinz Brandenburg* (Weimar, 1984); Helga Schultz, *Berlin 1659–1800. Sozialgeschichte einer Residenz* (Berlin, 1987); Ingrid Mittenzwei, *Preussen nach dem Siebenjährigen Krieg. Auseinandersetzung zwischen Bürgertum und Staat um die Wirtschaftspolitik* (Berlin, 1982).
12 Ingrid Mittenzwei, 'Die zwei Gesichter Preußens', *Forum* 32/19 (1978), pp. 8f.
13 Ingrid Mittenzwei, *Friedrich II von Preussen. Eine Biographie* (Berlin, 1979).
14 Ernst Engelberg, *Bismarck*, 2 vols (Berlin, 1985 and 1990).

Prussian tradition and brushed its more problematic aspects under the carpet. In 1980, on the occasion of the 200th anniversary of the birth of Clausewitz, the GDR officially honoured and celebrated him in a variety of ways. One looks in vain for GDR historians who problematized the militaristic ethos pervading the whole of Prussian society in the eighteenth and nineteenth centuries.

While the 'scientific' history in the GDR refuted Schmoller's Hohenzollern legend from early on, the popularized version of Prussia propagated in the GDR often picked up important elements of that legend. GDR television showed a series of largely positive portraits of Prussian generals and civil servants; Frederick II was portrayed as 'philosopher of Sanssouci'; and the Prussian–Russian military alliance of 1813 was frequently glorified, as was the whole of the 'patriotic movement' during the so-called 'Wars of Liberation'. The latter were widely and falsely associated with a rising of the 'people' for a unified and liberal Germany. Furthermore, Prussia's part in the division of Poland was not infrequently passed over in popular historical accounts, while Prussia's role in unifying Germany was routinely justified as 'historical necessity' in the best manner of nineteenth-century Prussianism. In other areas, GDR historians invented new myths to fit their own communist ideology. Thus, their aim to demonstrate that Prussian history was also the history of class struggles led them to over-interpret agrarian revolts and various people's protests. They became 'national upheavals' or forces which threatened the Prussian state with a 'revolution from below'. 'The people' were rapidly replacing the Hohenzollerns as the only positive actors in Prussian history, and in GDR historiography, the legend of the revolutionary potential of the people was replacing the Hohenzollern legend of old Prussianism.

The history of Prussia was also examined in great detail by Polish historians after 1945.[15] A Polish historiography of Prussia could look back on a string of works produced by the Cracow and Warsaw historical schools in the late nineteenth century, and by massive state-directed research projects carried out at the universities of Toruń, Lublin, Wilno, Poznań, Warsaw, Lwow and Cracow after the restoration of an independent Polish state in 1918. Popular themes of Polish research on Prussia included Poland's century-old struggle against the aggressive expansionism displayed by Brandenburg and the Teutonic knights, Prussia's role in the partitions of Poland, the eastern policies of the Hohenzollern dynasty, the Polish national movement, and the Germanization policies of Prussia in the nineteenth

---

15 Antoni Czubinski, 'Prussia as a Subject of Research in Polish Post-War Historiography', *Polish Western Affairs* 22 (1981), 127–50.

century. Following the ruthless repression and persecution of Polish historiography under German occupation in the Second World War, the traditional anti-Prussianism and anti-Germanism of Polish historians resurfaced after 1945. In particular, the Western Institute, founded in Poznań as early as 1945, came to occupy an influential position in organizing research on Prussia. Many volumes were now written to justify historically the movement of Poland to the West, which the Allies had agreed on at the conferences of Yalta and Potsdam. The areas incorporated into Poland after 1945 were widely perceived as 'ancient Polish lands'. However, in the 1950s, Polish historians began to criticize any one-sidedly negative stereotyping of Prussian history. In close co-operation with GDR historians, they now began to distinguish between Prussia's reactionary and progressive traditions. Special institutes for Pomeranian and Silesian history were established at the Institute of History of the Polish Academy of Sciences, founded in 1963. Under the impact of Marxist theory, Polish historians concentrated on agrarian and economic history, but, from the 1970s onwards, the focus was widened to include a wide array of political, legal, social and cultural studies. The steady stream of Polish publications on Prussian history tended to be steadfastly ignored by West German historians. With the Iron Curtain gone, co-operation between Polish and German historians to investigate manifold aspects of a mutual Prussian history is one of the important tasks for the future historiography of Prussia.

The history of Prussia after the end of Prussia: The FRG

Meinecke's *The German Catastrophe* of 1945 is notable for its attempt to link the victory of National Socialism in Germany to specific traditions in Prussian history. So, for example, he harshly criticized Prussian militarism and the allegedly weak bourgeoisie in Imperial Germany. Yet Meinecke was also enough of a pupil of Sybel to refer to geopolitics and to the 'authoritarian political systems of our neighbouring countries' to explain the success of Nazism in Germany. This did not, however, save him from being accused by many of his conservative fellow historians of fouling the national nest.

Historians such as Ritter, Hans-Joachim Schoeps (1909–80) and Walther Hubatsch (1915–84) were concerned with countering the view, held widely by the Western Allies, that Prussia was the epicentre of militarism, illiberalism and authoritarianism. So, for example, Ritter's *The Sword and the Sceptre* was specifically written to refute the charge that Prussia had always been the bearer of militarism and reaction. How powerful these conservative guardians of the Prussian tradition were in the early Federal Republic is highlighted by the successful prevention of the translation of Hans Rosenberg's study on *Bureaucracy, Aristocracy, and Autocracy. The Prussian Experience 1660– 1815*, first published in 1958. Rosenberg (1904–88) had been highly critical of the Prussian tradition, applying categories such as class, bureaucracy and power to the interpretation of the development of the Prussian state. Ritter prevented the translation with the argument that publication in German would not be in the national interest. Schoeps is a particularly interesting case because of his background. A Jewish émigré whose parents had perished in the Holocaust, he rigorously defended the Prussian tradition. In his view, Prussian conservatism, as represented by Leopold (1790–1861) and Ernst Ludwig von Gerlach (1795–1877), had always put law and justice before power and was fundamentally different from the ruthless power politics which became synonymous with Bismarck's unification policies. Once again, allegedly timeless Prussian values were propagated such as selflessness, sobriety, duty, simplicity, tolerance and justice. Prussianism now became an ethical phenomenon and the power politics were moved out of sight. After 1945, West German historians such as Hans Rothfels (1891–1976) and Ritter pointed out that the men and women who attempted to overthrow Hitler in July 1944 had been guided by this Prussian ethos. It was no coincidence, they argued, that it had been members of the great Prussian families, the Yorks, Moltkes, Schulenburgs and Schwerins, who formed the alleged core of opposition against Hitler. Prussian values, together with Prussia's tradition as a state honouring the rule of law, served to portray Prussia as the mirror opposite of the 'totalitarian' dictatorships of the twentieth century – Nazism and communism. Hence, Prussianism was refashioned to fit the country's Western integration and parliamentarization after 1949. An unreconstructed Prussianism remained the exception in the FRG, although there were those like Hubatsch who continued to defend even Prussia's part in the divisions of Poland.

The continuity in personnel and research agendas of German historiography beyond the watershed of 1945 is breathtaking. A number of books, such as Reinhard Höhn's *Scharnhorst's Vermächtnis* (first published in 1952), still propagated important parts of Nazi ideology; for example, its defence of militarism and total war as well as its anti-socialism and its *Volksgemeinschaft* ideal.[16] In 1965, Aubin republished a series of articles which

---

16 In the Third Reich Höhn had been a leading Nazi law professor at the University of Berlin and a high-ranking SS officer. His book went through several new editions in the Federal Republic and has appeared, since 1981, under the new title *Scharnhorst. Soldat, Staatsmann, Erzieher*.

had first appeared in 1937. They openly celebrated the *völkisch* view of history in which the Germans, from the Middle Ages onwards, had brought culture and civilization to a barbaric East. Cultural superiority was directly linked to the superiority of German over Slav blood – a theme which Aubin had already pursued when lecturing to Hans Frank in the capital of the *Generalgouvernment* in 1940 (at a time when his Polish colleagues perished in Nazi concentration camps).[17] Well into the 1960s, a whole string of publications on Prussian history were characterized by collective self-pity over the end of Prussia and by continued apologias for Prussian values and Prussian power politics.[18]

Historians such as Hinrichs, Richard Dietrich (1909–93) and Hans Herzfeld (1892–1982) also continued with their apologias of the Prussian tradition in a more modified form throughout the 1950s. Otto Hintze's work on Prussian history possibly had its greatest impact in the 1950s and 1960s. His opposition to National Socialism combined with his often apologetic view of Prussian history to serve a post-war generation of historians desperate to uphold a positive view of Prussia cleansed from its direct connotations with Hitler-Germany. At the same time, Hintze's work could also serve as an important inspiration for those who wanted to establish a comparative social history in the midst of the academic profession in the 1950s and 1960s. A majority of historians after 1949 supported the integration of the FRG into the political (European Union) and military (NATO) alliances of the West. In this context, it was clearly inopportune to persevere with the idea of a positive Prussian-German *Sonderweg* that was fundamentally different from the developmental paths of other Western European democracies such as Britain and France. Hence, Prussian history had to be reconciled with the Westernization of the FRG.

When Ritter published a new edition of his biography of Frederick II, the reference to Hitler was taken out. The emphasis was now on Frederick's progressive system of government and his objective role as the ruler who paved the way to German unity. He set the agenda which led, with historical necessity, to Bismarck and to the unity of Germany. So much for the old Prussianism. Yet Ritter also pointed out that the destruction of Prussia's military power and expertise was a severe blow in the fight of Western

---

17 Hermann Aubin, *Grundlagen und Perspektiven geschichtlicher Kulturraumforschung und Kulturmorphologie* (Bonn, 1965).
18 See, for example, Harald von Koenigswald and Hans-Joachim von Merkatz, eds, *Besinnung auf Preußen. Autorität und Freiheit – gestern und morgen* (Oldenburg, 1964); Hans-Joachim Netzer (ed.), *Preußen. Portrait einer politischen Kultur* (Munich, 1968); also Fritz Gause, *Deutsch-slawische Schicksalsgemeinschaft. Abriß einer Geschichte Ostdeutschlands und seiner Nachbarländer* (Kitzingen, 1952), who even manages, on pp. 182f., to justify the divisions of Poland as progressive.

civilization against the evils of Soviet communism. Anti-communism was the most important ideological bridge between the historians' commitment to National Socialism before 1945 and their commitment to a 'free' Western Europe after 1945. For former *Ostforscher* like Aubin, the East remained 'the enemy'. He was the key figure behind the foundation of the J. G. Herder Research Council in 1950, which was to become one of the major institutions for research on Prussia and the 'German East' in the Federal Republic.[19] Most West German researchers in the 1950s and 1960s continued to regard the areas of Prussia that had gone to Poland after 1945 as parts of Germany under 'alien administration',[20] and it was only from the 1970s onwards that a more realistic perception began to infiltrate research on Prussia.

That this kind of modified Prussianism had a significant impact on a new generation of Germans is confirmed by a representative survey among West German youth in 1961: Frederick II was not only widely known, but also extremely popular. He was outdone only by Bismarck and the Freiherr vom Stein, while more democratic figures such as Stresemann or Ebert trailed in popularity ratings. Even Stauffenberg was less popular than Frederick.

In the aftermath of the Fischer controversy about Germany's responsibility for the outbreak of the First World War in the 1960s, a 'critical school' of historiography was established in the FRG that consciously broke with the Prussian tradition. The tone had already been set by Ludwig Dehio (1888–1963) in 1961 when he drew a cautious line from the old Prussia to Bismarck and further to Hitler. Militarism, expansionism, authoritarianism were the red line connecting centuries of Prussian-German history.[21] From its inception in 1959, the Historical Commission played an important role in critically re-examining various aspects of Berlin and Prussian history. Under its first chairman, Herzfeld, much research on Prussian topics was initiated and from 1960 onwards the Commission also published its own journal entitled *Jahrbuch für die Geschichte Mittel- und Ostdeutschlands*. A new generation of historians now began to rediscover the earlier critics of Prussian history such as Mehring and Kehr. Under the influence of émigré historians, such as Rosenberg, they set out to destroy what they perceived as the myths of Prussianism. This generation also took account of the

---

19 On the institutional basis of Prussian history in the FRG after 1945, see Bernhart Jähnig, 'Die Landesgeschichtliche Forschung des Preußenlandes (Ost- und Westpreußen) seit 1960 im Überblick', *Jahrbuch für die Geschichte Mittel- und Ostdeutschlands* 38 (1989), 82–5.
20 See, for example, the book series established by the Herder Research Council and entitled 'East Germany under alien administration, 1945–1955'.
21 Ludwig Dehio, 'Preußisch-deutsche Geschichte 1640–1945. Dauer im Wechsel', *Aus Politik und Zeitgeschichte*, 18 January 1961.

historical writing in the GDR for the first time. In the harsh anti-communist climate of the 1950s, GDR historiography was widely ignored. In the 1960s, the beginnings of a yet very tentative dialogue became visible. Hans-Ulrich Wehler (*1931), Jürgen Kocka (*1941), Hans Mommsen (*1930) and Hans-Jürgen Puhle (*1940) are only some of the prominent names connected with that process. Inverting the concept of the German *Sonderweg*, they sought to investigate the specific Prussian and German traditions which had fed into the rise and victory of 'radical fascism' in Germany. The 'special path' of Prussia-Germany was no longer perceived as a positive counter-example to 'shallow Western civilization', quite the contrary: it was now portrayed as a fatal cul-de-sac that led to the rise of National Socialism. In particular, they examined the role of the Prussian Junkers and their long dominance over Prussian-German politics. Emphasis was put on the ability of the bureaucracy to create a modern state from above, on the fact that Prussia experienced an industrial revolution without a bourgeois political revolution, resulting in socio-economic modernization within an authoritarian state structure. If, as Wehler explicitly argued, 'Prussia helped to make Hitler possible',[22] then contemporary historians had a clear pedagogical task: by overcoming Prussianism, they would help to strengthen the parliamentary democracy of the Bonn republic and prevent the rise of a neo-Nazi movement. The Federal Republic was very much seen as the mirror image of the Prussian Reich created by Bismarck in 1871.

As has been pointed out, such an inversed Prussianism in fact built on many of the existing Prussian myths and just judged them differently. This is also why Thomas Nipperdey (1927–1993) could refer to Wehler as 'Treitschke redivivus'.[23] Ultimately, Prussianism, in its positive and negative versions, was really scrutinized only with the debate about the validity of theories of a German *Sonderweg*. Was Hitler the logical end point of a historical development leading back to eighteenth and nineteenth century Prussian history or was it a kind of perversion of 'true' Prussian-German traditions? The path-breaking critique of David Blackbourn (*1949) and Geoff Eley (*1949) especially has done much to stimulate research into many of the alleged peculiarities of German history.[24] Furthermore, the massive research project on the history of the German *Bürgertum*, initiated by Wehler and Kocka at the University of Bielefeld, undermined many

---

22 Hans-Ulrich Wehler, *Preussen ist wieder chic. Politik und Polemik in zwanzig Essays* (Frankfurt am Main, 1983), p. 70.
23 Thomas Nipperdey, 'Wehlers Kaiserreich: eine kritische Auseinandersetzung', *Geschichte und Gesselschaft* 1 (1975), pp. 539–60.
24 David Blackbourn and Geoff Eley, *The Peculiarities of German History. Bourgeois Society and Politics in Nineteenth-Century Germany* (Oxford, 1984).

theories about an alleged Prussian-German exceptionalism, so much so that Kocka, by the late 1980s, significantly modified the idea of a German *Sonderweg*.²⁵

Prussian history in the reunified Germany since 1990

The end of the GDR in 1990 sounded the death knell for GDR historiography. By 1996, it is estimated that about 90 per cent of all professional historians of the former GDR had been sacked for either political or academic reasons. The positions have been filled largely by West German historians. With reunification, Germany became bigger, but there was no effort to restore in any way the former state of Prussia. In any case, only a small part of this former state is part of today's Germany and even the attempted union of Berlin with Brandenburg failed in 1996, largely because the inhabitants of the latter baulked at the idea of shouldering the huge debts of Berlin. The political conditions for any revival of Prussianism seem to be remote. Indeed, several historians have pointed out that 1990 was significantly different from 1870–71 and that the new Federal Republic has little in common with the old Reich.

And yet, as Lothar Machtan (*1949) has argued, reunification has brought in its wake a 'return to the traditions of the Bismarckian Reich which belongs once again to the arsenal of nationalist propaganda in Germany'.²⁶ In addition, there have also been efforts to revive Prussia in the minds of Germans. These efforts did not start with reunification. They can look back to the 1980s, in particular to 1981, when a so-called 'Prussia wave' (*Preußenwelle*) rolled over the country. At its centre was a Berlin exhibition on Prussian history that drew crowds of more than half a million between the middle of August and the middle of October 1981. The 'year of Prussia' (*das Preußenjahr*) saw an additional 30 exhibitions on Prussian topics in different German cities and about 100 events surrounding the main exhibition in Berlin. A documentation of the media reaction to the exhibition filled three thick tomes.²⁷ Liberal-conservative historians such as

---

25 Jürgen Kocka, 'German History before Hitler: the Debate about the German *Sonderweg*', *Journal of Contemporary History* 23 (1988), 3–16.
26 Lothar Machtan, 'Einführung', in Lothar Machtan (ed.), *Bismarck und der deutsche National-Mythos* (Bremen, 1994), p. 9.
27 Karen Schoenwälder, 'Preussen-Renaissance, "deutsche Frage" und geopolitische Ambitionen', *Blätter für deutsche und internationale Politik* 28 (1983), 1,055–69.

Michael Stürmer (*1938), Hagen Schulze (*1943) and Karl Dietrich Erdmann (1910–1990) all evoked Prussia and Prussian history in order to cement an allegedly crumbling national identity of West Germany. Between 1985 and 1987, the so-called *Historikerstreit* raged in West Germany and brought renewed heated debates about the political lessons to be drawn from Prussian-German history. Historians, such as Stürmer, argued that only a rediscovery of Prussian-German traditions would prevent West Germany from losing all ties to its history. A 'history-less' people, according to Stürmer, might prove incapable of countering the alleged double threat constituted by the West German peace movement and Soviet communism. By contrast, left-liberal historians such as Wehler, Kocka and Heinrich August Winkler responded by stressing the dangers of reviving Prussian-German traditions that had been at least partially responsible for much of Germany's disastrous 75-year period of national unity. Rather than reviving Prussia's corpse, they upheld the allegedly Western values and political rights enshrined in the Basic Law as the best anchor point for West German identity. By 1987, it appeared as though the right-wing attempts to imbue West Germans with a new dose of Prussianism had been averted.

Yet, in the wake of the reunification of the country in 1990, the issue of Prussian-German traditions came to the fore once again. In 1992, the extreme right-wing historian Hellmut Diwald (1930–92) reminded his audience that one could talk only about 'partial reunification' in 1990, since Germany's eastern territory remained under Polish and Russian occupation.[28] Few have been as direct as Diwald, but it has become more common to refer to the former GDR as *Mitteldeutschland*, thereby indicating that there is an *Ostdeutschland* to the east of the present border with Poland. Thus, for example, Gerd Heinrich (*1931) has called for a 'rediscovery of the East' in view of the fact that 'Germany has two wings and a centre. One should not forget this'.[29] The chairman of the conservative Ranke Society, Michael Salewski (*1938), has also stressed the 'immortality' of the 'German East', which survived within Germany as 'spiritual history'. According to Salewski, its values and norms will allow the future Germany to act as a 'bridge' between Western and Eastern Europe. From there, his perspective becomes very long term when he writes ominously of 'historical raw material, from which maybe in centuries to come new historical-

---

28 Hellmut Diwald (ed.), *Handbuch zur deutschen Nation*, vol. 4, *Deutschlands Einigung und Europas Zukunft* (Tübingen, 1992), p. 8.
29 Gerd Heinrich, 'Brandenburgische Landesgeschichte und preußische Staatsgeschichte', in Reimer Hansen and Wolfgang Ribbe (eds), *Geschichtswissenschaften in Berlin im 19. und 20. Jahrhundert: Persönlichkeiten und Institutionen* (Berlin, 1992), p. 363.

political units will emerge'.³⁰ For Peter Moraw (*1935), 'a reunited Germany which simply encompassed the four zones of occupation, would only really seal the greatest catastrophe in German history'.³¹ Increasing reference is also being made to the alleged obligation of German historians to reassert the historical presence of Germans in Eastern Europe. There is a widespread discourse about the 'normality' of the nation state in contemporary Germany that includes hints of a new nationalism. In the historical writings of the new right represented by, among others, Karlheinz Weißmann (*1959), Rainer Zitelmann (*1957) and Ernst Nolte (*1923), Prussian traditions and values figure prominently as recipes for Germany's new national awakening. The maverick Arnulf Baring (*1932), for example, writes: 'Are we not lacking in all areas a feeling for the appropriate and congruent self-portrayal of our community such as was characteristic of Prussia in her best times?'³² Yet such views can be found only on the extreme margins of the profession today. In fact, as far as institutional back up for research on Prussia is concerned, not much has happened since 1990. The old Historical Commission, largely concerned with research on Prussia, was evaluated in the late 1980s and found wanting. It was subsequently replaced by a Prussia Institute under the directorship of Ernst Hinrichs. Its performance has also come in for substantial criticism, but if it has not excelled so far, this might well be related to constant financial problems owing to a basic unwillingness of Berlin and Brandenburg to provide adequate funds for the Institute. Within the mainstream historiography, a more critical perception of Prussia prevails. Despite some efforts to revive its corpse, nineteenth-century Prussianism will, one hopes, remain dead for good.

---

30 Michael Salewski, 'Der deutsche Osten und die deutsche Geschichte', *Geschichte in Wissenschaft und Unterricht* 42 (1991), 220–31.
31 Peter Moraw, 'Jüngste deutsche Geschichte und ältere deutsche Geschichte', *Geschichte in Wissenschaft und Unterricht* 41 (1990), 395.
32 Arnulf Baring, *Deutschland, was nun?* (Berlin, 1991), p. 205.

PART ONE

Conservatives and the Monarchy

CHAPTER TWO

Restoration Prussia, 1786–1848

THOMAS STAMM-KUHLMANN

Defining 'Restoration'

Historians customarily label the period of European history following the defeat of Napoleon and his forced abdication by the French legislature as the 'Restoration'. The name was derived from the title given by Karl Ludwig von Haller (1768–1854) to his book, *Restauration der Staatswissenschaften* (Restoration of the Science of the State), which appeared in six volumes between 1816 and 1834. Haller intended it to be much more than a mere proclamation of the re-enthronement of a handful of monarchs Napoleon had driven from power. When historians speak of 'restoration', however, it is exactly this process that is first and foremost in their minds.

In several instances, the return of former monarchs to their old thrones also signified deeper structural changes. In Spain, for example, not only was the king, Fernando VII, reinstated – he had been forced to renounce his throne by Napoleon in 1807 – but so, too, was traditional despotism, thus reversing, so to speak, the course of Spanish history. Even the Inquisition, which had been abolished by Napoleon, was set to work again.

In France, on the other hand, 'restoration' could not simply signify a return to the old. Louis XVIII was made king because the victorious Allies considered him to be the legitimate successor of his hapless brother, Louis XVI. As Prussia's former first minister, Baron von Stein, put it, the re-establishment of the Bourbons was the 'result of their ancestral right', which they had not lost in 'any valid manner'. Nevertheless, Louis XVIII was obliged to accept his crown from the French legislature. The architect of this transfer of power, Napoleon's former foreign minister, Charles-Maurice de Talleyrand, was compelled to explain the spirit of the times to his new royal master. According to Talleyrand, the epoch demanded that, in civilized states at least, supreme power be exercised with the support of representative bodies. Louis XVIII was consequently compelled to maintain both a lower house and a constitution, even though the latter was merely labelled a 'constitutional charter'. Church land nationalized during the early stages of the French Revolution remained in private hands, and Napoleon's marshals continued to command the Bourbon army. The reparation of émigrés who had returned in force after the fall of Napoleon became a hotly disputed issue in France, and a means by which the ultras – those who were 'more royalist than the king' – were able to exert pressure on Louis XVIII and his moderate government. Any attempt to turn back the course of history, as occurred during the Polignac ministry under Charles X, resulted in social and political upheaval – in this instance, the July Revolution of 1830. Post-Napoleonic France demonstrates, in other words, that the old dynasty could be restored and yet substantial elements of the revolutionary social and constitutional order be retained.

In Austria and Prussia, however, the word 'restoration' means little at all in the traditional sense of the word – nobody had to be restored because nobody had been deposed. For the Austrians, a long reform period had ended with the death of Emperor Leopold II in 1792. His successor, Francis II, who ruled until 1835, was not only ridden with the fear of revolution, but with the fear of the Enlightenment in general. He was 'a stupid and unimaginative defender of the status quo, [...] the single most influential Conservative in Germany throughout his long reign of forty-three years'.[1] The Austrian government had been the enemy of all progress long before Metternich appeared on the scene.

The reign of the King of Prussia, Frederick William III (1797–1840), covered roughly the same period as that of Francis II. Both monarchs came to rule before Napoleon seized power, and both died long after him. In Prussia, the spirit of the times demanded that some of the reforms inaugurated after the defeat of the Prussian army in 1806 – such as the liberation of the serfs, freedom of trade and the self-government of cities – were maintained independently of the existence of the Napoleonic empire. In fact, in Prussia, the continuity of rationalism in government, beginning with the accession of Frederick William III to the throne in 1797, was as firm as the continuity of the counter-enlightenment in Austria after 1792.

---

1   Klaus Epstein, *The Origins of Conservatism in Germany* (1966), p. 428.

The continuity of governmental practice, in other words, was tied to the personal continuity of the monarchs.

If the term 'restoration', and even more so that of a 'restoration period', is inadequate when referring to the Prussian monarchy, it can perhaps be used in regard to types of policies implemented by it. There are two considerations here. The first is that, as early as 1814, attempts to thwart the impulse of the Reform Movement were clear. The opposition that started to gather momentum after Stein's arrival in Memel (Prussia's provisional capital from 1807 to 1809) had more or less brought the 'Reform Period' to an end by 1819, the year of the Karlsbad Decrees, a set of regulations by the German Confederation to suppress liberal and democratic thought and the demand for political participation.[2] The Karlsbad Decrees were preceded by the Teplitz Agreement of 1819, an understanding between Prussia's state chancellor, Karl August von Hardenberg, and Austria's Metternich that meant, for the time being at least, Prussia would not introduce a general form of representative government. If 'restoration' is defined as the return to absolutism and the exclusion of any form of the separation of power, Teplitz may well correspond with the beginning of a 'restoration period' in Prussia. The term would then become synonymous with the end of all attempts to weaken traditional absolutism as it had been handed down from the days of the Great Elector. For Hardenberg, however, Teplitz did not include the renunciation of any long-term constitutional plans. According to him, the granting of a constitution was compatible with a rigid and authoritarian style of government. Generally speaking, however, the term 'restoration' suggests that somehow a new order had been replaced by elements of the old, in the same manner that Napoleon was replaced by Louis XVIII, or his brother Jérôme, King of Westphalia, was replaced by the Elector of Hesse. In this limited sense, there was, of course, no Restoration in Prussia.

The second consideration is that, despite attempts to thwart the Reform Movement, some decisive governmental policies introduced in the wake of Jena–Auerstedt remained untouched. An example is the laissez faire economic policy inaugurated by Hardenberg in 1810. By releasing trade and industry from the constraints of mercantilism and the relics of the guild system, Hardenberg had intended to create continuous economic growth to heal many of the deficiencies of a society of estates that no longer corresponded with the needs of a growing population. This policy of economic liberalism survived in Prussia until the Revolution of 1848.

---

2 An alternative date marking the end of reform is the Vienna conference of 1820 when the 'monarchical principle' was declared to be the decisive element for all German constitutions.

A sensible use of the term 'restoration', therefore, as applied to Prussia must differ from that used in general surveys of European history. Instead, we need to take a look at the major historical trends around 1800. It seems more appropriate to speak of a 'restoration party' than a 'restoration period' in Prussia.[3] It is possible to distinguish between various social, political and intellectual forces within Prussia according to the attitude adopted towards three key challenges: the philosophy of the Enlightenment; the idea of modern sovereignty; and the rise of a modern concept of natural law that made the idea of the social contract acceptable.

Restoration as the programme of a 'party'

Those in favour of these three tendencies formed what is known as the 'Party of Movement', made up of liberals, democrats and radicals.[4] Those who opposed these three tendencies represented a new force in society – conservatism (the term was taken from an article by the French political writer, Chateaubriand). One type of conservatism – 'reform conservatism' – attempted to ward off the dangers of popular sovereignty and revolution by the application of carefully dosed changes. Another type of conservatism was not directed against the Enlightenment, but used rationalism to develop its arguments against revolution.[5] These latter forces, which were directed against the Party of Movement as well as reform conservatism, together made up what can be referred to as the 'Restoration Party'. At its origins, the Restoration Party in Prussia-Germany fought its wars mostly on the intellectual front. At its height in 1819, it was able to put such heavy checks on the reform conservatism of Stein and the 'governmental liberalism' of Hardenberg that it nearly brought about the failure of the Reform Movement in Prussia.

---

3   One needs to keep in mind, however, that between 1790 and 1848 there were no political parties as we understand organized formations today. Even the British parliamentary parties of the time were not parties as we understand them. There was, however, much talk of '*Parteien*' in contemporary German discourse. It was widely felt that a conscious observer of the political stage had to take sides in this spectacular drama where the interests of humanity itself were felt to be at stake.
4   Klaus Epstein, in his wider survey of conservatism in Germany, includes socialism in the Party of Movement. Socialism, however, was not a serious force in German political life before 1840. Consequently, I prefer to use the term radicalism, which may include Jacobinism in Germany.
5   Cf. Jörn Garber, 'Drei Theoriemodelle frühkonservativer Revolutionsabwehr', *Jahrbuch des Instituts für deutsche Geschichte Tel Aviv* 8 (1979), 65–101, here p. 66.

The intellectual war involving reform versus conservative forces began during the French Revolution. In the years between 1790 and 1800, no less than 800 publications appeared in Germany criticizing the French Revolution or revolution in general. The political and social outlook of this critique of the Revolution has been labelled 'early conservative' (*frühkonservativ*),[6] even though the use of the term is anachronistic.[7] In fact, the question goes back even further than 1790. At the root of continental conservatism, we find the old European tradition of civil society (*societas civilis*) in opposition to the rise of the modern centralized state. Within the paradigm of *societas civilis*, as founded by Aristotle and continued by St Thomas Aquinas, no separation between household functions, economic and political status existed. Society was divided into estates, and each estate had its role to play in the home (*oikos*), agriculture, trade, war, the judiciary and government. Modern absolutism tended to monopolize all political functions at one central point, where sovereignty was located. If one accepted this paradigm, however, it did not matter whether sovereignty was imagined to be in the hands of a prince or in the hands of the people. Aristotelianism, it appears, still shaped European political thought, even if the tradition was implicit rather than explicit.

If the nobility and the traditional middle-class elements of the seventeenth and eighteenth centuries quite often regarded the prince with hostility, this attitude changed with the outbreak of the French Revolution. From that time on, the greatest threat to the political order was considered to be the different egalitarian elements within the Estates (notably within the Third), as the French example (and others before it) amply demonstrated. Consequently, conservatives rallied around the throne and the altar. Later, the Romantic movement portrayed this practical and somewhat opportunistic coalition between conservatives and the throne in terms of the chivalrous vassal protecting his lord.

The acceleration of the historical process towards the end of the eighteenth century brought about a more elaborated version of traditional conservatism. In Klaus Epstein's words: 'The *raison d'être* of conservatism as an articulate movement is conscious opposition to the deliberate efforts of the Party of Movement to transform society in a secular, egalitarian, and self-governing direction'.[8]

In conventional historiography, the Enlightenment or rationalism is often

---

6   The term was coined by Garber, ibid.
7   Fritz Valjavec, *Die Entstehung der politischen Strömungen in Deutschland: 1770–1815* (Munich, 1951), p. 10, claims: 'Wir müssen [...] die politischen Kennzeichnungen des 19. Jahrhunderts auch für die von uns behandelte Zeit verwenden, in der sie an sich noch nicht gebräuchlich waren.'
8   Epstein, *The Origins of Conservatism in Germany*, p. 5.

identified with the ideology of revolution, disrespect and atheism. This view was created by propagandists of the Restoration Party; it is to be found, for example, in the reasoning behind Frederick William II's religious edict (*Religionsedikt*) of 1788. Here we find the Enlightenment (*Aufklärung*) explicitly named as the cause of many defects of modern society. However, as a close study of the 800 German publications directed against the Revolution before 1800 reveals, there was also a long tradition of enlightened conservatism. About 100 of the 800 books, pamphlets and articles could be considered 'rational' or 'enlightened' conservative. Rational conservatism, as well as the 'enlightened despotism' incorporated in the Prussian General Legal Code (*Allgemeines Landrecht*) of 1794, proclaimed a homogeneous society of citizens (*Staatsbürgergesellschaft*), but maintained the necessity of keeping citizens in separate orders, which were essentially differentiated by their professional function.[9] A survey of the political and philosophical views of Metternich, the leading statesman of the Restoration, reveals him to be a disciple of the *Aufklärung*.[10] Nevertheless, the constant attacks against the *Aufklärung* in Germany helped give the Restoration Party its drive and fervour. Consequently, the Restoration Party's activity, not only in the political but also in the intellectual and religious sphere, needs to be studied.

At the core of political conservatism and, therefore, at the core of the Restoration Party, we find the interests of the traditionally privileged strata of society. These were sometimes middle-class (as in the case of the Osnabrück town jurist, Justus Möser), but, since Prussian towns were of little importance they were mostly aristocratic in character. 'Conservatism must be understood, in its fundamentals, as a political ideology defending the specific authority and class interest of the nobility'.[11]

Early anti-revolutionary proclamations

Inasmuch as conservatism, according to the Aristotelian tradition, started out as opposition to the monopolizing tendencies of the absolutist state, elements of it can be found in Prussia well before the French Revolution in areas where local interests were obliged to defend their position against an enlightened centralist government.

---

9   Cf. Garber, 'Drei Theoriemodelle frühkonservativer Revolutionsabwehr', p. 66.
10 See Heinrich Ritter von Srbik, *Metternich. Der Staatsmann und der Mensch*, 3 vols (Munich, 1925), i. p. 259.
11 Robert M. Berdahl, *The Politics of the Prussian Nobility. The Development of a Conservative Ideology 1770–1848* (Princeton, NJ, 1988), p. 7.

In 1783, the Estates of the Kurmark demanded to be heard before a new constitution for the courts of law (*Gerichtsverfassung*) was promulgated in the province.[12] We also know that in 1786, after the death of Frederick the Great, the Estates of East Prussia filed a petition (*Immediatsupplik*) to the new king and asked for a new system of consultation.[13] The Estates of Minden and Ravensberg demanded that every new law be communicated to them so that they could not only be consulted, but could also be asked for their consent.[14] Even before the Napoleonic wars, political opposition to absolutism fostered its own cultural climate. For example, nobles and intellectuals in Schleswig-Holstein were opposed to the tendencies of enlightened despotism that had made themselves felt under King Christian VII of Denmark (1766–1808). Count Friedrich Reventlow (1755–1828), a former Danish envoy to London, gathered around him a circle of friends at his country estate, Emkendorf. Reventlow, Count Friedrich Leopold Stolberg (1750–1819) and the journalist and poet Mathias Claudius (1740–1815) developed an 'intensified inwardness' (*Innerlichkeit*) which put feelings above reason. Their religious Pietism stressed the importance of biblical faith, remorse and atonement over the plain rational morality of many theologians and pastors of the day. Progressive and reactionary 'parties' all over Germany struggled in the different arcane formations of Freemasons and Illuminates on the one hand, and Jesuits, ex-Jesuits and Rosicrucians on the other. Each camp charged the other with conspiracy against the state.

The two most outspoken Prussian 'Restoration politicians' were Rosicrucians: Hans Rudolf von Bischoffwerder (1741–1803), aide-de-camp general to Frederick William II, and Johann Christof von Woellner (1732–1800), a theologian and the king's former teacher, who was made minister of justice and was given the department of religious affairs. Both men convinced the king that it was necessary to support Emperor Leopold in his attempt to save his sister in France, Marie-Antoinette. Although Prussia and Austria had recently come dangerously close to a confrontation, the two monarchs met at Pillnitz in Saxony (25 August 1791) to proclaim a state of ideological warfare between the French Revolution and the conservative powers. The Declaration of Pillnitz can be considered the first

---

12 Theodor Schieder, *Friedrich der Große. Ein Königtum der Widersprüche* (Berlin, 1983), p. 306.
13 Cf. Wolfgang Neugebauer, *Politischer Wandel im Osten. Ost- und Westpreußen von den alten Ständen zum Konstitutionalismus*. Quellen und Studien zur Geschichte des östlichen Europa, 36 (Stuttgart, 1992), p. 96 and *passim*.
14 Cf. Günter Birtsch, 'Gesetzgebung und Repräsentation im späten Absolutismus. Die Mitwirkung der preußischen Provinzialstände bei der Entstehung des Allgemeinen Landrechts', *Historische Zeitschrift* 208 (1969), 285.

declaration in the ideological confrontation that, much later, both Prince William of Prussia and the nineteenth-century historian, Leopold von Ranke, considered to be *the* major conflict of the nineteenth century: monarchical legitimacy versus popular sovereignty.

A moderate king, the reform ministers and their adversaries

In the years following Pillnitz, Prussian policy took a moderate and un-ideological path. The attempts to restore the Bourbon monarchy were curbed by the military successes of France. Moreover, many in the Prussian officer corps were not only sympathetic towards France, but mostly viewed its military threat within the framework of the traditional balance of power – that is, not in ideological terms. In the deliberations that surrounded the Peace of Basle (5 April 1795), which saw Prussia withdraw from the First Coalition, there was no mention of the possibility that implicit recognition of a revolutionary government might strengthen the forces of unrest at home.

On coming to power in 1797, Frederick William III was hailed as the reincarnation of Frederick the Great. The king believed himself to be an enlightened, tolerant ruler. He did away with the anti-enlightenment tendencies his father had implemented in the Church and in the education system that was still inextricably linked to it. Immediately after his ascent to the throne, the young monarch dismissed the Rosicrucian fanatics. He even generously extended his protection to the philosopher, Johann Gottlieb Fichte (1762–1814), despite Fichte being accused of atheism. At a time when Austria was putting her Jacobins on trial, the French Revolution was not a consideration in the early years of his reign.

The Christian faith of Frederick William III, however, was biblical. When drawing up regulations for elementary schools, for example, the king stressed that nobody should be taught more than was deemed necessary for that person to fit into the social order. In his world-view, everybody had to stay in the order into which he was born, a notion expressed by St Paul in the First Epistle to the Corinthians. In the king's opinion, too much learning created discontent. This reveals an aspect of his personality that the Restoration Party was to appeal to in later years. Frederick William III was not blind to the need for reforms in many branches of his state: he attempted changes in the military and the tax system. He even agreed to the abolition of serfdom on the royal domains. However, all these attempts obviously lacked energy.

It needed the crushing defeat of the Prussian army at the battles of Jena and Auerstedt (14 October 1806) and the humiliating Peace of Tilsit (9 July 1807), both severe blows to the self-esteem of the Prussian establishment, to shake Prussia out of its lethargy. In the period immediately following the collapse of the army, Baron von Stein was appointed first minister and granted considerable leeway by the king to reform the Prussian state. In the autumn of 1808, however, the king felt obliged to dismiss his headstrong minister. On this occasion, the influence of a 'court party' (*Hofpartei*) is notable. Between 1809 and 1811, when the reform of the army came up against a number of obstacles, there was also talk of the subversive activities of a 'party of moles' (*Maulwurfspartei*), as Hermann von Boyen, one of the architects of military reform, called it. It is often argued that the 'court party' comprised court officials, as opposed to government officials. Among the members of the 'court party', the queen's major-domo, Countess Sophie Marie Voss, and her chamberlain, Baron Schilden, are counted. This party supposedly also included nobles who were dissatisfied with agrarian reform, like Count Carl von Voss-Buch, and even the king's aide-de-camp, General Karl Leopold von Köckritz. It is, however, a misconception to assume that Queen Louise and her entourage were opposed to Stein's reforms from the beginning. In fact, they greeted Stein's appointment with enthusiasm. It was Stein's performance in office, including the dangerous mistake he made when a letter he wrote on the preparation of an anti-Napoleonic uprising was intercepted, that caused many of his supporters, including Hardenberg, to turn away from him.

In the meantime, the estates representing the privileged inhabitants and corporations of the different territories that constituted the monarchy had increased in importance. Traditionally, the influence of the estates grew whenever emergency situations demanded extraordinary measures. The war with France, defeat and Napoleon's consequent financial extortions created just such an emergency. In the Electoral March and in East Prussia, Estates Committees (*Ständische Komitees*) as well as Diets (*Landtage*) were assembled to apportion the financial burdens imposed on them by the French.

Nevertheless, the noble landowners knew best how to pursue their interests. In 1809, aside from the war contribution, the *Landtag* of the Kurmark was authorized by the king to debate further issues. The deputies decided that they would study Stein's decree of October 1807 (*Oktoberedikt*), which abolished serfdom throughout the monarchy and made the manors (*Rittergüter*) a free commodity. In the end, they were quite satisfied with most of it. They welcomed the notion that landed property should be 'mobilized' – that is, that it should be bought and sold without any restrictions and without any regard for the rights of the village community, the family of the noble owner, the peasant or the serf. A memorandum by the deputy von

Arnim-Neuensund dated 30 March 1809 employs the classic liberal phrase 'free use of forces' (*freier Gebrauch der Kräfte*).[15] The well-known Restoration spokesman, Friedrich August Ludwig von der Marwitz (1777–1837), introduced the modern methods of Albrecht von Thaer and the British agrarian revolution onto his own lands. If the estates came into conflict with the government over agrarian reforms, it was partly because the reforms did not serve their own economic interests as much as they desired.

Discontent among people like Marwitz grew with the appointment of Karl August von Hardenberg (1750–1822) as state chancellor in 1810. Hardenberg not only continued Stein's work on agrarian reform, he also attacked the institution of the estates in general. In each of the territories making up the Prussian monarchy that had either been conquered or inherited, different constitutions were observed and different privileges had been granted. The reformers now tried to construct a homogeneous nation out of this patchwork quilt of customs and privileges. Hardenberg intended to abolish the traditional estates and their financial institutions completely so that the restored state could be built from scratch.

Hardenberg's *Regulierungsedikt* (14 September 1811) paved the way for the peasants to pay off the feudal burdens they owed to the landlords and become free farmers. To the landlords, this offered the chance to round off their properties and establish large modernized agrarian enterprises. However, they came to fear the labour shortage that would have been one of the consequences of the abolition of traditional feudal labour duties. Therefore, they opposed any kind of agrarian reform that allowed a major portion of the population to become independent or that would allow people to leave the countryside.

Since the government intended on selling as much of the royal domains to private investors as possible to make up for its deficit, Prussia was well on the way to becoming, in the eyes of people like Marwitz, a 'new-fangled Jewish state'. It was thought that most of the available land would fall into the hands of Jews. Marwitz in general rejected the idea of 'mobilizing landed property'.[16] Increased economic efficiency was emphatically not meant to undercut the political prerogatives of the nobility or to question that the nobility was entitled to maintain large properties within the same families over centuries.

---

15 See Klaus Vetter, *Kurmärkischer Adel und preußische Reformen*. Veröffentlichungen des Staatsarchivs Potsdam, 15 (Weimar, 1979), p. 130.

16 'Wir wagen es zu sagen, daß, wenn der Grundsatz der Willkür, die Gleichmachung der Stände und die Mobilisierung des Grundeigentums wirklich durchgeführt werden, uns keine Rettung für diesen Staat [...] mehr erscheint.' Erich Meusel, *Friedrich August von der Marwitz. Ein märkischer Edelmann im Zeitalter der Befreiungskriege*, 2 vols (Berlin, 1913), ii. p. 21.

In 1813, the Estates of East Prussia gave another proof that they were still indispensable. They assembled without royal convocation and voted for the establishment of the militia (*Landwehr*) without waiting for a proposal from the king. Estate influence on agrarian policy reached its most spectacular success in 1814, when the county Estates (*Kreisstände*) of Mohrungen in East Prussia appealed to the king to reconsider Hardenberg's *Regulierungsedikt*. It was possibly the victory over the French Revolution, evident in Frederick William III's solemn entry into occupied Paris in 1814, that stirred in the king's mind the notion that perhaps there was no need for any further reform, since Prussia had achieved victory with the few that had already been carried out. In any case, the king, who was obviously moved by a very skilfully worded letter from Count Dohna-Schlodien, ordered Hardenberg to have the *Regulierungsedikt* rewritten. In the end, the Declaration of 29 May 1816 considerably reduced the number of peasants who could free themselves from any form of dependence on their lords and thus guaranteed that there would always be a sufficient supply of cheap labour.[17]

A little later, however, other representatives of the East Prussian Estates seriously considered ceding to the state the traditional jurisdiction of their districts (*Patrimonialgerichtsbarkeit*). Increasing demands on the quality of the legal services rendered by the patrimonial institutions had increased costs to a point where it seemed advisable to many owners of noble estates to renounce their rights over this part of the public sphere.[18] Those who thought they ought to give up some of their share in political domination did so out of self-interest, a motivation, if well understood, that can be a valuable factor in the development of a society. Adopting a position in defence of one's own interests, however, cannot simply be labelled 'reactionary'.

Romanticism and Restoration ideology

Romanticism, an intellectual movement rising about 1795, tended to glorify the Middle Ages. This suggests that romantic works might have been used as an ideological back-up for the political demands of the nobility, and it is necessary to examine the connections between Romanticism and the

---

17 Cf. Hartmut Harnisch, 'Vom Oktoberedikt des Jahres 1807 zur Deklaration von 1816. Problematik und Charakter der preußischen Agrarreformgesetzgebung zwischen 1807 und 1816,' *Jahrbuch für Wirtschaftsgeschichte* (1978), 268 and *passim*.
18 Cf. Neugebauer, *Politischer Wandel im Osten*, p. 267.

Restoration Party. In their rationalistic and anti-monarchical fervour, nineteenth-century liberals denounced Romantics as the toadies of absolutism, and they sometimes included Friedrich Gentz (1764–1832) among them even though Gentz, a student of Kant, was a classical spirit, a pupil of the Enlightenment. Carl Schmitt reminds us that Romanticism could be held just as responsible for the French Revolution as political reaction. Schmitt's explanation is sound: the Romantic does not wish to influence the course of the world. He takes only that event for real that is the occasion for *Stimmung*, a certain mood. When the French Revolution was the dominant force in Europe, the Romantic felt revolutionary.[19] When counter-revolution was the predominant force in post-Napoleonic Europe, the Romantic's preferences changed accordingly. Romantics loved polarities, and they loved to identify opposites. The poet Novalis (Friedrich von Hardenberg, 1772–1801), a distant nephew of the chancellor Hardenberg, praised the Middle Ages in his text 'Christianity or Europe' (*Die Christenheit oder Europa*) in 1799. In another text written the year before, Novalis typified this attitude of identifying opposites when he wrote: 'The real king will be a republic, the real republic will be king'. This line is taken from Novalis' panegyric of Frederick William III and Queen Louise, written in enigmatic language (*Raetselsprache*) under the title 'Faith and Love' (*Glauben und Liebe*). In fact, Novalis avoided taking sides. In his text 'Pollen' (*Blütenstaub*), he explained the revolution as an 'adolescent crisis'.[20] 'Faith and Love', on the other hand, 'has tendencies in about every political direction, and any assessment of its various interpretations depends on where one takes it literally and how one reads it figuratively'.[21] Frederick William III, a forthright, plain-spoken man, felt uneasy, as if brilliant young men like Novalis were mocking him. Perhaps he also felt strained. In any case, he expressed his displeasure with Novalis.

Marwitz, a dedicated defender of the society of estates, was able to secure the support of the newspaper *Berliner Abendblätter*, edited by the poet Heinrich von Kleist (1777–1811). He protested against the liberal agrarian legislation of Hardenberg, against Hardenberg's plans to raise the income of the state, his introduction of laissez-faire economics into Prussia, and his centralist tendencies.

The chief intellectual spokesman of the conservative movement in 1810–11 was Adam Müller (1779–1829), who published several articles in the *Berliner Abendblätter* until Hardenberg withdrew financial support from

---

19 Carl Schmitt-Dorotic, *Politische Romantik* (Munich and Leipzig, 1919), p. 92.
20 William Arctander O'Brien, *Novalis, Signs of Revolution* (Durham and London, 1995), p. 148.
21 O'Brien, *Novalis*, p. 168.

the paper. Müller, who was a theorist of considerable weight, developed an original system of political economy from the viewpoint of Romanticism. In his 'Elements of the Art of the State' (*Elemente der Staatskunst*) (1809), Müller described the state as a system of oppositions (*Gegensätze*) that needed each other to create a harmonious organism. The monarch depended on having the estates in opposition. While Adam Smith's economic theory was centred around the individual, Müller pointed to the importance of corporate organisms such as families. In his 'Lectures on Frederick II, Nature, Dignity and Destiny of the Prussian Monarchy' (*Vorlesungen über Friedrich II. und die Natur, Würde und Bestimmung der preussischen Monarchie*) (1810), Müller rejected the enlightened despotism of Frederick the Great and the individualism of Frederick's social theory and demanded the introduction of a state based on estates (*Ständestaat*).

In 1811, Müller and Ludwig Achim von Arnim-Wiepersdorf (1781–1831), the Romantic poet, founded the Christian-German Table Society (*Christlich-deutsche Tischgesellschaft*). This club, which excluded Jews from membership, was made up of Romantic intellectuals then living in Berlin, including Friedrich Carl von Savigny (1779–1861), founder of the 'historical school' in German law, Clemens Brentano (1778–1842), and Wilhelm (1789–1834) and Leopold von Gerlach (1790–1861). The latter proclaimed himself a devoted follower of Karl Ludwig von Haller and his theoretical vindication of Restoration. After the Wars of Liberation, a circle of even younger men continued the tradition of the *Tischgesellschaft* under the name of *Maikäferei* (which means ladybug, although the name was derived from the tavern where they met). This circle included Ernst Ludwig von Gerlach (1795–1877), who was soon to become the leading intellectual spokesman of Prussian conservatism after Adam Müller decided to try his luck in Metternich's Austria.

The *Tischgesellschaft* with its combination of 'Christianity' and 'Germandom' mobilized nationalism and religion for the support of the monarchy and the hierarchical social order in a manner that was to become the hallmark of Prussian conservatism. A poetic transfiguration of the Middle Ages helped the cause. Baron Friedrich Heinrich Carl de la Motte Fouqué (1777–1843), who came from a family with a long history of military service, married Caroline von Rochow, whose relatives belonged to the most resolute defenders of noble privileges in the Electoral March. While living as a lord of the manor, he wrote a popular novel, 'The Magic Ring' (*Der Zauberring*), which brought the age of the crusades back to life again. Fouqué's works nourished fantasies of medieval knighthood even among the princes of the ruling house. In 1818, the crown prince and his brothers and sisters staged the Feast of the White Rose (*Fest der weißen Rose*), a pageant that used Fouqués writings as blueprints. Fouqué was a Romantic poet, as was Achim von Arnim. And yet even Achim von Arnim, in his desire to bridge the gap between the *Volk* and the educated classes by means of a poetry common to both, had democratic elements in his thought. Romanticism, indeed, was used as an intellectual support for Restoration interests. Its impact, however, was equivocal. Romanticism has given strength to democratic as well as reactionary tendencies.

The Restoration Party gains ground

Even before the landowners had been able to score a success in the modification of agrarian reform, other influences were brought to bear on Frederick William III. Hardenberg had been able to secure his signature on a declaration, issued at Paris on 22 May 1815, that Prussia would receive a constitution and representative institutions. While the chancellor doggedly worked towards this goal, the king asked people in his entourage for their opinion. On this occasion, perhaps more than on any other, one can speak of the influence of a 'court party' (*Hofpartei*). After the premature death of Queen Louise in 1810, Frederick William gathered around him a kind of substitute family. It included Baron Schilden as well as the tutor to the crown prince, Johann Peter Friedrich Ancillon (1767–1837). Ancillon, a preacher of the French Huguenots in Berlin and author of historical works, was another example of 'rational conservatism'. He was among the first to warn against any concessions to the Party of Movement. In memoranda and letters to the king and in a book that he published in September 1815, Ancillon predicted that any conceivable national representation would strive to extend the scope of its powers. The idea of popular sovereignty would, he warned, lead to the despotism of a single man. The fate of France between the convocation of the Estates–General in 1789 and Napoleon's usurpation of power in 1799 was not accidental, but inevitable.

Frederick William was subject not only to internal pressures, but also to external pressures. He was led by the conviction that unity among the great powers, which in 1813 and again in 1815 had made the overthrow of Napoleon possible, was to be preserved under all circumstances. The opinions of the allied monarchs, therefore, were of utmost importance to him. When Emperor Alexander I of Russia (1770–1825), for example, who was not just an ally but a friend, began little by little to dissociate himself from his former liberal and constitutional ideas after 1815, this left an impression on Frederick William also.

In Vienna, the policy executed by the state chancellor, Prince Clemens von Metternich, was a perfect expression of the anxiety and the immobilization of his master, Emperor Francis of Austria. As the leading statesman of the leading German power, with interests and influence throughout the Balkans and the Italian peninsula, Metternich felt justified in meddling in the internal affairs of other states. On the occasion of the Congress of Aachen in 1818, for example, Metternich presented two memoranda to Frederick William III. One was entitled 'On the condition of the Prussian states' (*Über die Lage der preußischen Staaten*), the other 'On education, gymnastics and the freedom of the press' (*Über Erziehungswesen, Turnwesen und Pressfreiheit*). It is not surprising to find sport among the topics preoccupying the minds of European leaders when one considers that the *Turnbewegung* (Gymnastics Movement) in Germany was organized by nationalist teachers and students who practised gymnastics as a means of strengthening their military preparedness. In the memoranda, Metternich spoke out against a constitution for Prussia and warned the king that in Prussian secondary schools and universities a spirit of revolution was being nurtured. The Wartburgfest of 1817, a meeting of nationalist and liberal students from all over Germany to celebrate the victory over Napoleon at the battle of Leipzig, was proof of this assertion. It had already set going secret police operations against students and professors.

It is assumed that Metternich's memoranda were drawn up in cooperation with Prince Ludwig von Sayn-Wittgenstein-Hohenstein (1769–1843), another member of Frederick William's substitute family. He was Frederick William's grand chamberlain, and from 1812 chief of the secret police. In the past, he had been used on secret diplomatic missions. After the Wartburgfest in 1817, and again in 1819, Wittgenstein was able to offer the king intercepted letters of members of the opposition all over the country. This secret collaboration between Metternich and Wittgenstein has now become a historical fact of considerable importance. It was in this manner that the Austrian chancellor was able to implant his personal ideas into the mind of the King of Prussia, thus preparing the ground for the undisguised acts of repression in 1819 and after.

In 1819, when the Russian state councillor, August von Kotzebue, accused of spying for the Russian government, was assassinated by the student Karl Ludwig Sand in Mannheim, Metternich had the occasion he needed. It did not take much effort to win over Prussian authorities. On 7 July 1819, a wave of arrests took place during which further evidence on opposition activities was found. Frederick William even ordered that the most secret files on police inquiries in Prussia and several other German states be made accessible to Metternich. As a result, the Austrian minister became convinced that a widespread conspiracy aimed at overthrowing all the German governments existed and that, moreover, many high-ranking Prussian officials were involved in it. The centres of the conspiracy, Metternich believed, were universities outside Prussia, especially Jena, Heidelberg, Giessen and Freiburg. Somehow or other, Metternich believed, Prussian universities would have to be put under surveillance. The Prussian minister of religious, educational and medical affairs, Baron Altenstein, agreed, although he still wished to protect freedom of teaching as far as possible. Harmful professors were to be dismissed immediately; student associations (*Burschenschaften*) were to be suppressed.

In September 1819, Frederick William III and Hardenberg met with Metternich at Teplitz in Bohemia. The king allowed Metternich to 'bind' Hardenberg and the Prussian government, if necessary in writing, to make sure that no dangerous road towards a parliamentary system was taken. Moreover, Metternich and his aide Gentz decided that they would organize political repression all over Germany, but that they would circumvent the correct procedures prescribed by the Act of the German Confederation. These procedures, which were set up to protect the smaller member states of the German Confederation, made it impossible to push through laws that would put the smaller states under the surveillance of the great powers and would abolish due process of law.

Instead, ministers of the most important German states met in Karlsbad in 1819. An agreement was reached on future co-operation in Germany and later forced upon the Federal Diet. The resulting Karlsbad Decrees stipulated that all attempts to introduce freedom of the press in Germany were to be brought to an end. Individual states were made responsible towards the German Confederation for the correct execution of censorship. Universities were to receive government supervisors (*Kuratoren*). A central commission was to be set up in Mainz to investigate the activities of student associations and political clubs. Prussia was very quick to implement the Karlsbad Decrees, which were published in the law gazette on 18 October 1819. In December, the first student was sent to Mainz from Prussia to be interrogated by the commission. Friedrich Gentz hailed this policy as 'the greatest retrograde movement that has taken place in Europe for thirty years'.[22] The public climate in Germany had changed; the Restoration Party appeared to have gained the upper hand.

Other sources demonstrate that Metternich's views were no more and no less than those held by wider circles of opinion, especially those of the nobility. On 3 August 1819, for example, several noble landowners from Pomerania (including their prominent spokesman Ernst von Bülow-

---

22 Gentz to Pilat, Karlsbad, 1 September 1819 in Karl von Mendelssohn-Bartholdy (ed.), *Briefe von Friedrich von Gentz an Pilat. Ein Beitrag zur Geschichte Deutschlands im 19. Jahrhundert* 2 vols (Leipzig 1868), i. p. 411.

Cummerow) signed a petition complaining about the terrible state of affairs existing in schools and universities. The young generation had become totally politicized, they complained, and then went on to demonstrate that this unhappy state of affairs was more than a simple conspiracy among some students and officials. The whole reform administration, they argued, was unsuitable. There were too many civil servants and there was too much government expenditure. Everybody, it appeared to them, was aiming at the destruction of hereditary nobility because the nobility was the innate enemy of all revolutions. After the defeat of the nobility, the monarchy itself would collapse, until a man from the people would rise above everybody else and would try to establish a monarchy again.[23]

Hunting down the *Zeitgeist*

The police actions authorized by the Karlsbad Decrees, called 'prosecution of the demagogues' (*Demagogenverfolgung*) and unleashed in 1819, spoilt the career of many a young man in Germany. Prison sentences were rare, but students were expelled from universities, young graduates were banned from employment as civil servants, the public discourse was mutilated and censorship triumphed. Goethe's play, *Egmont*, depicting the resistance of Flanders against the rule of King Philip II of Spain, was suppressed in Prussia on 28 October 1819. The ban lasted until 1841. Despite censorship measures like this, theatres gained more and more attention during these years since the debate over the arts, especially theatre criticism, had replaced the debate over politics. While liberal newspapers and periodicals were effectively hindered and even threatened with suppression,[24] Restoration-minded officials and clergymen developed strategies to gain control over the *Zeitgeist*. Although the literal translation of the term means 'spirit of the times', *Zeitgeist* was used by the watchdogs of Restoration to signify rationalism, disrespect and emancipation. We can assess the degree to which this atmosphere of suspicion touched the intellectual life of the nation from a memorandum dated 15 February 1821 and signed by the bishop and court chaplain to the king, Rulemann Friedrich Eylert (1770–1852). There the whole course of contemporary idealistic philosophy was declared responsible for the general

---

23 Oskar Eggert, *Stände und Staat in Pommern im Anfang des 19. Jahrhunderts*. Veröffentlichungen der historischen Kommission für Pommern, 8 (Cologne, 1964), p. 408.
24 Cf. Franz Schneider, *Pressefreiheit und politische Öffentlichkeit. Studien zur politischen Geschichte Deutschlands bis 1848* (Berlin, 1966), pp. 273f.

spirit of disobedience. Contemporary philosophy, the memorandum said, refused revelation and denied the 'positive truths of the Christian religion'. Instead, it taught the moral autonomy of the individual conscience. (Indeed, Kotzebue's assassin claimed that he had committed the murder because his conscience demanded it.) To Eylert and his companions, the demand for popular sovereignty was a logical conclusion of this denial of any authority, earthly or divine.[25]

The Restoration Party was also strengthened by the fact that Enlightenment rationalism and idealistic philosophy had passed their zenith. The Christian faith revived and was used by many conservatives to back up their political arguments. Originating among Bavarian Catholics, a new religious awakening began to have wide repercussions in Germany across denominational borders – neo-Pietism. In Berlin, the Protestant pastors, Justus Gottfried Hermes and Johannes Jaenicke, gained reputations for their Pietist sermons. They emphasized the role of Jesus and his death on the cross for personal salvation. On the other hand, liberal theologians, such as Friedrich Daniel Schleiermacher (1768–1834), a professor at the University of Berlin, were suspected by the Restoration Party of not taking these elements of Christian belief seriously enough and of being politically unreliable. Listeners of Hermes and Jaenicke, and members of the *Maikäferei* who had settled down as landowners in Pomerania, brought the Awakening to the province where, for the next few decades, religious Pietism and the defence of noble class interests, including the ancient provincial estates, combined to make up the dominant mentality of the region. By the 1820s, Lutheran orthodoxy, Pietism and conservatism had formed a firm alliance in Prussia. Since the public debate was stifled, religious debates sometimes served as a medium of political struggle. In 1827, the young pastor Ernst Wilhelm Hengstenberg (1802–68), founded the *Evangelische Kirchenzeitung* (Evangelical Church Newspaper), which developed into a militant conservative journal. Ernst Ludwig von Gerlach was among its supporters, as was the theologian Friedrich August Tholuck (1799–1877). The *Kirchenzeitung* became notorious because of its attacks on the rationalist professors, Julius August Ludwig Wegscheider and Wilhelm Gesenius, both of whom had been quite successful teachers at the University of Halle. Before political conservatism developed into a modern organized party in the wake of the 1848 Revolution, conservatives identified themselves as the 'party of the *Kirchenzeitung*'.

---

25 Promemoria von Beckedorff, Eylert, Snethlage und Schultz, 15 February 1821 in Max Lenz, *Geschichte der Königlichen Friedrich-Wilhelms-Universität zu Berlin*, 4 vols (Halle, 1910), iv, pp. 390–401.

Transforming the military into an instrument of royal prerogative

The military was not spared from the attacks of the Restoration Party. In 1818, Queen Louisa's brother, Duke Charles of Mecklenburg, wrote a memorandum for the king in which he voiced his suspicion that the 'party of revolution' had gained a foothold among the top ranks of Prussia's bureaucracy. He also warned the king against democratic tendencies in the Prussian militia, called the *Landwehr*. The *Landwehr* mobilized ex-servicemen up to the age of 39. It had its own formations independent of active soldiers. *Landwehr* officers were more often bourgeois in origin. Since its soldiers were closely connected with civilian life, the *Landwehr* formations did not develop the spirit of military exclusiveness that was considered essential by conservatives if the military was to serve as the most important tool in the defence of the monarchy within state and society. In 1824, Duke Charles also wrote that officers coming from those classes of society that earned a wage (*Erwerbsklassen*) did not have the necessary chivalrous spirit; instead, they introduced attitudes from their own milieu.[26] In 1819, Hermann von Boyen, the author of the famous law of 1814 on the general conscription, resigned from his office as minister of war. He had wished to open the army to the middle class and the middle-class mentality. When, now, the king introduced several changes in the structure of the army, Boyen was afraid that the *Landwehr* would lose its character. With hindsight, his worries seem exaggerated. At the time, the king intended carrying out only superficial changes.[27] However, widespread mistrust of the *Landwehr* remained. Prince William, the king's second son and future king and kaiser, was also a strong advocate of a restoration in the composition of the military. William's intention to turn the army into an instrument of internal repression slowly began to appear in the decades before 1848. For William, the threat of revolution entailed two considerations. The first was that revolution was a danger that came from without, one that could be imported by a new wave of French expansionism. Indeed, during the Revolution of 1830, William feared that a second assault on the security of Europe, which would once again follow the Bonapartist pattern, was about to be launched. The second was that revolution was also a danger from

---

26 Cf. Alf Lüdtke, '"Wehrhafte Nation" und "innere Wohlfahrt". Zur militärischen Mobilisierbarkeit der bürgerlichen Gesellschaft', *Militaergeschichtliche Mitteilungen* 2 (1981), 49.
27 Cf. Dennis E. Showalter, 'The Prussian *Landwehr* and its Critics', *Central European History* 4 (1971), 3–33.

within, if the demagogues and other irreverent intellectuals were able to kindle popular unrest. To support the throne against the enemy from within, the army had to be turned into the king's exclusive instrument of power. Consequently, no independent *Landwehr* formations could survive. This 'restorative' aim was attained fully in the so-called 'reform' that William undertook with Albrecht von Roon soon after he became king in 1861. The case of the military demonstrates that some restorative attempts were obstinate and lasted far into the nineteenth century.

Conclusion

Hardenberg supported the 'prosecution of the demagogues'. He did not do so for purely tactical means – that is, to please the king and thereby persuade him to support the idea of a constitution. Instead, Hardenberg considered civil liberties to be the generous gift of a wise administration. The administration could withdraw them if it deemed proper, and it did so in 1819.

Historians have long been aware of Hardenberg's reform priorities. 'The reforms in which Hardenberg persisted were designed to achieve primarily economic ends, while those which he was willing to give up under pressure were motivated chiefly by socio-political or humanitarian ideas.'[28] Indeed, the core of his programme of economic liberalization remained untouched even after Hardenberg's death. It was defended by officials such as Maassen and Motz, both important ministers of finance, Rother, director of the important state enterprise 'Seehandlung' and minister of the treasury, Beuth, a privy councillor who supported early industrialization, and others. Hardenberg undermined his own position, and thus brought about the victory of conservative forces at court, because he stood by his false friend Prince Wittgenstein instead of building an alliance with Wilhelm von Humboldt (1767–1835) and Carl Friedrich von Beyme (1765–1838), the reform ministers who were dismissed in 1819, mainly because they dared to question Hardenberg's personal prerogatives.

For decades, historians have talked and written about monarchies without taking notice of the monarchs themselves. In Prussia, Frederick William III was a key figure in the struggle of the Restoration Party for influence. Understanding his personality makes it much easier to see why Reform and

---

28 Walter Michael Simon, *The Failure of the Prussian Reform Movement 1807–1819* (Ithaca, NJ, 1955), p. 95.

Restoration parties in Prussia tended to melt into one another. The image we have of him is, however, somewhat blurred, and this in turn blurs our interpretation of the period during which he reigned.

Frederick William III, a moderately conservative king, had attempted reforms himself and had accepted most of the proposals that Baron Stein had made. Shortly after the defeat of Napoleon in 1814, however, he began to assume that enough reforms had been carried through. From then on, it became easier to convince him that certain elements of reform policy were disadvantageous. The Pietist Baron Hans Ernst von Kottwitz (1757–1843), for example, was able to convince the king that freedom of trade – *Gewerbefreiheit* – might be dangerous because it caused unemployment. Unemployment was a misery, weighing heavily on the conscience of the ruler. Hardenberg, with all his theoretical background in physiocratic thinking and Enlightenment ideas, was not able to argue effectively against Kottwitz, who played on the king's religious feelings and his feeble conscience. Hardenberg began to fear that one of the cornerstones of his work might be removed. At the same time, Metternich manipulated the king masterfully. Therefore, if Prussia did not receive a constitution before 1848, it was largely the consequence of Frederick William's decision. In this respect, Hardenberg was aware that he had suffered a defeat, although he did not realize the extent to which Wittgenstein had betrayed him.

When Hardenberg died in 1822, the king and his sons agreed that the chancellor's reforms had done much harm to the 'good spirit' in Prussia. Indeed, shortly before his death, the crown prince had come to regard Hardenberg as his major adversary. Instead of a constitution and a general assembly, Prussia received only modernized provincial estates (*Provinzialstände*) by a law passed on 5 June 1823. Again, there were to be representatives of three of the social orders: noble landowners, farmer landowners and the cities. On the other hand, the provincial diets (*Provinziallandtage*) were to assemble in single homogeneous sessions; there was no separate debating and voting of the different estates. This was decidedly modern.

When the crown prince came to power in 1840 as Frederick William IV, he raised the hopes of many a liberal. While such hopes mostly went unfulfilled, there were some aspects to the king's policy that made him appear more progressive than his leading officials. For example, Frederick William IV took a decisive step away from the old state church system towards a modern understanding of the church as a mere corporation within the state by introducing the right of the individual to leave a church without joining another. For the first time in Prussian history, a citizen could be a citizen without being a member of any religious community. The king even attempted to reform the legal and economic status of the nobility. This ran into some opposition, as with the Rochow family, which included the minister of the interior Gustav von Rochow (1792–1847). This minister and several of his colleagues opposed any attempts on the part of the king to reform the Prussian nobility according to the British model and thereby bridge the gap between the nobility and the bourgeoisie.

The Rochows and the majority of the ministers of state were interested above all in a nobility that rallied around the throne and supported the state.[29] It was meant to stabilize the monarchy. As far as the conservative nobility was concerned, stabilizing the monarchy meant keeping the king from giving in to reformist tendencies, and from giving up his autocratic and romantic beliefs – a development that the Camarilla, the group of 'ultra conservatives' around Frederick William IV, feared more than anything else.

The term 'ultra' is in itself revealing. Indeed, both Hohenzollern kings of the pre-revolutionary period – Frederick William II and Frederick William III – were less extreme than some of their advisers. Consequently, a victory of the Restoration Party in Prussia presupposes a victory over the heart and mind of the king. Both monarchs had a tendency to follow the advice of the last person who had their ear. The lurching, unstable course that the monarchs thus took contributed to the image of a state that wavered between Restoration and Reform.

What of the bureaucracy in all this? The 'state' is an abstract notion; it can act only when its employees begin to act. What could bureaucrats do to stabilize the monarchy? From the viewpoint of the Restoration Party that existed in the 1790s, the bureaucracy itself was a dangerous enemy, especially in the shape that it had gained during the last decades of absolutism. And even for a conservative of the younger generation, like Ernst Ludwig von Gerlach, who was born in 1795, absolutism was as evil as revolution.[30] He nevertheless served as the employee of a government that up to 1848 remained formally absolutist. As Barbara Vogel has pointed out, the determined reformers, on the other hand, never made up more than a small group.[31] Even in the Hardenberg clique, opinions changed over the years as members grew older and views that formerly had been sharply accentuated began to mellow. In the educated circles of Prussia, one-time Romantics turned liberal, radicals turned conservative. The Prussian state apparatus in reality was a stronghold of rational reform conservatives who

---

29 Cf. Heinz Reif, 'Adelspolitik in Preußen zwischen Reformzeit und Revolution 1848', in Hans-Peter Ullmann and Clemens Zimmermann, eds, *Restaurationssystem und Reform politik. Süddeutschland and Preußen im Vergleich* (Munich, 1996), p. 222.
30 Cf. Hans-Christof Kraus, *Ernst Ludwig von Gerlach: Politisches Denken und Handeln eines preußischen Altkonservativen*, 2 vols (Göttingen, 1996), i, p. 204.
31 Cf. Barbara Vogel, *Allgemeine Gewerbefreiheit. Die Reformpolitik des preußischen Staatskanzlers Hardenberg (1810–1820)*. Kritische Studien zur Geschichtswissenschaft, 57 (Göttingen, 1983).

knew that the feudal state of Haller and his disciples was an illusion.[32] While it still may be possible to distinguish between 'liberals' and 'reactionaries' within the state apparatus itself, we must acknowledge that both party blocs 'cut across class planes'.[33] Both used different means of forming social cohesion, including 'cultural' instruments of orientation. As Eric Dorn Brose has pointed out, they formed friendship circles, salons, gatherings. In all of them, we find different shades and degrees of 'liberalism' and 'reaction'. This adds weight to the image described above – that of a state that wavered constantly between Restoration and Reform.

---

32 Lothar Dittmer, *Beamtenkonservativismus und Modernisierung. Untersuchungen zur Vorgeschichte der Konservativen Partei in Preußen 1810–1848/49*. Studien zur modernen Geschichte, 44 (Stuttgart, 1992), p. 407.
33 Eric Dorn Brose, *The Politics of Technological Change in Prussia. Out of the Shadow of Antiquity, 1809–1848* (Princeton, 1992), p. 259.

CHAPTER THREE

Revolution and counter-revolution in Prussia, 1840–50

DAVID E. BARCLAY

Prussia had never exactly been a 'classic' land of revolutions. Thus, when a real revolution did come to Berlin in March 1848, neither the revolutionaries nor their opponents knew exactly how to behave. In contrast to France, where revolution had been a form of grand public theatre for decades, Prussians on both sides of the barricades were unsure of the roles that they were supposed to play. As the commander of the Berlin garrison during the street fighting of 18–19 March 1848 later noted sardonically in his memoirs, 'In Prussia we had only known about revolutions from descriptions of them, but we had never experienced them ourselves'.[1] Despite their inexperience, the participants in these events quickly adapted to their new parts, becoming actors in a drama that turned out to be of far-reaching significance in the history of the Prussian state and Prussian society. The revolutions of 1848–50 represented far more than either a 'tragedy' or a 'farce', and they were certainly more than a 'turning point that failed to turn' or a mere prologue to Bismarck's *Reichsgründung* in 1871.[2] To be sure, the King of Prussia was not toppled from his throne in 1848, and after the revolution, Prussia's traditional elite groups – the monarchy, the bureaucracy, the military and the East Elbians – continued to enjoy a disproportionate share of power and authority in the

---

1 Karl Ludwig von Prittwitz, *Berlin 1848. Das Erinnerungswerk des Generalleutnants Karl Ludwig von Prittwitz und andere Quellen zur Berliner Märzrevolution und zur Geschichte Preußens um die Mitte des 19.Jahrhunderts*, ed. Gerd Heinrich (Berlin, 1985), p. 264.
2 The references here are to the famous opening sentences of Karl Marx's *Eighteenth Brumaire of Louis Bonaparte* and to George Macaulay Trevelyan's comments about the European revolutions of 1848 in general.

state. Moderate liberals and radical democrats alike were frustrated in their efforts to reshape the Prussian state according to their own ideals. In Prussia itself and in several other German states, the Prussian army brutally intervened after the spring of 1849 to restore 'order' and to suppress popular-democratic movements. Moreover, despite the pledges of King Frederick William IV in March 1848, Prussia did not thereafter take an effective lead in creating a greater form of German unity. By 1851, the old, and largely discredited, German Confederation of 1815 had been re-established; and, at the same time, renewed censorship and unprecedented forms of police surveillance had severely curtailed active forms of political opposition within Prussia and most of the rest of Germany.

Despite this admittedly depressing balance sheet, it would be grievously misleading to assume that the revolutions in Prussia represented little more than an exercise in vain political theatrics. As a result of the dramatic events between 1848 and 1850, Prussia did make a permanent transition to constitutionalism and parliamentarism. As the historian Günther Grünthal has noted, this transition was the result of a complex series of compromises in the late autumn of 1848 that involved the king, his conservative 'Camarilla' and key members of the cabinet.[3] Those compromises in turn required concessions to certain key liberal demands for a constitution and an elected parliament. Although constitutional and parliamentary institutions were in practice attenuated and limited, they created a lasting framework for the modernization of Prussian politics. As a result, anyone who was actively involved in the shaping of public policy, including the king and his closest advisers, had to accommodate himself to new political publics and to new forms of political mobilization, interest articulation, propaganda and organization. Conservative opponents of the revolution quickly realized that 'revolutionary' innovations like elections, newspapers, pressure groups and parliamentary caucuses could be turned to their own advantage; and thus, ironically, the radical transformation of conservative politics must be regarded as one of the major outcomes of the revolutions of 1848–50 in Prussia.

The coming of revolution, 1840–48

On 15 October 1840, the new King of Prussia, Frederick William IV, appeared before the royal palace in Berlin to receive the homage (*Huldigung*)

---

3 Günther Grünthal, 'Zwischen König, Kabinett und Kamarilla. Der Verfassungsoktroi in Preußen vom 5.12.1848', *Jahrbuch für die Geschichte Mittel- und Ostdeutschlands* 32 (1983), 119–74.

of the estates of the six western provinces of his realm. Along with the representatives of the estates and the *Bürgerschaft* of Berlin, 60,000 of the king's subjects were gathered in a driving rainstorm to observe the ceremony, which in Prussia was roughly equivalent to a coronation. Frederick William was a man who loved dramatic gestures, and this turned out to be one of his grandest moments. As a thoroughly modern man, he understood that, in an age of emerging mass publics and new forms of public opinion, monarchs could no longer justify themselves simply by virtue of their existence and their ancient lineage. Rather, they had to avail themselves of modern techniques of political persuasion in order to advance their interests. Accordingly, before taking his traditional oath to be a just and merciful ruler, the new king turned to his audience and delivered a rousing speech. Described even by his enemies as a compelling orator, Frederick William was the first Prussian monarch ever to address his civilian subjects so personally and so directly.

The king's speech elicited an enthusiastic and even ecstatic response from his listeners. After years of stagnation and paralysis at the top, it seemed that Prussia at last had an energetic ruler who was attuned to his times. As crown prince, Frederick William had regularly denounced the evils of bureaucratic despotism and political paralysis. He was well known for his patronage of the arts, especially architecture, and for his close association with prominent intellectuals like the great naturalist Alexander von Humboldt. Shortly after his accession to the throne in June 1840, he had attracted a great deal of positive attention by inviting a number of prominent writers and scholars to the University of Berlin, including several, like the Brothers Grimm, who were closely associated with the cause of liberal constitutionalism. Thus it was not surprising that the new king stirred liberal hopes for positive social and political change.[4] But, as the nineteenth-century historian Heinrich von Treitschke famously noted, both the monarch and liberal advocates of moderate change utterly misunderstood each other's intentions. Frederick William IV had his own political agenda, one that had little in common with the concerns of liberals or of other, more radical, reformers. As a result, during the last *Vormärz* years – that is, during the years that immediately preceded the eruption of March 1848 – the Prussian state was unable or unwilling to respond effectively to a variety of factors that, taken together, had by 1847 contributed to a generalized pre-revolutionary crisis. Those factors included the following:

First, sustained population growth had become a source of serious

---

4   For the preceding, see David E. Barclay, *Frederick William IV and the Prussian Monarchy 1840–1861* (Oxford, 1995), pp. 52–5.

concern to a number of critical observers by the 1830s and 1840s. In 1816, Prussia had a population of 10.32 million people, or 44 per cent of the total population of the German Confederation. By 1849, those figures had risen to 16.33 million and 47 per cent respectively.[5] As a result of the legislation of the Reform Era, ordinary people had become more mobile than ever before, contributing to what many contemporaries regarded as an alarmingly rapid rate of urbanization. That phenomenon was especially noticeable in Berlin, where between 1815 and 1848 the population grew from about 200,000 to over 400,000, making it the fourth largest city in Europe after London, Paris and St Petersburg.[6]

Second, related to rapid population growth and the increasing visibility of the poor, both in towns and in the countryside, was the equally visible reality of economic change, especially the crisis of handicraft production and proto-industry and the first signs of early industrialization. By the 1840s, a variety of factors, including population growth and competition from advanced British industry, had contributed to horrendous problems within the traditional artisanate. Similarly, many rural or small-town producers who had derived a growing share of their income from proto-industry – that is, decentralized home-based production organized according to the so-called putting-out system – were no longer able to make ends meet. The crises of these traditional sectors of the economy overlapped with the first stages of the industrialization process in Prussia, although the two phenomena were not as closely connected as some contemporaries thought. Prussia remained a pre-industrial society, and the increasingly impoverished 'lower orders' (*Unterschichten*) still derived their living from traditional agricultural and artisanal pursuits. Despite the rapid growth of railways during the 1840s, for example, Prussia did not experience a full-scale industrial 'take-off' until the 1850s; nor did early industrialization in Prussia contribute significantly to the crises of artisanal and proto-industrial production.[7] Still, many ordinary Prussians in the years just before 1848 sensed that their traditional way of life was being massively challenged,

---

5   Wolfram Fischer, Jochen Krengel and Jutta Wietog, *Sozialgeschichtliches Arbeitsbuch*, Vol. 1: *Materialien zur Statistik des Deutschen Bundes 1815–1870* (Munich, 1982), pp. 21–2.
6   Ilja Mieck, 'Ausländer und Immigranten in Berlin 1848', in Ilja Mieck, Horst Möller and Jürgen Voss (eds), *Paris und Berlin in der Revolution 1848/Paris et Berlin dans la révolution de 1848* (Sigmaringen, 1995), p. 215; Mieck, 'Von der Reformzeit zur Revolution (1806–1847)', in Wolfgang Ribbe (ed.), *Geschichte Berlins*, Vol. 1: *Von der Frühgeschichte bis zur Industrialisierung* (Munich, 1997), 480–4.
7   Cf. Hans-Ulrich Wehler, *Deutsche Gesellschaftsgeschichte*, Vol. 2: *Von der Reformära bis zur industriellen und politischen 'Deutschen Doppelrevolution' 1815–1845/49* (Munich, 1987), pp. 281–8; Wolfram Siemann, *Vom Staatenbund zum Nationalstaat. Deutschland 1806–1871* (Munich, 1995), pp. 152–8.

whether in the form of cheap British imports, structural unemployment, or new forms of homegrown, post-reform agrarian capitalism.

Third, the last *Vormärz* years thus witnessed a steady preoccupation with the social question and 'pauperism': that is, with worsening mass poverty in towns and cities and in the countryside. Across the political and ideological spectrum, contemporaries worried about the consequences of what seemed to them to be an unprecedentedly dangerous situation. In the well-known words of the conservative social reformer Joseph Maria von Radowitz, the social question represented 'the bleeding wound of the present'.[8] And in the years just before 1848, it could sometimes explode into violence, as in the Silesian weavers' revolt of 1844 (made famous by Heinrich Heine and Gerhart Hauptmann) and a wave of food riots, including the Berlin 'potato revolution', in the spring of 1847.[9] As the latter suggested, the situation was exacerbated by the bad harvests and potato blight of the years between 1846 and 1848.

Fourth, regional and confessional differences also contributed to the development of a pre-revolutionary situation in Prussia. In many respects, Prussia had always been an artificial state, an agglomeration of diverse territories that its rulers had acquired over the course of many generations. That territorial diversity became even more pronounced when Prussia acquired the Rhineland at the Congress of Vienna. Where Prussia had traditionally been Protestant and culturally 'eastern', the Rhineland was largely Catholic and 'western' in cultural orientation. It had been exposed to the transformations of the French Revolution and had been absorbed by Napoleon; accordingly, its legal and economic structures were more advanced than elsewhere in Prussia. Much of the country's early industrialization was focused on the Rhineland; and it is not surprising that a disproportionate number of moderate, constitutional-monarchical liberal activists were drawn from Rhenish business circles, including many who became politically prominent during the revolutions of 1848.

Discontent with Prussian rule often flared into confessional controversy, especially after the 1830s. In the latter part of that decade, a major conflict between the Prussian government and the Archbishop of Cologne had resulted in the latter's arrest; and, in 1844, hundreds of thousands of Catholics participated in a pilgrimage to Trier in what amounted to a form of grass-roots protest against the Protestant authorities. But it was not only Catholics who were unhappy with the Prussian state; the mid-1840s also

---

8 Quoted in Wehler, *Gesellschaftsgeschichte*, ii, p. 283.
9 On the hunger disturbances of 1847, see, above all, Manfred Gailus, *Straße und Brot. Sozialer Protest in den deutschen Staaten unter besonderer Berücksichtigung Preußens, 1847–1849* (Göttingen, 1990), ch. 4.

witnessed the emergence of the Friends of Light (*Lichtfreunde*), a group of Protestants, mostly around Magdeburg in central Germany, who embraced theological rationalism and opposed the conservative political and theological policies of Frederick William IV. As the writer and social critic Robert Prutz acidly observed in 1846, theology had become 'the centre of German life', a convenient vehicle for the articulation of what were really political differences.[10]

Fifth, the years just before 1848 were marked by the inability of Frederick William IV to transform the Prussian monarchy according to his conservative principles.[11] As a result, the Prussian state was unable adequately to respond to the social and economic problems of the 'Hungry Forties'. As crown prince before 1840, Frederick William had been the focal point for younger conservatives – the brothers Leopold and Ernst Ludwig von Gerlach, Joseph Maria von Radowitz, Count Carl von der Groeben, Baron Ernst Senfft von Pilsach, and others – who disapproved of 'bureaucratic absolutism' and who sought to recast the Prussian monarchy according to organic-corporatist principles. Frederick William IV's principal goal in life was to struggle against the 'revolution' (that 'monstrum horrendum ingens', he once called it) and all its works, by which he meant such 'French-modern' innovations as parliaments, constitutions and centralized state bureaucracies. The creation of a 'Christian-German' state on the basis of reinvigorated estates (*Stände*) and a rejuvenated, decentralized Protestant church would, he argued, represent a 'truly German' alternative to the horrors flowing from France. Moreover, he insisted, the introduction of a new structure of estates, in which people would be represented on the basis of 'historically' defined group rights and privileges, would permit him to fulfil his father's constitutional pledges of 1815 without actually agreeing to a constitution.

Frederick William's corporatist (*ständisch*) reforms represented something that was quite unprecedented in Prussian history: an attempt to come up with an ideological justification for monarchy on the basis of invented 'historical', institutional and theological traditions. As Sebastian Haffner has written, Prussia had always been a 'raw state based on reason'; and Frederick William's uncle, Count Friedrich Wilhelm von Brandenburg (1790–1850), liked to remind his nephew that Prussia was a 'centralized military and administrative state', nothing more and nothing less.[12] It had never sought

---

10 Cf. Wehler, *Gesellschaftsgeschichte*, ii, p. 467.
11 For the following, see Barclay, *Frederick William IV*, ch. 5.
12 Sebastian Haffner, *Preußen ohne Legende*, 2nd edn (Hamburg, 1979), p. 55; Friedrich Wilhelm Graf von Brandenburg to Frederick William IV, 4 September 1850, Geheimes Staatsarchiv Preußischer Kulturbesitz Berlin [hereafter: GStAPK], Brandenburg-Preußisches Hausarchiv, Rep. 50 J Nr. 212, Bl. 74.

to justify its existence by appealing to a non-existent medieval past or to divine sanction. But Frederick William, who literally believed that he was king by the grace of God, was trying to do just that. Between 1842 and 1847, he moved forward relentlessly with his *ständisch*-monarchical reform project, largely oblivious to the larger social and economic forces that were steering Prussia towards revolution. That project culminated with his February Patent in 1847, in which he announced that a United Diet (*Vereinigter Landtag*), composed of all the members of the provincial diets that had been established according to *ständisch* principles back in 1823, would meet in Berlin to consider urgent financial issues, including new loans and new taxes. When that body convened in April, however, it quickly turned into what Frederick William feared the most: a de facto parliament. To be sure, it was no assembly of Jacobin radicals. Composed largely of moderate conservatives and moderate liberals, it was not interested in overturning the established order. But it refused to approve new financial expenditures without a royal guarantee of 'periodicity' – that is, regular annual meetings of the United Diet – and the right of the Diet to approve future financial legislation. This was too much for Frederick William, and so the United Diet was allowed to adjourn without a resolution of any of the pressing financial problems that it was supposed to address. In the months that intervened between the summer of 1847 and March 1848, Prussia drifted aimlessly yet inexorably towards revolutionary violence.

Sixth, the United Diet itself presented a clear example of the resurgence of political activity in Prussia during the *Vormärz* period. That political activity extended across the entire ideological spectrum, from socialist, communist and radical-democratic movements on the left to monarchist and conservative organizations on the right. Recent years have witnessed an explosion of new research on all these movements, and especially on mid-century liberalism and conservatism; and we now know that both phenomena were far more variegated and far more complex than scholars used to think.[13] For the most part, Prussia's liberals, whether Rhenish businessmen or East Prussian aristocrats, were moderate modernizers. They were not interested in overturning monarchical authority, and would have been content with a moderate constitution and a government with a pro-business, pro-growth agenda that would also support the cause of the greater German national unity that most liberals supported. Although less effectively organized, Prussia's conservatives on the eve of revolution were far more 'ideological', especially the so-called 'high' conservatives who

---

13 See the excellent summary in Jonathan Sperber, *Revolutions, The European 1848–1851* (Cambridge, 1994) pp. 64–71.

shared the king's vision, though not always his tactics. At the same time, they were singularly unprepared for the tidal wave of change that swept over them in March 1848.

The liberal and democratic revolutions, spring–autumn 1848

'Satan is on the loose again.'[14] With these words, Frederick William IV reacted to the news of the February revolution that had toppled the July Monarchy in Paris. Almost immediately, he undertook a series of efforts to organize a common monarchical front against the contagion spreading from France, but these initiatives were far too little and far too late. As a popular agrarian revolution began to affect parts of southern and north-western Germany, the Aachen businessman David Hansemann called on 1 March for an all-German parliament and genuine representative political institutions; two days later, military authorities intervened in Cologne to break up a large-scale demonstration in that city. But such actions could not stem the tide of demonstrations, petitions and addresses that began to sweep across the entire monarchy in March. For the most part, Prussia's traditional ruling elites responded to these movements not with decisive action, but with a fear that bordered on paralysis, especially when they were faced with the horrifying prospect of a full-scale agrarian insurrection in places like Silesia. Indeed, the historian Gerd Heinrich has written of a generalized crisis in Prussia's 'primary leadership stratum' in the spring of 1848.[15] As Frederick William later put it to the historian Leopold von Ranke, 'In those days we were all lying on our bellies.'[16]

In fact, however, the King of Prussia responded to the revolution in a rather more measured fashion than most of his advisers, including his brother and heir, William, the Prince of Prussia (later Emperor William I). The older historical literature likes to depict Frederick William as a sobbing and hysterical monarch who had completely lost control of himself, but that picture is wildly overdrawn. Although the king was sometimes overcome by panic and depression during the March days, he responded to those events

---

14 Frederick William IV to Carl von der Groeben, 1 March 1848, GStAPK, Rep. 92 Graf Carl von der Groeben B Nr. 4e 1848, Bl. 6.
15 Introduction to Prittwitz, *Berlin 1848*, p. 1.
16 Leopold von Ranke, 'Friedrich Wilhelm IV., König von Preußen', in *Allgemeine Deutsche Biographie* (Berlin, 1968; orig. 1877), vii, p. 770.

with a series of timely concessions that helped to save lives and, possibly, his throne. In mid-March, as demonstrations and petition campaigns were mounting in Berlin itself, the king's chief minister, Ernst von Bodelschwingh (1794–1854), convinced the monarch on 17 March to abolish censorship, re-convene the United Diet, and pave the way for a constitution. In addition, the king agreed to appoint Count Adolf Heinrich von Arnim-Boitzenburg (1803–1868) to serve as the new chief minister and thus head Prussia's first constitutional government.

The new royal patents were issued on the morning of 18 March, and what happened immediately thereafter has frequently been described. A mass rally had already been scheduled to take place in front of the royal palace in the heart of Berlin. Now it turned into an occasion of thanksgiving, as several thousand demonstrators turned out to cheer the announcement, especially when the king himself showed up on the palace balcony to greet his subjects. As troops on the square tried to maintain order, however, some shots were discharged, and within hours barricades were being erected throughout the city amid charges that the king had betrayed his loyal people. Several thousand Berliners took part in the fighting. Despite the king's later contention that foreigners and outside agitators had been responsible for the violence, it is evident that, in fact, the participants in the violence mirrored the composition (and the social tensions) of the city itself. Of 303 civilians who were officially reported as having died on 18–19 March, 52 were listed as 'workers and proletarians', 115 were journeymen (including woodworkers, tailors, shoemakers and locksmiths), 11 were women, 34 were servants or small businessmen, and 15 came from the 'educated estates'.[17]

The new commander of the Berlin garrison, General Karl Ludwig von Prittwitz (1795–1885), was both tough and unimaginative. After hours of street fighting, he informed the king that the garrison, though numerically superior, would be able to hold out only for a few days, and urged a withdrawal preparatory to besieging and bombarding the city. To his credit, Frederick William did not want to kill his subjects, and, in the early hours of 19 March, drafted his famous decree 'To My Dear Berliners' (*An Meine lieben Berliner*). In it he suggested that the whole altercation had been a 'misunderstanding', and he stated that, if the barricades were taken down, Prittwitz's troops would also be withdrawn from the scenes of fighting. Despite the violent opposition of Prittwitz, the Prince of Prussia and other military leaders to this plan, the army returned to its barracks on the afternoon of the

---

17 Wolfram Siemann, *Die deutsche Revolution von 1848/49* (Frankfurt am Main, 1985), p. 69. Cf. Rüdiger Hachtmann, *Berlin 1848. Eine Politik- und Gesellschaftsgeschichte der Revolution* (Bonn, 1997), pp. 173–82.

nineteenth, and soon the palace itself, with the king and queen in it, was virtually unguarded. The revolution had apparently triumphed completely. Among other things, Frederick William and Queen Elisabeth were forced to pay homage as the bodies of those who had been killed in the street fighting (*die Märzgefallenen*) were paraded past them. The queen, described as 'white with fear', exclaimed that the 'only thing missing now is the guillotine'.[18] Two days later, on 21 March, Frederick William IV undertook one of the more bizarre public spectacles of his reign, riding openly through the streets of Berlin and proclaiming to his cheering subjects that Prussia, now a constitutional state, would take the lead in moving Germany towards a more genuine form of national unity, as the country's leading liberals had fervently advocated. Accompanied by the black–red–gold colours of the national movement, the King of Prussia proclaimed, 'Henceforth Prussia will merge into Germany'.[19] Finally, on 25 March, the king travelled to Potsdam to inform his unhappy officers that he felt quite safe in Berlin and that all was well. In fact, he was putting up a brave front. Although he had handled the pressures of the revolution reasonably well, most observers who saw him in the spring and summer of 1848 agreed that he seemed to be a broken man, by turns depressed, apathetic and querulous. By the end of March, he had left Berlin more or less permanently, settling in his usual summer quarters in Potsdam. There he increasingly seemed to be on the margins, removed from the centre of action in revolutionary Berlin.

In that city, Prussia's first constitutional government lasted for only ten days. On 29 March, Arnim-Boitzenburg was replaced as first minister by the respected Cologne businessman Ludolf Camphausen (1803–90), while the new finance minister was the Aachen entrepreneur David Hansemann (1790–1864). The moderate Rhenish liberals seemed to be firmly in the saddle, and their behaviour in office was entirely consistent with the programme that they had advocated for many years: to establish a pro-industry, pro-business, pro-growth parliamentary system based on a limited property franchise.[20] Although Marxist scholarship, beginning with Marx and Engels themselves, has long contended that the liberal bourgeoisie 'betrayed'

---

18 Prittwitz, *Berlin 1848*, pp. 329–31.
19 Adolf Wolff, *Berliner Revolutions-Chronik. Darstellung der Berliner Bewegungen im Jahre 1848 nach politischen, socialen und literarischen Beziehungen*, 3 vols (Berlin, 1851–54, repr. Vaduz, 1979), i, pp. 294–9; Veit Valentin, *Geschichte der deutschen Revolution von 1848–1849*, 2 vols (Cologne, 1977; orig. 1931–32), i, pp. 450–1; Hachtmann, *Berlin 1848*, pp. 208–13.
20 Rudolf Boch, 'David Hansemann: Das Kind der Industrie', in Sabine Freitag (ed.), *Die Achtundvierziger. Lebensbilder aus der deutschen Revolution 1848/49* (Munich, 1998), p. 178. For an important recent analysis of the Rhenish business elites, their economic interests and their political activities, see James M. Brophy, *Capitalism, Politics, and Railroads in Prussia, 1830–1870* (Columbus, Ohio, 1998).

the revolution in 1848, the liberals never made any attempt to disguise their long-term, evolutionary and constitutional-monarchical strategy. As the historian Rudolf Boch has recently observed, 'Their goal was to limit the power elite's concessions to what had already been agreed to during *Vormärz* and to stop the revolution as soon as possible'.[21]

Elections were among the first tasks that the Camphausen/Hansemann government faced. Qualified adult males – more than 3.6 million in all – were entitled to vote for electors, who in turn chose delegates for both a Prussian 'National' Assembly and for a genuinely German National Assembly. Those assemblies were intended to approve constitutions for Prussia and for a unified Germany respectively. They convened for the first time in May, the Prussian assembly mostly at the Singakademie in Berlin, and the German assembly at the Paulskirche in Frankfurt am Main. The results of these elections reflected the sharp divisions within Prussia itself in the wake of the March revolution. Where democratic forces triumphed in Prussia's Saxon province and in Silesia and the Rhineland, the old 'core' provinces of the Prussian state in Brandenburg, Pomerania and East Prussia voted for royalist and conservative candidates. The delegates to the Prussian National Assembly were more politically diverse than their colleagues at the Frankfurt Paulskirche; the 402 members included industrialists, merchants, peasants, artisans, government officials and aristocrats, but no professors or industrial workers. About 110 members belonged to the radical-democratic, republican left wing, which opposed the moderation of the Rhenish liberals and endorsed more thoroughgoing constitutional proposals than those which the Camphausen government submitted to the assembly in May. The assembly as a whole was unhappy with the government draft, and instead entrusted the radical democrat Benedikt Waldeck (1802–70) with the task of chairing a commission to develop a new constitutional draft.[22]

The difficulties that the Camphausen/Hansemann government encountered in the assembly paralleled the problems that it confronted outside that body. In contrast to France, Prussia experienced little in 1848 comparable to the few weeks of illusory popular consensus that followed the February Revolution in Paris. From the very beginning, sharp lines of division were visible in Prussia, some of which seemed to be driving the kingdom in a more radical direction. Only in recent years, for example, have historians paid much attention to the elemental popular movements in the countryside in the

---

21 Boch, 'Hansemann', p. 180.
22 Ilja Mieck, 'Preußen von 1807 bis 1850. Reformen, Restauration und Revolution', in Otto Büsch, ed., *Handbuch der preußischen Geschichte*, Vol. 2: *Das 19. Jahrhundert und Große Themen der Geschichte Preußens* (Berlin, 1992), pp. 252–5.

spring and summer of 1848. More than anything, perhaps, these agrarian upheavals in Prussia's East Elbian regions had shattered the confidence of the country's traditional rulers. Silesia was the focus of much of this activity, with peasants and other agricultural labourers united in their demands for a lessening of their obligations and for the elimination of the remaining privileges of the landed elite such as patrimonial justice and hunting rights. Although some estates were burned down during the spring, most political activity in the countryside became focused not so much on direct action as on the creation of new political associations (*Vereine*), a phenomenon that was one of the hallmarks of the revolution both in the cities and in the countryside. In Silesia, a network of 'rural societies' (*Rustikalvereine*) emerged in the spring that encouraged their members not to pay taxes or other dues until the government acceded to their demands; by August 1848, the societies had registered 200,000 members in 200 local organizations. Faced with this massive opposition, subsequent governments – including the counter-revolutionary cabinet of Count Brandenburg after November 1848 – agreed to a number of concessions that by early 1849 had taken the wind out of the sails of rural protest.[23]

The urban protests that accompanied the Prussian revolutions of 1848 have been much better documented than the rural revolts of that year. Throughout the spring and summer, Berlin and other major cities, from Königsberg in the east to Cologne and Düsseldorf in the west, were the locus of extraordinarily vigorous and multifaceted radical, democratic and socialist/communist movements of various kinds and with various kinds of supporters. These movements found expression in an astounding variety of local political clubs, regional and national associations, newspapers, leaflets, broadsheets and public rallies.[24] Although these movements represented the emergence of the 'working class' onto the historical stage, generalizations about 'workers' remain difficult. Thus, for example, some master artisans had to be reckoned as belonging to the middle strata of society (*Mittelschichten*), while less prosperous artisans, though nominally economically independent, clearly led 'semi-proletarian' existences close to the economic margins. In addition, the Prussian working classes also included vast numbers of journeymen, factory workers, formally 'unskilled'

---

23 Wehler, *Gesellschaftsgeschichte*, ii, pp. 713–14.
24 On the democratic movement in Rhenish Prussia, see the pioneering study of Jonathan Sperber, *Rhineland Radicals: The Democratic Movement and the Revolution of 1848–1849* (Princeton, 1991), esp. chs 5–7. For Berlin, the most accessible accounts can be found in G. Richter, 'Zwischen Revolution und Reichsgründung (1848–1870)', in Ribbe (ed.), *Geschichte Berlins*, ii, pp. 623–35; and, more recently, Hachtmann, *Berlin 1848*, pp. 272–88, 556–650.

workers (including most women employed in household service), and the urban underclass or *Lumpenproletariat*.[25]

Some clubs and newspapers represented the interests of skilled craft workers and artisans; and, indeed, many artisans were represented in the Citizens' Guards (*Bürgerwehr*) that emerged to maintain public order after the March revolution.[26] Some workers' groups managed to combine nostalgia for a pre-capitalist golden age with modern demands for state intervention on behalf of the labouring poor. Journeymen remained antagonistic to masters and ended up in August and September creating their own General German Workers' Brotherhood (*Arbeiterverbrüderung*) in Berlin to vent their grievances. On the whole, skilled workers remained divided from unskilled labourers, whose interests in turn were sometimes defended by disaffected bourgeois intellectuals. In short, as many recent scholars have noted, some workers' groups were socially conservative, others were reformist, and others, like the Cologne-based League of Communists (to which Karl Marx belonged), were truly revolutionary.[27]

The moderate constitutional liberals also, of course, had their own associations, newspapers and pamphleteers; but these were unable to save the Camphausen/Hansemann government, which was forced to resign on 20 June after radical crowds stormed the Berlin arsenal in an attempt to arm themselves, thus confirming the growth of popular radicalism, social polarization and street violence in Berlin during the summer. The Prussian assembly pressed on with its plans to prepare a more genuinely democratic constitutional draft, while Frederick William IV, still licking his wounds in Potsdam, appointed two more moderate governments – one in June and another in September – that immediately found themselves, like Camphausen's ill-fated cabinet, caught between the demands of the king, moderate constitutional liberals, the Prussian National Assembly, the radicalism of the streets and a newly resurgent conservatism. In the end, it was the latter that laid the foundation for the victory of counter-revolution and monarchical authority in Prussia.

---

25 These distinctions stem from the helpful article by Rüdiger Hachtmann, 'Die sozialen Unterschichten in der großstädtischen Revolution von 1848. Berlin, Wien und Paris im Vergleich', in Mieck *et al.* (eds), *Paris und Berlin*, pp. 108–10. See also Hachtmann, *Berlin 1848*, parts iv and v.
26 On the *Bürgerwehr* in Berlin, see Hachtmann, *Berlin 1848*, pp. 234–59, 586–604.
27 Siemann, *Revolution*, pp. 94–8.

Counter-revolution and compromise, spring 1848–January 1850

Of all the conservatives in Prussia, Ernst Ludwig von Gerlach (1795–1877) was perhaps the most tough-minded. As a prominent jurist in Magdeburg, he had grimly declared in March that 'I still have no hope [...]. We are facing years full of revolution'.[28] But Gerlach never allowed his pessimism to stand in the way of action. Deeply religious and an advocate of the 'high', organic-*ständisch* conservatism favoured by Frederick William IV, Gerlach was nevertheless fiercely critical of the monarch's many failings, despite the fact that his older brother, Leopold von Gerlach (1790–1861), had for years been one of the king's closest confidants. Even before March, Ludwig von Gerlach had castigated his fellow conservatives for their failure to organize themselves politically, and now he called upon them to learn from their enemies and make use of the same techniques that had helped liberals and radicals alike: political organization, agitation and propaganda. The forces of monarchical conservatism should renew themselves both by modernizing and by adhering fiercely to their principles: in an ideological age, Gerlach wanted to fashion a modern, ideological politics to help lead his fellow conservatives to victory over the revolution.

By the late spring of 1848, he had already started. He had gathered enough financial support to launch an ultra-conservative newspaper, the *Neue Preußische Zeitung*, popularly known, because of its masthead, as the *Kreuzzeitung*. Its first editor was the flamboyant and creative Hermann Wagener, who established the paper as an enormously influential voice of the 'high' conservatives, thanks above all to its vigorous and often vituperative journalistic style. At the same time as the newspaper was getting on its feet, other conservatives were beginning to organize new associations, clubs and societies to advance their goals: in short, they were doing the same kinds of things as liberals, democrats and radicals. By the summer of 1849, conservative organizations like the Society for King and Fatherland had enrolled some 60,000 members, many of them peasants, artisans and small businessmen, especially in the core regions of the Prussian state like the Mark Brandenburg, Pomerania and East Prussia.[29] At the same time, the

---

28 Gerlach to Ernst Wilhelm Hengstenberg, 27 March 1848, Staatsbibliothek Preußischer Kulturbesitz Berlin, Nachlaß Ernst Wilhelm Hengstenberg, Briefe Ernst Ludwig von Gerlachs 1829–1867, Bl. 159. On Gerlach, and on Prussian conservatism generally, see Hans-Christof Kraus, *Ernst Ludwig von Gerlach. Politisches Denken und Handeln eines preußischen Altkonservativen*, 2 vols (Göttingen, 1994).

29 On conservative associational life, see Wolfgang Schwentker, *Konservative Vereine und Revolution in Preußen 1848/49. Die Konstituierung des Konservativismus als Partei* (Düsseldorf, 1988).

country also experienced an outburst of pro-monarchist 'throne and altar' riots in 1848; of 81 disturbances of this sort that occurred in Germany between 1847 and 1849, 70 took place in Prussia.[30] In short, conservatives could reckon with a considerable reservoir of popular support for monarchical institutions and monarchical authority, and the victory of counter-revolution suggested that their calculations were correct.

Frederick William IV spent most of the long summer months of 1848 at the palace of Sanssouci outside Potsdam. There he was largely surrounded by an informal group of ultra-conservative advisers known as the 'Camarilla'. Its 'membership' was always small and shifting, but included two generals, Friedrich Wilhelm von Rauch and Leopold von Gerlach, high courtiers like Alexander von Keller and Ludwig von Massow, and, finally, people like Ludwig von Gerlach. Often described as a *ministre occulte* or backroom 'kitchen cabinet', the Camarilla was never as formidable, sinister, large or influential as the older historical literature sometimes suggests.[31] The king was himself too independent (or, as his detractors insisted, too inconstant and unpredictable) ever to submit himself to a single group of advisers. Rather, the Camarilla was a loosely organized group of individuals who shared similar views and a common loyalty to the monarchy, and who helped to push the monarch decisively in directions that he was in any case inclined to take.

By the late summer and early autumn of 1848, the opportunities for what the Camarilla member Edwin von Manteuffel called 'a carefully considered, carefully prepared Restoration' of monarchical authority were improving considerably.[32] In late August, for example, the Prussian government unilaterally concluded the armistice of Malmö with Denmark, thus bringing a temporary end to the 'Reich war' that had been precipitated by the Danish occupation of Schleswig in late March. The Danish seizure of what was regarded as German territory served for months as a rallying point for the national cause in Germany, and the liberals in the Frankfurt National Assembly had prevailed upon the Prussians to provide the bulk of the forces that were employed in the conflict. But Frederick William's advisers had never been enamoured of this enterprise; and when the

---

30 Gailus, *Straße und Brot*, pp. 129–32, ch. vi.
31 David E. Barclay, 'The Court Camarilla and the Politics of Monarchical Restoration in Prussia, 1848–58', in Larry Eugene Jones and James Retallack (eds), *Between Reform, Reaction, and Resistance: Studies in the History of German Conservatism from 1789 to 1945* (Providence and Oxford, 1993), pp. 123–56.
32 Edwin von Manteuffel, 'Anfang Juli 1848 (Ueber Revolutionen)', GStAPK, Brandenburg-Preußisches Hausarchiv Rep. 192 M Edwin von Manteuffel D Nr. 52, Bl. 7.

Prussians withdrew from the war, all the Frankfurt National Assembly could do was register its disappointment.[33]

But it was with the Prussian National Assembly in Berlin that Frederick William IV found himself on a collision course. In late July, the Assembly's constitutional commission, chaired by Benedikt Waldeck, had prepared a new constitutional draft – the so-called 'Charte Waldeck' – that was far more democratic and egalitarian than the original proposals of the former Camphausen/Hansemann cabinet. Its stipulations, which would have significantly limited the king's powers, were, of course, unacceptable to the monarch and his friends. Then, in early September, the Assembly passed a resolution that called upon army officers to 'distance themselves from all reactionary tendencies' and to demonstrate their loyalty to the new constitutional order by fraternizing with civilians. Finally, in October, the Assembly passed a decree that stripped Frederick William of his title as king 'by the Grace of God'. Unhappy with the efforts of his latest chief minister, the conciliatory Ernst von Pfuel, to resolve these conflicts, the monarch was now ready to listen to the Camarilla, which had its own candidate for minister-president waiting in the wings. Count Friedrich Wilhelm von Brandenburg, commander of the VI Army Corps in Breslau, was the king's uncle, and a tough-minded, traditional, pragmatic military conservative. In the words of Leopold von Gerlach, Count Brandenburg's main task would be to 'show in every possible way that the king, and not the Assembly, still rules in this country'.

Brandenburg assumed his new office at the beginning of November and almost immediately began a crackdown. On 9 November, he announced that the Prussian National Assembly would adjourn until the 27th, when it would meet in the city of Brandenburg rather than in Berlin. At the same time, 13,000 troops commanded by General Friedrich von Wrangel reoccupied Berlin. A state of siege was proclaimed, but Wrangel's forces encountered very little significant opposition. The fires of March had clearly been extinguished, at least in the capital city.[34]

But Brandenburg was no pliant instrument of the king or of the Camarilla. That group's influence, always fleeting, had reached its zenith with Brandenburg's appointment, and now the minister-president was determined to demonstrate his independence. He and his interior minister, Otto von Manteuffel (1805–82), were convinced that a simple policy of repression would not suffice; nor did they share the monarch's enthusiasm

---

33 David E. Barclay, *Anarchie und guter Wille. Friedrich Wilhelm IV. und die preußische Monarchie* (Berlin, 1995), p. 238.
34 On the military occupation of Berlin, see Hachtmann, *Berlin 1848*, pp. 739–63.

for allegedly 'historical', organic-*ständisch* institutions. Rather, Brandenburg and Manteuffel were aware that many moderate liberals would be willing to co-operate with them, if they in turn were willing to make substantive concessions to the ideas of constitutionalism and parliamentarism. In their view, it was impossible to pretend that the events of 1848 had not happened. Accordingly, on 5 December 1848, the new government announced that it was simultaneously dissolving the old Assembly and unilaterally promulgating (*oktroyieren*) a new constitution. Both the king and the Camarilla were aghast at the latter, but they really had no alternative to the Brandenburg/Manteuffel government, and they reluctantly went along with it. The new constitution was, all things considered, a surprisingly liberal document. Although the king retained his direct authority over the army (*Kommandogewalt*), the cabinet was to be responsible to the parliament, which itself was composed of an elected upper house, or First Chamber, and a more democratically elected lower house, or Second Chamber. In 1849 and early 1850, the original draft was amended, in consultation with the king and other constituencies; the final version incorporated the notorious 'three-class' suffrage system for the lower house that remained in effect in Prussia until 1918.[35] Although the monarch fought frantically against the constitution, a 'French-modern' scrap of paper that made him sick 'from his belly to his mouth', he finally bent to the will of his minister-president and took an oath to the revised constitution in February 1850.

The constitution of 1850 was thus the result of a series of compromises, beginning, as the historian Günther Grünthal has shown, with a triangular compromise in December 1848 among the king, the Camarilla and the cabinet.[36] In 1848, Prussia irrevocably set out on a constitutional and parliamentary road. Admittedly, both constitution and parliament were far from perfect. The former was based on a suffrage system that was heavily tilted towards wealth and status. As the events of the constitutional conflict after 1862 were to show, the army lay outside the purview of effective parliamentary control. Prussia's traditional elites retained a considerable amount of their former authority, especially in the countryside. Although Frederick William IV bemoaned the defeat of his *Vormärz* projects, he was able to retain an enormous amount of executive authority, and after 1848 the monarch remained at the centre of the Prussian state. Despite all of these limitations, Prussia's dominant elites had to accommodate themselves

---

35 Günther Grünthal, *Parlamentarismus in Preußen 1848/49–1857/58: Preußischer Konstitutionalismus – Parlament und Regierung in der Reaktionsära* (Düsseldorf, 1982), pp. 66–95.
36 Barclay, *Frederick William IV*, pp. 214–15; Grünthal, 'Zwischen König, Kabinett und Kamarilla'.

to a post-1848 world that had changed in significant ways. They had to learn how to justify themselves ideologically and programmatically. They had to edit newspapers, appeal to public opinion and work in political parties. In the wake of the revolution, politics in Prussia had become modernized, and so, too, as the recovery of the 1850s demonstrated, had economics and finance. These changes may not, in the final analysis, have been 'revolutionary'; but certainly they were enduring and important.

Aftershocks, 1849–50

If there were clear winners during the revolutions of 1848 in Prussia, there were certainly plenty of losers, including nationalists, democrats and radicals. The dreams of so many delegates to the Frankfurt National Assembly – that Germany could be unified on a constitutional-monarchical basis – were shattered when, in April 1849, Frederick William IV famously rejected the imperial crown that the Assembly proffered to him. In contrast to older conservatives like Metternich, the Prussian monarch had long been an enthusiast for 'higher' forms of German unity, although he always really hankered for a resuscitation of the defunct Holy Roman Empire. Thus, when the Frankfurt National Assembly elected him emperor on the basis of its 'little German' or *kleindeutsch* constitutional draft (i.e. excluding the Habsburg monarchy), he reacted with disdain. As he famously put it, the imperial crown was a 'dog collar with which they wanted to chain me to the revolution of '48'. With his rejection of this 'iron collar of servitude' that would have turned him 'into the serf of the revolution', the hopes of the Frankfurt National Assembly had been dashed.[37]

Having disappointed the hopes of German nationalists, the King of Prussia now turned his fury upon democrats and republicans who, in the spring and summer of 1849, became involved in a great grass-roots popular movement in support of the Frankfurt constitution (*Reichverfassungskampagne*). In Prussia itself, popular uprisings took place in Silesia, the Rhineland and Westphalia – that is, those areas that had been most turbulent or most anti-Prussian for years. Outside Prussia, popular upheavals threatened the stability of existing governments in Saxony, Baden and the Bavarian Palatinate. In all these cases, Prussian forces intervened with extreme

---

37 Frederick William IV to King Ernest Augustus of Hanover, 5 April 1849, and to Ernst Moritz Arndt, 15 March 1849, in Karl Haenchen, ed., *Revolutionsbriefe 1848. Ungedrucktes aus dem Nachlaß König Friedrich Wilhelms IV. von Preußen* (Leipzig, 1930), pp. 392, 436.

harshness to restore established authority. In May 1849, Prussian intervention led to the collapse of the great uprising in Dresden, and shortly thereafter Prussian forces, commanded by the Prince of Prussia himself, invaded Baden and crushed republican forces, who were finally forced to surrender in the fortress of Rastatt on 23 July 1849. Many republicans were summarily executed or sentenced to long prison terms. Others had to flee Germany, either to Switzerland, Great Britain, or the United States.[38]

But the upheavals of the revolutionary years were not quite over. One last aftershock was left, and it was primarily caused by the King of Prussia himself. Despite his rejection of the imperial crown and his violent suppression of the *Reichsverfassungskampagne*, Frederick William IV still wanted to be known for his 'positive' contribution to German unity. After the summer of 1849, he fell completely under the sway of his old friend Joseph Maria von Radowitz, an imaginative, intellectually creative, but politically isolated conservative social reformer. Radowitz believed that the two great issues of the age, embodied in the revolution itself, were the 'social question' and the 'national question'.[39] Conservative governments could and should address them both, he asserted; and Prussia in particular was destined to take the lead in showing the way to a conservative form of German unity. To that end, Radowitz proposed a Prussian plan of union, in which Prussia would dominate an inner core of German states, while Austria would be associated with a larger and looser group of German states. In 1849–50, assured of the king's support, Radowitz became the driving force of Prussian foreign policy, attempting to recast Prussia's German policy and, in effect, to ensure the hegemony of Prussia in non-Habsburg Germany. But he encountered increasingly virulent opposition to his plans, from the remnants of the Camarilla, from interior minister Otto von Manteuffel, from Tsar Nicholas I of Russia, and, above all, from a resurgent Austria that was determined to restore the old German Confederation of 1815. Everything finally came to a head in the autumn of 1850 when, in the space of a few weeks, Count Brandenburg suddenly died, Radowitz served briefly as foreign minister, and Austria and Prussia looked as if they were preparing for war. In the end, Prussia backed down. Frederick William reluctantly agreed to let Radowitz resign. Brandenburg's

---

38 On the *Reichsverfassungskampagne*, see esp. Siemann, *Revolution*, pp. 207–18; Sperber, *Rhineland Radicals*, part 3; and the numerous essays in the second half of the excellent exhibition catalogue edited by the Badisches Landesmuseum Karslruhe, *1848/49. Revolution der deutschen Demokraten in Baden* (Baden-Baden, 1998).

39 On Radowitz and the Union Project, see David E. Barclay, 'Ein deutscher "Tory Democrat"? Joseph Maria von Radowitz (1797–1853)', in Hans-Christof Kraus (ed.), *Konservative Politiker in Deutschland. Eine Auswahl biographischer Porträts aus zwei Jahrhunderten* (Berlin, 1995), pp. 37–67.

successor as minister-president, Otto von Manteuffel, travelled to the Bohemian city of Olmütz where he acceded to the demands of the Austrians and agreed to plans for a restoration of the German Confederation. By the end of 1850, in short, it seemed that the old order had been restored everywhere in Central Europe.

If anything, that old order was harsher than ever before. A decade of political reaction had ensued after 1848, marked by an intensification of censorship and police repression, the emigration and suppression of radicals and democrats, political corruption and apparent liberal quiescence. Although the reaction decade was more politically and socially complex than older historical writings suggest, there can be no doubt that, in the minds of many observers, the revolution had been liquidated throughout Central Europe, and especially in Prussia. But, as we have already seen, more had changed in Prussia than many people realized. Despite the disappointed hopes of moderates and radicals alike, politics and public life were in the process of becoming modern, while economically and socially Prussia was poised to enter an era of tumultuous change. In his own way, Frederick William IV recognized these facts. Revolution, he thought, had become a permanent fact of life. In 1857, shortly before his final illness, he wrote, 'The revolution is stalking the world once more. May God have mercy!'[40]

---

40 Frederick William IV to Carl von der Groeben, 29 June 1857, GStAPK, Rep. 92 Graf Carl von der Groeben B Nr. 4g 1855–1857, Bl. 45–46.

CHAPTER FOUR

The changing concerns of Prussian conservatism, 1830–1914

HERMANN BECK

From inveterate foes of royal absolutism to advocates of a strong monarchy, from a coterie of noblemen to a party with a mass following, from a social-minded group that regarded the nascent proletariat as a potential ally against the bourgeoisie to bitter antagonists of working-class influence: between 1830 and the eve of the First World War, Prussian conservatives underwent profound changes in ideology and organization. In their early days, conservatives prided themselves on the firmness of their principles: according to Ernst Ludwig von Gerlach, conservatism should mean more than postponing the loss of privileges and possessions in the march of time. After the turn of the century, however, Ernst von Heydebrand und der Lasa, 'the uncrowned king of Prussia' and influential leader of the conservative faction in the Prussian lower house (*Landtag*) from 1906 to 1918, made no bones about the fact that conservatives touted the material interests of the landed nobility. These shifts in conservative orientation were tied to the momentous changes Prussia itself had undergone. The thinly-populated agrarian backwater that was mired in financial difficulties for decades following the Napoleonic Wars – a great power in name only and barely taken seriously by the other great powers – had turned into an industrialized and vibrant engine that dominated the German Empire, the greatest power on the European continent, at once respected and feared by the others, as its once befitting modesty seemed to give way to a bullying arrogance.

Initially, Prussian conservatism was represented by a series of important personalities. There was no conservative party structure, and a conservative party as such came into being only in the 1850s in the form of different parliamentary groups, or *Fraktionen*, in the Prussian lower house;

conservative organization in its most rudimentary form began in the form of associations only during the Revolution of 1848. The first part of this chapter will concentrate, therefore, mostly on individuals, while subsequent sections focus on the political outlook of the party as a whole. The history of Prussian conservatism between 1830 and 1914 can be subdivided into three main periods.

The first encompasses the period from the foundation of the first organized conservative circle around the *Berliner Politisches Wochenblatt* in the early 1830s up to the crisis of the 1860s, when Bismarck's policies on unification divided the party and destroyed its *raison d'être*. It was during this first period that the theoretical foundations of Prussian conservatism were established. It was shaped by the great figures of 'old Prussian' conservatism, such as Leopold and Ernst Ludwig von Gerlach, Joseph Maria von Radowitz and, during the 1850s until early 1870s, Hermann Wagener, whose influence reached its height during the second period.

The second period covers the decade of restructuring and the search for a new identity between 1866 and 1876. This period witnessed the division and temporary decline of Prussian conservatism, the emergence of a new Free Conservative Party (*FreieKonservative Partei* or FKP)– the *Partei Bismarck sans phrase* as it was called, due to its unquestioning support of Bismarck's policies – and the regrouping of the old Prussian conservatives, which eventually led to the foundation of the German Conservative Party (*Deutsch-Konservative Partei* or DKP) in 1876, the main conservative party of the empire.

The third period covers the history of conservatism between 1876 and the beginning of the First World War that saw the development of the two conservative parties. In contrast to other German parties, notably the Social Democrats, conservatives had only rudimentary party organizations; instead, they relied on informal contacts among notables. This was true especially for the Free Conservative Party, renamed *Reichspartei* after 1871. The *Reichspartei* enjoyed some support outside Prussia's heartland, its East Elbian provinces, while the DKP, though officially paying lip service to the fact that it was a 'German' and not just an exclusively Prussian party, would always remain strongest east of the Elbe and had but few pockets of support in the west and south. In 1876, the DKP started out as a party that fully supported governmental policies, but in the years before 1914 it had become an opposition from the right to Bethmann-Hollweg's government, whose policies it thought weak, indecisive and unable to safeguard its own social interests and those of the nation. On the eve of the First World War, the fortunes of both conservative parties had noticeably declined.

The theoretical foundations of Prussian conservatism

In the beginning, fear of the spread of revolution fuelled conservative thought and policies: the first expressly conservative circle in Prussia was founded around the weekly *Berliner Politisches Wochenblatt* as a reaction to the July Revolution of 1830 in Paris. The personalities connected with the *Berliner Politisches Wochenblatt*, such as Leopold and Ludwig von Gerlach, Joseph Maria von Radowitz and Ernst Carl Jarcke, formed the hard core of Prussian conservatism and were to gain lasting importance. The Gerlach brothers, in particular, became mentors for others, such as Hermann Wagener and Otto von Bismarck, who rose to prominence after the 1848 Revolution. They laid the theoretical foundation of Prussian conservatism and shaped its identity, some aspects of which would remain in place until the eve of the First World War. Through their close association with the crown prince – after 1840, King Frederick William IV – they also wielded extraordinary political influence through informal channels until 1858.[1]

Their view of history, state and society can be summarized as follows: political legitimacy is bestowed by tradition and history; law, as well as any form of jurisdiction (*Recht*), is sanctioned by historical development. Man-made laws, therefore, do not carry the same authority as laws sanctioned by the process of historical evolution. An existing order is considered 'lawful' if it has evolved gradually over the course of centuries. 'The good and well acquired rights', on which special legal rights and privileges are based, are grounded in an organic development over centuries (here it becomes obvious that this is an ideology made for the aristocracy). In the same vein, social and legal institutions derive their legitimacy from a process of gradual maturation, that is, law as such is legitimate only as historically matured law. During the 1830s, dozens of articles in the *Berliner Politisches Wochenblatt* outlined a conservative ideology that set the tone for Prussian conservatism for the coming decades. Its main points included:

1. Opposition to 'absolutism' in all its forms, above all in the form of royal absolutism. The men around the *Berliner Politisches Wochenblatt* vehemently rejected the unlimited power of the crown that was considered to be the

---

1 David Barclay, 'The Court Camarilla and the Politics of Monarchical Restoration in Prussia, 1848–58', in Larry E. Jones and James N. Retallack (eds), *Between Reform, Reaction, and Resistance. Studies in the History of German Conservatism from 1789 to 1945* (Providence and Oxford, 1993), pp. 123–57.

main cause of revolution, since it transcended all *Recht*, that is, any limitations imposed by law. This opposition to royal absolutism would be modified after the 1848 Revolution. 'Absolutism' was to be fought in the same way as liberal constitutionalism, judged to infringe upon naturally evolved rights and privileges, and 'popular sovereignty', which conjured up not only the dreaded French Revolution, but also the more recent revolutionary upheavals of 1830.

2. Opposition to the use of 'abstract principles' in solving social problems or changing the 'organically grown' social and political conditions of society. Principles claiming general validity and rooted in natural law, such as 'sovereignty of the people' and 'human rights', were deemed suspect, as they were believed to run counter to the moral nature of man. In fact, abstraction of any kind was spurned: the French Revolution, to conservatives a symbol of the historic realization of the implementation of abstract principles, was held responsible for sucking the life out of society – everything 'has become abstract, the inner life has been squeezed out of things, nothing remains but fear, constraint and mere interest'.[2]

3. Antagonism to the emerging modern state and its all-encompassing power, which was regarded as a major opponent and deemed incompatible with 'true freedom'. Conservatives strongly opposed an activist state, which only reminded them of the great Revolution in France when all possible acts of violence could be justified in the name of the state. Equally, the uniformity of law, and the equality of citizens before the law, was viewed as unnatural since inequality was considered a natural condition of a God-ordained social order, while the uniformity of law would lead inevitably to increasing centralization of state power.

4. Hatred of the modern bureaucratic state and its representatives, Prussian officials, who were considered dangerous enemies. The bureaucracy, which emerged as a major policy-maker after the Reform Era, was denounced for having violated 'organically grown' social and political conditions. Conservatives objected to social change as such. They blamed officials for transforming the Prussian state, thereby obliterating the once strong position of the *Stände* (estates) and corporations.

5. Praise for the late medieval and early modern *Ständestaat*, their political ideal, with its implicit checks and balances and 'intermediary' powers, such as guilds, estates with their law courts, and corporations, all of which were considered essential ingredients of the social order. In

---

[2] *Berliner Politisches Wochenblatt*, 28 August 1841, p. 19.

former times, these served to curb the power of the prince who was merely *primus inter pares* among his nobles: the Quitzows, who had rebelled against the Hohenzollerns, when they came to the Mark Brandenburg in 1415, were looked upon as the real-life ideal of history. The organizations of the *Ständestaat* were praised for their controlling functions and for preserving the hierarchically structured, self-contained universe of the guilds – a static, immobile system, free of social change and mobility, in which everyone assumed an allotted place and performed an essential function.

6. Finally, pronounced antagonism to their main political adversary, the bourgeoisie – representatives of liberalism and constitutionalism – not the emerging proletariat, whose sad fate was viewed with sympathy and which was regarded as a potential ally against the overbearing might of 'the barons of industry'. Just then, during the 1830s, the beginnings of industrialization in Saxony, parts of Silesia and the Rhineland were perceived as threatening the social world of East Elbian conservatives.[3]

During the 1840s, Prussian conservatives began to relinquish their *ständisch* ideal. After the demise of the *Berliner Politisches Wochenblatt (BPW)* in 1841, Joseph Maria von Radowitz, one of the founding members of the group, modified the conservative tradition of the paper until his death in 1853. Radowitz became best known as Prussia's post-revolutionary foreign minister and architect of the ill-fated Prussian *Unionspolitik*. Domestically, he was the leading representative of the social conservative tradition in Prussia. Radowitz was convinced that conservatism, like socialism, stood for the realization of a higher principle in the state, while liberalism was merely the embodiment of materialism. Throughout all his writings, he never ceased stressing the inner relatedness of conservatism and socialism and made no bones about the fact that he clearly preferred socialists and Left Hegelian radicals to the liberal bourgeoisie.

Radowitz realized that the *ständisch* monarchy had disappeared from public consciousness and thus ceased to constitute a politically feasible solution. While his hatred for bureaucracy, the *Offiziantenregiment*, and what he called 'modern state absolutism', never abated, his attitude to the modern state differed markedly from that propagated by the *BPW*. Radowitz even envisaged active state involvement in the economy to help solve social problems. By the 1840s, the attitude of conservatives towards the state had generally undergone a momentous change. Prominent conservatives of the age, such as Viktor A. Huber, whose conservative

---

3 On the above, see Hermann Beck, *The Origins of the Authoritarian Welfare State in Prussia. Conservatives, Bureaucracy, and the Social Question, 1815–70* (Ann Arbor, 1995).

journal *Janus* was meant to replace the *BPW*, equally endorsed the strong role of the state, and Karl Rodbertus went so far as to outline a state socialist system to alleviate social misery.

Whereas the *BPW* had viewed the power of the monarch with misgivings, Radowitz wanted to see this power strengthened. To him, state and monarchy could be mutually reinforcing in that social policies promulgated by a monarch-led state would fortify the position of the sovereign and reflect well on the monarchy. In the ensuing 'social kingdom', royal power would thus be buttressed by the lower classes, which would become the natural allies of the monarchy. The potential of this social kingdom was appreciated by other conservatives, such as Hermann Wagener, and understandably dreaded by liberals.

This serves to highlight the continuity with the conservatism of the 1830s: Radowitz's main political enemy remained the liberal bourgeoisie. This political enmity was complemented by a metaphysical component: the hated materialism of the bourgeoisie. Radowitz railed against the 'servitude of mammon', bemoaned the growing power of money which, he lamented, would open all doors regardless of birth and inherited rank, and argued, as Ludwig von Gerlach had done before him, that the ownership of property should automatically carry obligations with it. Radowitz's anti-liberalism was a bridge to anti-modernism, and his anti-modernism, in turn, was interlaced with a loathing of industrial development: he decried the 'idolatry of industry', the increasing atomization of society, the dissolution of traditional bonds and the fact that the proper understanding of work and service had been lost. In this context, Radowitz reveals himself as nothing less than the first in a long line of German cultural critics.

Historians have characterized the age between Reform and Revolution as one of 'bureaucratic absolutism' given the elevated position of the Prussian bureaucracy. The members of the group around the BPW never realized that conservative patterns of argumentation that transcended political categories permeated the discourse of officials. The bureaucracy, so reviled and loathed by conservatives, was actually eminently conservative in its approach to society and politics. Officials were wrongly accused of redrawing society according to abstract principles; instead, they shared conservative assumptions in their various attempts to solve social and political problems.

A prime example of this can be found in a memorandum of the Prussian minister of culture, Karl von Altenstein, that recommended the elimination of the negative effects of factory work, but not 'through general institutions, ordinances, and laws for the whole state'.[4] Altenstein acknowledged that

---

4 Beck, *Origins*, p. 204; and Hermann Beck, 'The Social Policies of Prussian Officials: The Bureaucracy in a new Light', *Journal of Modern History* 64 (1992), 262–98.

'nature, circumstances, people in different provinces vary so greatly' that restrictive measures may be needed in one province while in another industrial development might have to be promoted. Altenstein continually emphasized the importance of allowing for historically-grown traditions and the prevailing diversity of local conditions, while adamantly rejecting the application of general laws.

A similar mindset is to be found in other memoranda written after the Revolution, in which leading officials rejected abstract principles and their application to society, and insisted instead on accounting for historically-grown differences and particular conditions of circumstance and location in their legislation. They demanded that the mutual interdependence of social conditions be acknowledged, dismissed all-encompassing state measures and, like August von der Heydt, Prussian minister of commerce between 1848 and 1862, rejected the possibility that any universal system could solve all social problems.[5]

1848 was a great watershed for conservative organization: throughout Prussia, a vast number of conservative associations were founded, though, as time went on, it became clear that there was less inclination among conservatives than among liberals or socialists to organize, since party organization seemed to indicate an endorsement of a parliamentary form of government. Conservative associations included aristocrats, journeymen and day-labourers. During the summer of 1849, there were more than 300 of them in Prussia with at least 60,000 members, most prominent of which was the *Verein für König und Vaterland* founded in July 1848, which counted Ludwig von Gerlach, Viktor A. Huber and Bismarck among its founding members.[6]

With the passing of a constitution, conservative parliamentary groups, or *Fraktionen*, made their appearance in the Prussian *Landtag*. These included the *Hochkonservativen* (ultra-conservatives) led by Ludwig von Gerlach, who rejected constitutional government and continued advocating the reintroduction of the *Ständestaat*. Their disdain for party politics made them despise the parliamentary process which, to them, seemed incompatible with monarchical government. In contrast to the ultra-conservatives who were opposed to the semi-absolute Manteuffel government of the 1850s, another, numerically less significant, conservative group, that of Arnim and

---

5   7 July, 1849, 'Vorschläge zur Lösung der sozialen Frage und Massnahmen wegen Abwendung eines Nothstandes, 1848–1860', Geheimes Staatsarchiv Preußischer Kulturbesitz Dahlem, Rep. 120BB, VII, 1, pp. 84–94.
6   Wolfgang Schwentker, *Konservative Vereine und Revolution in Preußen 1848/49. Die Konstituierung des Konservatismus als Partei* (Düsseldorf, 1988).

Heinrichsdorf, lent unquestioning support to the Manteuffel government, while the *Fraktion* of Alexander and Moritz von Lavergne-Peguilhen evinced a strong interest in social issues.[7] The liberal-conservative group, the *Fraktion* of August von Bethmann-Hollweg, or *Wochenblattpartei*, supported constitutional government and, during the Crimean War, broke with conservative tradition by advocating an alliance with England, while Ludwig von Gerlach, in keeping with conservative custom, remained a steadfast supporter of an alliance with the autocratic Russian Empire.[8] The liberal conservatism of the parliamentary group around Bethmann-Hollweg would later appear in the *FreiKonservative Partei*.

Politically, conservatives dominated the Prussian *Landtag* up to 1858, but lost their supremacy with the beginning of the New Era when the manipulation of elections in favour of conservatives came to an end. In an attempt to be in tune with the spirit of the age, the new regent, William I, appointed a moderately liberal government, thereby giving rise to hopes for a liberal future, including the creation of a nation state. These hopes not only exceeded, but were in downright opposition to William's original intentions. The ascendancy of liberalism, indeed, soon became overpowering. The goals of Prussia's new strong liberal party, the Progressive Party founded in 1861, foremost among which were the attainment of national unity and the realization of constitutional liberties, naturally ran counter to the interests of the Prussian monarchy and aristocracy. Conservatives, fearing an erosion of local and regionally-based privileges as well as the loss of a specific Prussian identity, opposed a national unity that seemed to make parliamentarization of government and majority rule inevitable. In 1862, when no solution to the conflict between the monarchy and a parliament dominated by the Progressive Party over the issue of the army reform (favoured by the king, but rejected by the parliament's liberal majority) seemed possible, the Prussian king, on the verge of abdication, called in Otto von Bismarck as a last resort.

The search for a new identity

Bismarck, who became Prussian prime minister in September 1862, was so determined to implement the army reforms dear to the heart of the Prussian king that he was even prepared to adopt a course of constitutional

---

7   Günther Grünthal, *Parlamentarismus in Preußen 1848/49–1857/58* (Düsseldorf, 1982).
8   Michael Behnen, *Das Politische Wochenblatt 1851–1861. Nationalkonservative Publizistik gegen Ständestaat und Polizeistaat* (Göttingen, 1971).

illegality. As the liberal majority's veto of the fiscal budget could not be broken by constitutional means, Bismarck ruled without parliament, relying on the bureaucracy instead. Hermann Wagener, the former editor-in-chief of the main conservative party organ, the *Kreuzzeitung*, founded in 1848, was one of Bismarck's most influential political advisers during the 1860s. Wagener, who also served as a conservative deputy in the Prussian *Landtag*, the Diet of the North German Confederation (1867–1871), and later in the Imperial Diet (1871–1873), had an astute sense of power politics. As a *Realpolitiker*, he evinced a keen interest in widening the popular appeal of conservatism. Wagener realized early on the potential of the lower classes to act as a mass base of support for Bismarck's policies against the liberal majority in parliament. Convinced that the outlook of the masses was essentially royalist and conservative, Wagener hoped that a socially-minded monarch might be in a position to create a counterweight to the rising strength of the bourgeoisie by furthering the interests of the lower classes. Wagener argued that the alliance between the monarchy and the lower classes had tangible advantages for both sides: a strong lower class following would allow the monarchy to survive, albeit in the form of a 'social kingdom', while the standard of living of urban workers and unemployed journeymen would be raised considerably with the help of royal intervention. In 1861, he created the *Preußischer Volksverein* to establish a counterweight to the growing strength of liberalism. Moritz von Blankenburg, Bismarck's close friend, and Wagener himself jointly led the organization, whose membership was made up of civil servants, officers, clergymen and artisans opposed to freedom of trade.[9]

In sharp contrast to Prussian liberals, Wagener favoured the introduction of universal suffrage, which, in his estimation, would strengthen the conservative cause. He rejected Prussia's three-class franchise as too plutocratic and one which furthered the interests of the liberal bourgeoisie. Wagener's conservatism was thus undoubtedly more modern than that of his erstwhile mentor, Ludwig von Gerlach. Traditional conservatives like Ludwig von Gerlach never lost their distrust of the *Volksverein*, whose programme, shaped by Wagener's social conservative ideas, smacked too much of populism to be compatible with their brand of conservatism.

A striking feature of Wagener's conservatism was his affinity with socialist ideas. Wagener was intimately acquainted with the writings of Saint Simon, Marx and Lassalle; like Radowitz, he saw the working class as the unspoiled counterpart of the bourgeoisie. He never tired of praising the ethical

---

9 See Hans-Ulrich Wehler, *Deutsche Gesellschaftsgeschichte 1849–1914* (Munich, 1994), iii, pp. 343–4.

idealism of socialism, with its emphasis on timeless values, and of contrasting it favourably with what he considered to be the mere profit-seeking impetus of liberalism. One of Wagener's closest collaborators on his multi-volume encyclopaedia, the *Staats- und Gesellschaftslexikon* (which had a distinctly conservative slant) was Bruno Bauer, formerly a figurehead of Left Hegelianism. There were also noticeable communalities between the policies of the conservative Wagener and the socialist Ferdinand Lassalle, who, equally, had offered his services to Bismarck by holding out the promise of mass support in return for a worker-friendly, anti-liberal policy. Wagener and Lassalle both stressed the importance of universal suffrage, preferred the public organization of labour to free competition, favoured the predominance of public investment over private capital and the drive towards corporate organization, were agreed that the strengthening of a monarchic central power would favour their overall purpose, and evinced a hatred of liberalism that transcended the immediate sphere of politics.

While Bismarck showed interest in Wagener's ideas without feeling the need to act upon them, Wagener's continued advocacy of protective legislation for workers and for an active social policy alienated him from the traditional ultra-conservatives, especially from Ludwig von Gerlach, who was still widely recognized as the undisputed elder statesman of Prussian conservatism and head of the loosely organized Prussian conservative establishment. Gerlach had been equally suspicious of Bismarck's political motives for some time. Called to office with the express purpose of combating the liberal majority in parliament and strengthening the hand of the king, Bismarck appeared as the natural figurehead of Prussian conservatism. While the genuineness of his conservatism had never been doubted, the Gerlachs and others had often questioned his methods. When it became apparent that the conservative prime minister was actively pursuing a liberal policy of unification, traditional conservatives – Ludwig von Gerlach foremost among them – took exception to his policies. Bismarck's policies after 1866 gave them good reason to accuse him of betraying conservative ideals on more scores than one: his anti-Austrian policies that undermined the European security system created in 1815; his anti-legitimist policies, such as the annexation of the Kingdom of Hanover, electoral Hesse and Nassau after the war of 1866 (conservatives labelled it *Kronenraub*); the introduction of universal suffrage in the North German Diet and, after 1871, the German Empire; and his shocking readiness to enter into alliances with 'revolutionary' national movements in Italy and Germany. It was naturally offensive to conservatives that, after 1866, he based his policies on the support of the National Liberal Party. His very success with his erstwhile liberal opponents made conservatives suspicious. Bismarck's indemnity bill, a post-factum endorsement of his unconstitutional policies, was perceived by conservatives as both a misguided effort to be granted absolution by parliament and a weakened resolve to act decisively in the defence of the imperilled conservative cause. Gerlach, on the other hand, prided himself on the firmness of his principles: 'I would rather become the porter of a democratic minister', he once stated, 'than soil myself through alliances with a politics à la Cavour'.[10]

The extraordinary success of Bismarck's policies, their popularity with the broad population and the extent and unexpected speed of his military success first against Austria and then France, weakened the old Prussian conservative party. After the foundation of the Empire, Prussian conservatives found themselves in opposition to the liberal *Zeitgeist*. They could not fully take part in the great wave of enthusiasm that accompanied the process of unification, for they feared the loss of Prussian particularism, strongly objected to Bismarck's liberal economic policies, and were naturally opposed to the vast process of standardization, such as the adoption of a uniform law code, which the creation of the German Empire entailed.

Prussian conservatives thus found themselves in an inexorable predicament, since their natural champion, Bismarck – once called in with the express purpose of blocking the advance of liberalism – now seemed to carry out a liberal programme. In contrast to the governmental policies of the early 1870s, many conservatives during the *Kulturkampf* favoured church involvement in public education – the *kirchliche Schulaufsicht* the government wanted to see abolished – and were adamantly opposed to the extension of state power. When, against the wishes of a majority of conservatives, the new *Kreisordnung*, curtailing seigneurial policing powers, was pushed through in 1873, the party divided owing to the intransigent hostility shown by the *Hochkonservativen*. Subsequently, a minority of 45 deputies, led by Bismarck's brother Bernhard, formed a 'New Conservative faction'. But even this new creation had no electoral success.

The party's hostile yet unclarified attitude towards Bismarck's policies at the time when the German chancellor was at his most influential, brought with it the real danger that Prussian conservatism would recede into insignificance. In the Prussian elections in the autumn of 1873, the old conservative party, or *Altkonservativen*, obtained a mere four mandates, while the *Neukonservativen*, who were more favourably disposed towards Bismarck's policies, gained 28.[11] Symptomatic of the breach with Bismarck were the so-called *Ära Artikel* of 1875 in the *Kreuzzeitung*, the main press organ of the Conservative Party. This series of articles, entitled 'The Economic Policies

---

10 Hans-Christof Kraus, *Ernst Ludwig von Gerlach: Politisches Denken und Handeln eines preußischen Altkonservativen* (Göttingen, 1994), ii, p. 795.
11 Hans Fenske, *Deutsche Parteiengeschichte* (Paderborn and Munich, 1994), p. 135.

of the Era Bleichröder–Delbrück–Camphausen', argued that Bismarck was under the influence of financial advisers who pursued a strictly capitalist policy driven by mere profit-seeking. When an enraged Bismarck called on subscribers and backers of the *Kreuzzeitung* – who included the better part of the Prussian aristocracy and many of his long-time allies – to discontinue their subscription, a large number of prominent aristocrats delivered a declaration of loyalty to their paper (the so-called *Deklaranten*). Bismarck, in return, felt compelled to sever ties with some of his oldest followers.

The development of conservatism in the empire

Due to the ebbing electoral fortunes of conservatism, it was a matter of survival and not just reassertion that the Conservative Party reconstituted itself as *Deutsch-Konservative Partei* (DKP) on 7 June 1876 in Frankfurt. The new name already signified a positive reorientation towards the newly founded empire.

The DKP was primarily a Prussian party: among the 285 mandates the party won at Reichstag elections between 1890 and 1912, only 53, that is, less than one-fifth, came from non-Prussian areas: among the 74 mandates the party gained in the 1887 Reichstag election, 13 were gained outside Prussia; in 1903, there were a mere six out of 51, and in 1912, only four non-Prussians among the 43 Reichstag conservatives.[12] Outside Prussia, the party enjoyed some support in Saxony, Mecklenburg and Baden; in other German states, such as Bavaria, conservatives voted for the Catholic Centre Party, in Hanover they voted for the *Welfen*. In the Prussian *Landtag*, the vast majority of deputies came from the old provinces east of the Elbe, notably from East Prussia, Pomerania and Brandenburg, with the ratio gradually changing in favour of the east. In 1880, there were 77 deputies from east of the Elbe as compared to 27 from western electoral districts; by 1886, the ratio had altered to 102 easterners compared to 30 from the west, and in 1913, 125 from the east had a mere 18 counterparts from western districts.[13] From the first, the DKP made it clear that it supported Bismarck's policies unconditionally; those of the *Deklaranten* who wished to join, no matter how prominent they may have been, abjectly had to beg Bismarck's forgiveness for their former waywardness. But, initially at least, political support for

---

12 Hans Booms, *Die Deutsch-Konservative Partei. Preußischer Charakter, Reichsauffassung, Nationalbegriff* (Düsseldorf, 1954), p. 7.
13 Ibid.

governmental policies was given wholeheartedly as in the case of the introduction of protective tariffs and the anti-socialist law of 1879.

Strength

The formation of the new party boosted the strength of the conservative position: the number of conservative seats – not counting Free Conservatives – in the Imperial Diet rose from 22 (in 1874) to 40 (in 1877), 59 (in 1878), and finally, after the dip to 50 after the 1881 elections, to 78 (in 1884) and even 80 (in 1887). Thereafter, the electoral fortunes of the party steadily declined until it was left with a mere 43 seats after the elections in 1912. Numbers of seats gained were no adequate reflection of the party's electoral strength, since the undue preference given to rural electoral districts (where conservative strength was congregated) distorted the party's support. The Social Democrats, on the other hand, whose voters came from the rapidly growing cities of Saxony, Hamburg and the Ruhr, were severely handicapped, since the initial carving up of electoral districts failed to allow for the internal migration that had taken place since the foundation of the empire.

Characteristics

The DKP was characterized by its belief in authority, rejection of majority rule, fear of the power of the emerging masses, and belief in a strong role for the monarchy. The party was opposed to further parliamentarization of the empire and wanted to see traditional hierarchies upheld. Conservatives stressed the importance of Christianity in a sea of ever rising disbelief and vehemently defended Prussian particularism. There was also a pronounced streak of anti-capitalism: a mistrust of big capital that stemmed from the financial scandals of the *Gründerzeit*, and a rejection of the ruthlessness of economic competition. Some conservatives even considered limiting stock-exchange activity. This pronounced anti-capitalism lay at the root of the strong misgivings over the alliance with the National Liberal Party, loudly voiced in the second half of the 1880s. Bismarck's past collaboration with National Liberals between 1867 and 1873 and the Industrial Code of 1869 seemed to bode ill for the future.

After 1879, conservatives formed the strongest party in the Prussian *Landtag*; here lay their main power base, which they defended with extraordinary tenacity. In Prussia, which accounted for two-thirds of the empire's population and size, the three-class franchise remained operative until 1918, and with its help Prussian conservatives could successfully block reform in the entire Reich through Prussia's veto in the federal council, or *Bundesrat*. The three-class electoral system put conservatives at an advantage, for it gave undue weight to estate owners in rural districts, who were almost invariably put into the first electoral bracket. Since voting was public, estate owners could often prevail upon their peasants to vote for conservative candidates.

Organization

Except for the short-lived attempt to create a mass party for conservatism through Hermann Wagener's *Preußische Volksvereine* in the 1860s, the Conservative Party remained an elite organization without a party apparatus even after 1876. This was true especially for the *Reichs- und Freikonservative Partei*, which essentially consisted of a number of illustrious individuals, who had won a mandate in their electoral districts by dint of their local reputation. In terms of organizational structure, however, this party never succeeded in graduating beyond its parliamentary group status. A considerable number of Free Conservative deputies came from the ranks of the Silesian aristocracy or Rhenish magnates and loathed the very idea of party organization.

The DKP, on the other hand, was led by a steering committee, after 1892 named the 'Committee of Fifty', though the parliamentary groups in the Imperial Diet (Reichstag), the Prussian *Landtag* and the Prussian Upper House (*Herrenhaus*) remained relatively independent of each other. To coordinate their activities, a 'Committee of Eleven' was established in 1889, composed of four deputies from the Imperial Diet, three from each of the Prussian chambers and one non-Prussian candidate. Since 80 per cent of Reichstag deputies came from Prussia as well, the non-Prussian element in the power structure was completely insignificant. The Committee of Eleven (another member was added in 1902) quickly became the executive body of the party. This committee, as well as most of the provincial committees, was dominated by the aristocracy.[14]

Christian social movement and *Kreuzzeitung* group

At the beginning of the 1880s, aspirations of appealing to a broader electorate prompted party leaders to envisage widening their electoral

---

14 James Retallack, *Notables of the Right. The Conservative Party and Political Mobilization in Germany, 1876–1918* (Boston, 1988), pp. 235–44.

appeal by giving more room to the Christian social movement within party ranks. This opened up the tantalizing prospect of garnering votes outside Prussia's East Elbian provinces. The Christian Social Party was more or less a continuation of the social conservative tradition reaching back into the *Vormärz*. It had been created in 1878 as a 'Christian Social Workers' Party' by the charismatic court preacher Adolf Stoecker in order to provide working men with a conservative alternative to the Social Democratic Party, which Stoecker rejected as anti-Christian and unpatriotic. In 1881, the small and relatively insignificant party joined the *Deutsch-Konservative Partei* as an independent group, dropping the epithet 'Workers' from the party name. Though Stoecker's anti-liberal and anti-Semitic propaganda succeeded in raising the conservative vote in Berlin from about 14,000 (1878) to 56,000 (1884), his support remained limited to the petty bourgeoisie and small artisanate. Within the DKP, the Christian Social Party (CSP) collaborated closely with the *Kreuzzeitung* group around Wilhelm von Hammerstein; together they formed an intra-party opposition group to Otto von Helldorf-Bedra. A majority of conservatives, led by Helldorf-Bedra, supported Bismarck's *Kartell* policies, his alliance with the National Liberals and the Free Conservative Party. The alliance with the National Liberals was especially unpopular with Stoecker and the *Kreuzzeitung* group, who were loath to eradicate differences between liberalism and conservatism. They favoured instead an alliance with the Centre Party, which seemed to represent conservative politics more convincingly. Intent on creating a conservative *Volkspartei*, they strove for independence from Bismarck's policies and for closer co-operation between the Protestant and Catholic churches, whose political influence they wanted to see consolidated and strengthened. Bismarck, Stoecker asserted, was about to deprive Germany of its inner life, since he lacked any understanding of the peculiarities of the nation's mind and emotional life.[15] The anti-liberalism of Stoecker and the *Kreuzzeitungspartei* was more pronounced, their anti-Semitism more overt, and their social concerns more loudly voiced than was the case with the remainder of conservatives. In January 1888, Hammerstein wrote in the *Kreuzzeitung*: 'In many respects we stand much closer to the Socialists than we do to heartless, mammonistic Manchesterism.'[16]

Yet, Stoecker, a gifted orator and shrewd demagogue, was more a man of the rostrum than the pen. After having vainly tried to win over Protestant workers by weaning them away from the Social Democratic Party, while

---

15 Walter Frank, *Hofprediger Adolf Stoecker und die christlichsoziale Bewegung*, 2nd ed (Hamburg, 1935), p. 156.
16 Retallack, *Notables of the Right*, p. 46.

augmenting the influence of the Protestant church, he appealed with more success to the lower middle classes through anti-Semitic propaganda in the 1880s, and in April 1892, Stoecker and Hammerstein emerged victorious from their long-standing rivalry with Otto von Helldorf-Bedra, who was forced to resign the party leadership. At the beginning of the 1890s, the influence of Christian socialism within Conservative Party ranks still seemed strong and would soon be reflected in the revised conservative programme of 1892, the so-called Tivoli programme. This new conservative platform, which would remain in operation until 1918, affirmed that the Conservative Party was determined to fight the 'demoralizing Jewish influence upon the life of our people', and voiced opposition to the powerful position of great capital, while emphasizing the importance of protective legislation for agriculture and industry. The Social Democratic Party was cited as the single most dangerous political enemy.[17] It was made quite explicit that henceforth the Conservative Party was bent on pursuing policies that would benefit primarily the Junker class.

The increasing success of a host of other radical anti-Semitic parties, which reached the pinnacle of their influence in 1893 with a total of 16 mandates (up from five in 1890 and one in 1887) and 263,861 votes, soon cut into the following of the CSP, lessening its attractiveness for conservatives, though internecine bickering of the anti-Semitic splinter groups reduced them to insignificance again within a matter of years.[18] Rendered obsolete as a vote getter, the standing of the CSP within the Conservative Party fell steadily, and in February 1896, Stoecker was forced to resign, first from the party's steering committee, the *Elfer Ausschuß*, then from the party itself, following a scandal that involved his long-time ally Wilhelm von Hammerstein. Hammerstein was found guilty of embezzling large sums to maintain a lifestyle not commensurate with his income. In the course of the criminal investigation, Hammerstein's private papers were subjected to minute scrutiny, revealing a letter Stoecker had written to him on 14 August 1888, in which the leader of the CSP had suggested a strategy designed to sow discord between Bismarck and the young emperor, thereby ultimately undermining the viability of the *Kartell*. To the dismay of conservatives, this notorious *Scheiterhaufenbrief*, literally 'funeral pyre letter', was published by the Social Democratic Party newspaper *Vorwärts* on 5 September 1895 after Stoecker had vainly denied his authorship. In the *Scheiterhaufenbrief*, Stoecker

---

17 Edgar Hartwig, 'Konservative Partei', in Dieter Fricke et al., *Lexikon zur Parteiengeschichte* (Leipzig, 1983–86), iii, pp. 283–309, esp. 293.
18 Richard S. Levy, *The Downfall of the Anti-Semitic Political Parties in Imperial Germany* (New Haven and London, 1975); Dieter Fricke, 'Antisemitische Parteien 1879–1894', in *Lexikon zur Parteiengeschichte*, i, pp. 77–88, esp. p. 77.

suggested that Hammerstein erect a metaphorical ring of 'funeral pyres' around Bismarck and sow dissension between Bismarck and the emperor by focusing attention on issues on which both obviously disagreed.[19] The publication of this letter naturally called into question the moral stature of the court preacher. After Stoecker's resignation, the CSP reasserted its independence from the conservatives, but lingered in obscurity. Following Stoecker's death in 1909, its anti-Semitic rhetoric was toned down, but by then it had already forfeited all political importance: in 1907, the party counted a mere 9,000 members and in 1918 it merged into the German National People's Party (DNVP).[20]

The politics of the DKP after 1890

After Bismarck's fall from office, Prussian conservatives were less abashed than before in their pursuit of a policy designed to further conservative and agrarian interests. In the years before 1914, their brazen realization of interest policies became especially noticeable in three specific instances: first, in the conservative protest against the commercial policies of Bismarck's successor, Leo von Caprivi, which resulted in the foundation of a conservative-agrarian pressure group in February 1893, the *Bund der Landwirte*; second, in the refusal to countenance the construction of the *Mittellandkanal*, a projected commercial and military artery connecting the Prussian Rhine province with East Elbia; third, in the breaking up of the Bülow bloc in 1909, a political alliance of the former *Kartell* (Conservatives, Free Conservatives and National Liberals) with the left liberal parties. This alliance, the mainstay of Bülow's policies since December 1906, was renounced by conservatives over the issue of imperial financial reform, which, if implemented as envisaged, threatened conservative landowners with an inheritance tax. In destroying the bloc, conservatives brought down Bülow's government and ended his chancellorship.

1. The introduction of protective tariffs among European states in the 1880s without prior agreements presaged steady tariff increases and trade wars. To obviate these and secure markets for German products, Caprivi concluded a series of commercial treaties with a number of European states: Austria, Italy and Belgium (in 1891), Switzerland, Serbia and Romania (in 1892), and finally Russia. As part of these treaties, Germany agreed to reduce its tariff on wheat and rye from 50 to 35 marks per ton

---

19 Erich Eyck, *Bismarck. Leben und Werk* (Zürich, 1944), iii, p. 550.
20 Dieter Fricke, 'Christlichsoziale Partei, 1878–1918', *Lexikon zur Parteiengeschichte*, i, pp. 440–54.

in exchange for being granted favourable export conditions for manufactured goods. While the Reichstag endorsed the first commercial treaties by an overwhelming margin, approval proved harder to gain when, due to continued good harvests and inexpensive grain imports from abroad, the price of some cereals, such as rye, was cut in half. Though the reduced tariff was, in itself, not the main factor for the collapsing price, conservative opposition to Caprivi's policies grew increasingly vehement, even though industry and commerce were in favour of the commercial agreements. This optimism proved well-founded, for the agreement enhanced the demand for industrial labour, virtually put an end to German overseas migration, doubled German exports, and eventually speeded up German industrial development. Conservative protest against Caprivi's commercial policies led to unrestrained promotion of agrarian interests and eventually to the foundation of the Agrarian League. This association provided an alternative mass basis for conservatives, who were now less dependent on support from the urban petty bourgeoisie than they had been during the 1880s. From the beginning, the Agrarian League was a mass organization that grew to more than 300,000 members by 1913, though its influence remained negligible outside Prussia. For the more traditional leaders of the conservatives, the popular orientation of the CSP, its appeal to the lower classes and its excessively popular and demagogic style had always been suspect. The Agrarian League, on the other hand, was led by East Elbian estate owners; it was centrally organized, well funded, had its own press organs, and was altogether more predictable than the volatile CSP. The existence of the Agrarian League further consolidated the tie between Prussia's rural East Elbian provinces and the conservative party; there was now less incentive than ever to gain a mass following in the more heavily urbanized West.

2. In Prussia, plans had been circulating since the 1850s to connect the western with the eastern parts of the monarchy through a waterway from the Rhine to the Elbe rivers. This *Mittellandkanal*, as it was to be called, would be a great expeditor for any kind of traffic. Even though the potential importance for military usage was extolled in no uncertain terms (an argument that ought to have struck a sensitive chord with conservatives), the conservative bastion in the Prussian *Landtag* rejected the project, believing the canal would bring cheaply exported grain to the eastern provinces and depress grain prices there. Conservative Prussian officials who, as conservative *Landtag* deputies, voted against the government plan, were subjected to disciplinary measures and forced to take an early retirement. After a renewed rejection of the scheme in

1901, the *Kanalvorlage* was finally approved in 1904, after Bülow had managed to procure conservative support through the passing of the 1902 Tariff Law that again raised duties on imported grain to the former high level. Yet, bowing to conservative demands, the final (and all-important) link between Hanover and the Elbe was never built so that the project remained essentially a torso. By then, it had become clear that conservative political support for governmental policies depended on the reception with which their own political demands, such as protective tariffs, were met.

3. By 1907, mounting expenses for the navy, which had risen to half the army budget, necessitated a large-scale financial reform to boost tax revenues, lest the empire remain mired in ever rising national debt. Between 1906 and 1909 alone, the debt of the empire had increased by 1.5 billion marks to a total of 5 billion, while, in 1908, the annual budget stood at a mere 2.5 billion marks.[21] Income taxes already lay in the purview of the individual states, while a limitless increase of indirect taxes on various products would hurt low income households and be grist for the mills of social democracy; augmenting revenue through an inheritance tax thus appeared to be a logical solution. Yet, the Conservative Party, an important component of the Bülow bloc, was loath to consider an inheritance tax for a number of reasons: first, to assess the proper level of taxation, landed properties in the east would have to be appraised, thereby revealing their actual pecuniary circumstances; second, taxes on the national level were under the jurisdiction of the Imperial Diet, elected on the basis of universal manhood suffrage, where the Conservative Party had a mere 60 seats (after the 1907 election), and was therefore unable to wield decisive influence. In the Prussian *Landtag*, on the other hand, where the three-class franchise was still in operation, they occupied a dominant position. Keenly aware of the root of their influence, they were anxious to avoid any reform of that electoral system, however outdated it might seem to contemporaries. Their democratic opponents might well come to prevail some day, but, as their parliamentary leader Heydebrand stated with candour, conservatives would do their utmost to postpone that evil day for as long as possible. Since Bülow had declared his intention to reform the Prussian electoral system, the demise of his government would, therefore, be no great loss to conservatives. They were thus all

---

21 Johannes Ziekursch, *Politische Geschichte des neuen deutschen Kaiserreiches* (Frankfurt, 1930), iii, p. 213; Erich Eyck, *Das persönliche Regiment Wilhelms II* (Zürich, 1948), p. 527.

the more adamant in considering the inheritance tax, even though the compromise package that had been worked out left 90 per cent of landed property untouched (due to a large tax-exempt allowance). The demise of the chancellor, who had lost the confidence of his sovereign over his handling of the *Daily Telegraph* affair, followed upon the disintegration of the Bülow bloc. But conservatives' ruthless pursuit of interest policies proved to be counter-productive, for in the elections of 1912, the party found itself reduced to a mere 43 mandates.

The two decades before 1914 witnessed the rise of a host of nationalistic pressure groups with an ever growing membership. Some of the better known included the Pan-German League, which counted Bismarck among its honorary members, with over 20,000 members (in 1900); the Colonial Society with over 40,000 (in 1914); the Society for the Eastern Marches with 54,000 (in 1914), and the Navy League, which, counting all, including corporate ones, had more than a million members. These nationalistic pressure groups were mostly led, not by the aristocracy, but by the educated bourgeoisie, the *Bildungsbürgertum*, a socio-cultural group more influential and respected in Germany than elsewhere in Europe, which had forsaken its former liberal persuasions for nationalistic fervour. The members of these nationalistic pressure groups formed a 'new right': they did not necessarily vote for the Conservative Party, but they popularized and radicalized nationalistic ideals, eventually changed the nature of conservatism, and prepared the ground for extending its influence to areas west of the Elbe. The all-inclusive national conservative movement of the wartime years, the *Vaterlandspartei*, a reservoir for those with conservative, national-liberal, and annexationist leanings, was well represented throughout the German Empire, and the *Deutschnationale Volkspartei*, the main conservative party of the Weimar Republic, succeeded in winning almost half its mandates to the National Assembly in electoral districts west of the Elbe.

PART TWO

The urban and rural environments

CHAPTER FIVE

The Prussian Zollverein and the bid for economic superiority

HANS-JOACHIM VOTH

To an astute political observer pondering the German question at the beginning of the nineteenth century, the founding of the Reich in 1871 under Prussian leadership was anything but a foregone conclusion. There was no reason why a Prussian king, ruling a patchwork of economically, socially and culturally distinct areas, should succeed in unifying Germany. Prussia was also lagging behind the rest of Germany economically, with an unusually high proportion of the labour force employed in agriculture. Not only was Prussia economically backward, but the humiliating defeats suffered at Jena–Auerstedt at the hands of Napoleon's armies in 1806 had put to rest the myth of its invincible military might. Socially and culturally, the Reform Movement under Stein and Hardenberg was struggling to achieve the degree of legal and social modernization that other states, such as France and Britain, had achieved long ago. Despite these obstacles, it was Prussia that succeeded in unifying Germany. A number of historians have argued that the Zollverein, or Customs Union, was a crucial catalyst for Prussia's transformation into Germany's economic and political powerhouse.

At the end of the eighteenth century, the area that was to be unified in 1871 was remarkably backward in economic terms. At a time when less than half the English population was still working the land, the figure in Germany was probably closer to 80 per cent. Incomes and life expectancy were low even by the standards of the time; infant mortality was high. Germany, divided into hundreds of states, wielded little political influence. By the end of the nineteenth century, however, it had undergone a classic 'rags-to-riches' transformation. National income and population size had rapidly increased, and the prowess of its export industries earned it admiration and caused consternation abroad. In the leading sectors of the so-called Second Industrial Revolution – chemicals and electrical engineering – its dominance was absolute. Every year, German scientists habitually took a disproportionate share of Nobel Prizes in the sciences, and the Reich's High Seas Fleet was preparing to challenge the Royal Navy. Germany's transformation into one of the leading economies is also often partly attributed to the Zollverein. By extending market size and abolishing onerous tariff barriers, the basis for the business empires of Siemens, of Deutsche Bank and Krupp and their worldwide successes had been laid.

The Zollverein has long played an almost mythical role in explanations of Prussia's eventual rise to political and economic supremacy in Germany, and of Germany's rise as an economic power. This chapter revisits the debate in an attempt to demonstrate that there is, in fact, precious little evidence to suggest that the Zollverein strengthened Prussia's position either directly or indirectly with the German Confederation. Also, one could argue that the economic consequences of the Zollverein for Germany as a whole were probably largely detrimental. The Customs Union probably mattered little either as a stimulus to growth or as a catalyst for Prussia's rise.

Launchpad for take-off or precursor of unification?

The historical literature falls into two main categories. One strand of research is primarily concerned with the economic consequences of the Zollverein; the other is mainly interested in its political and social effects. Following an intellectual tradition dating back to the economist and politician, Friedrich List (1789–1846), many scholars have argued that the economic effects of the Zollverein were vital for Germany's transition into self-sustaining growth. According to this view, industrialization was significantly accelerated by the creation of external tariff barriers and a larger domestic market. List argued that without tariff protection Germany would have soon been reduced to the position of an English colony specializing in agricultural goods – to become, in his words, a nation of 'hewers of wood and drawers of water for the Brits'.[1] In the 1960s,

---

[1] Cited in Hans-Ulrich Wehler, *Deutsche Gesellschaftsgeschichte*, 3 vols (Munich, 1994), ii, p. 133. I first explored some of the issues discussed in this chapter during 'The Struggle for Mastery in Germany' lecture series at the History Faculty, Cambridge University. I am grateful to Brendan Simms and Jonathan Steinberg for stimulating comments.

Walter G. Hoffmann and Hans Mottek argued that 1834 was a turning point in German economic history precisely because the Zollverein helped to reduce English competition and allowed German industry to flourish behind a system of protective tariffs.[2] F. Lütge's textbook, widely used in universities, argued for a similar interpretation.[3] Having gained a breathing space from British competition, German industry eventually developed sufficiently to take up the challenge not only at home (behind tariff barriers), but on world markets as well.

More recently, however, scholars have begun to doubt the supposed large benefits of the Zollverein. Did the Customs Union lead to a permanent increase in Gross Domestic Product (GDP)? Did it raise the rate of growth? Rolf Dumke's contributions have been crucial in casting doubt on the supposed welfare gains derived from the Zollverein. He calculated the highest possible gains that could be attributed to the Customs Union, systematically formulating assumptions towards finding beneficial effects. Despite this, Dumke found that even in the most favoured areas – the southern member states – total gains were no more than approximately one per cent of national income.[4] Improvements in growth rates for the cotton industry were equally unspectacular, as his examination of G. Kirchhain's data shows.[5] If industries with an important fixed-cost component such as cotton showed such small net benefits, it is highly likely that they were even smaller in other sectors of the economy where economies of scale were negligible. Finally, the gains in sectors such as cotton have to be balanced against losses in proto-industrial sectors that now were made to feel domestic competition more acutely.[6] The economic significance of the Zollverein is also undermined by the work done by Richard Tilly and Sidney Pollard. They argue that, far from harming German economic development, British competition was actually

---

2   W. G. Hoffmann, 'The Take-Off in Germany', in W. Rostow (ed.), *The Economics of Take-Off into Sustained Growth* (London, 1968), pp. 95–118; and H. Mottek, *Wirtschaftsgeschichte Deutschlands*, 2 vols (East Berlin, 1964), ii, pp. 56–68.
3   F. Lütge, *Deutsche Wirtschafts- und Sozialgeschichte* (Berlin, 1966).
4   R. Dumke, 'The Political Economy of German Economc Unification: Tariffs, Trade and Politics of the Zollverein Era' (PhD, University of Wisconsin, Madison, 1976); R. Dumke, 'Die wirtschaftlichen Folgen des Zollvereins', in W. Abelshauser and D. Petzina, eds, *Deutsche Wirtschaftsgeschichte im Industriezeitalter* (Düsseldorf, 1981), pp. 341–73.
5   G. Kirchhain, *Das Wachstum der deutschen Baumwollindustrie im 19. Jahrhundert* (New York, 1977).
6   R. Dumke, 'Tariffs and Market Structure: The German Zollverein as a Model for Economic Integration', in R. Lee (ed.), *German Industry and Industrialisation* (London, 1991), p. 86. Note that the welfare loss arising from a reallocation of the labour force from proto-industry to other sectors is transitory, and will eventually be compensated for by the higher productivity of the viable sectors in the economy.

beneficial.⁷ As a consequence, one could argue that the attempt to reduce competitive pressure by means of the Zollverein (whose tariff rates were in any event too low to achieve such an objective) was not necessarily beneficial. The revisionist literature, however, has not met with universal success: Hans-Ulrich Wehler, for example, still portrays the Zollverein as an important stepping stone in the industrialization process.⁸

The economic consequences of the Zollverein are therefore still open to debate. The same is true of political motives and consequences. The nineteenth-century German historian, Heinrich von Treitschke, put it most bluntly: at the inception of the Zollverein, 'the thunder of Königgrätz [...] resounded from afar'.⁹ Later historians such as Helmut Böhme and Ernst-Rudolf Huber continued to see the Zollverein as a potent weapon in Prussian power politics.¹⁰ Austria's repeated attempts to be admitted into the Zollverein became so fierce because the ultimate outcome of the struggle for mastery in Germany was at stake – it was assumed that political union would naturally follow from economic union. Both Wolfram Fischer and William Henderson have cast doubt on the notion that political union would naturally follow from economic union by stressing the extent to which the smaller member states joined because of fiscal pressures during the 1830s and 1840s. While they sought to retain and even strengthen their political links with Austria, they more or less reluctantly joined the Customs Union out of financial necessity. No automatic mechanism guaranteed the political success of Prussia; rather, the Zollverein should be seen as a 'system of expedients'.¹¹ This interpretation also received support from a study of the Hessian states by Hans-Werner Hahn.¹²

A similar line has been taken by Rolf Dumke, who sees the Zollverein as a way of rationalizing revenue collection for the member states. Many German states relied on tariff revenue to a significant extent because of one important advantage – in contrast to taxes, tariffs did not have to be approved by parliaments. A higher net yield of the tariffs (after expenses)

---

7 R. Tilly, 'Los von England: Probleme des Nationalismus in der deutschen Wirtschaftsgeschichte', in R. Tilly, *Kapital, Staat und sozialer Protest in der deutschen Industrialisierung* (Göttingen, 1980), pp. 97–209; S. Pollard, *Peaceful Conquest* (Oxford, 1981), pp. 636–45.
8 Wehler, *Deutsche Gesellschaftsgeschichte*, ii, p. 134.
9 Heinrich von Treitschke, *Deutsche Geschichte im 19. Jahrhundert* (Leipzig, 1918), iv, p. 379.
10 H. Böhme, *Deutschlands Weg zur Großmacht* (Cologne, 1966), pp. 211–15; E. R. Huber, *Deutsche Verfassungsgeschichte*, 8 vols (Stuttgart, 1957), i, pp. 814–16.
11 W. Fischer, 'The Zollverein. A Case Study in Customs Union', *Kyklos* 13 (1960), 65–89; W. Henderson, *The Zollverein* (London, 1984).
12 H-W. Hahn, *Wirtschaftliche Integration im 19. Jahrhundert. Die hessischen Staaten und der Deutsche Zollverein* (Göttingen, 1982).

strengthened the hand of conservative governments.[13] Therefore, the more efficient collection mechanism provided by the Zollverein was of particular benefit to those governments engaged in repeated conflict with their parliaments over budgetary issues. In short, while historians have traditionally argued for a causal connection between the Zollverein and the founding of the Reich in 1871, recent interpretations see a much more tenuous link. It is largely because liberalism in the smaller states was held at bay (parliaments were less potent because of Zollverein customs revenues) that the political preconditions for unification under Prussian leadership existed.

Hans-Ulrich Wehler has recently suggested a new twist to the tale. Even if the ultimate, direct political pay-off to Prussia was disappointing, its own position within the group of German states was strengthened markedly in economic terms.[14] According to Wehler, it was Prussia's industries that benefited most from tariff protection and a larger domestic market. Independent of the price paid in terms of customs revenue shared with the smaller states, Prussia gained sufficiently in economic weight to compensate for this cost.[15] While the large agricultural producers in the eastern regions of Prussia suffered a decline in their terms of trade, the industries of both Prussia and Saxony prospered. The process of structural change, leading to a higher share of the labour force employed in industry, was thereby accelerated. It is this superior degree of economic development that underpinned Prussian political influence and military muscle. The Zollverein, therefore, mattered because it provided Prussia with the economic tools to accomplish unification.[16]

There are, therefore, three hypotheses that require further investigation. First, the economic consequences of the Zollverein for Germany as a whole need to be clarified. Second, the political consequences of the Zollverein for the unification process are in need of further attention. Third, Prussia's economic development as a result of its role in the Zollverein of 1834 needs to be examined more closely.

German economic development

Much of the writing on the economic consequences of the Zollverein has adopted a regional or industry perspective. Investigations of individual

---

13 Dumke, 'Tariffs and Market Structure', p. 84.
14 Wehler, *Deutsche Gesellschaftsgeschichte*, iii, pp. 288f.
15 Wehler, *Deutsche Gesellschaftsgeschichte*, iii, p. 556.
16 Wehler, *Deutsche Gesellschaftsgeschichte*, ii, pp. 134f.

industries or single areas have great analytic potential in illuminating economic issues that are highly localized or specific, such as the effect of industry-specific shocks. What these investigations add at the level of economies as a whole is somewhat less clear: there is no reason to believe that they are representative of changes at large. Dumke's studies come closest to examining the overall impact of the Zollverein. However, it is perhaps worth pursuing a complementary strategy – that of placing German economic development when the Zollverein was at its zenith within the context of an international perspective.[17] We should expect German growth to outpace that of other industrializing nations – if the customs issue acted as an important drag on economic development, the removal of this bottleneck should have led to a period of unusually high growth rates. The second prediction concerns the pattern of trade. If large benefits resulted from unifying Germany economically through the Zollverein, and flourishing industries gained in competitiveness, an export boom should have ensued.

The Zollverein grew out of extensions of the Prussian customs laws which abolished internal tariff barriers in 1818. Initially, smaller states that were surrounded by Prussian territory, such as Anhalt-Köthen and Anhalt-Dessau, were simply absorbed by the Prussian customs laws. A second step towards a customs union occurred after the incorporation of Hessen-Darmstadt allowed Prussia to combine its eastern and western provinces into a single customs area in 1828. That same year, the Prussian Customs Union joined forces with Bavaria-Württemberg. Finally, after a trade area agreement in the middle of Germany, instigated by Metternich, had effectively collapsed, the Zollverein of 1834 came into being and incorporated the vast majority of Germans outside Austria. In 1835, Baden, Nassau and Frankfurt joined. In 1841, Braunschweig and Luxemburg were incorporated. By the end of the 1830s, more than 88 per cent of the German population lived in member states of the Zollverein.[18] The period 1840–60 is, therefore, when the Zollverein's influence was at its peak. Before 1840, numerous states were still absent. After the Zollverein joined the Cobden–Chevalier Treaty in 1862, which had already radically lowered tariff barriers between England and France, the degree of protection was too low to claim that it exerted much influence.

---

17 Wehler, *Deutsche Gesellschaftsgeschichte*, ii. p. 135 has recently rejected Dumke's calculations as mere 'speculation' – in terms of real history, the Zollverein mattered because entrepreneurs adapted to it. For a leading protagonist of a school of German historians that once sought to remodel history as a social science, this is a highly illuminating statement – nothing could be further from a 'social science history' approach than to substitute condescending comment for rigorous analysis.

18 Wehler, *Deutsche Gesellschaftsgeschichte*, ii. p. 129.

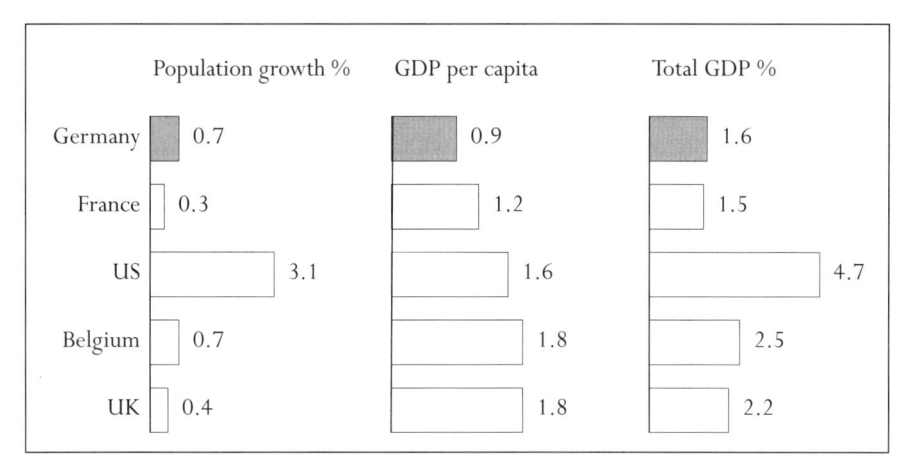

	Population growth %	GDP per capita	Total GDP %
Germany	0.7	0.9	1.6
France	0.3	1.2	1.5
US	3.1	1.6	4.7
Belgium	0.7	1.8	2.5
UK	0.4	1.8	2.2

Figure 5.1: Measures of economic performance: Population growth and GDP growth per annum in per cent, 1840–60.

Source: data from Maddison 1991

During the heyday of the Zollverein, Germany's macro-economic performance was disappointing on most counts. Growth in total GDP was unspectacular – the rate of annual increase was a mere 1.6 per cent, compared with 2.1 in the UK, 2.4 in Belgium, and 4.7 in the US.[19] Only France saw aggregate GDP rise at a (marginally) slower rate of 1.5 per cent per annum. Nor was this the result of slow population growth – as Figure 5.1 shows, Germany's GDP per capita growth was particularly disappointing over the period compared with its neighbours and constitutes the prime reason for slow growth of total GDP. The only reason why total German GDP increased more rapidly than French GDP is the latter's particularly low rate of demographic growth. The productivity of the population – measured by per capita GDP – did not grow at impressive rates, and the total economic power of the country – calculated as total GDP – also failed to live up to expectations. During the very period when Germany, supported by the enlightened trade policies of Prussia, should have prospered, the growth record was dismal. If trade distortions acted as powerful restraints on economic development before 1834, and if the erection of an external trade barrier combined with a larger domestic market allowed the exploitation of economies of scale, then why did Germany grow much more slowly than its rivals?

---

19 Angus Maddison, *Dynamic Forces in Capitalist Development: A Long-run Comparative View* (Oxford and New York, 1991), table A.5, pp. 206ff., and table B.1, p. 226ff.

Germany's economic potential in 1834 was not low. With per capita income far below British levels, the chances for 'catch-up growth' were enormous. 'Catch-up' is the phrase used by economists for growth generated by applying technologies and organizational advances developed elsewhere. Instead of becoming more productive through new inventions and innovations, catch-up growth occurs when individual countries increase output by copying from the technology leader.[20] Nor was Germany's ability to transfer the leading technologies of the time, and thus to narrow the productivity gap, small. Economists do not agree on all the factors that enable catch-up growth to occur, but on most of the measures normally mentioned, such as human capital stock, security of property rights and the rule of law, Germany scored well.[21] To attribute a positive influence to the Zollverein is to argue that Germany would have grown even more slowly if it had not been for the Zollverein. This was unlikely, however, as the following demonstrates.

Germany failed to integrate as rapidly into the world economy as its neighbours. During the period 1840–60, the Zollverein came to include almost all German states save Austria. Intra-German trade was booming, but export volumes to the rest of the world failed to rise as rapidly as in other countries. As Figure 5.2 shows, exports from Britain, Belgium and France increased by more than 200 per cent during the period. On average, the countries in our sample saw volumes rise by 175 per cent. German exports, however, increased by 128 per cent, or little more than half the international average. It could be argued that Germany's lack of colonies was responsible for this disappointing performance, but other countries in the same situation also showed more rapid export growth – e.g. the United States. To be sure, Germany's dismal export record could be excused on other counts. Nonetheless, there is precious little to suggest that the Zollverein rapidly boosted the competitiveness of Germany's exports.

Might the two phenomena – the Zollverein and the lack of export growth – be connected? In his classic study, Jacob Viner distinguished two consequences of customs unions – trade creation and trade diversion.[22] Trade creation between the new members of a joint customs area is unambiguously beneficial – individual areas leverage their specific

---

20 W. Baumol, 'Productivity Growth, Convergence, and Welfare: What the Long-Run Data Show', *American Economic Review* 76 (1986), 1072–85. For a critique, cf. B. DeLong, 'Productivity Growth, Convergence, and Welfare: Comment', *American Economic Review* 78 (1988), 1138–54. R. Barro, 'Economic Growth in a Cross Section of Countries', *Quarterly Journal of Economics* 106 (1991), 407–43 presents the most conclusive evidence.

21 On the influence of human capital, cf. J. Temple and H-J. Voth, 'Human Capital, Equipment Investment, and Industrialization', *European Economic Review* 42 (1998), 1343–62.

22 J. Viner, *The* Zollverein *Issue* (New York, 1950), p. 97.

Chart Data

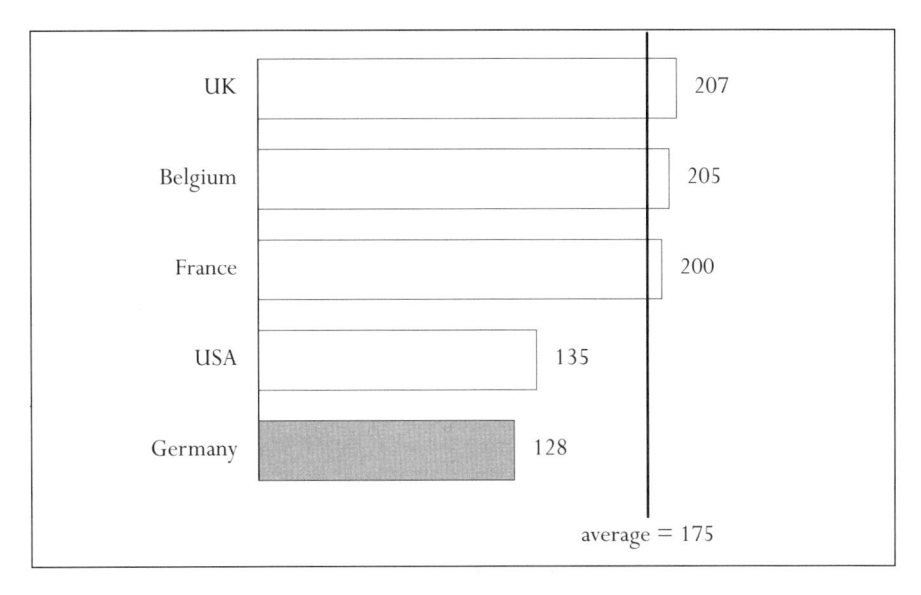

Country	Value
UK	207
Belgium	205
France	200
USA	135
Germany	128

average = 175

Figure 5.2 Development of export volumes: Change in volume of exports in per cent, 1840–60 (1840 = 100).

Source: data from Maddison 1991

strengths by exploiting country-specific advantages such as rich endowments of particular natural resources.[23] Trade diversion, however, involves the substitution of trade between member states and external states for trade within the customs area. The consequences are obviously harmful – comparative advantages are no longer exploited to the full, and economic resources are misallocated. The layman's suspicion that the cost of trade diversion falls mainly on nations excluded from a customs union is wrong: most of the burden is borne by the member states that can no longer buy from the cheapest suppliers.[24] Protectionism is almost always most costly for the nation instituting protectionist practices. The creation of a customs union causes both trade creation and trade diversion. The net benefit or cost depends on the magnitudes of these two effects. Might a similar explanation be useful for understanding Germany's disappointing growth record during the heyday of the Zollverein?

---

23 The classic example is Britain's intensive use of coal. On the disadvantages of not having access to domestic coal deposits, cf. C. Bardini, 'Without Coal in the Age of Steam', *Journal of Economic History* 57 (1997), 633–53.

24 P. Krugman and M. Obstfeld, *International Economics: Theory and Policy* (New York, 1997), pp. 227–35.

Before 1834, Germany was not composed of states committed to free trade. Most German states levied stiff tariffs and, in many cases, joining the Zollverein implied a lowering of actual tariff rates. At the same time, there was a clear discrimination in favour of Zollverein member states, and commensurate disadvantages for exporters outside the Zollverein area. The main cost was borne by consumers. Prussia's textile manufacturers in Westphalia would never have been able to compete against Lancashire under free trade. Nor would most German states have been large buyers of Prussian cloth before the founding of the Zollverein – tariffs discriminated equally against Prussian and English cloth, and therefore did nothing to reduce the competitive disadvantage of the former. Thanks to the tariff barriers, however, German customers everywhere now found themselves forced to purchase Prussian textiles. It is not clear, however, if the lowering of internal tariff barriers compensated fully for two factors that now tended to raise the price of textile products – the increased market power of domestic textile producers, and the need to buy from (comparatively) inefficient manufacturers. Also, the sudden advantage of Prussian textile manufacturers – and other industries largely freed from the pressures of English competition – encouraged a diversion of economic resources. Without the distortions introduced by the Zollverein, Prussia (and other industrial areas of Germany) might have specialized in industries in which relative factor cost gave them a natural advantage.

In short, the consequences of the Zollverein were, on the whole, negative for Germany's economic development, even though Prussia may have benefited at the expense of its German neighbours. This may help explain Prussia's eventual role in the unification process.

Prussia's political influence

The Zollverein was undoubtedly one of the most politically charged issues in Germany between 1834 and 1866. Austria's repeated attempts to force its way into the Zollverein, and Prussia's successful tactics to keep Austria at bay, have been described elsewhere.[25] As already mentioned, Böhme saw Prussia's forging of the Zollverein as a vital step in achieving political dominance in Germany.[26] Most member states relied heavily on customs

---

25 Wehler, *Deutsche Gesellschaftsgeschichte*, iii, pp. 225ff.
26 Böhme, *Deutschlands Weg zur Großmacht*, pp. 210–15.

duties, and the Zollverein was seen to be a success largely because it boosted tariff revenues.[27] They thus came to depend economically on Prussia. In this perspective, the way in which Bismarck forced the acceptance of the Cobden–Chevalier Treaty – thus excluding Austria from the Zollverein for good – demonstrated that the member states could be held to ransom by Prussia by economic means.

As Hans-Ulrich Wehler has recently emphasized, Königgrätz did not predetermine the outcome of the struggle for mastery in Germany. Austria and Prussia competed fiercely for influence and prestige among the smaller German states, and the Zollverein provided yet another outlet for these competitive pressures. In terms of trade policy, Prussia may have wielded great influence, and even managed to force Bavaria and Württemberg into submission. Yet the ultimate arbiter in the conflict of states is war, not trade, and this was the case in the nineteenth century even more so than today. The Austro-Prussian War saw most of the Zollverein member states joining forces with Austria. In the moment of truth, all its skill at the bargaining table and all its supposed economic influence bought Prussia precious few allies. If the battle of Königgrätz had ended in an Austrian victory,[28] it is more than likely that today the Zollverein would be seen as a futile Prussian attempt to shore up some support in its struggle with Austria.

One of the reasons for the minimal influence of Zollverein membership as an instrument of power politics lies in its modest contribution to government revenues. Economic dependence on Prussia or freedom from the budgetary powers of parliaments have been attributed to the allegedly large increases in government income coming from tariffs. As Figure 5.3 demonstrates, however, these claims are hard to sustain. Before and after joining the Zollverein, all member states generated the vast majority of their revenues by means other than tariffs. On average, some 90 per cent of revenues came from alternative sources prior to joining the Zollverein. By around 1850, this had decreased to 82 per cent – hardly a dramatic shift over a 16-year period. Customs revenues were not, therefore, the lifeblood of the member states' governments. They may have become gradually more important over time, but even by the middle of the century, the volume of customs revenue was dwarfed almost everywhere by income from the state domains, forests and fisheries, and direct and indirect

---

27 For a similar view, cf. Dumke, 'Tariffs and Market Structure', p. 94.
28 For most of the day, the outcome was anything but clear. Bismarck contemplated that, in the case of defeat, he might be hanged on his return to Berlin (Wehler, *Deutsche Gesellschaftsgeschichte*, iii, p. 294).

	Prior to customs union*		1850*	
Prussia	86	14	83	17
Bavaria	93	7	84	16
Baden	92	8	80	20
Württemberg	93	7	85	15
Hessen-Darmstadt	92	8	86	14
Hessen-Kassel	88	12	82	18
Nassau	86	14	74	26

non-tariff revenue / tariff revenue · non-tariff revenue / tariff revenue

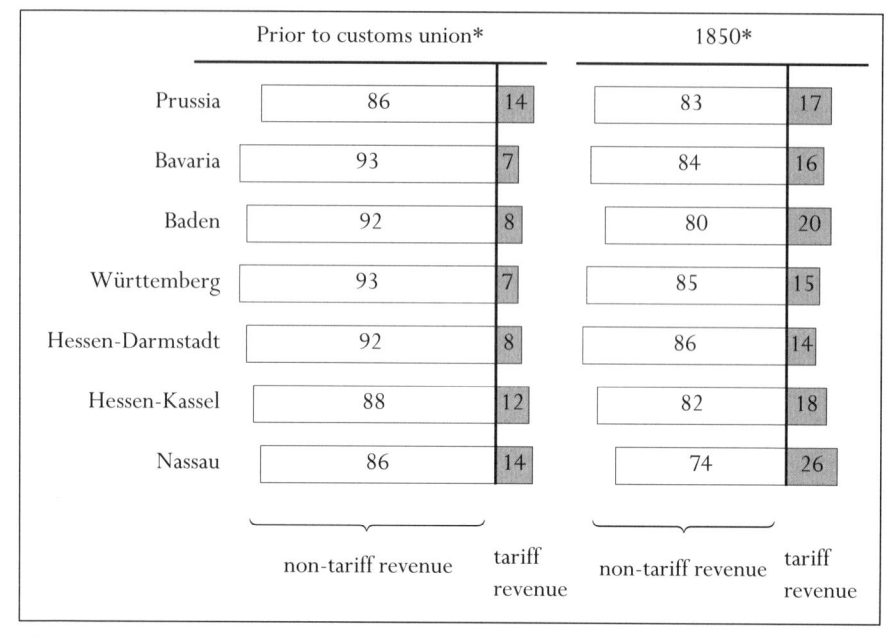

Figure 5.3 Contribution of customs duties: Percentage of total government revenue.

* nearest available date
Source: Dumke, 1991

taxes.[29] It is also less than clear if the revenue gains over this period can be attributed to the Zollverein. Export and import volumes everywhere had a tendency to grow more rapidly than national income – in the European states examined in Figure 5.2, by a factor of 4:1. Even without the Zollverein, it would have been natural to expect that tariff revenue would have expanded more quickly than other forms of taxation that depend on income.

Prussia's economic power

Historians traditionally view the Zollverein's main contribution as that of strengthening the economy of Prussia. Consequently, some scholars continue

---

29 Dumke, 'Tariffs and Market Structure', p. 89, argues that the Zollverein held huge benefits mainly because revenue collection became more efficient. This may have been true of the Palatinate and small states such as Kurhessen or Hessen-Darmstadt. It probably made little difference for Bavaria, Württemberg or Prussia. Cf. Dumke, 'Tariffs and Market Structure', table 3.2, p. 112.

to believe that Prussia's eventual political supremacy in Germany was partly founded on its organizing the Zollverein. The Zollverein may not have brought it any important allies, but it fostered the growth of its industry – and it is this growth that underpinned its successes on the battlefield. If one looks closer at this argument, however, one can see that it is flawed on two counts: success on the battlefield during the wars of German unification was not determined by economic factors; and, more importantly, the Zollverein did not bring any significant benefits to the economy of Prussia.

If war provides the opportunity to use stockpiles of weapons and ammunition that were produced before the outbreak of hostilities, the influence of economic factors is consequently reduced considerably. The First World War became a bitter struggle in which not only armies but entire economies were pitted against each other because the stockpiles of arms and ammunition available in 1914 paled into insignificance in comparison with the demands placed upon industrial production during the course of the war. The Seven Weeks' War of 1866 and the Franco-Prussian War of 1870–71 were not wars of attrition; industrial might played less of a role in the Wars of Unification than some accounts imply. Moltke's plans to supply his armies in Austria by rail nearly ended in catastrophe. The Prussian supply trains did not catch up with the troops until the battle of Königgrätz was won. Despite all meticulous planning to supply the troops by rail, Moltke's army, like Frederick the Great's, lived off the country, by quartering or purchases.[30] Nor was a single field gun or cartridge fired by the Prussian armies that had not been manufactured before the outbreak of hostilities in 1866.[31] In short, industrial development, powerful logistics and economic capacity did not play a role as far as the supply of guns and butter during the military confrontation was concerned.

There is a second reason why the Zollverein probably mattered less than has previously been thought – Prussia's economy arguably derived little benefit from it. This is not necessarily true for individual regions or industries, notably the textile manufacturers in Westphalia who saw windfall profits. The problem is trying to assess whether these are simply local distortions resulting from a protectionist tariff regime, or harbingers of self-sustaining growth and industrialization. Estimates of output growth per capita and other standard measures of economic performance are not available in sufficient detail at the state level. Fortunately, a simple substitute for the level of economic development exists – the share of the population employed in agriculture. The development of an industrial economy is

---

30 M. van Creveld, *Supplying War: Logistics from Wallenstein to Patton* (Cambridge, 1977), pp. 79–80.
31 Creveld, *Supplying War*, p. 81.

normally accompanied by a falling share of the workforce employed on the land.[32] As agricultural productivity rises, more people can be fed in the towns where they engage in industrial production. In England in 1870, a mere 15 per cent of the labour force was still employed in the primary sector.[33] In France, on the other hand, 49 per cent of the labour force was employed in agriculture and related activities.

At the beginning of the eighteenth century, Prussia was predominantly agricultural with more than 70 per cent of the workforce engaged in producing primary products. Throughout Germany, as economic development slowly increased, the share of the population in agriculture fell. In Baden and Württemberg, for example, less than half the labour force was engaged in agriculture by 1870. In Prussia, on the other hand, the share of the agricultural labour force remained remarkably high. After the creation of the Zollverein, this proportion fell, but at a very slow pace, and there is no sign that the downward trend might have accelerated after 1834. Even after unification, a little less than 70 per cent of the population of Prussia was still working the land, one and half times above the average for the rest of Germany.[34] In other words, the unusually slow expansion of the industrial and services sectors in Germany (compared to the European norm) is almost entirely due to Prussia's retardation.[35] One additional statistic easily demonstrates how little economic factors determined the outcome of the struggle for mastery in Germany – Austria actually had a lower proportion of the population employed in agriculture than Prussia, indicating a lower level of industrial backwardness.[36] Austria also achieved a level of output per man-hour that was on a par with the German average. Even if the equivalent figures for Prussia don't exist, the high proportion of agricultural employment, accompanied by a sizeable productivity gap in agriculture vis-à-vis the industrial sector, strongly suggest that Prussia may have lagged behind Austria on this count.[37]

This evidence is reinforced by an examination of the composition of

---

32 E. A. Wrigley, *People, Cities and Wealth* (Oxford, 1987), pp. 157–93.
33 N. F. R. Crafts, *British Economic Growth During the Industrial Revolution* (Oxford 1985), p. 59.
34 Cf. R. Tilly, 'La Formacion de Capital en Alemania del siglo XIX', *Historia Economica de Europa* (Madrid and Cambridge, 1987), vii, pp. 543–625; Wehler, *Deutsche Gesellschaftsgeschichte*, iii, 46, 34.
35 Crafts, *British Economic Growth*, pp. 48–69; Wehler, *Deutsche Gesellschaftsgeschichte*, iii, p. 46.
36 Crafts, *British Economic Growth*, p. 57. Note that the figure is for 1880, and refers to the the area of present-day Austria. A. Maddison, *Dynamic Forces in Capitalist Development. A Long-Run Comparative View* (Oxford and New York, 1991), p. 248 gives a somewhat higher ratio for 1870, but still below the Prussian level.
37 Maddison, *Dynamic Forces*, table C. 11, p. 274.

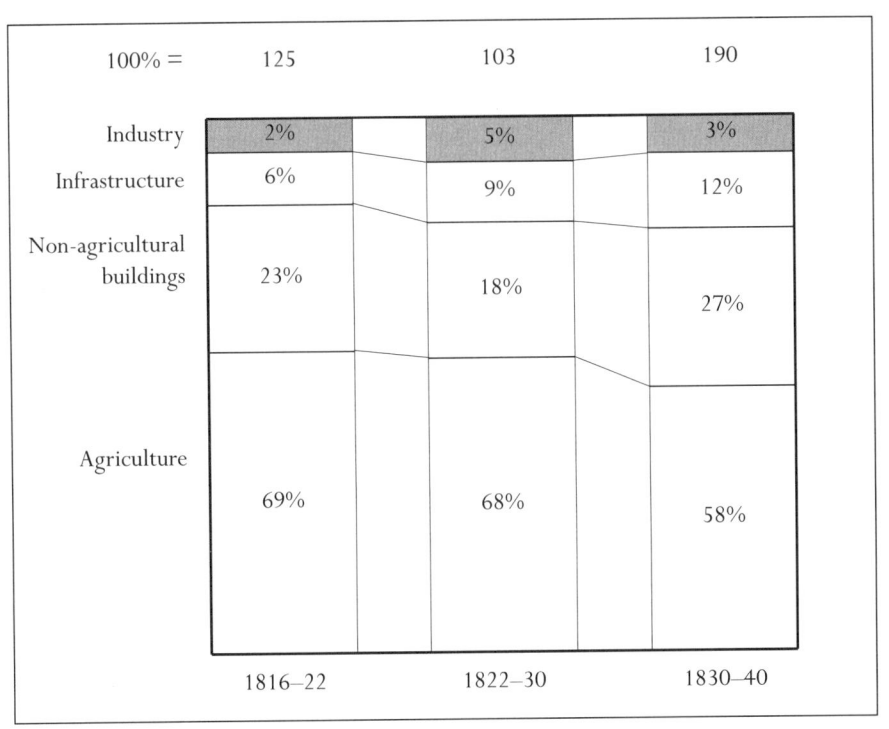

THE PRUSSIAN ZOLLVEREIN AND ECONOMIC SUPERIORITY

	1816–22	1822–30	1830–40
100% =	125	103	190
Industry	2%	5%	3%
Infrastructure	6%	9%	12%
Non-agricultural buildings	23%	18%	27%
Agriculture	69%	68%	58%

Figure 5.4 Composition of investment in Prussia, 1816–40: Annual net investment in millions of 1913 marks.

Source: Wehler, 1994 ii

Prussian investment. Figure 5.4 shows the net capital formation in Prussia between 1816 and 1840. If the Zollverein had enabled Prussian industry to experience accelerated growth due to tariff protection and a larger domestic market, the influence should have made itself felt strongly in investment activity – faster growth would normally be accompanied by high rates of investment and rapid growth of the capital stock. The last period before the founding of the Zollverein for which we can construct the necessary data shows – as is only to be expected in an economy dominated by agriculture – that more than two-thirds of capital formation took place in the primary sector; a mere 5 per cent went to industry. For the period before and after the founding of the Zollverein, the agricultural share declined somewhat. Most of the capital gains, however, went into buildings. Industry actually saw its share of investment reduced sharply, falling from 5 to 3 per cent. This 3 per cent was, to be sure, a share of a markedly larger pie. Yet even in absolute numbers, the growth was unspectacular: investment in industry grew from 5.1 million marks in 1822–30 to 5.6 million in 1830–40, while investment in agriculture over the same period increased from 70.4 to 109.6 million.

According to this, the most robust indicator of economic development, Prussia was one of Germany's most backward states in 1830. It remained in that position after the founding of the Zollverein. There is no evidence that growth was accelerated by the Zollverein, or that Prussia began to catch up with its German rivals because of it.

Conclusion

Bismarck spoke of German unification as having been achieved by 'blood and iron'. By 'iron', he was probably referring to arms, not industrial output. And rightly so. If Prussia had had to rely on economic might rather than the strength of its armies and the ruthlessness of its political leaders, it would not in all likelihood have emerged victorious from the struggle for mastery in Germany. The Zollverein did not strengthen Prussia's position in Germany, either economically or politically. First, economic power did not automatically imply political power in nineteenth-century Germany, and industrial backwardness was not tantamount to strategic impotence. If this had been the case, it would be hard to understand why it was Prussia that succeeded in unifying Germany and not Austria. Second, there is no indication that Prussia exerted any political influence and power over the other member states of the Zollverein when it mattered most – in time of war. Third, the Zollverein provided few tangible economic benefits for the country as a whole. Germany's growth record lagged behind that of other nations with similar economic conditions. The idea of a customs union may have excited the hearts and minds of contemporary bourgeois commentators, but it did little to boost economic performance. The Zollverein thus appears to have provided simply another arena in which Austria and Prussia tested each other's resolve diplomatically. The whole question was as overcharged with the images and emotions of power politics as it has been overrated as a matter of political and economic significance. Its influence as a catalyst for German economic development has been similarly exaggerated. By the standards of the time, the Zollverein did not accelerate economic growth. Germany was falling behind its competitors during the period when almost all German states had joined the customs union. Its meteoric rise came only after 1870. In explaining this dramatic change, future research should focus on factors that distinguished the Reich from the Zollverein.

The question which now must be posed is why so many historians have decided to believe in the crucial importance of a more or less marginal institutional arrangement? Two intellectual traditions contributed to this tendency. Post-war German historians began to taste a fruit that had previously been forbidden – the use of a Marxist paradigm with its emphasis on economic and social factors as an explanation of political outcomes. What had long been regarded as vulgar Marxism in the pre-war era, acquired the cachet of advant-garde analysis during the 1960s and 1970s. In an intellectual environment that saw itself as gratifyingly liberated from the taboos of days past, it was often considered sufficient simply to point to economic antecedents as a way of proving a point.[38] In the case of the Zollverein, this new enthusiasm for economic explanations was reinforced by the fact that fervently Borussian historians such as Treitschke had argued that it had primarily been a means of achieving political dominance. Political suspicion, combined with a seemingly powerful socio-economic analysis, resulted in an appeal that few historians of the self-styled, left-wing 'new school' could resist.

Our analysis suggests that historians' infatuation with the Zollverein should largely be regarded as a phenomenon of intellectual history. There is, however, one sense in which our main argument could be undermined. Since the 1970s, the theory of international trade has undergone a revolution associated with the name of Paul Krugman.[39] At the heart of the 'new trade theory' are economies of scale. They provide a new lease of life for the potentially positive impact of protective measures. If it could be demonstrated that economies of scale were sufficiently large in leading sectors in Germany such as cotton or steel, and that the Zollverein tariffs were set at the right level to allow development of the domestic industries, then some of the conclusions presented in this chapter may well have to be revised. This will be true, however, only if a sufficiently convincing alternative explanation can be found for the disappointing growth performance in Germany at the height of the Zollverein.

---

38 This is especially true of Böhme, *Deutschlands Weg zur Großmacht*, pp. 211ff.
39 Cf. Krugman and Obstfeld, *International Economics*, pp. 35–86.

CHAPTER SIX

The Prussian labour movement, 1871–1914

DICK GEARY

The national context

In several German states in the 1860s, working men formed friendly societies, co-operatives, educational associations and trade unions. Even more remarkably, two working-class political parties came into existence: Ferdinand Lassalle's General Union of German Workers, based primarily in Prussia, and the 'Eisenach' party of August Bebel, which found its support in Saxony, Germany's most industrial state at this time. By the late 1860s, both parties spoke the language of class and subscribed to some form of socialism.

The common experience of workers in the industrial disputes of the early 1870s, unification under Prussia and an increasingly repressive government pushed the two organizations together into a single party in 1875. The German Social Democratic Party (SPD) was outlawed from 1878 to 1890, when the anti-socialist law proscribed all organizations suspected of socialist sympathies, banned their books, seized their assets and imprisoned many of their members. Unions, some of which had hitherto been either apolitical (printers) or inclined towards liberalism (engineering workers), were also closed down. The persecution failed miserably: in 1871, the SPD had won just 3.2 per cent of votes in the national elections, but it secured 9.1 per cent in 1877 and almost 20 per cent in 1890. The exile of Social Democrats from centres of party strength served to spread the message to formerly barren districts, while the SPD's rank and file were radicalized and Marxism became ideologically dominant within the party, culminating in the Erfurt Programme of 1891.

Between 1890 and 1914, German Social Democracy enjoyed spectacular success. In the national elections of 1912, the SPD won 34.8 per cent of the popular vote and could count on over 1 million individual members only two years later. It also spawned a plethora of ancillary organizations: there were SPD choirs, educational and ramblers' associations, drama, cycling, sports, chess and even smoking clubs! By 1914, their total membership embraced around 600,000 workers.[1]

No less impressive was the increased participation of workers in strikes and trade unions, as the figures in Tables 6.1 and 6.2 indicate.

Table 6.1 Participation of workers in strikes

Year	Industrial disputes	Numbers involved
1890/91	226	38,536
1898	985	60,162
1905	2,657	542,564
1910	3,228	390,706
1912	2,834	493,749

Table 6.2 Participation of workers in unions

Year	Membership of the Free Unions
1890	294,551
1900	680,427
1913	2,525,042*

* Klaus Tenfelde and Heinrich Volkmann (eds), *Streik* (Munich, 1981); Klaus Schönhoven, *Expansion und Konzentration* (Stuttgart, 1980); Wolfgang Mommsen and Hans-Gerhard Husung, eds, *Trade Unionism in Great Britain and Germany* (London, 1989); Michael Schneider, *A Brief History of the German Trade Unions* (Bonn, 1989).

1 Jürgen Kocka, *Lohnarbeit und Klassenbildung* (Berlin, 1983); Toni Offermann, *Arbeiterbewegung und liberales Bürgertum* (Bonn, 1979); Gunther Bergmann, *Das Sozialistengesetz im rechtsrheinischen Industriegebiet* (Hanover, 1970); Vernon L. Lidtke, *The Outlawed Party* (Princeton, 1966); Eduard Bernstein, *Die Geschichte der Berliner Arbeiterbewegung* (Berlin, 1910); Roger Fletcher (ed.), *From Bernstein to Brandt* (London, 1987); Dieter Groh, *Negative Integration und revolutionärer Attentismus* (Frankfurt am Main, 1973); W. L. Guttsmann, *The German Social Democratic Party* (London, 1981); Guenther Roth, *Social Democrats in Imperial Germany* (Totowa, NJ, 1963); Carl E. Schorske, *German Social Democracy* (Cambridge, Mass., 1955); Gerhard A. Ritter (ed.), *Der Aufstieg der deutschen Arbeiterbewegung* (Munich, 1991); Mary Nolan, *Social Democracy and Society* (Cambridge, 1981); Adelheid von Saldern, *Auf dem Wege zum Arbeiterreformismus* (Frankfurt am Main, 1984).

These developments can in part be explained by the increase in the number of industrial workers in Germany: in 1870, approximately half the active population was still employed in agriculture; by 1913, less than a third was so employed. That this change correlates with the rise of the SPD is indisputable: with other variables (ethnicity, religious confession) constant, the more industrial workers in a constituency, the higher was the party's vote. The membership was also recruited overwhelmingly (80–90 per cent) from manual workers, the great majority of whom were male, skilled, Protestant and had served apprenticeships.[2]

As important for the emergence of labour organization was the dramatic expansion of German towns in these years, as Table 6.3 shows.

Table 6.3 Expansion of German towns

	Population in	
	1875	1910
Breslau	239,050	512,105
Chemnitz	78,209	287,807
Leipzig	127,387	589,580
Munich	193,024	596,467
Nuremberg	91,018	333,142

Urbanization was accompanied by an increase in the significance of towns of over 100,000 inhabitants: whereas 1,969,000 people had lived in such urban centres in 1871 (4.8 per cent of Reich's population), by 1910, the figure had risen to 13,823,000 (21.3 per cent). This concentration of the population also correlates strongly with the growth of the SPD. Holding other variables (ethnicity, religious affiliation) constant, the larger the town, the greater, both absolutely and proportionately, the number of votes cast for the party. Conversely, the SPD's performance in rural areas and small provincial towns was disproportionately poor. A similar picture of mobilization applies to the free trade unions, which were close to the party: in the large towns, 42 per cent of all those employed in industry, trade and manufacture were free union members in 1911; in towns of between 2,000 and 100,000, the percentage dropped to 16.4 per cent, and in villages with fewer than 2,000 to a paltry 1.2 per cent.[3]

---

2 Ritter, Introduction to *Aufstieg*, p. xvi; Adelheid von Saldern, 'Wer ging in die SPD?', in Ritter, *Aufstieg*, pp. 163–71.
3 Dieter Fricke, 'Die Organization der SPD und die Sozialstruktur ihrer Mitglieder und Reichstagskandidaten', in Ritter, *Aufstieg*, p. 158; and Klaus Schönhoven, 'Die regionale Ausbreitung der deutschen Gewerkschaften im Kaiserreich', in Ritter, *Aufstieg*, p. 350.

The emergence of a large socialist party was no automatic consequence of industrialization and urbanization, however, for these factors produced no such outcome in the United States or Britain before 1914. Other factors played a major role in the politicization and radicalization of working men and women: a repressive and unrepresentative political system, the intransigence of employers and an at least partial middle-class renunciation of political liberalism. These points will be explored below with specific reference to Prussia. At the same time, certain other factors served to hinder the formation of a unitary and radical working class: ethnic, gender and religious divisions, distance migration and high labour turnover. These factors further explain the varieties of labour in Prussia before the First World War. For stretching from Saarbrücken in the west to Königsberg in the east, Prussia included three-fifths of all workers and 50 per cent of all free trade union members in the Reich. It was also a state of extremes, with the highest levels of union and socialist mobilization in some of its larger cities and with the lowest levels in the agrarian east.

Varieties of Prussian labour

The socialist stronghold: Berlin

Lassalle's General Union of German Workers mobilized support above all in Prussia, with strongholds in Berlin, Düsseldorf and Solingen. In the Reichstag elections of 1877, the SPD won 39.2 per cent of the votes in the capital (in the Reich as a whole, 9.1 per cent); in 1891, 56.1 per cent (Reich 19.7 per cent); and by 1912, a staggering 74.9 per cent (Reich 37.4 per cent). In 1910, three of the five largest local party branches were located in the Berlin area, and four years later the Greater Berlin social democratic organization had 121,689 members, making it the largest in the country. Its women's group of 20,039 was also the biggest and most active in the Reich.

---

4   Rudolf Blank, 'Die soziale Zusammensetzung der sozialdemokratischen Wahlerschaft', in Otto Büsch *et al.* (eds), *Wählerbewegungen in der deutschen Geschichte* (Berlin, 1978), p. 185; Gerhard A. Ritter, 'The Social Bases of German Political Parties', in Karl Rohe (ed.), *Elections, Parties, Political Traditions* (Oxford, 1990), p. 33; Franz Osterroth and Dieter Schuster, *Chronik der deutschen Sozialdemokratie* (Berlin, 1975), pp. 23, 34f, 41–7; Francis L. Carsten, *August Bebel und die Organization der Massen* (Berlin, 1991), pp. 27 and 213f; Dieter Hertz-Eichenrode, 'Parteiorganization und Wahlkämpfe der Sozialdemokratie in Berlin', in Ritter, *Aufstieg*, pp.

In Berlin, 301,644 workers (43 per cent of the total in the city) also belonged to the free trade unions in 1911.[4]

Explanations of the strength of social democracy in Imperial Berlin mirror the general patterns of SPD strength. First, Berlin was a major industrial city: already a centre of the textile and garment industries, major engineering firms, such as Borsig, settled there in mid-century. By 1914, electro-technology was represented by the giant Siemens and AEG concerns. In 1907, 53 per cent of economically active Berliners were employed in trade and industry and manual workers made up 61 per cent of the capital's labour force.

Second, Berlin was the archetypal *Grossstadt* (large town). Between 1875 and 1910, the city's population grew from 966,859 to 2,071,257. This rapid expansion had appalling consequences: the average number of tenants per building was depressingly high in most of Imperial Germany's major cities in 1905 (36.53 in Munich, 51.97 in Breslau), but especially shocking in Berlin at 77.54. This was a consequence of high-rise tenement building: in 1895, 67.1 per cent of all buildings in the city had four or more storeys, often stretching back to two, three or as many as six interior, badly-lit yards. Within these buildings, conditions were cramped, with the smallest flats occupied by four people or more. Few apartments would have had more than one heated room, let alone a toilet or bath; and many Berliners (100,000 in 1890) inhabited dank and dismal cellars.

These conditions had important consequences for the socialization of Berlin workers: there was little room for a family-oriented private life or leisure. Within the working-class home, the whole family (and possibly the lodger, too) would meet in the one heated room. From infancy, socialization took place in the corridors, on the staircases, in the yards and on the streets of the working-class neighbourhood. Such overcrowding led many men, especially the young and single, to spend their time in public places and above all in the public house. It was here that the clubs and branches of the labour movement had their base, not least because civic buildings were closed to social democratic meetings in repressive Prussia. The connection between the pub and SPD success was spelled out by Kautsky in 1891: 'The pub is the only bulwark of the proletarian's freedom, of which he can so easily be deprived [...] Without the pub there would not only be no social but also no political life for the German proletarian'. The pub thus acted

---

219–54; Detlef Lehnert, 'Das "rote" Berlin', in Gert-Joachim Glaessner *et al.* (eds), *Studien zur Arbeiterbewegung und Arbeiterkultur in Berlin* (Berlin, 1989), pp. 1–36; Heinz Niggemann, *Emanzipation zwischen Sozialismus und Feminismus* (Wuppertal, 1981), p. 79; Friedhelm Boll, 'Arbeitskampf und Region', in Ritter, *Aufstieg*, pp. 387–94.

not only as a place of leisure, but also as the backbone of political mobilization and solidarity.[5]

A third reason for the strength of the SPD in Imperial Berlin resided in the city's confessional structure: in 1910, there were, for every 10,000 Berliners, 8,155 Protestants, 1,173 Catholics, 434 Jews and 84 'others'. Throughout the Reich, the party was weakest in Catholic areas (Cologne, Aachen, the Saarland, Silesia) and strongest in Protestant towns (Magdeburg, Kiel, Hanover, Hamburg, Leipzig, Dresden).[6]

If anything was responsible for the scale of socialist support in Germany before the First World War, however, it was the nature of the German state in general and the Prussian state in particular. A semi-autocratic constitutional system produced a labour movement that was neither wholeheartedly radical nor uniformly reformist. Whereas the more liberal states of south Germany gave rise to a predominantly reformist SPD, which was prepared to vote for state budgets and collaborate with the local (liberal) bourgeoisie, a repressive and discriminatory regime in Prussia created more radical party branches. It was the imperial state in general, and the Prussian government in particular, which united, politicized and radicalized the German working class by a combination of discriminatory economic policies, discriminatory constitutions, the discriminatory application of the laws and outright repression.

We will first examine the national scene, then turn to Prussia. There was a national parliament (Reichstag) elected by all German males aged 25 and over. However, it was far from sovereign. Foreign policy was reserved for the Kaiser, who appointed the chancellor, who in turn was responsible to the monarch and not to parliament. This chancellor appointed ministers, who were not dependent on parliamentary majorities. Thus, the SPD, although the largest party, could be excluded from national government until the very last days of the First World War. The Federal Council, a non-elected upper chamber, had the power to veto legislation, whilst electoral boundaries were drawn to minimize socialist representation (rural areas were over- and large cities under-represented).

The policies of Reich governments reflected this unrepresentative system. Agricultural tariffs and state subsidies protected large landowners but

---

5 Gesine Amus (ed.), *Hinterhof, Keller, Mansarde* (Reinbek, 1982); Johann Friedrich Geist, *Das Berliner Mietshaus* (Munich, 1984); Gerhard A. Ritter and Klaus Tenfelde, *Arbeiter im deutschen Kaiserreich* (Bonn, 1992), pp. 582–617. The Kautsky quotation comes from *Die Neue Zeit* 9 (1891), 2, pp. 107f.
6 Eric Dorn Brose, *Christian Labour and the Politics of Frustration* (Washington DC, 1985); Michael Schneider, *Geschichte der Christlichen Gewerkschaften* (Bonn, 1982); Klaus Klöcker, 'Konfession und sozialdemokratische Wählerschaft', in Büsch, *Wählerbewegungen*, pp. 197–207.

increased food prices, as the SPD pointed out repeatedly. The absence of a national system of progressive, direct taxation before the war meant that the working class was penalized by indirect taxes on consumables, which increased as state expenditure exploded in the arms race. The anti-socialist laws, trials of Social Democrats for 'insulting' the Kaiser and armed governmental intervention in industrial disputes served to lay bare the class nature of the Prusso-German state. However, levels of autocracy and repression varied from state to state, being significantly less in Baden than in Prussia.

The suffrage for the lower house of the Prussian parliament (*Landtag*) was especially discriminatory. The electorate was divided into three groups based on income. Each class of electors elected the same number of delegates to an electoral college, which then voted for the deputies to the house. Thus, a relatively small number of rich Class I electors had the same voting power as a much larger number of less wealthy voters in Class II, who in turn disposed of as many votes as a very much larger number of voters in Class III. In 1903, a Social Democrat claimed that 238,885 electors in Class I were matched by 856,914 in Class II and over 6,000,000 Class III electors in the *Landtag* elections of that year, yet each class had the same voting power. This discrimination was compounded by various underhand practices at election times: in 1903, many polling stations opened only in the early hours of the afternoon; in Potsdam in 1890, conservative thugs acted as 'bouncers' at the entrance to polling stations, and in others only conservative voting slips were displayed. Crucially, the *Landtag* ballot was not secret.[7]

Hence, it is scarcely surprising that the SPD resolved in 1893 not to participate in elections to the Prussian *Landtag*. However, the fact that this reactionary institution nearly enacted more repressive legislation soon thereafter led the party to reconsider. In 1897, the party conference left it to individual branches to decide whether to participate, and it was only in 1903 that a general campaign was launched. Aware of the political realities, however, fewer workers participated in the *Landtag* than the Reichstag elections, for the 179,591 votes cast for the SPD in the *Landtag* election of 1908 (out of a total of 243,942) produced only six mandates in the House of Deputies. Even in 1913, the party held just ten seats there! Municipal franchises in Prussia also tended to be restrictive.

In 1874, a wave of persecution was unleashed in Prussia by the state

---

7 Helmut Trotnow, *Karl Liebknecht* (Cologne, 1980), p. 113; Paul Hirsch, *Der Weg zur Macht in Preussen* (Berlin, 1929), p. 26; Bernstein, *Berliner Arbeiterbewegung*, iii, p. 186; Guttsman, *Social Democratic Party*, pp. 138ff.

prosecutor, Hermann Tessendorf. He dissolved the General Union of German Workers in most towns and brought before the courts on charges of violating the Prussian Law of Association a large number of trade union and party organizers. That same law forbade the involvement of women or minors in political activity, and their presence at meetings was used to close them down before its replacement by an Imperial Law in 1908. The implementation of the anti-socialist law in Prussia tended to be harsher than elsewhere. Some trade unionists and suspected Social Democrats were dragged from their beds in the middle of the night. In some cases, they died in police custody. The 'minor state of siege' was imposed on several cities, enabling the authorities to arrest and deport suspected agitators, and this they often did without the requisite legal notice. In 1878 alone, 67 people were expelled from Berlin, and in the whole period of the law, 294 activists were kicked out of the city.[8]

This persecution had a huge impact on the SPD's identity. As an SPD deputy stated in the Reichstag: 'Your anti-socialist law has created a bond for us, the bond of all the persecuted […] this bond unites us […] Herr von Puttkammer [Prussian Minister of the interior], you have made us into a true party'.[9] In fact, Puttkammer proved incapable of distinguishing between industrial discontent and political radicalism: the Prussian police moved violently against pickets in 1886 and used the Law of Association to close both the local branches and the central associations of some trade unions. All trade-union meetings were banned in Berlin and employers encouraged to 'purify' their factories.[10]

Many of the laws used against labour activists remained on the statute book after 1890. Social democratic editors were charged with 'insulting the Kaiser'; party meetings were often closed on the grounds that a window had been left open and thus were 'public', or because they reduced church attendance! Workers' sports clubs and trade-union locals were deemed 'political' in Prussia in 1912 and thus made subject to the provisions of associational legislation. In the same year, more pickets were arrested in the Ruhr miners' strike than in the previous ten years. The problem was not just the law, however, but also its discriminatory application. At the Congress of Free Trade Unions in 1896, their chairman commented that the real problem stemmed less from the law itself than from the 'arbitrariness' of the

---

8 Hirsch, *Weg zur Macht*, p. 26; articles by Karl Kautsky in *Die Neue Zeit* 15 (1898) 2, pp. 275–82 and 580–90, as well as 22 (1905) 1, pp. 255–81; Osterroth and Schuster, *Chronik*, pp. 47f; Bernstein, *Berliner Arbeiterbewegung*, ii; Dieter Fricke, *Bismarcks Prätorianer* (Berlin, 1962).
9 Quoted in Reinhard Höhn (ed.), *Die vaterlandslosen Gesellen* (Cologne, 1964), p. xxv.
10 Quoted in Lidtke, *Outlawed Party*, p. 247.

police. The laws themselves did create difficulties, though: the Prussian Servants Law (*Gesindeordnung*), for example, forbade the organization of rural labourers.[11]

The SPD's strength in Berlin was created by the industrial, residential and confessional structure of the city. It was also a consequence of autocratic government. Independent working-class politics in the capital also stemmed from the general hostility of bourgeois politics towards the labour movement. The isolation of the SPD was partly brought upon itself by its inflexible Marxist ideology; but this was not the whole story. In the run-offs in the second round of elections, other parties usually did deals to prevent the election of socialist candidates. In the *Landtag* elections of 1908, the left-liberals did not back SPD candidates in the run-off, and in some places the percentage of votes gained by socialist candidates in the second round actually fell between 1893 and 1912. There was an electoral agreement between the Social Democrats and Progressives in this latter year; but it was SPD voters rather than the liberals who kept to this agreement. In fact, the vigorous campaigns Prussian social democracy mounted against the suffrage alienated liberals; and its fight for suffrage reform distinguished the SPD from all other parties. In this respect, Prussian Social Democrats found themselves in a situation unlike that of their comrades in Baden, Bavaria and Hesse-Darmstadt, where the prospects of collaboration with liberals were much higher.[12]

The fight for suffrage reform in Prussia brought vast numbers of workers onto the streets of Berlin (260,000 on 10 April 1910); and on the issue of a mass strike to bring about such reform, the Prussian party conference was invariably more radical than its national counterpart. Even some moderate local organizations, such as that in Breslau, backed the idea. Street demonstrations on this issue constituted an unusual combination of social democracy's more normal caution with direct action, which sometimes led to clashes with the police and to violence, as in the Berlin district of Rixdorf in

---

11 Klaus Saul, 'Zwischen Repression und Integration', in Tenfelde and Volkmann, *Streik*, pp. 209ff and 269–82; Klaus Tenfelde, *Sozialgeschichte der Bergarbeiterschaft an der Ruhr* (Bonn, 1977), p. 216; Michael Gruttner, 'Working-Class Crime and the Labour Movement', in Richard J. Evans (ed.), *The German Working Class* (London, 1982), pp. 67, 74 and 79; Evans, 'Introduction' to *German Working Class*, p. 36. That persecution became worse around 1912 is shown in Osterroth and Schuster, *Chronik*, p. 44; Schorske, *Social Democracy*, p. 258; Carsten, *Bebel*, pp. 216f and 225.

12 Peter-Christian Witt, 'Friedrich Ebert: Studien der Forschung nach 1945', in Rudolf König *et al.*, eds, *Friedrich Ebert und seine Zeit* (Munich, 1990), p. 26; Carsten, *Bebel*, pp. 217f; Peter Steinbach, 'Die SPD im Parteien- und Wahlsystem des deutschen Reiches', in Ritter, *Aufstieg*, pp. 2 and 23ff; Bernhard Mann, 'Die SPD und die preussischen Landtagwahlen', in ibid., pp. 45f.

February 1910 and in Moabit later the same year. A party right-winger, Max Maurenbrecher, claimed that calls for suffrage reform were giving way to a more dangerous campaign for 'the right of the streets', as workers resisted police intrusion into their neighbourhoods.[13]

The SPD further demonstrated its presence in Berlin by the organization of huge anti-militarist and anti-war demonstrations: on 3 September 1911, for example, 200,000 Social Democrats demonstrated for peace in the city's Treptower Park. Even more impressive were the demonstrations held in the capital in late July 1914: half a million Berliners turned out for these demonstrations.[14]

Berlin was only one of many Prussian towns that were social democratic strongholds. Among others were the cutlery towns of Remscheid and Solingen, the engineering centre of Bielefeld, and Breslau in Silesia, which were industrial, Protestant and housed a large number of skilled workers. Typical of such places was the town of Harburg, where almost two-thirds of voters gave their support to the SPD in January 1912, where the party found itself confronted by hostile liberals, who were not prepared to support the reform of a restrictive communal franchise, and where over 60 per cent of its members were skilled workers. Such workers developed a rich associational life and inhabited what has been described as a social democratic milieu.[15] Not all areas of Prussia, however, produced such a 'milieu' before 1914; and it is to these that we must now turn.

Mixed fortunes: the Ruhr

The Ruhr seemed a natural home for unions and the socialist movement. The sinking of deep coal mines from the 1840s and the development of steel firms, such as the Gute Hoffnungshütte in Oberhausen, Thyssen in Mühlheim, Krupp in Essen, the Bochumer Verein and the Dortmunder Union, led to a massive demand for labour and explosive urban growth, as shown in Table 6.4.

Workers in mining and manufacture constituted a high percentage of Ruhr labour (74.5% in Bochum and 80% in Gelsenkirchen in 1907). What is more, levels of industrial concentration were especially high here, with

---

13 See n. 9 above. Also Osterroth and Schuster, *Chronik*, pp. 130, 135, 140, 144, 147; *Vorwärts* 6, 7 and 8 March 1910; *Sozialistische Monatshefte* 23 (1910), iii, pp. 1655ff.
14 Osterroth and Schuster, *Chronik*, p. 147; *Vorwärts* 26, 27, 28 and 30 July 1914.
15 Peter Witt, 'Die Entstehung einer "sozialdemokratischen Stadt": Harburg', in Ritter, *Aufstieg*, p. 283.

Table 6.4 Population growth in towns of the Ruhr

	1875	Population in 1910	Growth%
Dortmund	57,742	214,226	271.0
Duisburg	37,380	229,438	513.8
Essen	54,790	294,653	437.8

large firms predominant. Here was a 'modern' urban and industrial labour force; but here the free trade unions and the SPD were weak. Whereas 42 per cent of the nation's big-city dwellers in trade and industry belonged to a free union in 1911, in Dortmund only 16.8 per cent, in Essen a mere 16 per cent and in Duisburg a paltry 9.9 per cent had joined. When the SPD was getting almost 75 per cent of the vote in Berlin in 1912, it secured only 22.8 per cent in the Ruhr as a whole, 19.1 per cent in Dortmund, 13.4 per cent in Duisburg, 12.3 per cent in Essen and 11.9 per cent in Bochum. The percentage of voters who were party members was also low in the region. After a decline in the socialist share of the vote in the western Ruhr between 1867 and 1878, the party did make advances. In some of the Protestant mining villages, the great strike of 1889 broke the hold of paternalism and of the National Liberals, though nothing analogous happened among the steel workers. Some significant gains were also made by the SPD after 1904. The SPD had become the largest party in the Ruhr by 1912, but its electoral support was not rooted in the kind of large membership and cultural activities that characterized the party in Berlin.[16]

The strength of Catholicism, the power of employers, ethnic diversity, patterns of residence, the high percentage of migrants from rural backgrounds and high levels of labour turnover help to explain the differences between the Ruhr and Berlin. In the Ruhr, as in the Reich generally, the SPD enjoyed greater support from Protestants than Catholics, but here the confessional composition of the population was very different from that of Berlin's. For every 10,000 Westphalians in 1910, there were 4,722 Protestants, 5,143 Catholics, 58 'others' and 51 Jews. These Catholics were far less likely to leave their church than Protestants; their church was not discredited by identification with the Prussian state, and it did attempt to address the social question. Stung by the competition and the irreligiosity of

---

16 Karl Rohe, 'Party Alignments and Re-alignments in the Ruhr', in Rohe, *Elections*, pp. 110–35; Karl Rohe, 'Die Ruhrgebietssozialdemokratie im wilhelminischen Kaiserreich', in Ritter, *Aufstieg*, pp. 318–43; Schönhoven, 'Ausbreitung', p. 350.

Social Democrats, German Catholics developed their own associational life. The fruits of this initiative were Catholic gym and soccer clubs, and journeymen's, apprentices' and workers' associations, which had approximately 500,000 members by 1914.

Catholic mobilization in the Ruhr also gave rise to the 'Christian Unions'. In principle of mixed confession, these recruited 90 per cent of their membership from Catholics and were most successful in the Ruhr, the Rhineland and Silesia. The Christian Miners' Union had 63,000 members by 1914 and was strongest in this region, whilst the total membership of the Christian Unions had reached 343,000 on the eve of war. Founded by priests and initially committed to industrial peace, the growth of these organizations stemmed from the fact that they came to resemble their free trade union competitors: they went on strike, gave out strike pay and became increasingly independent of clerical control. Political Catholicism in Germany also adapted to the age of mass politics with great success. Although the SPD began to make some inroads into the Catholic vote in the Ruhr before 1914, these were limited and usually related to the presence of Catholic immigrants rather than support from the resident Catholic community. Where the Centre Party failed to recruit Catholic votes between 1898 and 1912, this is explained less by a switch of allegiance to the SPD than by Polish migration into the Ruhr, for Polish Catholics supported neither the Centre Party nor Social Democracy.[17]

The juxtaposition of Catholics and Protestants in the Ruhr gave the local Evangelical Church a vibrancy that it lacked in the solidly Protestant but staunchly secular cities of north Germany and Saxony. Here were cases of Protestant workers voting for a socialist candidate in the first round of elections, but for a conservative in the run-off, because the opponent was a Catholic. Evangelical workers' associations also seem to have had more of a life here than in Berlin.[18]

The strength of Catholicism constituted a hindrance to social democracy in the Ruhr. The division of the trade-union movement into socialist and Christian wings also weakened labour in its conflict with employers, as in the miners' strike of 1912, though there were times when the two organizations fought side by side, as in the pit stoppages of 1905. Division compounded the difficulties of workers when they came into conflict with

---

17 Rohe, 'Ruhrgebietssozialdemokratie', pp. 325f. See also n. 7.
18 Ritter and Tenfelde, *Arbeiter*, pp. 598f; Hugh McLeod, 'Protestantism and the Working Class in Imperial Germany', *European Studies Review* 12 (1982), 352f; Wilfried Spohn, 'Religion and Working-Class Formation in Imperial Germany, 1871–1914', *Politics and Society* 19 (1991), 109–32.

their employers, and in the strength of those employers lies another reason for the weakness of the free trade unions and the SPD in the region.

Ruhr industrialists were noted for both paternalism and autocratic management. The Bochumer Verein created a day nursery for the children of its employees; Krupp canteens, a savings bank and schools. Many firms laid on lavish anniversary and Christmas celebrations, and many workers in the iron and steel industry were covered by company pension schemes. Most famously, the larger employers built houses and dormitories for their workers. As early as 1889, the Bochumer Verein owned over 1,000 dwellings, and Krupp over 6,000 by 1906. The standard of such housing was in general higher, the space greater and the rents lower than in the private sector. These welfare measures were dictated by the need to attract and retain workers in areas of new industry, and they were part of a strategy of control. They were directed at some groups of workers rather than others – white-collar, skilled – and served to accentuate divisions in the labour force. The threat of withdrawing benefits became a mechanism in the prevention of labour unrest and socialist agitation: those living in company housing faced eviction on the same day if they became involved in labour disputes, joined independent unions or the SPD, while workers' contributions to pension schemes could be forfeited in the same circumstances. The authoritarian attitude of employers was further reflected in the almost total absence of collective wage agreements in German heavy industry before the First World War.

Tough postures could be adopted where labour was relatively unskilled (truer of the Ruhr than Berlin), where confessional and ethnic divisions weakened labour and where the regional economy was controlled by a small number of very large firms, as in the Ruhr but not in the capital. The Ruhr was also the centre of the 'yellow' unions: founded and funded by the employers, these company unions had a membership of 279,000 by 1914. They were strong in the iron and steel plants of the region, were committed to support the firm and could rely on a range of welfare benefits to maintain loyalty. Conversely, the socialist Metalworkers' Union (DMV) recruited more from engineering than iron and steel, and was strongest in Berlin, Brunswick, Stuttgart and Saxony, where labour was more skilled and firms smaller.[19]

---

19 Schneider, *Geschichte*; Dick Geary, 'The Industrial Bourgeoisie and Labour Relations in Germany', in David Blackbourn and Richard J. Evans (eds), *The German Bourgeoisie* (London, 1990), pp. 140–52; Peter Ullmann, *Tarifverträge und Tarifpolitik in Deutschland* (Frankfurt am Main, 1977); Peter Ullmann, 'Unternehmerschaft, Arbeitgeberverbände und Streikbewegung', in Tenfelde and Volkmann, *Streik*, p. 198; Klaus Mattheier, *Die Gelben* (Düsseldorf, 1973).

The barriers faced by the free unions and the SPD in the Ruhr were further compounded by the rapidity of industrial growth and by the large numbers of migrants from rural backgrounds for whom absenteeism and changing employer were common, and because many of the newcomers were Poles. By 1914, over 17 per cent of Hamborn's, 21 per cent of Herne's and 23 per cent of Recklinghausen's populations were Polish. Being Polish did not imply an absence of class consciousness. Indeed, being a Pole in the Ruhr could mean nothing but being a worker, and Poles participated in and often initiated strike actions, including the 'Herne Polish Revolts' of 1899. But in the main, Polish workers stayed away from the Free Unions and the SPD, forming their own Polish Union and voting for the cause of Polish nationalism. Masurian immigrants, who were Protestant but also came from the east, on the other hand, did not like their Polish neighbours, but they tended to vote for the National Liberals and reject socialism.

Another area of mixed fortunes for the German labour movement was Silesia. Breslau was a centre of SPD strength, with 45.6 per cent of the electorate casting their votes for the party in 1907. Yet, despite the stark class differences in this region and the fact that the army was used more unsparingly here than anywhere else, Silesia as a whole was infertile soil for Free Union organization or socialist politics. Many of the reasons for this situation resembled those in operation in the Ruhr, but in yet crasser form. Labour turnover and absenteeism were high, many workers still possessed plots of land, employers were powerful and authoritarian, and Catholic industrial workers were more likely to join the Christian unions. Above all, relations between Germans and Poles in Silesia were tense, though there were occasions of joint industrial action, as in the Upper Silesian coalfield in 1913.[20]

Deserts – regional and social

Parts of the Catholic Rhineland were industrial, yet election results here were even less favourable to the SPD than those in the Ruhr. In Cologne and Aachen together, the party won only 21.3 per cent of the vote in 1912. It was here that the centres of the Christian Textile Workers' Union

---

20 Rohe, 'Ruhrgebietssozialdemokratie', p. 326; Christoph Klessmann, *Polnische Bergarbeiter im Ruhrgebiet* (Göttingen, 1978); Richard Charles Murphy, *Guestworkers in the German Reich* (Boulder, 1983); John H. Kulczycki, *The Foreign Worker and the German Labour Movement* (Oxford, 1994); Ritter and Tenfelde, *Arbeiter*, p. 603; Richard Blanke, *Prussian Poland in the German Empire* (Boulder, 1981); Lawrence Shofer, *The Formation of a Modern Labor Force* (Berkeley, 1975); Ritter and Tenfelde, *Arbeiter*, p. 604; Rudolf Blank in Büsch, *Wählerbewegungen*, pp. 186f.

(Aachen, Krefeld, Mönchen-Gladbach) were to be found and the Centre Party remained dominant. If the situation in the Rhineland was bad for the Free Unions and the SPD, however, in the Saar it was catastrophic: in 1914, the party had only 777 members in the Saar, the Free Miners' Union only 1,665, despite the fact that this was a mining region. As one contemporary reported in 1891, 'here it's either holy or kingly'. Here the unions and the SPD actually experienced reversals with the march of time: in the constituency of Ottweiler-St Wendel-Meisenheim, for example, the party's share of the vote went down from 10 per cent in 1890 to only 0.5 per cent in 1903. In the first six months of 1912, even the Christian Union of Miners lost three-fifths of its membership (from 17,000 to 7,000). These two developments testify to the signal aspects of the situation in the Saar. Something like three-quarters of pit workers owed allegiance to the Catholic Church; and the region was dominated by one of the most powerful of employers, Stumm-Halberg. It was Stumm's candidacy in the Ottweiler constituency that explains the collapse of the socialist vote, and he became both a Reichstag and *Landtag* deputy. Furthermore, this 'Sheikh of Saraby' was an advocate of 'factory feudalism', forbidding his workers to join either the free unions or the SPD. The significance of religion was also demonstrated in 1912 by a dramatic decline in support for the Christian Miners' Union when it refused to give its support to the Centre Party in the election. Shortly before the First World War, there were a few signs that some Protestant mineworkers were moving towards the SPD; but, in general, the 25 per cent of Saar miners who were Evangelical were also beyond the party's reach, enjoying better promotion prospects than their Catholic workmates, whom they tended to despise.[21]

The most barren areas for the unions and the SPD were to be found in the Prussian countryside. In 1903, when 70.1 per cent of voters in Altona and over 62 per cent in Hamburg gave their support to the SPD, the figures for West Prussia, Hohenzollern and Posen were 8 per cent, 3.8 per cent and 2.7 per cent respectively. The absence of an agrarian programme scarcely helped the party; but more seriously, the SPD, as a party of urban consumers, attacked agricultural protection and stood for lower food prices. In any case, the party's chances were severely limited by the power of the local landowner, who was often the local magistrate, by repressive legislation in the shape of the *Gesindeordnung* and by forms of non-cash payment that tied rural labourers to their landowner. In these communities, the press was in conservative hands, local pastors preached against the 'red peril', the authorities forbade meetings, often on specious grounds, and communi-

---

21 Ritter, *Aufstieg*, p. 41; Ritter and Tenfelde, *Arbeiter*, pp. 416 and 598ff.

cations were poor. The fact that it was young males, precisely those who were likely to challenge established authority, who deserted the villages and farms of the east for industrial Berlin, Saxony and the Ruhr, further compounded the problems of socialist and union organizers. The SPD remained a party of the big cities.[22]

The socialist desert also had certain social characteristics. Both unions and the SPD were dominated by skilled workers, who had served apprenticeships and were relatively well paid. Skilled engineering, wood and building workers had long traditions of organization and a strong sense of the dignity of labour, inculcated by apprenticeship. Most trade unionists and Social Democrats were also male. The 174,000 women who had joined the SPD by 1914 constituted only 16.09 per cent of the party's total membership. There was a similar deficit in the trade union movement. In 1907, there were only two trades in which female union density was higher than male: cobbling and bookbinding. The Free Union of Factory Workers in Harburg had recruited 4,157 male but only 377 female employees in 1911; and in the following year, just 7.9 per cent of Christian and 8.7 per cent of Free Union members were women.

Female workers were concentrated in unskilled and poorly paid occupations: non-residential domestic service (Reich figures – 1.5 million in 1907), residential domestic service (1.25 million) and agriculture (4.5 million). Only 1 million females found jobs in trade and commerce, and 2 million in industry, and many of these jobs were located in home-based domestic production. With unskilled males, women workers shared low expectations and little bargaining power. They mostly lacked the traditions of organization on which the labour movement of skilled males was built. Women's wages were even lower, their hours (compounded by domestic chores) longer than those of German men; and female workers were even more deprived of the resources – time, money, energy – to invest in union and party activities. What is more, many German women did not work outside the home for most of their adult life: those in factory employment were usually single and under 24 years of age. For many such workers, industrial labour preceded marriage or childbirth and ceased thereafter.

Women were also more closely tied to organized religion than men: by the 1890s, women formed a clear majority of communicants in all Protestant state churches, while 62 per cent of adults leaving the church in three working-class Berlin districts in 1913 were male. Arguably, the continued religious commitment of many Prussian women compounded the problems

---

22 Mann in Ritter, *Aufstieg*, p. 41; Fricke in ibid., p. 157; Ritter and Tenfelde, *Arbeiter*, pp. 23, 230f; Blank in Büsch, *Wählerbewegungen*, p. 185.

of social democratic recruitment. So did the attitudes of many working men. Although trade unions and the SPD were officially committed to equality of the sexes, there is no doubt that many of their members saw the employment of women as a threat to their jobs and wages. Indeed, in the 1880s and 1890s, male weavers in the Rhineland protested against the employment of female 'wage-cutters'. The leaders of the socialist textile union refused to give women members a permanent seat on their executive committee, despite female pressure; and, more generally, the unions and the SPD refused to see any real value in work performed in the home. Additionally, the cultural organizations of German social democracy almost invariably held their meetings in the male territory of the public house and embraced predominantly masculine virtues (physical strength, high alcohol consumption).

Of course, working-class wives and daughters did play an indispensable role in supporting striking husbands and brothers by caring for offspring and providing sustenance on picket lines. The work of women in the home created the space and time for the union and party activities of males. Women took in washing, sewing and lodgers to supplement family income. Though relatively few female workers joined unions, a higher percentage of unorganized women participated in some of the great strikes than did men. Many did go on strike and female union members in cobbling, tailoring, textiles and tobacco manufacture were more likely to strike than their male counterparts. Kathleen Canning has further identified female textile workers with a work-based culture, who did return to the factory after childbirth and who turned to the Free Textile Union in ever increasing numbers. Women made up 37 per cent of its membership by 1907. It has also to be remembered that it was illegal for women in Prussia to join political parties before 1908, but thereafter things began to move. By 1913, 21 per cent of the Göttingen SPD membership were women; and the 174,000 who had joined the national party's women's organization constituted the largest women's movement anywhere, though they were often the wives of social democratic workers and rarely worked outside the home. Before 1919, German females also remained disenfranchised.

Yet, the fact remains that the Prussian and German labour movements were still overwhelmingly male before the First World War, as the percentage figures for national membership demonstrate clearly. Furthermore, Canning's depiction of female textile workers tells us relatively little about politics, not least because textiles proved barren for SPD recruitment in the main. In any case, free union density in textiles, at 15.5 per cent, was low, compared to that in predominantly male occupations such as metalwork (32 per cent in general and higher in its engineering branches), woodwork (34.6 per cent) and printing (60 per cent).[23]

White-collar workers were also absent from the free unions and the SPD. In Harburg, for example, only 7.5 per cent of white-collar employees belonged to a Free Union. Enjoying closer contact with management, pension rights and holiday entitlements, paid by seniority and not suffering the insecurity and declining earnings of manual workers in old age, accorded separate treatment by private and state insurance schemes, white-collar workers belonged to neither the industrial nor the political organizations of the socialist labour movement. Some joined the German National Union of Commercial Employees, but this organization subscribed to an anti-socialist, nationalist, imperialist and racist ideology.[24]

Epilogue: Prussian labour in the Weimar Republic

By 1914, Prussian Social Democracy had recorded enormous successes. Its political influence remained negligible, however, not only because of the constitutional system, governmental repression, the power of employers and the hostility of liberals, but also because it failed to recruit women, Catholics and provincial and rural Prussians on any great scale. It took the First World War to break this impasse. The war – or, more precisely, defeat at its end – temporarily broke the forces of social control, including the military, and created a space in which social upheaval could take place. The material deprivations of war radicalized the German working class and saw protest grip formerly unorganized groups (rural labourers, white-collar workers, working women), though in some places (Berlin, Remscheid, Stuttgart) and

---

23 See n. 3 and n. 4 above. Also Hans Beyer, 'Die Frau in der politischen Entscheidung', in Büsch, *Wählerbewegungen*, p. 301; von Saldern in Ritter, *Aufstieg*, p. 180; Hugh McLeod in *European Studies Review*, 52; Robyn Dasey, 'Women's Work and the Family', in Richard J. Evans and W. R. Lee (eds), *The German Family* (London, 1981), pp. 221–55; Ute Frevert, 'Women Workers, Workers' Wives and Social Democracy in Imperial Germany', in Fletcher, *From Bernstein to Brandt*, pp. 34–44. More generally, Richard J. Evans, *Sozialdemokratie und Frauenemanzipation* (Bonn, 1979); Niggemann, *Emanzipation*; Jean Quataert, *Reluctant Feminists* (Princeton, 1979); Stefan Bajohr, *Die Hälfte der Fabrik* (Frankfurt am Main, 1982). For the recent argument that factory work was central to the culture of at least some women in Imperial Germany (and the USA), see Kathleen Canning, *Languages of Labour and Gender* (Ithaca, NJ, 1996); and by the same author, 'Gender and the Politics of Class Formation: Rethinking German Labour History', *American Historical Review* 97 (1992), 736–68.
24 Jürgen Kocka, *Unternehmensverwaltung und Angestelltenschaft* (Göttingen, 1975); Jürgen Kocka, *Die Angestellte in der deutschen Geschichte* (Göttingen, 1981); Iris Hamel, *Völkischer Verband und nationale Gewerkschaft* (Frankfurt am Main, 1967).

among some groups of workers (skilled engineers, construction workers), this radicalism had pre-war roots. The Revolution of 1918 brought into existence a new constitutional structure. It failed to destroy German capitalism or the military, but the Weimar Republic was not the Second Reich reborn.

Parliamentary sovereignty and the fact that elected representatives now formed administrations at Reich, *Land* and municipal level, meant that the SPD could play a role in national, regional and local government. The introduction of direct, equal and universal suffrage for all citizens aged 21 or over for all elections, combined with absolute proportional representation, put an end to electoral discrimination against urban residents and those on lower incomes. It enabled the SPD to participate in national (1918–23, 1928–30), regional (Prussia became a social democratic bastion) and local (most large towns gained socialist administrations) government, albeit in coalition with other parties. This led to a sea change in labour legislation, granting new recognition to unions, and the creation of a welfare state. Welfare benefits were increased and extended, including a national system of unemployment insurance. Locally, social democratic councils provided social housing and created an impressive system of child and youth welfare. This ambitious welfare state was now underpinned by direct taxation far more equitable than had prevailed under the empire. It is thus not surprising that Social Democrats were the initial beneficiaries of the new Republic. In the national elections of January 1919, the SPD mobilised 37.9 per cent of the popular vote, whilst party membership peaked at 1,261,000 four years later. Female and white-collar support for the party exceeded pre-war levels, and the leisure associations of German social democracy expanded both their range of activities and their membership.

Despite such auspicious beginnings, the history of the SPD in Weimar was to turn out disastrously. Many workers resented the fact that the Revolution of 1918–19 had stopped short of full-blown revolution, and these workers deserted first to the Independent Social Democratic Party (USPD) and then to the Communist Party (KPD). This was especially true of young working-class males and the unemployed. The SPD in government also presided over policies unpopular with many workers. An SPD administration in Prussia dismissed communist civil servants and policed demonstrations of the unemployed. On May Day 1929, it was the Berlin social democratic police chief, Zörgiebel, who sent armed men against marchers with catastrophic results, whilst socialist town councils, confronted with massive financial problems in the Depression, found themselves having to sack their employees.

The mass unemployment of the Depression saw the SPD lose large numbers of votes to the Communists (and some to the Nazis) and increased the social divide between the constituencies of the SPD and the KPD. While the SPD remained a party primarily of older, skilled, employed workers, the ranks of the KPD were dominated by the young unemployed with very different interests. The Depression also fragmented the German working class along lines of age, gender and region; and it destroyed the possibility of working-class resistance to both the progressive destruction of Weimar's welfare system, the removal of the socialist Prussian government in mid-1932, and the rise of Nazism. Those in work wanted to hold on to their jobs at the same time as unemployment robbed the jobless of industrial muscle. What is more, although Social Democrats and Communists could still count on the votes of two-thirds of Berliners in July 1932, many groups of workers outside the big cities, employed in domestic or artisan production, and rural labourers actually turned to the Nazis in large numbers, especially in Prussia's Protestant east. The disintegration of the Prussian labour movement was thus well advanced before Adolf Hitler became chancellor.[25]

---

25 There is a massive literature on war, revolution, the SPD and the KPD in the Weimar Republic, welfare policy, and the rise of Nazism. Some of the more accessible works are mentioned in Suggestions for further reading.

CHAPTER SEVEN

Agrarian transformation and right radicalism: Economics and politics in rural Prussia, 1830–1947

SHELLEY BARANOWSKI

Nazism has weighed so heavily on the history of Prussia and Germany both that we cannot divorce the long-term development of Prussia's rural economy from an assessment of its political consequences. In an essay written during the Second World War that was to influence profoundly post-war interpretations of the rise of National Socialism, the émigré economic historian Alexander Gerschenkron identified agricultural protectionism that privileged the Prussian landed elite, the Junkers, as responsible for sustaining authoritarianism in Germany after 1871. Tariffs against grain imports and other forms of government subvention impeded agrarian modernization, and those in turn sustained a 'feudal', grain-producing landlord class that ultimately installed Adolf Hitler in power. Peasants followed the Junkers partly because they failed to adjust to market conditions that discouraged cereal production, and partly because they found irresistible the 'irrational notion of homogeneous agriculture', the ideological centrepiece of the Junker-led pressure group, the Agrarian League (*Bund der Landwirte*). Thus, according to Gerschenkron, democratizing Germany after the war would succeed only if landed estates in the Prussian provinces east of the Elbe River were expropriated and a smaller, more efficient, livestock-based primary sector was nurtured.[1]

Historians have grown sceptical of Gerschenkron's claim as to the backwardness of German agriculture and protective tariffs as evidence of it, for recent scholarship suggests that an agricultural 'revolution' occurred

---

1 Alexander Gerschenkron, *Bread and Democracy in Germany*, with a new foreword by Charles S. Maier (Ithaca and London, 1989), pp. 71–80.

during the nineteenth century. One leading German historian, Hartmut Harnisch, has even argued, although not without resistance, that through capital accumulation, the demand in the countryside for industrial products, and increased productivity on the land which released excess labour, agrarian modernization ignited the industrial revolution in the German states.[2] Moreover, Gerschenkron's identification of the Junkers as the villains of his analysis not only belies the social diversity of Prussian estate owners, it also ignores the populist variants of agrarian conservatism and the social and religious identities that informed them. Finally, Gerschenkron's depiction of irrational peasants who passively followed the Junkers no longer suffices, for peasants responded logically to changing market conditions and asserted their independence from estate owners when their interests diverged. Nevertheless, Gerschenkron's sensitivity to the relationship between agricultural development, agricultural policy and right-wing demagoguery defined one of the most crucial problems in Prussian and German history, the affinity of the countryside to right radicalism, and ultimately to National Socialism. Furthermore, his focus on the detrimental political and economic power of estate owners, one which other influential historians such as Hans Rosenberg, Hans-Ulrich Wehler and Hans-Jürgen Puhle have elaborated upon, identified a salient element of Prussia's and Germany's past.

Agricultural change and political mobilization, 1830–1914

By 1830, the upheavals of the Napoleonic wars and the Prussian reforms had completed the transformation from a subsistence to a market-based agriculture. The elimination of serfdom, although modified by the East Elbian nobility's political influence in local assemblies, could not forestall the growth of a large group of independent peasants with medium and large holdings (5 to 20 and 20 to 100 hectares respectively). Smaller peasant holdings multiplied, especially with Prussia's annexation of the western provinces of Westphalia and the Rhineland in 1815. Those peasants who could not acquire land of their own became a free labour pool for large

---

2 Hartmut Harnisch, *Kapitalistische Agrarreform und Industrielle Revolution. Agrarhistorische Untersuchungen über das ostelbische Preußen zwischen Spätfeudalismus und bürgerlich-demokratischer Revolution von 1848/49 unter besonderer Berücksichtigung der Provinz Brandenburg* (Weimar, 1984).

landowners, who substantially expanded their own holdings. Yet the social make-up of estate owners, that is, those who farmed holdings in excess of 100 hectares, underwent profound recomposition as well.[3] The *de jure* recognition of bourgeois ownership of knights' estates, and the post-war collapse of grain prices that extended well into the 1820s, accelerated the conversion of the East Elbian elite from a noble caste of true Junkers, many of whose families could trace their ancestry to the German colonization of the Middle Ages ('young noblemen' was the original meaning of the term), to a mixed entrepreneurial class of old nobles, the recently ennobled and commoners. Because the high value of estates made them attractive prospects for exchange, that trend continued throughout the nineteenth century to the point where commoners significantly outnumbered noblemen, save for estates exceeding 1,000 hectares, which remained in the possession of the oldest Junker families.[4] In the western provinces, Catholic nobles responded to their incorporation in Protestant Prussia and the subsequent diminution of their status by adding to their holdings and rationalizing their agriculture, which in turned allowed them to become prosperous.[5] Geared to both regional and international markets, agrarian modernization consisted of four components: the expansion of arable land followed by the diversification and intensification of production, improved yields per hectare, mechanization, and the creation of a low-cost, flexible labour force.

The abandonment of fallowing, the rotation of new fodder crops, the elimination of common lands, the draining of marshes, and the construction of dykes expanded the amount of land under cultivation. Yields per hectare grew dramatically across the German states, fortified by population growth and urbanization, as well as the robust demand from Great Britain after 1846, the year the Corn Laws were lifted. By the early 1850s, rye and wheat yields had increased by 119 per cent, barley by 138 per cent and oats by 160 per cent.[6] The 'golden age' of Prussian and German agriculture, which stretched from the 1830s to the 1870s when strong grain prices reigned, owed relatively little to mechanization. By the

---

3 Hans Rosenberg, 'Die Pseudodemokratisierung der Rittergutsbesitzerklasse', in Hans Rosenberg (ed.), *Machteliten und Wirtschaftskonjunkturen: Studien zur neueren deutschen Sozial- und Wirtschaftsgeschichte*, (Göttingen, 1978), pp. 83–101.
4 Ilona Buchsteiner, 'Wirtschaftlicher und sozialer Wandel in ostdeutschen Gutswirtschaften', *Archiv für Sozialgeschichte* 36 (1996), 93.
5 Heinz Reif, *Westfälischer Adel 1770–1860. Vom Herrschaftsstand zur regionalen Elite* (Göttingen, 1979), pp. 213–40.
6 Hans-Ulrich Wehler, *Deutsche Gesellschaftsgeschichte*, Vol. 2, *Von der Reformära bis zur industriellen und politischen 'Deutschen Doppelrevolution' 1815–1845/49* (Munich, 1987), p. 42.

last quarter of the nineteenth century, however, reapers, threshing machines and steam-powered ploughs appeared with greater frequency. Mechanization occurred not merely on the estates, but also on many smaller holdings, for peasants shared equipment to compensate for labour shortages. The use of synthetic fertilizers, the product of German scientific sophistication, became routine. Not surprisingly, the large estates figured prominently in agrarian development, but not exclusively. Despite formidable obstacles that confronted peasants in the post-emancipation period, among them less access than estate owners to credit at favourable interest rates, medium- and large-sized peasant holdings adopted new methods and deepened their ties to local and distant markets. Moreover, the Prussian state took an active interest in modernization. Agricultural associations of semi-official status multiplied throughout the nineteenth century to promote new farming methods. In the 1890s, Prussia led Germany in founding chambers of agriculture as fully public institutions with rights of taxation.

Cereals were not the only source of profit, for livestock, especially horses, cattle and pigs, grew increasingly important, not merely as a source of fertilizer and labour power, but also as generators of food for market. The planting and rotation of new fodder crops permitted larger herds. Although, as Gerschenkron noted, the large estates of the Prussian east concentrated on grains while peasants emphasized livestock breeding, agricultural producers of all sizes avoided monoculture because it reduced their ability to respond to changing demand. In fact, the estate owners who weathered the collapse of grain prices in the 1820s did so by raising sheep, the wool from which they sold as a substitute for grain until the fall in wool prices and the decline in consumer demand for mutton later in the century forced them to reduce their herds. Furthermore, depending on soil and climate conditions, which dictated what could be planted, estate owners practised intensive cultivation, using root crops such as the potato and sugar beet in order to maximize output per unit of land through the efficient deployment of capital, entrepreneurship and labour. Beginning in the 1850s, root-crop production showed impressive increases in yields per hectare to such an extent that by 1899 the average sugar-beet harvest was 14 times that of wheat.[7] The impact of sugar-beet cultivation was not limited to agricultural output alone. It stimulated the growth of the artificial fertilizer industry and the manufacture of steam-powered ploughs. Sugar beets became the staple of the 'black earth' region of Prussian Saxony with its rich soil and relatively long growing season, while the potato emerged as the root crop of choice in

---

7   J. A. Perkins, 'The Agricultural Revolution in Germany 1815–1914', *Journal of European Economic History* 10 (1981), 75–6.

the sandier soils and colder climate of Pomerania east of the Oder River. There the potato's role as a source for nourishment, the distilling of spirits and fodder for animals was sufficiently important to warrant monuments in its honour.[8]

A sufficient labour pool at the disposal of primary producers was essential, but growers increasingly assessed that supply in terms of cost effectiveness, choosing short-term for long-term commitments whenever possible. Peasants, especially those who owned 20 hectares and less, operated effectively with the labour of family members alone, while larger peasant holdings used hired hands to supplement family labour in periods of peak demand. Both solutions signified the virtual disappearance by the end of the nineteenth century of a once common practice, that of engaging workers (*Heuerlinge*), who in return for a long-term lease and other benefits provided labour services to their peasant employers. Obviously, the large estates relied the most on non-family workers. Their employees ranged from a core of permanent workers, who were essential to the ongoing management of the estate, to day labourers hired for short periods. Frequently, estate owners claimed the labour of their workers' wives and children, who assisted in such tasks as milking and gardening. Like peasants, however, estate owners strove to balance need with cost. As the nineteenth century progressed, the estates abandoned as unprofitable the practice whereby workers received a share of the grain threshed following the harvest, and they also reduced the amount of land that labourers received on which they raised their own crops and livestock. Finally, employers reduced the number of employees whom they engaged year-round because machines eliminated the need for manual threshing over the winter. Instead, the *Deputat* system came to define the compensation of regular workers, who received a fixed payment in kind, a small cash wage, as well as a rent-free cottage and a tiny plot of land. For those workers engaged solely during the growing season, cash wages were the rule.

Regional variations applied, even in East Elbia. On many estates along the Baltic coast, the *Deputat* system survived until the end of the Third Reich and the patriarchalism of resident owners coexisted uneasily with their thoroughly capitalist attention to profit and loss. Despite their obligations to their owners and their tiny plots, which should have provided little more than subsistence, regular workers and their families accounted for most of the estates' swine breeding and pork production. As producers themselves, such workers straddled the normal boundaries between the wage-earning

---

8   Christian Graf von Krockow, *Die Reise nach Pommern. Bericht aus einem verschwiegenen Land* (Stuttgart, 1985), p. 144.

proletariat and the petit bourgeoisie.⁹ Yet in sugar-beet regions such as Prussian Saxony, employers opted mainly for seasonal labour, notably migrants from Prussian Poland and Galicia, who settled for piece rates and temporary housing in barracks, the living conditions of which could be charitably described as sub-standard. The legal proscriptions certified in the Prussian Servants' Law (*Gesindeordnung*) of 1854 against breach of contract, unionization and strikes, however, applied to all agricultural labourers, a prime reason why socialist efforts to unionize agricultural workers made little impact until after the First World War.

Indeed, after mid-century, the agricultural labour force in East Elbia grew increasingly stratified by skill, duration of the labour contract and ethnicity. For German seasonal workers, a livelihood that often did not suffice to survive the winter without a second income had to be garnered in a few short months, usually under the watchful eyes of overseers, who bulldozed their employees in pursuit of profits for their employers. Rather than sparing workers from physical exhaustion, mechanization made their jobs more punishing, to which the autobiography of the agricultural labourer, Franz Rehbein, testified. 'The work goes as fast as the "sweat box" [thresher] can swallow the grain. Man has to keep pace with the machine; he becomes its slave, himself a part of the machine. Picture to yourself the uninterrupted howling and rumbling of the thresher and the almost impenetrable dust that envelops it, and you can imagine what this sort of machine threshing means for the worker.'¹⁰ Little wonder that many German farmhands left the region in search of better opportunities in industry. Employment there not only offered higher wages and shorter hours, Germany's burgeoning urban centres also provided a degree of individual autonomy and excitement that villages could not provide. In part, hiring Polish workers, most of them women and children forced to work in Germany because of overpopulation at home, compensated for the declining German labour pool. Against criticism from nationalist interest groups and government officials that the influx of Slavic workers endangered the German character of the eastern Prussian provinces, estate owners decried the 'flight from the land' (*Landflucht*) by native workers that left them little choice but to hire foreigners. Yet the recourse to Polish labour also reflected the cost calculations of employers who, by paying piece rates to Poles, strove to reduce the upward pressure on wages for Germans. Polish workers were

---

9   Bernd Kölling, *Familienwirtschaft und Klassenbildung. Landarbeiter im Arbeitskonflikt: Das ostelbische Pommern und die norditalienische Lomellina 1901–1921* (Greifswald, 1996), pp. 159–333.
10 *The German Worker. Working-Class Autobiographies from the Age of Industrialization*, translated, edited and with an introduction by Alfred Kelly (Berkeley, 1987), p. 198.

consigned to the most poorly-paid, unpleasant and physically-demanding jobs, thus occupying the bottom rung of the rural hierarchy. Ultimately, the clash between the labour needs of the large estates and the desire to preserve German ethnicity resulted in a compromise of no small consequence: first issued in 1890 and supplemented thereafter, regulations that restricted Polish immigration to the growing season alone and limited the freedom of movement of Poles while in Germany, guided the subsequent discrimination of foreign labour that reached its apogee during the Third Reich.

The 'Great Depression' that extended from the 1870s to the early 1890s halted an over 40-year span of strong prices, particularly for grains. Quite apart from its uneven impact on growers, however, its effect on the rural economy was to stimulate modernization, rather than to impede it. Overall, increases in productivity and yields continued unabated until the First World War, especially in provinces such as Brandenburg, Pomerania, Mecklenburg-Schwerin and Strelitz, where large estates dominated the landscape. Between 1880 and 1910, the average yield per hectare of rye rose by 60.2 per cent in Mecklenburg and 121 per cent in Pomerania, while wheat increased by 60.9 per cent in Mecklenburg and 91.5 per cent in Brandenburg.[11] Growers adjusted in response to the unsettling price fluctuations and the competition of better and less expensive grains from the United States, Latin America and Russia. Peasants used the grain that they produced as fodder for their pigs, thus demonstrating, contrary to Gerschenkron, the seamless connection between grain production and animal husbandry. Large landowners, on the other hand, stepped up their breeding of livestock, as well as their cultivation of root crops and wheat. Arguably, bourgeois estate owners proved more aggressive than nobles in responding to structural shifts in the market, as evidenced by the growing size of their swine herds compared to cattle or sheep. By contrast, many nobles entailed their estates with the encouragement of the Prussian state, and persisted in a less-productive extensive agriculture. The relatively high levels of indebtedness that characterized estate owners, however, once considered a sign of their weakness for conspicuous consumption, signified further investment in modernization.[12]

Yet if the 'depression' was not as severe as scholars once believed, the downturn in commodity prices encouraged the politicization of food

---

11 Buchsteiner, 'Wirtschaftlicher und sozialer Wandel' p. 107.
12 Buchsteiner, 'Wirtschaftlicher und sozialer Wandel' pp. 101–9; Klaus Heß, *Junker und bürgerliche Großgrundbesitzer im Kaiserreich. Landwirtschaftlicher Großbetrieb, Großgrundbesitz und Familienfideikommiß in Preußen (1867/71–1914)* (Stuttgart, 1990), pp. 101–214, 215–312.

producers. The timing of the decline, coming just two years after the consolidation of the German Empire, amplified not only the competition of foreign commodities, but also that of other economic interests in a radically-expanded domestic political arena. In the wake of its victory over Austria in 1866, Prussia itself had grown to include Hanover, Hessen-Nassau, Hessen-Cassel and Schleswig-Holstein, and following unification in 1871, it absorbed two new provinces, Mecklenburg-Schwerin and Strelitz, as Prussia joined a still-larger empire. Industrialization and urban growth, which the Bismarckian unification quickened, stimulated the importing of foodstuffs. Despite the productivity of German agriculture as a whole, it failed to meet a demand that was not only expanding, but also becoming more insistent on variety. Furthermore, the pressure to keep food prices affordable grew severe, not only from the urban working classes for whom food constituted a sizeable percentage of the household budget, but also from industrialists, who had no wish to raise wages to meet higher living costs.

In many ways, cultural and religious conflict laid the foundations for the politicization of Prussian agriculture in the 1890s. Although regional Catholic peasant associations did not form a national umbrella association until after the Agrarian League forced them to reach a comparable level of organization, the peasant associations of Westphalia, the Rhineland and Silesia pioneered in mobilizing rural Germans as early as the 1860s. Led by Catholic noblemen, such as the Westphalian aristocrat Burgfried Freiherr von Schorlemer-Alst, the peasant associations sought independence from state-sponsored agrarian improvement organizations. Closely allied with the Catholic Centre Party, their existence mirrored the religious tensions stemming from the minority status of Catholics in Prussia and the antagonism of Catholic nobles towards the Protestant Hohenzollerns that existed well before the *Kulturkampf* of the 1870s. They drew first from anti-rationalist Catholic nobleman, whose position as lay church leaders reinforced their secular advocacy of agriculture, and then from the proliferation of bourgeois Catholic voluntary associations rooted in the rural, small-town anti-Protestantism that reflected not only the confessional divide of Imperial Germany, but also an entrenched populist suspicion of Junkers. The passage of the grain tariff of 1879, the so-called 're-founding' of the Reich, which forged a 'compromise' between heavy industry and East Elbian estate owners, testified instead to the political impact of Catholic agriculture. Crucial to protectionism was the Centre's desire to break out of its political isolation to which the *Kulturkampf* had consigned it, while Catholic peasants believed that the revenue generated by the tariff would bring a reduction in their property taxes. By contrast, the then reflexive commitment of Protestant estate owners to free trade and the position of the East Elbian nobility in civil administration, the officer corps and diplomatic service retarded that contingent's mobilization until the state directly threatened its interests.[13]

The loss of once secure overseas markets, especially in Great Britain, and the emergence of policies designed to promote industry at agriculture's expense, prompted East Elbian estate owners to assume the populist mantle. When in the early 1890s, Bismarck's successor Leo von Caprivi proposed commercial agreements with eastern European states that necessitated a reduction in import duties, the Agrarian League forged a powerful counter-insurgency under the banner of protectionism. Founded in 1893, the Agrarian League's agitation not only forced Caprivi's resignation, it also undermined the tariff reductions stipulated in the trade treaties. By the following decade, agrarian protectionism became once more a fixture of imperial commercial policy. The tariffs of 1902 and 1906 specified significant increases over previous levels set in 1887. Without the tariff, cereal prices would have been significantly lower, along with the value of the estates, many of them mortgaged to secure capital for modernization.[14] Yet the tariff was not the only form of protection. Other measures designed to encourage the export of cereals, sugar and spirits prevented an overproduction of those commodities that would have deflated their value. Estate districts (*Gutsbezirke*) and entailed estates (*Fideikommiße*) received tax benefits that left them all but exempt, a testimony to the sympathy of district officials (*Landräte*), many of them scions of the nobility. The varieties of protection testified to the political and economic impact of growers in the Kaiserreich. Moreover, because of Prussia's dominant position in the German Empire, protectionism also attested to the influence of rural Prussian notables, be they Westphalian and Catholic or Protestant East Elbian, which in turn spoke for a real, if ironic, convergence of interest between Protestant and Catholic agrarians. During the same period, the landed elite in Germany's principal industrial rival, Great Britain, enjoyed no such leverage. Urban, especially working-class, consumers paid the price in higher food costs, which in turn solidified one of the major fault lines in modern German history, the urban–rural divide.

Because the Agrarian League mushroomed into the largest agricultural interest organization in Imperial Germany, a mass-based pressure group par excellence, its angry coalition of estate owners and small producers has appeared for Gerschenkron's intellectual heirs, notably Hans-Jürgen Puhle,

---

[13] Wolfram Pyta, *Landwirtschaftliche Interessenpolitik im Deutschen Kaiserreich. Der Einfluß agrarischer Interessen auf die Neuordnung der Finanz- und Wirtschaftspolitik am Ende der 70er Jahre am Beispiel von Rheinland und Westfalen* (Stuttgart, 1991).

[14] Wehler, *Deutsche Gesellschaftsgeschichte*, iii, *Von der 'Deutschen Doppelrevolution' bis zum Beginn des Ersten Weltkrieges 1849–1914* (Munich, 1994), p. 689.

as a 'prefascist' forerunner of the Junker-dominated, right-radical constituency that spawned Nazism later.[15] Yet, as recent critics of that position have made clear, Geoff Eley among them, the Agrarian League was no mere plaything of East Elbian estate owners, despite their prominence in its formation. The interpenetration of the Agrarian League and the interests of estate owners was most pronounced in the eastern Prussian provinces where estate agriculture was firmly entrenched. Furthermore, the Agrarian League's success in winning a national membership was not only confined to Protestants, it depended at least as much on catering to the material interests of small producers as it did on the ability of estate owners to mesmerize peasants with the scapegoats of liberalism, socialism and international Jewry. The platforms of the Agrarian League, which included the demand for lower taxes, targeted the practical needs of a broad rural constituency. The size of the Agrarian League enabled it to secure reduced prices for fertilizer, machinery and insurance, and to establish credit unions, an obvious stimulus to modernization. Finally, the Agrarian League advocated protective legislation of special value to peasants and farm workers, such as veterinary regulations against imported animal and dairy products. The Agrarian League evolved into an alliance of diverse agricultural producers, while its day-to-day management lay in the hands of middle-class political organizers such as Diederich Hahn. Recognizing its broad-based support, however, should not obscure the Agrarian League's most insidious contributions to the demagoguery that characterized German politics after 1890. First, it drew Protestant estate owners to mass politics: an arena that they certainly could not manipulate at will and one that they often distrusted, but one that broadened the possibilities for an aggressive defence of their interests. In fact, to achieve a reliable following in Protestant rural areas, neither the National Liberal Party nor especially the most agrarian of the Imperial German parties, the Conservatives, could survive without the Agrarian League's endorsement. Second, by integrating its explicit material concerns in an ugly rhetoric of anti-urbanism, anti-socialism and anti-Semitism, the Agrarian League implicitly challenged the legitimacy of parliamentary and bureaucratic negotiation among competing interests, thus weakening the prospects for a 'moderate' conservatism that could have accepted and adjusted to the inevitable compromises of parliamentary politics.

---

15 Hans-Jürgen Puhle, *Agrarischer Interessenpolitik und preussischer Konservatismus im wilhelminischen Reich (1893–1914)*, 2nd edn (Bonn-Bad Godesberg, 1975).

By the eve of the First World War, Prussian growers could credit themselves with a century of impressive gains in productivity, diversification and political organization. To be sure, industry had overtaken agriculture not only as a source of employment and livelihood, but also as a contributor to the net national product, a fact that encouraged rural interest organizations to proclaim a 'crisis' in a sector that they considered foundational to Prussian and German culture. Then, too, although Germany exported sugar, rye and oats, its imports of other grains, butter and meat to satisfy consumer demand provided the context for the emerging concern as to the insufficiency of Germany's food supply.[16] Nevertheless, because of agriculture's ability to define commercial policy, or at least level the playing field between industry and itself, we cannot view the Kaiserreich as the source of agriculture's protracted decline. The combined influence of estate owners and peasants, Conservatives and the Centre Party, contributed mightily to agriculture's political weight and agriculture's very political effectiveness owed much to its economic achievements. Rather, global war would undermine the economic viability and political compromises that sustained Prussian and German growers.

War-making, urban priorities and the decline of agrarian influence, 1914–33

In July 1914, Germany's decision to endorse Austria–Hungary's ultimatum to Serbia triggered a protracted global war that yielded unprecedented devastation, loss of life, and material deprivation for soldiers and civilians alike. The consequences for German agriculture were enormous, for the imperial government's attempt to master the war's exactions on the battlefield and 'home front' had the effect of weakening the rural economy and eroding agriculture's political influence. First, shortages of fertilizer, capital and machinery parts, which reflected the priority accorded to armaments, and the drastic declines in draught animals and human labour drawn to military service, reversed the increases in yields that characterized the 'long' nineteenth century. Between 1913 and 1916, yields per hectare in Prussia alone, excluding Mecklenburg-Schwerin and Strelitz, fell from slightly over 1,840 kilos to 1,490 kilos for rye, 2,430 kilos to 1,990 for wheat,

---

16 James Retallack, *Germany in the Age of Kaiser Wilhelm II* (London and New York, 1996), pp. 16–19; Rita Aldenhoff, 'Agriculture', in Roger Chickering (ed.), *Imperial Germany: A Historiographical Companion* (Westport, Conn., 1996), pp. 34–5.

and from 15,450 kilos to 9,410 for potatoes.[17] Second, the government's need to provide the cities with an affordable supply of food so as to suppress the demand for wage increases necessitated a system of requisitions and price controls known as the Controlled Economy (*Zwangswirtschaft*) that came into effect in the autumn of 1914. Tariffs on food imports disappeared with the new regulations. Although it was insufficiently comprehensive and only marginally effective in securing food at low cost, food producers resented the Controlled Economy, complaining of artificially low commodity prices and the frequent government confiscations of grain reserves. In turn, growers tried to evade the Controlled Economy by hoarding to force price increases, producing foodstuffs not subject to mandatory deliveries, and selling on the black market. Urban consumers grew embittered as their hunger increased and the black market flourished, convinced that farmers were starving the cities to further their own interests.

With the kaiser's abdication and Germany's defeat in November 1918, urban–rural conflicts intensified. The one-time pariahs, the Social Democrats, whose political weight as advocates for consumer interests the war had only magnified, assumed the leadership of the provisional government, the Council of People's Commissars. The necessity of preventing strikes during the hostilities so as not to jeopardize production allowed the SPD a degree of leverage that could not be eroded after the war ended. Because the new government, the SPD included, feared popular unrest that the Independent Socialists (USPD) and the Spartacists could exploit, it extended the Controlled Economy, thus reinforcing the link between cheap food and 'Marxism' in the eyes of food producers. Even in eastern Prussian provinces such as Pomerania, where estate owners perceived the popular risings that accompanied the collapse of the Kaiserreich with unabashed loathing, the Controlled Economy fostered an abiding anti-urban activism that united large landowners, peasants and many agricultural labourers. Crop thefts by city dwellers desperate for food personified the assault of urban interests against the countryside.

In contrast to the relatively favourable conditions of the empire, the Weimar Republic that came into being in 1919 seemed nightmarish for Prussian agriculture. The increased powers of the Reichstag and the corporatist logrolling among competing economic interests that characterized Weimar had the effect of confirming the primary sector's waning influence. The disproportionate weight that rural districts once enjoyed evaporated, and the three-class franchise in Prussia, one of the most important props of estate-owning power, existed no longer. To make matters

---

17 *Statistisches Jahrbuch für das Deutsche Reich* (1913), p. 40, and (1918), p. 16.

worse, the SPD dominated the state government of Prussia until mid-1932. Moreover, the Republic legalized strikes by farm workers, collective bargaining and overtime pay, thus endorsing some of the important acts of the provisional government, the repeal of the Servants' Law and subsequent decrees that protected the rights of farm labour. Finally, the post-war peace settlement meant the loss of most of West Prussia and Posen, as well as parts of East Prussia, Pomerania and, ultimately, Upper Silesia. The elimination of so much of Prussia's agricultural land factored into the steep decline in the production of grain and potatoes from their 1913 levels that the war initiated. In Prussia minus Mecklenburg-Schwerin and Strelitz, rye fell from slightly over 8.8 million metric tons in 1913 to less than 4.4 million by 1924. Wheat dropped from roughly 2.75 million metric tons to 1.5 million during the same period. Potatoes fell from slightly under 35 million metric tons in 1913 to less than 25 million in 1924. Livestock herds languished well below their pre-war numbers.[18]

Arguably, the Weimar system represented as much the containment of leftist radicalism as it did social and political transformation, for, in early 1919, the army and Freikorps violently suppressed the Spartacists and the USPD failed to survive beyond 1920. If right-wing elites in business and agriculture, the military, the civil service and the judiciary could not prevent the establishment of parliamentary democracy, their continuing influence, which the SPD sanctioned, circumscribed economic and social redistribution. Thus, a proposal that would have expropriated non-viable East Elbian estates for settlement was watered down because even the socialists feared it would undermine food production. A promising unionization campaign in the German Farm Labour Union (*Deutscher Landarbeiterverein*) that arose with the termination of the Servants' Law sharply contracted in the wake of a lethal combination of countermeasures. The Labour Union's tactical blunders, the provisional and then Weimar government's oppositions to strikes that could disrupt the harvest, and then the counter-attack of estate owners, who fired union members for 'insubordination', hired Freikorpsmen as scabs, and promoted their own 'economically peaceful' (*wirtschaftsfriedlich*) unions, soon undermined the attempt at independent representation for farm workers.[19] The creation of the National Rural League (*Reichslandbund*), the Agrarian League's successor, and the re-emergence of the peasant associations in Catholic regions of Prussia, despite competition from the newly-emerging Free Peasantry, signified the

---

18 *Statistisches Jahrbuch für das Deutsche Reich* (1913), pp. 41, 49, and (1924), pp. 58–9, and 64.
19 Jens Flemming, *Landwirtschaftliche Interessen und Demokratie: Ländliche Gesellschaft, Agrarverbände und Staat 1890–1925* (Bonn, 1978).

revitalization of pre-war agrarian interest representation. In Protestant areas, the Rural League forged strong ties to the German National People's Party, the post-war successor to the Conservatives, while in Catholic districts the peasant associations maintained their ties with the Centre. Nevertheless, the government's decision to continue grain levies and the disequilibrium between fixed prices for commodities and the skyrocketing rate of inflation, reflected the increased influence of urban interests, and minimized the salutary effects of a depreciating currency on rural indebtedness.

In 1924, the resolution of the Ruhr crisis and stabilization brought the hyperinflation under control. Nevertheless, the insurmountable combination of carry-over debt and disadvantageous government policy had a catastrophic impact on agriculture. Rising interest rates that resulted from the inability of rural credit unions to provide low-cost loans, as well as spiralling indebtedness, the consequence of the revaluation of the mark and incautious investments during the inflation, joined with tax liabilities that significantly exceeded those of the Kaiserreich to force many food producers into bankruptcy. Although all holdings suffered grievously, large estates proved especially vulnerable, not merely because of their high levels of debt, but also because the Erzberger and post-stabilization tax reforms conspired to eliminate their previous exemptions.[20] Consumer preferences that rejected important components of Prussian agriculture, such as rye and potatoes, and an increasingly glutted international commodities market drove prices down, thus jeopardizing efforts to bring yields to their pre-war levels. The 'price scissors', that is, the disjunction between high production costs and low returns, exemplified the structural weaknesses of the primary sector for the remainder of the Republic. Despite the left's at best modest success in unionizing agricultural workers, the introduction of government-sponsored mediation between management and labour caused wages to rise in the countryside, an especially nettlesome problem in Prussia, according to employers, because of the SPD's leading position in the Prussian ruling coalition. All food producers lamented the Weimar Republic's commercial policies that promoted bilateral agreements so as to boost industrial exports, despite the introduction of the 'small' tariff in 1925 and subsequent increases to it. Food imports continued to rise unabated, especially dairy products and processed foods that tripled between 1925 and 1928.[21]

Beginning in 1928, poor harvests and the primary sector's relative powerlessness encouraged the escalation of rural agitation against the

---

20 Heinrich Becker, *Handlungsspielräume der Agrarpolitik in der Weimarer Republik Zwischen 1923 und 1929* (Stuttgart, 1990), pp. 210–49.
21 John Hiden, *Republican and Fascist Germany. Themes and Variations in the History of Weimar and the Third Reich 1918–1945* (London and New York, 1996), p. 154.

Weimar system, much of it arising in the midst of foreclosures and public auctions of bankrupt farms. In Prussia's Catholic regions, the Centre Party retained most of its rural supporters, who eschewed closer ties with the largely Protestant German National People's Party (DNVP) and the National Rural League, despite the mounting unhappiness of Catholic growers with the party's participation in Weimar cabinets and the declining membership of peasant-based interest groups. If the Centre Party proved relatively impervious to electoral decline, its rightward drift after 1928 under its new prelate chairman, Ludwig Kaas, hardly boded well for the survival of the Republic. The Centre did not endorse the demands of Catholic agrarians for autarky, for had it done so it would have alienated its sizeable working-class following. Yet the increasing opposition to the parliamentary system among party leaders conformed to the sentiments of Catholic peasants and nobles alike. In the Protestant countryside, a plethora of special interest groups, most notably the Christian National Peasants and Rural People's Party (*Christlich-Nationale Bauern- und Landvolkpartei*, or CNBLP), signified the decomposition of the major liberal and conservative bourgeois parties. This trend did not spare the right-wing German National People's Party (DNVP) that had most consistently championed agrarian interests. The DNVP's participation in republican cabinets since stabilization, a tactic designed to elevate the party's political influence, had produced few tangible benefits for agriculture as its post-stabilization crisis worsened. The bitterness was especially pronounced east of the Elbe, not only because of the presence of so many large estates and the resentment against the post-war territorial settlement, but also because that region's industrial underdevelopment deepened its dependence on agriculture and thus its virulent anti-republicanism.

One of the most volatile expressions of agrarian discontent emerged first in Schleswig-Holstein and then radiated outwards. The so-called Rural People Movement (*Landvolkbewegung*) reflected not only the accumulated rage of peasants against high taxes and trade treaties that allowed the importing of frozen meat, but also the anger of village artisans and small retailers, who challenged the Republic's putative bias towards big business and organized labour. Those sometimes violent protests signified a brand of populism that established rural associations and elites found it increasingly difficult to manage, not least because it betrayed a level of hostility towards estate owners unmatched by peasant protest under the Kaiserreich. Agrarian populism protest after 1928 took aim at the scandalous Weimar relief programme known as Eastern Aid (*Osthilfe*), which protected unsalvageable estates from foreclosure while providing little relief from the crippling interest rates that oppressed small-scale producers. Agricultural workers, especially those who could not deliver family members to their employers as additional labour, suffered lay-offs while Polish replacements, according to widespread rumours, mysteriously appeared on the large estates. Neither the vehemently anti-republican course of the DNVP after 1928, which the party assumed under its new chairman, Alfred Hugenberg, nor the National Rural League's less radical attempts to organize a national 'green front' so as to increase agriculture's political leverage, stemmed the radicalization of the Protestant countryside. The NSDAP became the principal beneficiary of electoral volatility, forging a disparate following of peasants, agricultural labourers, artisans, shopkeepers and even some estate owners in a powerful protest bloc. In the September 1930 Reichstag elections, the Hitler movement mutated from a small movement residing at the fringes of the Weimar party system into the second largest party in the Reichstag, drawing crucial support from the villages and small towns of central and eastern Germany. The referendum against the rescheduling of Germany's reparations payments, known as the Young Plan, that Hugenberg had instigated during the previous year gave the Nazi Party valuable exposure and legitimacy even though it failed to win the votes necessary to achieve its goal.

Despite the anti-elitism embedded in the rural populist explosion, a major contribution to the DNVP's electoral decline, the relationship between elite and populist anti-republicanism was in practice more symbiotic than parasitic. To begin with, the anti-republican militancy of many estate owners fuelled the frustrations of the Protestant countryside, discrediting the DNVP in the process. In the estate villages, such as those of Pomerania, employers co-opted popular dissatisfaction by using the Rural People Movement to mobilize peasants, estate workers and shopkeepers against an unsympathetic and corrupt 'Marxist' system. The agitation of estate owners against the Young Plan incorporated various means of coercion, subtle and crass, to force their workers to endorse an initiative that condemned as treasonous government officials who signed the new reparations agreement. On the other hand, even as the NSDAP attacked the DNVP as the party of 'reactionaries', the Nazis cultivated village leaders, including estate owners, so as to profit from the cachet of familiar and respected notables.[22] The Hitler movement exerted a strong attraction for young nobles in particular, and even Junkers who remained committed to the DNVP showed more willingness to oppose the Republic outright rather than defend their interests within the system. The open and consistent expression of concern from

---

22 Wolfram Pyta, *Dorfgemeinschaft und Parteipolitik 1918–1933. Die Verschränkung von Milieu und Parteien in den protestantischen Landgebieten Deutschlands in der Weimarer Republik* (Düsseldorf, 1996), pp. 94–107, 163–84, 291–311 and 336–53.

estate owners as to the Nazis' anti-elitism arose only after the party's electoral breakthrough abetted its anti-Junker fulminations. The staunchly conservative Pomeranian Junker, Ewald von Kleist-Schmenzin, suffices as a good example of belatedly-articulated reservations. As a monarchist, patriarchal landlord and outspoken supporter of the Hugenberg wing of the DNVP, Kleist backed the referendum against the Young Plan that had required co-ordination between his party and the NSDAP. By 1932, however, Kleist had come to condemn the Nazis for their materialism, irreligion, 'Marxism' and contempt for traditional elites, apparently unwilling to confront the 'old' right's contributions to the Nazi ascendancy.[23]

The anti-republicanism in the Prussian countryside, which was only slightly less volatile among Catholics than among Protestants, magnified the destructiveness of Prussian agrarian elites, Protestant and Catholic, at the highest levels. To be sure, Adolf Hitler could never have emerged as a serious candidate for chancellor without the collapse of the bourgeois parties and the NSDAP's stunning electoral growth. Yet even in the Reichstag election of July 1932, their best performance before coming to power, the Nazis drew only 37.4 per cent of the vote nationally. Thus, non-Nazi conservatives remained essential to undermining the Republic and installing an authoritarian coalition of the right. In 1932, prominent East Elbian estate owners, who were unhappy with the proposed settlement of bankrupt estates by the unemployed, sabotaged the governments of Heinrich Brüning and Kurt Schleicher, using their access to a crucial ally, Reich President Hindenburg, to make their case. Furthermore, the short-lived government of the Westphalian Catholic aristocrat, Franz von Papen, a Centre Party renegade who had been a consistent advocate of agrarian protectionism, offered a preview of the horror to come. Papen's demolition of the Prussian state government in July 1932 and his transformation of the Prussian police into an unambiguous assault weapon against the left comprised essential preconditions for the even more violent Nazi dictatorship later. Finally, Papen may well have conceived his role in the negotiations that led to Hitler's appointment as chancellor in January 1933 as a way to contain the Nazi juggernaut, yet, at a deeper level, his involvement exposed the lethal alliance of convenience between the Nazi and non-Nazi right. A common rural antagonism towards the Republic, the force of which elided the confessional divisions among agrarians at crucial moments, contributed significantly to the birth of the Third Reich.

---

23 'Der Nationalsozialismus – Eine Gefahr', in Bodo Scheurig, *Ewald von Kleist-Schmenzin. Ein Konservativer gegen Hitler* (Oldenburg and Hamburg, 1968), pp. 255–64.

Unkept promises: Prussian agriculture from the Third Reich to the occupation, 1933–47

Nazism's popularity, especially in the Protestant districts of the Prussian east, owed much to its anti-Marxism and its promises to preserve family, religion and the sacred vocation of tilling the soil. In that context, it endorsed specific measures that had long been staples of agrarian agitation, including tax relief, protection against foreign imports, lower costs for fertilizer and electricity, reduced interest rates and even autarky. Between 1930 and 1933, the party solidified its rural presence by extending its Agrarian Apparatus (AA) under the leadership of Richard Walther Darré, a 'blood-and-soil' agronomist with ties to Heinrich Himmler. All told, the Hitler movement promised to restore agriculture's rightful place in the economy, a claim that seemed credible because the NSDAP had not compromised itself by accepting portfolios in Weimar cabinets as had other bourgeois parties with once-significant rural constituencies. Shortly after taking power, the Nazi regime strove to prove its goodwill towards the primary sector. Under Darré's direction, the Reich Food Estate (*Reichsnährstand*) fixed prices and regulated commodity production so as to secure a steady food supply and shield growers from international competition. Consistent with its racial and propagandistic crusade on behalf of a 'healthy' peasantry, the regime instituted the Hereditary Entail Law (*Erbhofgesetz*). Initiated first in Prussia, the law secured inheritance by primogeniture, protected heirs against having to compensate younger siblings, and prevented the foreclosure of peasant holdings for the non-payment of debts. Yet, despite the Nazi Party's shrill attacks on Junker 'reactionaries', the 'socialist' overtones of the Nazi Party's 1920 programme, which threatened estate owners with expropriation, and the party's valorization of the peasantry, pragmatism governed the Nazi regime's approach to the large estates. Its eastern settlement programme created just slightly over a third of the new holdings created by the modest initiative of the Weimar Republic,[24] for, ironically, the regime arrived at the same conclusion as the SPD had in 1918 and 1919. Breaking up estates would compromise food production. The *Osthilfe* subsidies that had been biased so notoriously in favour of estate owners continued until 1936.

Regardless, if the Nazi era did not reproduce the political alignments that had so disadvantaged agriculture during the First World War – the concentration camps, after all, testified eloquently to the regime's brutal

---

24 Hiden, *Republican and Fascist Germany*, p. 161.

suppression of the left – its war preparations belied its agrarian romanticism. Farm incomes and profits did improve for several years after the Nazi takeover, but they could not match those in industry and handicrafts. Agriculture's share of the national income continued its decline, from 12.2 per cent in 1927 to 9.8 per cent by 1939.[25] Rising incomes represented enough of an improvement over the Weimar era to keep rural discontent at manageable levels, and in response to peasant complaints, local Nazi officials often mitigated the most restrictive clauses of the regime's farm legislation, among them primogeniture. Yet the gargantuan claims of rearmament, especially after the institution of the Four Year Plan in 1936, further eroded the position of growers. The regime's 'battle for production' (*Erzeugungsschlacht*), which was supposed to raise farm output, increased working hours on the land at the very moment when an unintended consequence of the Entail Law, the migration of younger siblings from the countryside, reinforced industry's status as a magnet for dissatisfied rural dwellers. A diminishing labour pool resulted in declining output relative to demand and a slower rate of modernization. Finally, rising consumer pressures on the food supply that the achievement of full employment did little to undermine, reinforced a long-standing trend, greater dependence on imports, now supplemented by food from the less-developed Danube and Balkan states that had fallen into Germany's orbit.

Ultimately, the regime expected that its racially-defined reorganization of the continent would not only provide 'living space' (*Lebensraum*) for armed German agricultural settlements, it would also remedy the Third Reich's food, labour and raw materials deficits. Walther Darré's political decline after 1936 paralleled the rise of his one-time subordinate, Herbert Backe, who, as head of the agrarian section of the Four Year Plan and by 1942 minister of agriculture, proved more capable than his supervisor of tailoring agriculture to the needs of rearmament and expansion. An economist who specialized in Russian agriculture, Backe gave less priority to building a healthy peasant stock at home than to Germanizing the east and exploiting its resources. By August 1944, in fact, every second worker in agriculture was a foreign conscript, as good an indication as any as to the regime's temporary ability to realize its expansionist goals.[26] Yet the second total war of the twentieth century not only brought Germany's defeat, it also resulted

---

25 Gustavo Corni, *Hitler and the Peasants. Agrarian Policy of the Third Reich*, trans. David Kerr (New York, Oxford and Munich, 1990), p. 261.
26 Ulrich Herbert, *A History of Foreign Labour in Germany, 1880–1980. Seasonal Workers/Forced Labourers/Guest Workers*, trans. William Templer (Ann Arbor, Mich., 1990), p. 153.

in the loss of a substantial share of Prussia's food-producing land to Poland and even in Prussia's dissolution. Countless members of the Prussian nobility died fighting, especially on the Eastern Front, and Hitler added to those numbers by executing Junkers who participated in the 20 July 1944 plot against him. Even before German communists and the Soviet Military Administration formally instituted land reform in the Soviet zone of occupation, millions of German civilians had fled westward ahead of the invading Soviet armies, while hundreds of estate owners and their families lost their lives and property. By 1949, when the German Democratic Republic came into being, the expropriation of large estates had affected more than 8,000 families.[27] Ironically, agrarian conservatism, which in all its complexity had done so much to facilitate the Nazi rise to power, led indirectly to the realization of Alexander Gerschenkron's fondest wish, the elimination of the East Elbian estates.

---

27 Norman Naimark, *The Russians in Germany. A History of the Soviet Zone of Occupation, 1945–1949* (Cambridge, Mass. and London, 1995), pp. 85–6, 142–56.

PART THREE

Religion in State and Society

CHAPTER EIGHT

Religious conflicts and German national identity in Prussia, 1866–1914

MARJORIE LAMBERTI

With a population of nearly 16 million Protestants and over 8 million Catholics in 1871, Prussia formed the Protestant core of the newly established German national state, and yet it contained twice as many Catholics as did Bavaria, and more than half of the entire Catholic population of Imperial Germany. The social reality of Prussia reveals a more heterogeneous state than the stereotypical idea of Prussia. Its cultural landscape was marked less by unity than by confessional division and distrust. The Prussian state's assault on the Catholic Church during the *Kulturkampf* in the 1870s was a critical juncture in the history of Prusso-Germany. This conflict politicized the division between the two religious communities and cemented confessional antagonism in political life. The confessional segmentation of society, reflected in the organization of Catholics and Protestants in separate subcultural milieus and in political parties dependent on the cohesion of each self-enclosed milieu, had a profound and enduring impact on public life in Prussia.

In the past, historical research on German Catholics and Protestants was generally confined to the spheres of church and intellectual history. Even with the ascendancy of social history after 1970, confessional identity and religious culture were seldom taken as seriously as the influence of class and material interests when historians sought to explain the political orientations and behaviour of social groupings. A deeper appreciation of the centrality and force of confessionalism in Prussian social and political life came from new scholarship on the *Kulturkampf*, that placed this state–church struggle in the context of the unstable process of German nation state building and cultural coalescence, and from research on the social history of Catholicism in Germany, that focused on its distinctive subculture and massive associational life in the years after 1870. This historical scholarship has shed new light on two significant questions. How and why did confessional solidarities and conflicts come to play a central role in society and politics? What were the long-term historical consequences of the polarization and political mobilization of Catholics and Protestants for the national polity?

The tendency of Catholics and Protestants to live in homogeneous areas marked the geographical terrain of Prussia with distinct confessional lines. Protestants constituted 95 per cent or more of the population in 13 governmental districts located in the eastern provinces of old Prussia and in the territory of Hanover annexed by Prussia in 1866. Although the Rhine Province, Silesia and Westphalia had more confessionally mixed populations, many counties here were confessionally homogeneous enclaves, with Catholics or Protestants forming a commanding majority of 80 per cent or more. The rural–urban migration that came in the wake of industrialization brought Catholics and Protestants closer together in Berlin, Breslau and other cities in the northern Rhineland and Westphalia. But even where Catholics and Protestants lived in close proximity, they formed segregated communities and sent their children to separate public schools. Over 90 per cent of the Catholic and Protestant schoolchildren in Prussia were instructed in elementary schools designated for their confession.

Protestant liberals and Catholics in the era of national unification

Protestant liberals and Catholics in Prussia formed two opposing camps on the question of national unification in the 1860s. Middle-class, Protestant liberals organized in the German National Association and German Protestant Association were advocates of constitutional freedom and unity in a smaller German national state that would be established under Prussia's Protestant monarchy and would be exclusive of Catholic Austria. They associated Protestantism with political and material progress and the emancipation of the individual from clericalism and irrational dogma. The triumph of freedom in the new national state, they believed, could be achieved only on the basis of the humanistic and rational principles represented by liberal Protestantism – the autonomy of the human personality, communal self-government in a constitutional monarchy, and freedom in the search for knowledge and in teaching. In their view, these principles and goals constituted Protestantism's superiority over the

Catholic Church, which aspired to political domination through the authority of the hierarchy and the subjugation of the individual conscience. They regarded the Roman papacy's temporal and spiritual claims and the sympathy of Catholics for a large, federally organized German state inclusive of Austria as obstacles to the realization of their national programme. When the Prussian army defeated Austria and France in the wars of national unification, Protestantism was linked to German nationalism in the triumphant euphoria.[1]

The conduct of Catholics in Prussia during these years gave some substance to the liberals' perceptions of political Catholicism as an intransigent and unpatriotic opposition. The Catholic caucus in the Prussian House of Deputies and Catholic publicists supported the idea of greater-German unity, which would be created by reforming the existing loose confederation of the German states. They opposed any form of national unity that would be forged by civil war and the forcible overthrow of legitimate authority. Catholic deputies disapproved of the power politics of Prussia's minister-president, Otto von Bismarck, and refused to vote war credits for Prussia's war against Denmark in 1864. When Prussia fought Austria in 1866, the mobilization of the army reserves in Catholic areas of the Rhine Province and Westphalia was accompanied by resistance and riots. The clergy here made no secret of their pro-Austrian sympathies and denounced the liberals as warmongers and atheistic enemies of Christianity. In the autumn of 1866, the Catholic caucus voted against Prussia's annexation of Hanover and Hesse and the dotation bill rewarding Bismarck and the generals for the military victory.

In the elections for the Reichstag of the new North German Confederation in February 1867, priests campaigned for the oppositional candidates put up by Catholic election committees. When the Reichstag refused to incorporate into the constitution drafted by Bismarck articles guaranteeing the autonomy of the church, freedom of religious belief and other civil liberties, Catholic deputies voted against the constitution as a whole. In 1870, when the Reichstag voted on the treaties with the south German states to complete the creation of the national state, Catholic deputies from Prussia abstained or voted against them. When the Reichstag adopted an address to the throne asking King William of Prussia to accept the imperial crown, they abstained or were absent during the vote.[2]

---

1   Wolfgang Altgeld, *Katholizismus, Protestantismus, Judentum: über religiös begründete Gegensätze und nationalreligiöse Ideen in der Geschichte des deutschen Nationalismus* (Mainz, 1992), pp. 66ff.; Helmut Walser Smith, *German Nationalism and Religious Conflict: Culture, Ideology, Politics, 1870–1914* (Princeton, NJ, 1995), pp. 21ff.
2   George Windell, *The Catholics and German Unity 1866–1871* (Minneapolis, 1954), pp. 6ff.

The opposition of Prussian Catholics to Bismarck's politics did not mean a fundamental rejection of the national state of 1871. With remarkable swiftness, politically conscious Catholics reconciled themselves to the founding of the German Empire. However, the way in which Protestant liberals constructed national identity and propagated a sense of what it was to be German led Catholics to maintain a reserved distance towards the empire.[3] Protestant liberals of the educated bourgeoisie viewed the beliefs and rituals of the Catholic Church as irrational dogma and idolatry. From their point of view, the forms of popular piety cultivated in the revival of ultramontane Catholicism after 1850 kept the Catholic populace in ignorance and superstition and under clerical subjugation. This perception was reinforced by the condemnation of liberalism and modernity in Pope Pius IX's encyclical of 1864. When the liberals grounded German national culture in the traditions of Protestantism, they gave an exclusive definition of belonging to the national community and marginalized the Catholics. The widely-read master narratives of German nationhood written by Droysen, Treitschke and other historians of National Liberal persuasion enshrouded the idea of Prussia's destiny in a mystique, identified the Prussian state and the principles of Protestantism as the agents of social progress and German national unity, and projected an image of Catholicism as the brake on the iron wheel of history.[4]

What also aroused the apprehensions of Catholics was the kind of state and national community that they thought the National Liberal Party and the smaller, left-liberal Progressive Party were striving to create. Elevating the state from an instrument of brute political power into a cultural and moral entity, Rudolf von Gneist and other liberals made expansive claims for the sovereignty of the national state and the primacy of the citizen's identity with and loyalty to it. National Liberal politicians in the Prussian House of Deputies assumed that they could concede full sovereignty to the state and at the same time bind this authority to the rule of law and a representative constitution. Convinced that cultural uniformity was a prerequisite for the building of a modern national state, they looked to the power of the state to efface confessional particularism and ethnic-linguistic differences and to carry out reforms that would emancipate the public elementary school from the Church and provide a common education for Catholic and Protestant children in interconfessional schools.

---

3   Rudolf Lill, 'Die deutschen Katholiken und Bismarcks Reichsgründung', in Theodor Schieder and Ernst Deuerlein (eds), *Reichsgründung 1870–71* (Stuttgart, 1970), pp. 345–54.
4   Smith, *German Nationalism*, pp. 27ff.

Catholic clergymen and politically active laymen criticized the liberals' conception of a powerful, centralizing state and sought to preserve the cultural diversity of the German people in the structure of the new national state. When Ludwig Windthorst, Hermann von Mallinckrodt and other Catholics in the Prussian House of Deputies and the Reichstag invoked constitutional principles, they argued for federalism and defended the conscience of the individual and the autonomy of the Church against the intrusions of an authoritarian state. To Catholics, the idea of emancipation in liberalism's world-view spelt the rule of secularism, which would encourage materialism and egotism in society and lead to moral decadence. In their view, genuine tolerance was to be attained not through a confessionally integrated school system, but through the peaceful endurance of religious differences and the recognition of Catholics and Protestants as equal compatriots.

Bismarck's collaboration with the National Liberals in parliamentary politics and the frightening prospect of anti-Catholic measures in Prussia made the organization of a party of Catholics seem necessary to Peter Reichensperger and other Catholic politicians in the western provinces of Prussia. Out of a feeling of uneasiness and defensiveness, they took the initiative in founding the Centre Party in October 1870. The choice of a neutral name reflected their belief – prior to the *Kulturkampf* – that a confessional party would be 'a great misfortune' for Catholics. The organizers of the party found the elements of a political machine in existence and quickly acquired mass electoral support. After the revolutionary upheavals of 1848–49, Catholic clergymen promoted forms of popular piety that enhanced their own authority and anchored the sociability of the laity in a religious milieu. Catholic political clubs were formed in many cities in the late 1860s. When the elections for the Reichstag of the North German Confederation were held in 1867, the bishops in Prussia issued pastoral letters that mobilized the lower clergy for political campaigning. Parish priests exerted all the strength of their influential position on behalf of Catholic candidates in sermons and in door-to-door canvassing. The outcome of the elections in constituencies in the Rhineland and Westphalia showed that the clergy could wield enormous political influence under the empire's democratic system of equal suffrage and direct balloting. The triumph of organized political Catholicism was repeated in the Reichstag election of 1871 and even in the 1870 election for the Prussian House of Deputies based on the three-class franchise. Once again, the bishops' pastoral letters called on the faithful to vote for devout Catholics. The lower clergy engaged in aggressive electoral agitation, denouncing the liberals as godless atheists and enemies of the Pope and warning their parishioners that it was a sin to vote for candidates of the 'anti-religious party'.5

The *Kulturkampf*

Bismarck's perceptions of the new Catholic party played a major role in his decision to launch the *Kulturkampf*. For many years, Bismarck harboured a deep distrust of the political ambitions of the Catholic Church and believed that the Hohenzollern monarchy as the chief Protestant power in continental Europe was the target of a widespread ultramontane conspiracy. At a time when Bismarck was concerned with the problems of consolidating the new national state, especially disturbing to him were the Catholic clergy's use of the Polish language and cultivation of Polish ethnic identity in the eastern border regions of Prussia, where a Polish-Catholic minority of over 2 million lived. The founding of the Centre Party appeared to Bismarck to be yet another instance of Catholic aggression against the state. He saw the Centre Party as a magnet for all those malcontented groups within the empire who resisted national assimilation and clung to their separate identities.

The *Kulturkampf* was not a political strategem devised by Bismarck to lure the liberals into an anticlerical crusade and to distract them from constitutional issues in a conscious effort to hinder the development of responsible parliamentary government, as historians have contended in the past. Bismarck launched the *Kulturkampf* to wage an 'internal preventive war' against real and imagined dangers that threatened the consolidation of the empire. 'There can be little doubt', Otto Pflanze states, 'that Bismarck actually believed that the Catholic opposition was willing to ally with any subversive force in order to undermine the authority of the government.'6 Bismarck's other motive was to reduce the public authority of the Church. Through the appointment of clergymen as school inspectors and the precedence given to religious instruction in the elementary school curriculum, the Catholic and Protestant churches had traditionally exercised immense influence in Prussia's educational system. Bismarck suspected Catholic priests of disloyalty to the German national state. He believed that county school inspectors in the Polish-speaking areas were sabotaging the

---

5 Margaret Anderson, *Windthorst: A Political Biography* (Oxford, 1981), pp. 134–8; Jonathan Sperber, *Popular Catholicism in Nineteenth-Century Germany* (Princeton, 1984), pp. 164–8.
6 Otto Pflanze, *Bismarck and the Development of Germany*, 2 vols (Princeton, 1990), ii, pp. 188–200.

government's policy of Germanization and were not enforcing its regulations for the instruction of Polish schoolchildren in the German language.[7] Bismarck did not foresee a long conflict. Arrogant and overconfident, he overestimated the capacity of state power to mould reality and underestimated the tenacity with which the Catholics would resist the political persecution of their Church.

Far from being manipulated by Bismarck, the liberals entered the *Kulturkampf* with the idealism of secular crusaders. They saw no tension between freedom and force in this struggle. Historical explanations of their motives that ignore their positive goals remain incomplete. Adolf Birke approaches the issue of motivation by asking why the liberals squandered their political and moral energy in a conflict against ultramontanism when they should have concentrated their efforts on advancing the parliamentary development of the new empire. He contends that, after 1848, the liberals had abandoned their old principles and ceased to be a movement striving to safeguard the freedom of individuals and social groups from state power. Showing themselves to be heirs of Hegel, the liberals waged the struggle against the Church to strengthen the sovereignty of the state vis-à-vis particularistic claims.[8] On the other hand, Geoff Eley argues that the *Kulturkampf* was for the liberals an integral part of the process of nation state building, an attempt to create – through the intervention of state power – a coherent nation across confessional lines. His thesis emphasizes the 'positive objectives' pursued by the liberals, for whom the *Kulturkampf* was a struggle to emancipate German society from archaic institutions that obstructed cultural integration and social progress.[9]

The *Kulturkampf* legislation was intended to enhance the authority of the state over church affairs and to reduce the influence of the Catholic clergy in public life. The Reichstag passed a law in the summer of 1871 prohibiting 'the misuse' of the pulpit for political purposes. Another law in 1872 excluded the Society of Jesus from Germany and forbade individual Jesuits from administering the sacraments, conducting missions and teaching in schools. In May 1873, the Prussian *Landtag* passed a set of laws violating the autonomy of the Church. Under the May Laws, bishops were required to register clerical appointments with the provincial governors for approval.

---

7   Marjorie Lamberti, *State, Society, and the Elementary School in Imperial Germany* (New York, 1989), pp. 42–3 and ch. 4.
8   Adolf Birke, 'Zur Entwicklung und politischen Funktion des bürgerlichen *Kulturkampf*verständnisses in Preussen-Deutschland', in Dietrich Kurze (ed.), *Aus Theorie und Praxis der Geschichtswissenschaft* (Berlin, 1970), pp. 258–63.
9   Geoff Eley, 'State Formation, Nationalism and Political Culture in Nineteenth-Century Germany', in Eley (ed.), *From Unification to Nazism: Reinterpreting the German Past* (Boston, 1986), pp. 69–73.

These state officials could veto out of political considerations the appointment of any priest to a parish within 30 days after the bishop's notification. Some accounts of the *Kulturkampf* contend that the Prussian government possessed neither a bureaucracy and police force of sufficient size nor the unquestioning loyalty of county and municipal officials of the Catholic faith to be able to enforce these anticlerical laws rigorously. David Blackbourn argues more convincingly that the *Kulturkampf* was 'more violent than often supposed' and that it is 'important not to play down [its] coercive aspects'.[10]

Another dimension of the *Kulturkampf* in Prussia was the fight over the state's educational system. In the cities of the western provinces, while liberal clubs devoted to educational reform (*Bildungsvereine*) propagated the cause of interconfessional schooling, liberals in the municipal councils and school reformers in the provincial bureaucracy seized the opportunity to carry out innovations.[11] In 1871, the Prussian government introduced a bill to place elementary school supervision under the exclusive jurisdiction of the state and to clarify the status of school inspectors as state officials. After the enactment of the School Supervision Law, the government swiftly ousted Catholic clergymen from school inspection offices in the Polish-speaking districts. The movement to secularize the school inspectorate in the Rhine Province and Westphalia gained momentum in 1873, when the May Laws provoked many priests into political activism. Priests who campaigned for Centre Party candidates and were charged with 'agitation hostile to the state' were removed from their school positions. By 1878, professional educators – secondary schoolteachers, school principals and instructors from teachers' training seminaries – were appointed as full-time county school inspectors throughout the western provinces.

The ministry of education also approved the opening of interconfessional elementary schools in predominantly Catholic cities of the Rhineland. A long-standing goal of pedagogical reformers, confessionally integrated schooling became embroiled in partisan politics when *Kulturkämpfer* in the National Liberal and Progressive parties took up the cause. Protestant liberals criticized the confessional school system as a breeding ground of intolerance and an obstacle to cultural integration. They charged that Catholic schools instilled in the children complete devotion to the Church at

---

10 Sperber, *Popular Catholicism*, pp. 208, 241–5; Ronald Ross, 'Enforcing the *Kulturkampf* in the Bismarckian State and the Limits of Coercion in Imperial Germany', *Journal of Modern History* 56 (1984), 456–82; David Blackbourn, 'Progress and Piety: Liberals, Catholics and the State in Bismarck's Germany', in Blackbourn (ed.), *Populists and Patricians: Essays in Modern German History* (London, 1987), pp. 156, 166.
11 Lamberti, *State, Society, and the Elementary School*, ch. 2.

the expense of patriotism and emotional bonds to the fatherland. The civil consciousness of German society, they argued, could not be nationalized by preserving in sharp extremity the differences of confession and politics that divided citizens into hostile camps. Through a common educational experience for Catholic and Protestant youths, they hoped to diminish confessional particularism, create shared political loyalties, and establish the primacy of the relationship of the citizen to the national state.

Adalbert Falk, whom Bismarck selected as the Prussian minister of education and religious affairs in January 1872, openly stated in the House of Deputies his sympathies for the interconfessional school and the appointment of professionally-trained and experienced educators as school inspectors. For reasons of political expediency related to the opposition of politically influential Protestant groups in the Conservative Party and Prussian *Landeskirche*, the ministry did not extend these innovations to other regions where the population was predominantly Protestant. The reforms were confined to areas where the Catholics constituted the majority, and were experienced by them as discriminatory measures and acts of persecution against their Church.

The Catholic clergy resisted the *Kulturkampf* courageously and could not be browbeaten into submission. Prosecuted by the Prussian state for acting in defiance of the May Laws, five bishops were deposed from their episcopal offices. Many priests, especially in the dioceses of Breslau, Cologne, Gniezno-Poznan, Paderborn and Trier, were sentenced to prison. By 1880, more than 900 pastoral offices in parishes throughout Prussia were vacant. The Mainz Association of German Catholics, founded in 1872 to defend the freedom and rights of the Church, mobilized the Catholic population of the western provinces. Local clubs affiliated with the Mainz Association organized public rallies, where Catholic politicians and clergymen addressed crowds numbering a thousand and more. The Centre Party's leadership built up a mass political movement in the 1870s by invoking the image of an embattled Church and its persecuted priests and by defining the issues as the defence of religion, Christian schools and the rights of the family against liberalism's revolutionary concept of the 'omnipotent state'.

By the end of the decade, it was clear to Bismarck that repressive laws and administrative persecution had failed to achieve what he had hoped for. The struggle against the Church had politicized the Catholic populace and justified the very existence of the Centre Party. In the Reichstag elections of 1878, the Centre retained its electoral strength while the National Liberals and Progressives lost votes heavily to the two conservative parties. Falk's school policies had alienated Protestant conservatives and churchmen, and the opposition from this quarter upset Emperor William I. Even before Falk's resignation in 1879, Bismarck had decided to end his alliance with the

National Liberals in domestic politics and to make peace with Rome. Bismarck found Pope Leo XIII more conciliatory than his predecessor and obtained a concession that spared him from the humiliation of a full retreat. When the Peace Laws of 1886 and 1887 repealed or revised sections of the May Laws, the obligation of the bishops in Prussia to notify the state authorities of the appointment of priests to church offices was retained.

Religious cleavages and antagonisms in public life

Rather than unifying the new national state culturally, the *Kulturkampf* deepened the rift between Protestants and Catholics. In the following years, anti-Catholic prejudice, informal discrimination in the allocation of power and influence and mutual distrust between the two groups acted as a brake upon the forces of integration. Protestants and Catholics emphasized their confessional identity in manifold ways in public and private life, in the selection of the newspapers they read, the parties they voted for and the clubs they joined. Veterans' associations and nationalist leagues never became an agency of integration and had a predominantly Protestant membership. Few Catholics joined the Navy League and Pan-German League because their conspicuous ties to notorious Catholic-baiters in the Evangelical League and Imperial League against Ultramontanism belied their claims to be above confession.[12]

The propensity of German citizens to define their identity in terms of confession suggests that the extent to which they abandoned the beliefs and rituals of established religion should not be overstated. The secularization of German society was an uneven process. In small towns and the countryside, the number of church-going Protestants was high among artisans, shopkeepers and farmers. In confessionally mixed areas, where religious tensions led the two groups to define themselves against the 'other', the level of religious observance for Protestants was higher than in confessionally homogeneous regions. Active participation in church life declined among male Protestants of the educated and entrepreneurial bourgeoisie and the industrial working class. The relative distance of these sections of the Protestant community from church life did not necessarily mean irreligiosity and the complete loss of religious culture. Religious observance maintained a high constancy among all strata of the Catholic bourgeoisie in cities and

---

12 Roger Chickering, *We Men Who Feel Most German. A Cultural Study of the Pan-German League, 1886–1914* (Boston, 1984), pp. 138ff.

small towns. After 1900, signs of Catholic industrial workers' indifference toward religious culture – membership of socialist-oriented trade unions and the high incidence of mixed marriages in big cities – suggest that the influence of ultramontane Catholicism was slowly eroding.[13]

Why did religious cleavages and antagonisms persist in the political life of Prussia-Germany after 1886? First, the *Kulturkampf* had the effect of radicalizing the social distance between Catholics and Protestants. The years after 1870 witnessed the formation of socio-cultural milieus – more cohesive and dense for Catholics than for Protestants – that isolated the two confessions from each other. A web of voluntary associations organized and socialized massive numbers of Catholics and Protestants in separate subcultures.[14] Second, the 'modernity' of the political environment in Germany after 1890, characterized by an expansion of the national 'public space', a proliferation of voluntary associations to articulate and represent the opinion and interests of various constituencies, and a high level of political mobilization and participation in elections, provided the conditions for the politicization of confessional differences and antagonisms. Third, a 'new confessionalism' exceeding the traditional religious framework emerged as social and economic problems were increasingly observed and experienced through the category of confession. Fourth, anti-Catholic prejudice within the Protestant, educated middle class and the highest official circles of Prussia kept in place an informal discrimination in the allocation of political influence and the distribution of professional opportunities. The Catholics' fight for parity placed confessionalism at the centre of public life and heightened public consciousness of Protestant dominance and 'Catholic inferiority' with respect to higher education and to achievement and success in the civil service, free professions and business world.

Although the Catholic population was socially heterogeneous, a shared religious faith and adherence to the Church, the experience and memories of the *Kulturkampf*, and a specific Catholic consciousness that was shaped in the attacks of the state and liberalism on the traditional rights and influence of the Church, bound together Catholics of diverse occupations and material interests in a separate socio-cultural milieu. The carriers of the Catholic subculture were a network of voluntary associations under clerical

---

13 Thomas Nipperdey, *Religion im Umbruch: Deutschland 1870–1918* (Munich, 1988), pp. 22–3, 118–20.
14 Olaf Blaschke and Frank-Michael Kuhlemann, 'Religion in Geschichte und Gesellschaft. Sozialhistorische Perspektiven für die vergleichende Erforschung religiöser Mentalitäten und Milieus', in Blaschke and Kuhlemann (eds), *Religion im Kaiserreich. Milieu-Mentalitäten-Krisen*, 2 vols (Gütersloh, 1996), ii, pp. 22–41.

and lay leadership. The Catholic milieu provided a system of symbols and values and prescribed a manner of behaviour that helped individual Catholics to define and orientate themselves in public life.[15] The Catholic subculture was characterized by distrust of Prussian state power and bureaucracy, dedication to constitutionalism and the rule of law, and opposition to exceptional legislation and state encroachments on the conscience of the individual and the autonomy of the Church. The Catholic milieu was strongest in rural and small-town areas, where the material interests of farmers, artisans and shopkeepers intertwined with the social conservatism of the Church to produce a defensive outlook towards modernity and laissez-faire liberalism.

Catholic voluntary associations worked to solidify the base of support for the Centre Party. At the annual gathering of Catholics at the four-day-long *Katholikentag* (Congress of German Catholics), clerical and lay politicians displayed a talent for populist oratory when they defended the freedom of the Church against the 'omnipotent' state and assailed liberalism and socialism as the 'foes of Christianity'. From the 1880s on, this annual assembly assumed a plebiscitary function and became a mass political spectacle, which drew 10,000 to 15,000 participants and many more thousands of Catholics as spectators and marchers in the highly symbolic workers' procession held on the opening day. The People's Association for Catholic Germany (*Volksverein für das katholische Deutschland*), which was founded in 1890 to foster interclass unity and to conduct propaganda against socialism, issued news releases to the Catholic press, produced pamphlets for political education and election campaigning, and cultivated ties between the party and the Catholic electorate. A highly successful mass organization, the *Volksverein*, recruited a membership of 151,000 in 1901 and around 800,000 by 1914.[16]

The membership of the *Volksverein* suggests the areas where the Catholic social milieu attained its greatest cohesion and strength. Its headquarters were located in Mönchen-Gladbach in the heart of the Ruhr, and the vast majority of its members lived in the western half of Prussia. It was more successful in recruiting members among the rural and small-town *Mittelstand*

---

15 David Blackbourn, 'Catholics and Politics in Imperial Germany: the Centre Party and its Constituency', in *Populists and Patricians*, pp. 199ff. Wilfried Loth stresses the evolution of the Centre Party after 1890 into a 'coalition of social milieus' as a result of the social differentiation of Catholics and the penetration of economic interests in politics, in *Katholiken im Kaiserreich. Der politische Katholizismus in der Krise des wilhelminischen Deutschlands* (Düsseldorf, 1984), pp. 18–35.

16 Nipperdey, *Religion im Umbruch*, pp. 24–31; Josef Mooser, 'Volk, Arbeiter und Bürger in der katholischen Öffentlichkeit des Kaiserreichs: Zur Sozial- und Funktionsgeschichte der deutschen Katholikentage 1871–1913', in Hans-Jürgen Puhle (ed.), *Bürger in der Gesellschaft der Neuzeit* (Göttingen, 1991), pp. 261–70.

than among the working class in the industrial cities. The Christian (mostly Catholic) trade unions founded in 1894 had greater success in integrating Catholic workers into the milieu of political Catholicism, and were for many years a barrier to the recruitment efforts of the socialist-oriented labour movement. The Centre Party's remarkably stable popular vote – another indicator of the cohesion of the Catholic milieu – did not suffer any erosion until 1912.

The socially and politically fractured Protestant population never achieved the same degree of cohesion as the Catholics, but it would be misleading to portray the differences between liberals and conservatives within the Protestant Church too starkly by applying the concept of 'pillarization'.[17] Besides the common structure of the Prussian *Landeskirche*, many ideological affinities bound both groups – German nationalism, a sense of Protestant cultural hegemony, distrust of political Catholicism and hostility to social democracy. After 1870, German nationalism penetrated deeply into the Protestant Church and religious culture. Protestant chaplains appointed for each reserve and regular corps of the Prussian army and other politicized pastors espoused an ideology that blended Protestant religiosity, fervent support for the imperial state system, German nationalism and anti-Catholicism.[18]

Protestant clergymen and laymen who were unhappy with Bismarck's decision to wind down the *Kulturkampf* and make peace with the Vatican organized the Evangelical League in 1886. Willibald Beyschlag, a professor of theology and a leading figure in the Synod of the Prussian *Landeskirche*, and the other founders of the league were bent on continuing the struggle against 'ultramontanism' – the alleged striving of the Roman Church for secular political power and domination under the cloak of and through the exploitation of religion. They observed with deep anxiety the unity and resurgent power of political Catholicism against the divided and debilitated condition of Protestantism. In the following years, the league waged an unrelenting propaganda war against the Catholic Church and the Centre Party. The ideologues of the league saw the vast web of Catholic organizations as a conspiracy threatening to divide the nation into two alien and antagonistic parties. Local chapters of the league promoted a confessionally framed German nationalism in their celebrations of holidays commemorating the Protestant heroes of the Reformation and the Thirty Years' War. After the turn of the century, the league's younger generation of

---

17 Gangolf Hübinger, 'Kulturprotestantismus, Bürgerkirche und liberaler Revisionismus im wilhelminischen Deutschland', in Wolfgang Schieder (ed.), *Religion und Gesellschaft im 19. Jahrhundert* (Stuttgart, 1993), pp. 277–8.
18 For the ideological 'consensus' within Protestantism, see Nipperdey, *Religion im Umbruch*, pp. 93–105.

leaders, who espoused integral nationalism and great-power imperialism, maintained a warm relationship with the nationalist leagues.

The large membership that the Evangelical League recruited, 100,000 by 1897 and 509,000 by 1913, suggests the extent to which anti-Catholicism was still smouldering within German society more than three decades after the *Kulturkampf*. Protestant pastors shared leadership roles with academics, professional and managerial men, and high civil servants, many of whom were affiliated with the National Liberal and Free Conservative parties. One of the league's most pugnacious activists was Albert Hackenberg, a pastor and National Liberal in the Prussian House of Deputies, who frequently provoked exchanges with Centre deputies by Catholic-baiting. In Prussia, the league's stronghold was the confessionally mixed and urban areas of the Rhine Province and Westphalia. It was less successful in recruiting members in the more agrarian and homogeneously Protestant provinces in the east. Helmut Walser Smith contends that the support base of anti-ultramontane activity consisted of middle-class groups distinguished by their education and social standing – 'the most forward-looking of Protestant citizens' – and that 'anti-Catholicism cannot be explained by reference to groups threatened materially by modernization'. Other historians see in the agitation of these activists a defensive ideology that combined cultural pessimism, social anxieties and integral nationalism.[19]

The upsurge of political mobilization affected the fortunes and behaviour of the Centre and two liberal parties. Protestant middle-class voters, upon whom National Liberal and Progressive candidates traditionally depended, became politically volatile and were prone to defect to other established parties or the new populistic splinter parties appealing to the economic interests and disaffection of shopkeepers and farmers. In electoral districts where National Liberal notables once did little campaigning to win, the elections became hotly contested fights. With opportunism and political plasticity, National Liberal politicians resorted to anti-ultramontane and anti-socialist rhetoric in election campaigning in order to isolate their rivals and unify Protestant voters. The heavy losses which the National Liberals suffered to the two conservative parties in the elections of 1878 and 1879 for the Reichstag and Prussian House of Deputies started a downward trend that reduced the liberal movement to a permanent minority. In comparison, the Centre Party thrived in the new political terrain. Catholic clerical and

---

19 Smith, *German Nationalism*, pp. 102–4; Dieter Langewiesche, *Liberalismus in Deutschland* (Frankfurt am Main, 1988), pp. 180–7; Gangolf Hübinger, *Kulturprotestantismus und Politik. Zum Verhältnis von Liberalismus und Protestantismus im wilhelminischen Deutschland* (Tübingen, 1994), pp. 34–7, 47, 308.

lay politicians were no less demagogic in striving to neutralize class differences within the Catholic electorate and to prevent defection. Besides emphasizing confessional and cultural issues, they portrayed German Catholicism as an embattled religious community threatened by 'outsiders' – liberals, socialists, Protestants, and Freemasons. Catholic priests in the countryside and small towns functioned as a reliable and efficient political machine for the Centre Party, transmitting political information to the electorate and getting voters to the polls. Male Catholic citizens were stable, habitual voters and affirmed their loyalty to the Church and solidarity with their confessional community at the polls. With a large bloc of votes in the Reichstag and Prussian House of Deputies, the Catholic party acquired a position that the National Liberals envied. Its support was indispensable to the government for the passage of important pieces of legislation.

In the 1890s, the Centre Party's fight to abolish the legacy of the *Kulturkampf* evolved into a campaign for parity. The annual debates on the state's budget were the occasion for Catholic deputies to protest at the disparities in public school facilities for the two confessions and the unequal treatment of Catholic and Protestant clergymen in the appointment of county school inspectors. Deputies from the Rhineland and Westphalia, reflecting the ambitions of the region's sizeable number of Catholic middle-class professionals, fought for parity between Protestants and Catholics in the distribution of opportunities for civil service appointments and promotions. They attributed the disproportionately low number of Catholics in the state administration to bias and discrimination. For the Protestant middle and upper classes, the campaign for parity was another demonstration of the Centre Party's 'narrow-minded' confessionalism. Government spokesmen and National Liberal deputies rebuffed Catholic criticism by contending that the Centre Party was proposing a mechanical system of quotas based on confession as a qualification for appointment. Protestant polemicists blamed the Catholics themselves and pointed to the 'educational deficiency' of the Catholic population and the weak Catholic enrolments at the universities. The debates over parity – extending over a decade – aggravated confessional relations and released a host of Catholic resentments and insecurities.[20]

School politics was a constant ground for confessional conflict in Prussian public life, as the example of the debate over the elementary school bill of 1892 reveals.[21] The school bill, proposed by the Conservative minister of

---

20 Martin Baumeister, *Parität und katholische Inferiorität. Untersuchungen zur Stellung des Katholizismus im Deutschen Kaiserreich* (Paderborn, 1987), pp. 13ff.
21 Lamberti, *State, Society, and the Elementary School*, pp. 161–71.

education, Robert von Zedlitz, defined expansively the rights of the church in respect to the supervision of religious instruction and the examination of candidates for the teacher's licence. It provided that, as a rule, schoolchildren were to be instructed by teachers of their own confession, and required the opening of a separate public school even for small numbers of children belonging to the confessional minority in a school district. Another provision made it easier to secure state permission for the establishment of private schools. While the Catholic bishops and Centre Party welcomed the school bill enthusiastically, the two liberal parties attacked the concessions to the Church and confessional interests. Liberal opponents of the school bill saw in the powers granted to the clergy on the local school boards and in the examination for the teacher's licence a threat to the state's control of public education. Leo von Caprivi, the Prussian Minister-President and Imperial Chancellor, reacted to the criticism by stating bluntly his determination to push the school bill through the *Landtag* irrespective of the National Liberals' opposition. The government intended to conciliate the Catholics and to obtain the Centre Party's co-operation for the passage of bills in the Reichstag.

National Liberal politicians and ideologues of the Evangelical League injected a strong anti-Catholic tone in the agitation against the school bill. The league charged that the school bill granted the Roman Church an augmentation of power that would be dangerous to the state and the Protestant Church. Asserting that priests would gain control over the training and certification of Catholic teachers, the league's widely circulated manifesto warned that 'given the ideological orientation in the Roman Church today, the cultivation of patriotic feeling and national culture could not be expected from such teachers'. The league also objected to the provisions for private schools and heightened public fears by making exaggerated predictions about the opening of 'Jesuit schools'. Beyschlag demanded that the school bill disqualify Catholic priests from teaching in private schools, explaining contemptuously that 'persons who alienate themselves from the fatherland by the oaths of their religious order and are obliged to unconditional obedience to a foreign authority cannot fulfil the task of the German *Volksschule*'. The National Liberals' unrestrained battle against the school bill in the Prussian parliament and press made a deep impression on a small circle of high state officials close to Emperor William II. William's closest confidants disliked Caprivi's policy of appeasing the Centre. They expressed their misgivings about 'the all-too-pro-Catholic sections' of the proposed law, and persuaded the emperor to resolve the political crisis by burying the school bill.

Two aspects of the emotionally charged controversy over the school bill in 1892 should be emphasized. First, the National Liberals and Evangelical

League were very effective in arousing anti-Catholic anxieties among Protestants. Protestant conservatives who supported the school bill lamented how much hysterical fears of the Catholic Church, grounded in bigotry, pervaded the debate. The conservative *Kreuzzeitung* chided Protestant pastors for allying with liberal opponents of the confessional school because of imaginary fears that the proposed law would enhance the power of the Catholic hierarchy and enable it to threaten Protestantism.

Second, the Protestant ruling elite's resentment of the pivotal position of the Centre Party in parliamentary politics was a key factor in the political intrigues of William's circle of confidants and in the vehemence with which the National Liberals fought the school bill. They wanted Caprivi to subdue rather than to court and make concessions to the 'clericals'. His strategy of governing with the support of a parliamentary coalition of conservatives and political Catholicism threatened to change the character of the German national state, as they understood it. This resentment surfaced again in the years from 1900 to 1905, when, given the declining electoral strength of the National Liberals and the growing number of Social Democrats in the Reichstag, Chancellor Bülow could see no other alternative than to keep the Centre Party in a pro-government position. Bülow told the Prussian Cabinet of Ministers in 1903 that the repeal of article two of the Jesuit law of 1872 was a political necessity.

After 1890, Catholic integralism with its self-isolating and defensive tendencies waned, and the reconciliation of Catholics with the German Empire and the 'nationalization' of political Catholicism gained momentum. The group that came to dominate the Centre Party in Prussia consisted of Catholics who longed for acceptance in the national community and for peace between Protestants and Catholics based on a shared patriotism and loyalty to the monarchy and a common Christian front against social democracy. In the Rhineland and Westphalia, where a sizeable self-confident, Catholic middle class emerged, the presence of clergymen in positions of leadership in the Centre Party declined. A new generation of lay leaders, many of whom were lawyers, civil servants and successful businessmen, wanted to be political 'insiders' and to transform the Centre from the party of a pariah community into a party of national co-operation. Typical of this generation was Julius Bachem, a publisher in Cologne, who argued that the Centre Party should move out of its confessional 'tower' and collaborate with the conservatives so that Catholics could dispel Protestant fears of ultramontanism and achieve full parity in German society. To prove their national reliability and gain social respectability within high official circles, Centre politicians supported the government's imperialist programme and bills to strengthen the army and navy. They distanced themselves from Polish Catholics in the eastern provinces who protested at the Prussian government's Germanization policy in the schools.22

The national integration of Catholics was an unsteady process. Firmly set Protestant identities did not change quickly. Integral nationalists in the Evangelical League, Navy League and other associations could not reconcile themselves to the government's policy of drawing the Centre Party into the coalition of national unity to fight social democracy because it implied the recognition of Catholics as equal compatriots and undermined the exclusive association of German nationalism with Protestant traditions. They thought that Catholics, whose highest spiritual authority resided in Rome, would never feel true German sentiment. The resurgence of anti-Catholicism in the nationalistic atmosphere of the Reichstag election campaign of 1907 aroused Catholic anxieties of a 'second *Kulturkampf*'. William II and his coterie of close advisers had an ingrained prejudice against Catholics and thought that the Centre Party should be kept in a subordinate role. The Centre Party opposed exceptional laws as a matter of principle, and the contribution of Catholic parliamentarians to the defeat of several government bills aimed at repressing the Social Democratic Party confirmed the emperor in his dislike of the party. 'Scoundrels without a fatherland' was his description of these German Catholics.

The historical consequences

The formation of socio-cultural milieus and a party system segregated along class and religious lines in Imperial Germany had, as M. Rainer Lepsius pointed out in a seminal essay in 1966, a profound impact on the society and politics of Prussia-Germany. Although historians may challenge Lepsius' contention that parties that remained fixated on a single social grouping and subculture – in contrast to the parties of integration in the United States – were another manifestation of the 'historical particularity' of Germany, his analysis offered valuable insights and opened the discussion on the persistence of confessional solidarities and antagonisms in political life and the consequences of these conditions for the national polity.23 The

---

22 Rudolf Morsey, 'Die deutschen Katholiken und der Nationalstaat zwischen *Kulturkampf* und Erstem Weltkrieg', in Gerhard A. Ritter (ed.), *Deutsche Parteien vor 1918* (Cologne, 1973), pp. 275–83; Ronald Ross, *Beleaguered Tower: the Dilemma of Political Catholicism in Wilhelmine Germany* (Notre Dame, 1976), pp. 42, 63–4.
23 M. Rainer Lepsius, 'Parteiensystem und Sozialstruktur: zum Problem der Demokratisierung der deutschen Gesellschaft', in Ritter (ed.), *Deutsche Parteien*, pp. 56–80.

assertion of Protestant cultural hegemony, the identification of German nationalism with Protestant traditions, and the intrusion of confessionalism in public life produced an atmosphere of aggressive intolerance and hostile stereotyping in the confessionally mixed areas of Prussia, and undermined attempts to create a cohesive nation and tolerant pluralistic society. After unification, Protestant liberals propagated a view of German national culture and history that marginalized Catholic citizens. The ostracism of Catholics from the national community and the political persecution of their Church during the *Kulturkampf* reinforced and radically politicized Catholic isolation.

The formation of the Centre Party bound to church and confessional interests and dependent on subcultural cohesion and solidarity hindered the development of interconfessional and interparty co-operation that was essential to promote parliamentary government and democracy. The 'declericalization' of the Centre Party's leadership did not diminish the value that the party assigned to confessional interests and cultural policy. Centre politicians such as Wilhelm Marx of Düsseldorf, who organized in 1912 the Catholic School Organization for the defence of confessional schooling in Prussia, knew that confessional identity and interests held the disparate sectional groups within the Catholic community together. The balance of parties in the Reichstag made the Centre Party decisive for any majority coalition of either the right or the left. The Centre Party chose to align with the conservatives who stood for the preservation of the three-class suffrage in Prussia and the political status quo rather than with the reformers in the Social Democratic and left-liberal Progressive parties. This choice was determined not only by the Catholics' aspirations for social acceptance and public influence, but also by their defence of the confessional school and their social and moral conservatism vis-à-vis modernity. The Centre's leadership could not make compromises on questions of cultural policy without alienating the church hierarchy and without undermining their subcultural identity, which had been defined again and again against that of the 'other'.

CHAPTER NINE

Prussian Protestantism

NICHOLAS HOPE

This subject raises the question, bearing the Nazi racial dictatorship in mind, have we given too much attention until recently to a substantially Prussocentric interpretation of Protestant Church and State in modern Germany, to Prussian Protestant high politics, to deference to church hierarchy and its bureaucratic procedure centred in Berlin, and to Prussian senior clergy leading a new German national triumphalism in sermons praising Prussian arms at the expense of the parish congregation and parish democracy? Protestant German church historians, too, have often preferred to record the progress of modern Protestant academic (read 'scientific') theology, a German nineteenth-century university speciality, in Prussian universities and its personification in Prussian church government.[1] Fair enough, perhaps, given the dominant political and cultural role in Germany played by expanded Prussia after 1867, and the fact that both *Kulturkampf* and *Kirchenkampf* were coined (1873, 1933) and fought out to a considerable extent on Prussian soil (see Marjorie Lamberti in this volume). Even one of the pacemakers of twentieth-century Protestant ecumenism, the Swedish archbishop (1914–31) Söderblom, who saw modern national churches as provinces within the Christian Church, could write in August 1909 in an article projecting intercommunion between the Swedish and

---

1 The outstanding patristic scholar of his generation, Adolf von Harnack, quipped about theological progress from Neo-Lutheran and Positive (pre-1817) to Liberal-Protestant: 'The Prussian church was coloured in 1866 by Hengstenberg, in 1890 by Kögel, in 1900 by von der Goltz, and today (1911) she stands under Dryander, Kahl and Kaftan. This is tremendous progress. The wheel of history cannot be rotated more rapidly!', Agnes Zahn-Harnack, *Adolf von Harnack*, 2nd edn (Berlin, 1951), p. 309.

Anglican churches, that in Germany: '[...] one can never entertain any real fairplay between religious denominations so long as the Catholic church's bishops, taking into account their specific historical, social, and even economic situation, face [Protestant] clergy acting as quasi civil servants governed centrally by [equal numbers of] lawyers and theologians in Berlin'.[2] Söderblom was thinking of the Prussian organ of church government, the Upper Consistory (*Oberkirchenrat*), established in 1850.

Such a view also obtained in the Weimar Republic. Otto Dibelius (1880–1967), general superintendent of the Kurmark (1925–33), a Prussian church reformer much impressed by the Scottish Presbyterian self-government he had encountered on a Scottish visit in 1906 (published as a book in 1911), and a keen participant at the Stockholm 'Life and Work' conference in 1925, thus wrote with Söderblom and the post-war Swedish ecclesiological revival in mind in his purple-covered bestseller, *Das Jahrhundert der Kirche* (1926), of November 1918 as 'the thunderstorm which cleared the air' in Protestant Germany. The end of the monarchy and the realignment of Germany's (read Prussia's) territorial borders freed at long last the Protestant Church from the heavy hand of Berlin and the *Landeskirche* mentality, meaning an exclusive and deferential Protestant frame of mind handed down via the bond of the local ruler and his church since the Reformation.[3] Needless to say, Dibelius's optimism in a self-governing Protestant Church headed by bishops was swiftly swept aside by the Protestant theologian Karl Barth's (1886–1968) radical questioning of the prevailing liberal theology, which bracketed, so Barth alleged, a fundamentally erroneous synthesis between theology and culture; by the Nazi 'German-Christian Church Movement' advocating a new bond between Nazism and Christianity, and by the local conciliar or synodical framework of the 'Confessing Church' (1933–45) formed by a group of Protestant German clergy and laity as an informal church of confessors for the faith in opposition to German-Christianity sponsored by the Nazis.

In other words, a Prussian Protestant identity and the larger Protestant German whole can all too easily be lumped together nationally, though both have influenced each other as anomalous and plural customary orders of church provinces continuously since the Reformation. One can mention

---

2   N. Söderblom, 'Canterbury och Uppsala', in *Svenska kyrkans kropp och själ* (Stockholm, 1916), p. 122.

3   Otto Dibelius, '*Das befreiende Gewitter*', *Das Jahrhundert der Kirche* (Berlin, 1927), pp. 75–7.
    Dibelius had in mind, especially, the loss of Posen, Danzig, Memel and Upper Silesia, though German Protestants there remained members of the mother Prussian church. Scotland, *Das kirchliche Leben Schottlands* (Giessen, 1911). Revelatory, Dibelius's pamphlet, *Staatsgrenzen und Kirchengrenzen: Eine Studie zur gegenwärtigen Lage des Protestantismus* (Berlin, 1921).

here the Brandenburg-Nuremberg church order (1533), and its observance of the structure of the Ordinary and Proper of the Latin mass contained in Luther's *Formula Missae et communionis* (1523). And even regarding Protestant Prussia as such, it can be argued very plausibly that, until the outbreak of the Second World War, its historic Reformation church order and worship, modified by time and custom in church provinces such as Lutheran Brandenburg or Lutheran East Prussia and Reformed Westphalia or the Reformed Rhineland, mattered far more than the Prussian whole. Berlin, too, was almost a church province. It might not be too fanciful to imagine Thomas Hardy's 'Wessex': several south-western English counties setting the scene of his novels at the dawn of our modern industrial age. One has to go to Prussia's church provinces to understand the larger Prussian whole. National histories and high politics can cloud the life of such provincial Reformation churches, from their peculiar historical gestation to what they shared to and fro. This chapter, therefore, can be only a very selective survey of the Protestant Prussian church order and its development in the period under consideration. Comparison with the rest of Protestant Germany remains largely unsaid; an attempt is made in my recent book.[4]

A search for identity and establishment

The Prussian United Church was, in the sense of an established royal Anglican or Swedish Lutheran Church, an early nineteenth-century creation. But, in contrast to both latter historic Reformation churches, Prussian kings had to manufacture a traditional establishment like the Church of England. However, as the largest grouping of Protestant German churches, under a royal supreme bishop since 1867 and significantly modified by constitutional reform in 1876, their established church outlasted the nineteenth century by little more than a decade and a half. It vanished with the abdication of Kaiser-King William II on 28 November 1918. On the other hand, the pains which Prussian kings took as supreme bishops, particularly in the capital, Berlin, was not forgotten after 1918 in troubled republican Protestant Prussia.

The Prussian United Church of October 1817 (comprising Reformed minority and Lutheran majority) was an act of state, and its ecclesiology was designed by the propriety and liturgical fancy of Frederick William III (1797–1840), and the aesthetic taste of Frederick William IV (1840–61).

---

4 Nicholas Hope, *German and Scandinavian Protestantism 1700–1918* (Oxford, 1995).

Frederick William IV, in particular, dreamt of the basilica, the form of the building for Christian worship in the first three Christian centuries, the church art and church music of the quattrocento, and the contemporary Anglo-Catholic revival at Oxford holding a 'high' doctrine of the church and sacraments as models. Its German setting, however, was the lengthy debate about a suitable modern Protestant church order and liturgy (whether to unite Lutheran and Reformed churches) in the period of liturgical enlightenment c.1770–1840 – in Prussia at Königsberg and Berlin – which both kings disliked. The irony was that Berlin thereafter gave a lead in the revival of the choral liturgy in Protestant Germany.[5] 'Bishops', in the Anglican and Swedish sense as guardians of their new established church, thus appealed to both monarchs. Frederick William III had already ordered that the word 'Evangelical', expressing subscription to Bible and Gospel, replace 'Protestant' in official correspondence in 1821, since he associated the adjective 'Protestant' with the Enlightenment and political representation.[6]

On the other hand, this royal church, and even its republican successor, 'The Evangelical Church of the Old-Prussian Union', until its destruction by the Nazis in 1934, really masked, as mentioned above, the survival of the customary order of historic 'Brandenburg-Prussia' as an archipelago of many little and large local Reformation churches (*Landeskirchen*) keenly conscious of their separate Lutheran and Reformed identities. This was visible in their princely and urban church orders and liturgies. Such pluralism dictated, on the whole, tolerant church government by Reformed Hohenzollerns since 1613 because immigration, which included religious minorities such as the Huguenots and Mennonites, was essential for the growth of Brandenburg-Prussia as a state. Prussia therefore shared much structurally with a much larger, disorderly, plural, Protestant German whole (over 350 church orders and liturgies before 1806) both before and after the tidying-up of political and religious boundaries in the period 1806–15.

A principal division between a Reformed Prussian west – the new Prussian Rhineland and Westphalian provinces since 1815, with Reformed pockets also in western and eastern Prussia – and a Lutheran Prussian east – Brandenburg, western and eastern Prussia since Polish division between 1772–95 and Silesia – became noticeable in modern Prussian church politics for the first time in a bitter public reaction to Frederick William III's imposition of his 'Catholic' 1822 rite. It was also made explicit by the contemporaneous creation of a synodal church order in 1835 for Reformed Rhineland and Westphalia.

---

5   Ibid., chs 13, 17, and 20.
6   'Bishops' were introduced in 1816; clerical dress five years earlier in 1811.

The latter tried to mix Reformed presbytery (the majority) with Lutheran consistory (the minority). It was also, therefore, a solution, given borders adjacent to contemporaneous Dutch and Swiss early nineteenth-century Reformed *Reveil*, which was coloured by such Dutch and Swiss synodalism. The Reformed churches in these new nations liked the new western European constitutional movement. Needless to say, the same development took place in south-western Germany; the Reformed in Baden and the Rhine Palatinate gained with their Lutheran neighbours 'constitutions' in 1821.

This new church-political development had the effect, however, of reinforcing a customary allegiance to local church order both in Protestant Prussia and in Germany. The Reformed Rhineland and Westphalia managed to keep their particular synodal order intact with only a few modifications (it favoured a Reformed understanding) even after 1918. A modern historian of republican Prussia's Protestant Church thus concedes that, 'since most congregations formally retained either Reformed or Lutheran identities, the union [1817] remained incomplete in the Weimar period as an organizational, sacramental, and liturgical union'.[7]

This complex Protestant Prussian and German map, and the growth of nineteenth-century Protestant synodal churchmanship, remains today outside of Protestant Prussia a controversial Protestant German reality, despite the momentous political changes that took place in Germany in the twentieth century. Neither a Nazi German-Christian Church (*Reichskirche*) under a Nazi archbishop to impose its will (June 1933–July 1935), nor the division of Germany and the massive shift and mixing of religious persuasions that the military map of 1945 produced, nor the reconstitution of post-war German political division after more than 40 years in 1990, have altered this legacy of the German Reformation. Nothing resembling a national Protestant German church has yet appeared.

Peculiar to Protestant Prussia in this period was not its continued piecemeal assimilation of Lutheran and Reformed church provinces (first east, with the conquest of Silesia in 1742 and the three Polish partitions in 1772, 1793 and 1795, then west in 1815 and 1864–66), but their piecemeal loss in the first half of the twentieth century. The transregional Prussian United Church of 1817, which easily dominated Protestant Germany after 1867, remained stable only for some 50 years until 1919, when Prussia shed, under the terms of the Versailles peace treaty, much of its eastern Lutheran heartland. Prussian legislation (1921–22) recognized, too, the independence of the 'new' church provinces – Schleswig-Holstein, Hanover, Electoral

---

7   Daniel R. Borg, *The Old-Prussian Church and the Weimar Republic: A Study in Political Adjustment, 1917–1927* (Hanover and London, 1984), p. xiii.

Hesse, Frankfurt am Main and Nassau – gained by annexation in 1864 and 1866. The Allied military Map of Unconditional Surrender in 1945 finally hived off the historic Prussian east, and divided its former capital, Berlin.

Briefly, Silesia, West Prussia and Polish Posen (gains of the three Polish divisions 1772–95) added not only very poor rural Lutheran parishes and Lutherans acutely conscious of their identity as a church in danger in a Catholic churchscape, but also a substantial and equally sensitive poor Catholic population (20 per cent), and the first Catholic bishoprics of Breslau, Kulm and Frauenburg (Ermland). The territories ceded to Prussia in 1815 brought 57.5 per cent of Lutheran Saxony, including Wittenberg, and the rest of Lutheran Pomerania (*Vorpommern*), provinces that were very conscious of their shared conservative Lutheran Reformation. Just as important in the west, given their place in a Catholic churchscape, was the equally self-conscious Reformed Westphalia and Rhineland. Protestant Prussia's Catholic population rose to two-fifths, with Cologne, Münster and Paderborn adding substantial weight to the Catholic eastern Prussian bishoprics. The new provinces to the left of the Rhine which subscribed to the French *Code Civil* made it difficult if not impossible to return to the old church-state. In other words, these big political changes forced upon Protestant Prussians the touchy leading question whether Reformation churches could be governed 'constitutionally' at all.

The Prussian answer, given the new sovereign power of the early nineteenth-century German state, was subordination of the church, following the French example, under a new minister for church affairs and education (1817). Also, the three new major Prussian universities, Berlin (1809), Breslau (1811), which absorbed Reformed Frankfurt-on-Oder, and Bonn (1818), were emphatically Prussian state universities whose theology faculties fell increasingly under the supervision of state education and finance departments. Such reasoning implied, however, a huge expansion of central church administration in Berlin (seen as a common Protestant Prussian capital only since the Polish divisions) over an ever more hopelessly complex archipelago of church provinces. The immediate result was a bitter conflict in both east and west with the restored Catholic Church (in 1821) over the upbringing of children, marriage resulting from the mixing of populations created by these boundary changes, and about a state university or Catholic seminary education. Protestant and Catholic divided as worlds, and nationality, too, began to cause friction, since Prussian Protestants usually equated Poles with Catholicism. This foreshadowed the course of Bismarck's 'national-liberal' inspired *Kulturkampf* (1871–87), modelled on similar Badenese liberal legislation (1860–70), which 'produced the modern cleavage between Protestant and Catholic Germany in family, school, work and political preferences which finally played both churches into Hitler's hands in 1933'.[8] Such expansion also exposed Berlin to Reformed synodal democracy, active already in 1815–16 in the Rhineland and Westphalia, and, at this time of awakened churchmanship, to a more or less inevitable strong neo-Lutheran reaction against the new United Church and its synodical modification along parliamentary lines. Neo-Lutherans rediscovered and re-emphasized instead the authority of the Lutheran office (*Amt*), subscription to Lutheran religious articles and Luther's *Formula Missae* retained in local Lutheran liturgies, and the deferential rural Lutheran social order of 'estates'. Particularly divisive was a decade and a half of Silesian Lutheran opposition to the 1822 royal rite. Their obstinate retention of the old liturgy of worship in their parish churches led to an embarrassing use of the Prussian army. Official permission for 'Old Lutherans' to emigrate from Silesia in September 1837 stamped this as the last emigration for religious reasons in Germany.

On the other hand, in the long run, however long it took to grasp officially, the idea of Protestant self-government, meaning 'constitutions' coloured by Reformed 'Orders' – offices comprising doctors of divinity, pastors, elders and deacons – giving laymen a sense of their own worth in church affairs, did take root, however limited in practice.[9] Prussia, in the more associative climate of the 1840s, and under a king, Frederick William IV, who wished to sink religious differences, became a pacemaker like Baden in making room for the Church (Protestant and Catholic) as a corporation in modern public law. This was dictated by new state legislation which increasingly dispensed with religious ties in education and economic affairs. 'The development of the constitution [of the Protestant Church] towards greater independence', the general aim of the first Protestant German general synod ever, held in Berlin in 1846, was thus:

> [...] a wistful, but nevertheless fundamental step away from the old dependent Reformation order of *cuius regio*. It implied a grudging, but growing recognition of congregational rights; separation of the religious parish from the civil parish (notably in social welfare), and a gradual abandonment of the canon law principle [...] which obliged parishioners to use and pay for the services of the home parish clergyman.[10]

---

8 Hope, *German and Scandinavian Protestantism*, p. 460; Baden is discussed in ibid., pp. 492–3. Baden's progressive 1821 Protestant church constitution was replaced in 1861 by a new constitution mixing presbytery and consistory on Rhine-Westphalian lines (1835) under a senior consistory at Karlsruhe.
9 The consistory, the Lutheran organ of church government since the Reformation mixing equal numbers of lawyers and theologians, tended to prevail until 1918.
10 Ibid., p. 460. '*Pfarrzwang*' was abolished in most German states between 1818 and 1903.

The expansion of a new and growing labour market based on wages made this inevitable. Prussian Protestant self-government, also in the rest of Protestant Germany, developed, however, behind the scenes in the period of unification during the *Kulturkampf* and in the midst of a new and very vocal Protestant German nationalism (*c*.1840–90).

A fragile new constitutional ('synodal') church order

If Prussia went only a short way down the 'peoples' church' path, observing the basic modern constitutional rule – every religious denomination to be governed independently, but subject to laws of a state that allowed none to enjoy special privileges – as both the Frankfurt parliament and Danish June constitution did in 1849, its revised January 1850 constitution did recognize for the first time Protestant and Catholic self-government.[11] The growth of Protestant German transregional self-government in the shape of the biennial Eisenach church conference (1855–1919) influenced this new direction too. Prussia's 'new' church provinces – Schleswig-Holstein, Hanover, Electoral Hesse, Frankfurt am Main and Nassau, gained in 1864 and 1866 – were allowed to govern themselves separately under overall supervision by Berlin. In turn, their particular synodal legislation added weight to this synodal direction.[12] Protestant Prussia remained, after 1871, a loose provincial gathering of churches. Their relationship with the new *Reich* remained undefined. Bismarck preferred this for the sake of religious peace.

Although mocked miserably by Bismarck's *Kulturkampf* legislation, the idea of a constitutional Protestant Church paved the way for the application in 1876 of a 'General Synodal Order' or a 'Church Constitution' for the eight older provinces of the monarchy.[13] This united three new basic constitutional principles in Prussian church government until 1918: self-government by presbytery and synod, administration by Berlin's Upper Consistory (1850), and the continuance of the Prussian king as supreme bishop. If this introduced

---

11 Art. 15: E.R. Huber and W. Huber, eds, *Staat und Kirche im 19. Und 20. Jahrhundert*, (Berlin, 1973) ii, no.11.
12 Hope, *German and Scandinavian Protestantism*, pp. 494–6.
13 Brandenburg, Pomerania, West and East Prussia (united as a single province 1828–79), Posen, and Silesia, Rhineland and Westphalia. Compare this 'constitution' in Huber and Huber, *Staat und Kirche*, ii. no. 449, with the very different Brandenburg-Nuremberg Reformation 'church order' in E. Sehling (ed.), *Die evangelischen Kirchenordnungen des XVI. Jahrhunderts, Bayern: Franken* (Tübingen, 1961), xi. pp. 140–283.

to Prussia exclusive church parties who were divided between positive (conservative) and liberal tendencies, and led to some dubious decisions in doctrinal matters by Berlin's Upper Consistory and General Synod (a questionable Heresy Law appeared in 1910), the habit of increasing synodal meetings brought more common-sense debate to church affairs.[14] Even liturgical matters became less acrimonious. The controversial revised royal rite (1829) was revised by Prussia's new general synod uncontroversially. Its authorized two-volume rite in 1895 offered more choice to Lutheran and Reformed congregations and was quickly accepted everywhere without any element of coercion.[15]

What is very striking about this new growing synodal framework is its very detailed constitutional regulation on paper of the historic parish and its anomalous economic structure. For example, the new church constitution regulated in order, building and maintenance, the collection of church dues, state supervision of parish registration (since the introduction of the register office in 1875), the purchase and sale of church property, the sale of objects which had historic or artistic value, loans, new fees and the changing of fees, new buildings, the siting of graveyards and their use once they became redundant, church collections outside the parish church, and the use of church property for other than official purposes. Parish democracy and the economics of the church went hand in hand. On the other hand, consistories and the Prussian state retained the right, first enunciated in the Prussian Code (1794), to look into parish accounts and use law enforcement if irregularities occurred.

Significant, too, was such regulation in the last third of the century. The first accurate church statistics commissioned by the Eisenach church conference (after 1862), and a generally improving supervision and management of Protestant parish churches and their records throughout Protestant Germany, gave for the first time some sense of the haphazard development of Protestant church patronage and economics since the Reformation. In Prussia, the question of who was responsible for appointing the vicar and for the upkeep of the parish church – private patron, municipality, or parish congregation – became especially acute at this time of rapid Prussian labour mobility and urbanization. It led to a string of bitterly contested lawsuits, particularly in Berlin. The first legal histories of local patronage in the decade before 1914 apologized for poor Prussian recording and unfair appraisal after a century that saw only the very

---

14 Hope, *German and Scandinavian Protestantism*, pp. 575–80.
15 Ibid., p. 554.

gradual distinction in law between parish (*Kirchengemeinde*) and municipality (*Ortsgemeinde*).[16]

Far more serious was a sudden realization by Prussian senior and junior clergy, on the basis of the new church statistics, that they and their church had really lost out in a very rapidly growing national money economy and urban-industrial order. Berlin, in particular, had jumped from 264,590 inhabitants in 1834, to 825,937 in 1871, and 2,040,148 in 1905.[17] Church provision and pastoral care, particularly in a new suburban jungle open to the SPD parole 'religion is a private matter', was as bad in Berlin and in the cities comprising the new Ruhr industrial belt as that in neighbouring urban-industrial Saxony. Specific also to Prussia was its miserably-paid Lutheran and Reformed parish clergy. This had already been laid bare by the Prussian Code, and was the subject of many worried memoranda written by Berlin's senior clergy in the period 1800–20. How could one dare to think of a United Church and a uniform liturgy, given such poverty and low esteem among parish clergy? But little happened subsequently. More money was not an option for ministers of state who disliked the idea of a more self-confident church; such proposals never reached the royal desk – kings should not be disturbed by a poor church. But a basic official Prussian neglect since the Reformation, and huge stipendiary variation in country and town and between province and province, had produced 'starvation' stipends for a majority of parish clergy by 1875.[18] Most eked out a living from the little that came from tithe in a good harvest year, working the glebe when they could, and all relied heavily on occasional fees and freewill offerings. Once in office, they remained there as long as they could. Age, living into one's eighties, paid. Small wonder that most clergy worried much about the loss of fees with the introduction of national civil registration in 1875. Therefore, in this new synodal environment, clergy began to suggest municipal and state subsidies to improve their stipends. If the new Prussian-led nation could improve the salaries of its civil servants after 1871, why could it not do something for the clergy, since they were regarded by Berlin as poorly-paid civil servants?[19]

Moreover, the increasing role of the state in this synodal management of

---

16 See preface in J. Niedner's, *Die Entwicklung des städtischen Patronats in der Mark Brandenburg: Ein Beitrag zur Geschichte der kirchlichen Lokalverwaltung* (Stuttgart, 1911); critical, G. Arndt, 'Die kirchliche Baulast in der Mark Brandenburg' *Jahrbuch für Berlin-Brandenburgische Kirchengeschichte* 13 (1917), pp. 20–1.
17 'Brandenburg II', *Theologische Realencyklopädie* (1977–), p. 119.
18 Hope, *German and Scandinavian Protestantism*, p. 517.
19 O. Janz, *Bürger besonderer Art: Evangelische Pfarrer in Preußen 1850–1914* (Berlin and New York, 1994), pp. 362–83.

church finance raised the question of a church tax levied by the state after consultation with General Synod and Upper Consistory. Prussian state and church laws of 1892, issued for both the old and new church provinces, eventually abolished fees for baptism, marriage and the publication of banns, and replaced them with a state annuity. A Prussian church tax was introduced with a clutch of laws passed during 1903–06. However, the new church tax (*Ortskirchensteuer*, 1905) in Prussia was defined as a subsidiary source of income for a church that received a state subsidy already according to needs. The Prussian state rejected any notion of 'endowment', given a very painful official memory of the cost of Catholic secularization in Prussia in 1810. Ministers argued that the Protestant Church was too much a part of the social fabric for the Prussian state to act simply as a pay office making bequests without strings attached. This 1905 legislation introduced the first regular stipends and pensions for Protestant and Catholic clergy alike in Prussia.[20]

In vocational terms, both Awakening (Protestant religious revival 1800–50) and industrialization proved very influential with the late nineteenth-century Prussian pastorate. If the former gave clergy a new sense of dignity in their calling both as pastor and as celebrants at parish worship, industry and suburb exposed a new pastoral distance to congregations. The latter became apparent in the work of Berlin's new City Mission (1874) under Adolf Stoecker (1835–1909), and in a rapidly proliferating new network of urban diaconates. Stoecker and his experiment with Christian Socialism, needless to say, proved very controversial, but he nevertheless exercised a lasting influence into the Weimar Republic in Berlin's working-class parishes. In turn, this new urban pastoral problem pushed many pastors towards a new practical theology around 1900 associated with 'Liberal Protestantism' and the work of the Evangelical-Social Congress (1890–1945). Even a more radical-minded pastor like Günther Dehn in working-class Moabit (1911–30) noted that much could still be done among his parishioners: they still took rites like baptism and confirmation seriously. As Hugh McLeod has recently written in his thoughtful comparison of working-class religion in Berlin, London and New York before 1914, 'the churches entered people's lives at many points, and few people had a wholly secular view of the world'.[21] Tradition and custom counted here, too. But this new urban-industrial pastoral conscience and commitment was only a beginning in 1914. Clergy families in their poor,

---

20 Hope, *German and Scandinavian Protestantism*, p. 583.
21 Hugh McLeod, *Piety and Poverty: Working-class Religion in Berlin, London and New York* (New York and London, 1996), p. 177.

deferential, and genteel pre-war Prussian churchscapes had little idea of the new national, secular and industrial age that was already upon them. Both Niemöller brothers, Martin (b.1892) and Wilhelm (b.1898), future symbols of Protestant opposition to National Socialism, for instance, drew great spiritual strength from their pious, patriarchal and punctilious clergy home in Elberfeld and Lippstadt.[22] Loyalty to king (emperor) and country (Bismarck's new nation) united father and sons.

War and peace

The Prussian Protestant church leadership and its clergy were thus, like their colleagues elsewhere in Germany, wholly unprepared for the military state and industrial war that followed the lead given in patriotic sermons by Berlin's senior court preachers such as Ernst von Dryander and Bruno Doehring in August 1914. One needs only to dip into Doehring's two-volume popular edition of 1914 war sermons, *Ein feste Burg*, to see an illusory national euphoria that few clergy could subsequently dispense with. Hence their bitter resentment about revolution, defeat and loss of the monarchy in 1917 and 1918. Sentiments like the following expressed in Doehring's preface, '1914 gave our people quite extraordinary religious impulses', and the idealistic little copper prints depicting scenes like the Prussian military at prayer, Frederick the Great and his guards, or Bismarck with Excalibur clad in armour (*Wir Deutsche fürchten Gott sonst nichts auf der Welt*) framing sermons and speeches with headings like 'Fearless and Loyal', 'Heroism', or 'The National Spirit', give this mood away.[23] The just national war bonded theologians and clergy against the reality of there being no national Protestant Church at the German front. Prussia's United Church, based on military church orders of 1832 and 1902, went to war with three other major churches: Lutheran Saxony, Lutheran Württemberg and Protestant Bavaria. The response of Germany's *Landeskirchen*, given a continuing habit of independent action, was woefully inadequate in what became prolonged trench warfare and the huge scale of military operations. Common purpose, like the development of the new fragile pre-war synodal church order, collapsed. Instead, German Protestant churches, especially

---

22 M. Niemöller, *Vom U-Boot zur Kanzel* (Berlin, 1934), p. 208 and *passim*.
23 '*Furchtlos und treu*' (Bruno Doehring), *Ein feste Burg: Predigten und Reden aus eherner Zeit*, (Berlin, 1914) i, pp. 9–13; and '*Heldentum*' (Reinhold Seeberg), and '*Vom nationalen Selbst*' (Kalweit), ibid., ii, pp. 339–53, 354–76.

Prussia's as the largest collection, became mouthpieces for the directives of the Supreme Army Command (1916). But the war economy wrecked the fabric and the finance of the mother churches with demands for organ pipes, church bells, inventory like church plate, and cash from church funds, donations, and bequests for nine war bonds. In November 1918, little was left in the mother churches: few if any bells rang; Protestant Prussia, along with Protestant Germany, collapsed from within.

Most important of all, defeat stifled the chances of picking up the new pre-war synodal order, particularly in Prussia, in what Dibelius (see earlier) had hoped was fresh air. The outcome of the Great War added another massive step backwards to that after the *Kulturkampf*. The new collective Protestant German mentality, the nationalist homiletic 'spirit of 1914', proved a much stronger emotional bond with Prussia's church leadership and its parish clergy than thinking about the place of their 'church' in a new democratic republic inert in religious affairs. Instead, many flocked in 1918 to the new conservative German Nationalist Party (DNVP) as a Protestant Centre Party, and many, within some 15 years, misjudged completely the year 1933. It was certainly not a year of Protestant religious renewal.

August 1914 had begun in Protestant Prussian terms as a fatherland war anyway. East Prussian parishes were also occupied immediately by a destructive Russian army; memories were reawakened of Russian occupation in the Seven Years' War and Napoleon's Grand Army; from there it was not a long way in royalist East Prussia to collective clerical horror at the Russian revolutions of 1917, and a bitter defence of the Prussian/ German Protestant eastern church provinces both against barbaric Russia and an evil new Bolshevik atheist state bent on subversion of the Christian world order.[24] Defence of the exposed Protestant Prussian east against such contamination became more or less inevitably a post-war shibboleth.

Ironic, however, in the longer term was the way essential reorganization after 1917 of the East Prussian church, and replacing almost 25 per cent of its parish clergy lost in the war, turned East Prussia eventually into one of the citadels of the Confessing Church (see below).

In contrast to the defence of Protestant Prussia and Germany in danger, Christian peace initiatives, whether associated with Pope Benedict XV's peace declaration (1 August 1917), or Söderblom's first Uppsala peace

---

24 A. Nietzki (ed.), *Was wir in der Russennot 1914 erlebten. Siebzehn Berichte ostpreußischer Pfarrer* (Königsberg, 1915), and *Zweiundzwanzig neue Berichte ostpreußischer Pfarrer mit 9 Kunstbildern* (Königsberg, 1916). These were published in large editions of *c*.11,000 each to finance repairs to damaged churches. On East Prussian royalism: M. Lackner, *Ein ostpreußischer Geistlicher: Sein Werden und sein Wirken* (Königsberg, 1921), p. 14.

initiative (14 December) outlining the principles behind the Stockholm 'Life and Work' (1925) conference (organizing the practical co-operation of the Christian churches without consideration of doctrinal differences), were stamped by the nationalist Protestant German church press of whatever colour as akin to a betrayal. German delegations, often led by Prussian church leaders, to the first post-war Protestant ecumenical conferences, particularly Stockholm (1925) and Lausanne (1927), thus preferred to conjure up allied injury to Germany, rather than an honest Protestant peaceful sinking of national differences and a search for a meaningful Protestant ethic in a disturbing new world which seemed to have little time for the Christian Church. Few were prepared to see what Hindenburg and Ludendorff's ill-managed military state had done to their Protestant churches. Even Dibelius failed to see 'November 1918' as its consequence, rather than his being freed from his oath to king and Prussian state. He also seemed to learn little from the advice he gave in his popular best-seller. Within less than a decade, Dibelius made the colossal misjudgement both to open and bless the new Nazi parliament at Potsdam on 21 March 1933, and to give a sermon unhappily repeating Dryander's August 1914 text 'if God be for us, who can stand against us?' (Romans 8:31). Dibelius quickly learnt the hard way about the new freedom of the church he preached: Prussia's new Nazi state commissioner promptly sacked him in June.

Prussian Protestantism after 1918, therefore, stood for a church politicized ideologically by the lost war and the loss of its king. The directing royal hand in nineteenth-century Prussian church affairs was still really felt. Loss of the monarchy was thus a 'crime' for many. Also, Prussia reverted to *Land* status, and lost its voice in the 1871 federal council. The unresolved question of Prussia within Germany seemed to suggest a new provincialism. Prussia's 'new' church provinces (1864–66) were hived off in a series of laws passed between December 1920 and April 1921.[25] The loose order of the Old-Prussian Union Church thus returned with important boundary modifications (see below) to being in 1924 the eight church provinces of the period 1817–66, with the Rhineland and Westphalia managing once again special constitutional status. The terms of the Versailles peace positioned Protestant Prussia also so much closer to the Russian Bolshevik revolution, and unreformed Prussian rural church patronage next door to the new national smallholder republics, Poland and the three Baltic states. They cleared out the old Lutheran German ruling class: the baronial descendants of the Teutonic knights and other aristocratic German landholders. A deep sense of hurt connected with such losses held sway. Could Protestant

---

25 Huber and Huber, *Staat und Kirche*, iv, no. 279.

Prussians honestly serve a democratic republic 'neutral' in religious affairs? Prussia was moreover a 'free state' after November 1920, and was governed until von Papen's *coup d'état* of July 1932 by a coalition of SPD, German Democratic Party and Centre governed by three socialist ministers (Hirsch, Severing and Braun) bent on creating more responsible democratic government.[26]

The political answer was more Prussian Protestant support for the DNVP, and in church affairs the hotly contested introduction during the years 1919–22 of another self-governing Protestant church under a general synod. A new 'Constitution for the Evangelical Church of the Old-Prussian Union' (29 September 1922), confirmed by the Prussian state on 8 April 1924, came into force on 1 October for its eight old church provinces in order of size: Brandenburg, Prussian Saxony, Silesia, Westphalia, Rhine, East Prussia, Pomerania and a new 'Border Mark' (see below). Berlin's Protestant population, only 75 per cent of the total with the inclusion of its outlying suburbs in 1920, reached 3,039,390 in 1925. Thus, larger than any of the other eight, Berlin confirmed its continuing role as an almost special Prussian church province. Protestants remained minorities in Catholic 'Upper Silesia' 10 per cent, Rhineland 29 per cent, Westphalia 46 per cent. In numerical strength, Prussia remained the largest Protestant land in the Weimar Republic (18,700,000).[27]

But how difficult it was to change old Prussian ways; to balance necessary reform with provincial church tradition, which many felt had been sorely hurt. Loss of the monarch implied finding a replacement for his role as supreme bishop. A fiction was quickly found. It was argued that this authority returned to the Church in November 1918: to all of its members who were invested with the right to elect a legislative assembly. But the church party lists in the constituent elections (1922) showed the weight of tradition: 140 to those who stood for 'Confession', 50 to the middle, and only 19 to the liberals (12 'above party').[28] On paper, however, the 1922 constitution took the congregation (*Gemeinde*) as the source of Protestant Prussian self-government far more seriously than either the revised constitution of 1850 or the general synod of 1876.[29] Quite distinctive were the very detailed 165 articles defining offices and procedures. They bore

---

26 On democratic staffing, see A. Glees, 'Albert C. Grzesinski and the Politics of Prusssia 1926–1930', *English Historical Review* 89 (1974), 814–34.
27 Borg, *Old-Prussian Church*, pp. xii–xiii.
28 K. Kupisch, 'Die deutschen Landeskirchen im 19. und 20. Jahrhundert', in K. D. Schmidt and E. Wolf (eds), *Die Kirche in ihrer Geschichte* (Göttingen, 1966), iv, pp. 111–12.
29 '*Die Kirche baut sich aus der Gemeinde auf*', Art. 4 (1), Huber and Huber, *Staat und Kirche*, iv. no. 280.

little resemblance to *Obrigkeit* (the high authority of a prince or town council) and the vivid soteriological language contained in Prussia's Reformation church orders. Modern constitutional prose sought to secure the voice of the layman. Here the past was past. Provincial synods, consistories and general superintendents became equal partners under a legislative General Synod (two-thirds lay; one-third clergy), a church senate as supreme bishop, and a new solely administrative Senior Consistory (*Oberkirchenrat*). But what did such synodal progress mean in this emotional environment mourning the loss of monarchy? In the passionate debates behind these paragraphs, the old issues resurfaced, such as confession – in what sense could a people's church (*Volkskirche*) be a church with a confession; eligibility in 'church' elections; the ratio of laity to clergy in synods; the appointment of clergy (private patronage was still widespread); the status of general superintendents – but here the question whether to have 'bishops' remained unresolved. It proved too hot an issue.

The financial regulation of disestablishment which this constitution presented was extremely controversial, too.[30] The pre-war question of how to pay for a Reformation church and clergy stipends in a modern parliamentary nation state returned with a vengeance to these eight Prussian church provinces. Church tax seemed very insecure. The growth of the church's social commitment before and during the war, the enormous cost of the war to churches and parishes and inflation worried many clergy. Would the new free state also allow the new church tax to continue? The state was no longer Christian. Would the church have to make a treaty with the state to secure its material status in future? If it was luck that the Weimar Constitution (article 137) regarded the Protestant Church as a public corporation with the right to raise taxes to pay for its clergy as officials (Prussia reaffirmed its 1905 legislation as law in August 1920), its open position on 'state contributions' (article 173) was less clear. Here the Prussian state was generous in December 1920 in covering the deficits of poor congregations. However, the way inflation ate into income from church property and church tax meant that such legal regulation constantly raised the question of adequacy. This was to some extent regulated by a law of April 1928, which assured state contributions slightly higher than in 1914, and a law passed in May 1929 reassessing the amount of church tax. And how did one pay for this constitution's implied large and cumbersome church administration? A compromise of sorts was reached in parliament with a law of October 1924. The state obliged with a commitment to

---

30 Huber and Huber, *Staat und Kirche*, iv. nos 119, 124, 127, 132–34; commentary in Borg, *Old-Prussian Church*, pp. 116–22.

paying an adjustable annual lump sum to cover the cost of church administration, salaries, pensions and benefits. Officials in church administration finally threw off their status as Prussian civil servants. But sounder church finance implied nevertheless political scrutiny of some kind. The spectre of parliamentary control over higher church officials apparent in Prussian parliamentary debate dominated by SPD and Centre for many clergy forced them in the direction of a future treaty with the Prussian state. Could a treaty be made between a disestablished church and a 'free state'? Church opinion divided bitterly once again. Nevertheless, an accord was felt as very urgent, given an expanding Catholic Church: 1923 had seen the appointment of a bishop-coadjutor in Berlin (bishop, 1930) for the apostolic vicariate Brandenburg and Pomerania (1921), and after a Prussian concordat (June 1929), the restoration of Aachen as a bishopric and the elevation of Breslau and Paderborn to archbishoprics. A controversial Protestant Church Treaty of May 1931 swiftly followed, but it left unresolved the disputed right of the state to influence appointments to church government.[31]

The establishment of this new democratic church order could only be halting. These eight self-conscious church provinces found it very difficult to find a home in the Prussian free state and in the republic. Berlin's Senior Consistory failed to stand by democratic Prussia in crisis in July 1932. Aggrieved local Prussian pride stood in the way. In particular, Protestant Prussia was worst affected of all Protestant German churches by the Versailles peace. A new 'Polish Corridor' giving the new Polish republic access to the Baltic sea implied the loss of 75 per cent of West Prussia (language in 1910 census: 59 per cent German; 32 per cent Polish), the reconstitution of Lutheran Danzig (95 per cent German) as a Free City, and separation from the old Prussian Lutheran heart, East Prussia. Posen (Prussian since 1815) and the Memel district went too, though the loss of West Prussia and Posen was eventually compensated for with the creation in December 1922 of the Border Mark (*Grenzmark*) with a General Superintendency in Schneidemühl. Silesia was divided (1922). Even if these reconstituted Prussian provinces became more visibly German-speaking and Protestant, their exposed borderland status and the Polish Corridor produced a profound identity crisis among local Protestant clergy and parishioners.

In the rural social order of these eastern provinces dominated by the patronage of the large estate and its deferential order, the result was a preference for the DNVP and likeminded political groupings demanding border revision in favour of Germany. Most clergy were still born in the

---

31 Huber and Huber, *Staat und Kirche*, iv, no. 309.

home province or in adjacent provinces, and most followed father's footsteps. Pomerania, and western and eastern Prussia were also provinces where to take cloth was not rated highly; social occasions in the manors rarely included pastors. Clergy could say little to landowners. The patron's exclusive right to name the parish clergyman meant favouring candidates of a conservative political persuasion. This political custom in this new climate of official disestablishment worried consistories enough to feel that church 'neutrality' was in question. Post-war visitations noted into the 1930s 'great devotion' to the old black, white and red flag. Reports in Pomerania repeated that 'the patron and pastor were, in the villages at any rate, predominant in the congregation. What they precribed was not only done; it was right and good. The parish councils were, in most cases, hardly responsible bodies'.[32] Republican visitations really showed that war and revolution hardly changed the old values of deference, worthy causes personified in countesses supporting *Innere Mission* work, the customary round of family evenings and visits, and singing the praises of the intact village community in the clergy-led 'village-church movement' (*Dorfkirchenbewegung*). Kurt Scharf, one of the future leaders of the Confessing Church, noted as pastor in Friesack in Brandenburg (1928–31) how a neighbouring vicar, leader of the local village-church movement, even recommended to his colleagues texts from the Brothers Grimm fairy-tales like *Snow White* and *Briar Rose* for their Sunday sermons. Such a superstitious lead could only strengthen at a time of rapidly rising unemployment a receptiveness to the attractions of the Nazi Labour Service and Hitler Youth.[33] Small wonder, then, that the nationalist political ticket, the DNVP anti-Bolshevik ticket (its subversion of Christian marriage and schooling), Versailles as a sell-out, and anti-Catholicism fuelled by great anxiety about Catholic advances next door in the new Polish smallholder republic, should be so persuasive.

Protestant Prussia thus became a new testing ground also in Protestant German church affairs: between its new, but easily bruised, democratic Protestant church order and this post-war Protestant neo-Conservatism, and between the historic plural order of Protestant German provincial churches held together loosely in a new republican federation (1922) and a Nazi centralist *Reichskirche* in the four decisive years 1931–34.

However, it was certainly not an easy task to destroy the new Prussian

---

32 S. Baranowski, 'Continuity and contingency: agrarian elites, conservative institutions and East Elbia in modern German history', *Social History* 12 (1987), 294.
33 K. Scharf, 'Kirchlicher Widerstand im Dritten Reich – Bekennende Kirche', in M. Richter (ed.), *Kirche in Preußen: Gestalten und Geschichte* (Stuttgart, 1983), pp. 178–9; K. Scharf, *Widerstehen und Versöhnen: Rückblicke und Ausblicke* (Stuttgart, 1987), pp. 69–73.

democratic framework of disestablished church and free state. Papen's political destruction of democratic Prussia by a coup in July 1932 had to be completed by a two-stage coup in its constitutional Protestant Church. The Prussian church elections of 13 November 1932 saw the engineered successful installation of the Nazi German Christians (*c.* one-third) by the Gauleiter of the new *Ostmark*, Wilhelm Kube. He was one of the few Nazis who really knew this new post-war Protestant church order, since he was a member of the parish council in Berlin's Gethsemane parish and of Berlin's district city synod III. These church election results showed clearly the provincial profile and preferences mentioned above. In the new Border Mark, in East Prussia and in Pomerania, nearly 50 per cent voted for the German Christians; in contrast, the old synodal tradition of Westphalia and the Rhineland seemed to dictate a very measured response – only a fifth; Brandenburg, Prussian Saxony, Silesia and Berlin returned below a third, but Berlin's rural hinterland well over a third.[34] But this was only a start. The Nazis had to use the stratagem of exploiting loopholes in the 1931 Prussian Church Treaty and murky intrigue of the kind hidden behind President Hindenburg's back. In brief, Hermann Kapler (the very worried and frustrated president of the Prussian Senior Consistory) begged the Prussian church senate in June 1933 to be retired. This gave the new Nazi Prussian minister of church affairs, Bernhard Rust (wits playing with military vocabulary like armoury and rapid mobilization dubbed Rust's love of swift directives a 'Rüst' in time), the chance to claim illegality because the 'political clause 7' of the church treaty ruled that the church senate was bound to ask the government whether there were reservations of a political nature against the proposed candidate.[35] Rust's henchman, August Jäger, head of the church section in his ministry, was promptly installed as a state commissioner for all of Prussia's provincial churches. The floodgates opened: Jäger sacked the Prussian church leadership, including Dibelius, and ordered the SA to occupy the Prussian church press offices and intimidate the various church associations and local synods. Elected church representatives were replaced by German Christians. But even then, President Hindenburg felt he had to call Hitler to halt Jäger's terror tactics for fear of dividing the nation.[36] It really needed the engineered 70 per cent return in the national church elections of 23 July to install a German Christian leadership in Protestant Prussia excepting Westphalia. The disestablished Old-Prussian Union Church thus came to an end a year after the Prussian free state; it

---

34 K. Scholder, *Kirchen und das Dritte Reich* (Frankfurt am Main/Berlin, 1977) i, p. 273.
35 Art. 7, Huber and Huber, *Staat und Kirche*, iv, no. 309.
36 Hindenburg's letter to Hitler, 30 June 1933, ibid., no. 410.

was integrated officially with the new Nazi *Reichskirche* on 1 March 1934.

Nevertheless, Protestant Prussia's transregional character made it easier than elsewhere for a Protestant church opposition to a centralist *Reichskirche* to build. Already in July 1933, clergy in the Rhineland and Westphalia organized against the local German Christians, and Reformed colleagues established a so-called 'Coetus' in September; in opposition to the introduction of the April 1933 Aryan paragraph by the Nazified Prussian general synod (5 September), Martin Niemöller called into being the Pastors' Emergency League (soon, very roughly, 6,000 pastors: a third of Protestant German clergy). This paved the way for the first 'Confessing Synods' in January 1934, and the appearance of a 'Confessing Church' in Westphalian Barmen in late May 1934 and in Berlin-Dahlem (Niemöller's upper-class parish) in late October. Twelve Prussian synods followed until the last held in Breslau in 1943. Under Barth's influential hand, mainly young clergy organized as a 'brotherhood', and they espoused a Reformed ecclesiology in sharp contrast to any idea of episcopacy which Dibelius might have entertained. To this extent, the Prussian-led Confessing Church was a constitutional child of the Prussian presbytery and synod in the church constitution of 1924. Kurt Scharf (see above), in his humble and understated way, called this a very halting 'process of learning step by step'. A new clergy generation in Prussia learnt once again to respect the visible church: church organization, its authorized prayer, liturgy and explanation of the Bible; also, especially in these years of hardship and unemployment, that parishioners in need and care of the underprivileged took precedence over any theological fashion. This opened a way to the modern ecumenical movement, which injured Prussian and German Protestant pride had prevented in the 1920s.[37]

However, this was a religious renewal that happened not only in Barmen and Berlin-Dahlem, but also in distant Königsberg, given the reorganization of the East Prussian church after 1917 by general superintendent Paul Gennrich. The appointment of the Silesian, Hans-Joachim Iwand, as inspector to Königsberg's Lutheran seminary, the Lutherheim, in 1923, and the Elberfelder, Julius Schniewind, to the university as professor of New Testament studies in 1925, was seminal. They taught this new generation of Lutheran ordinands that Hegelian 'spiritual renewal' (*geistige Erneuerung*) called for by the new Nazified German university theology had nothing to do with the Greek 'renewing of the Holy Ghost' in Titus 3:5. The Old and New Testaments belonged together; Hebrew was just as important as Greek and Latin in an ordinand's training; daily prayer and still meditation were

---

37 Scharf, 'Kirchlicher Widerstand im Dritten Reich', in Richter (ed.), *Kirchen in Preußen*, pp. 180–1.

the foundation of a Christian office responsible to a visible church in its surrounding society.³⁸

Whether one should couple the adjective 'Prussian' with Protestantism and emphasize it, was a question which this very small and scattered, but nevertheless active, opposition learnt to ask the hard way of experience in these terrible years. It happened by circumstance that they experienced as Christian individuals in a Prussian churchscape what Protestantism under a racial dictatorship meant. Bonhoeffer was well aware of this.³⁹ The Confessing Church, however, polarized Protestant Prussia far more than was the case elsewhere in Protestant Germany. The remnants of the Old-Prussian Union Church after its official destruction by the Nazis in 1934 vanished eventually during the Second World War. There remained the individual witness of some of its members as martyrs after 20 July 1944. What actually happened in the 1940s is only now beginning to be written up.

---

38 N. Hope, 'Zum heutigen Verständnis des protestantischen und katholischen Widerstandes in Großbritannien', in J. Kuropka (ed.), *Clemens August Graf von Galen Menschenrechte, Widerstand, Euthanasie, Neubeginn* (Münster, 1998), p. 158.

39 E. Bethge, 'Dietrich Bonhoeffer – Widerstand in preußischer Tradition?', in Richter (ed.), *Kirche in Preußen*, pp. 107–25.

PART FOUR

Prussia, The State and Prussianism

CHAPTER TEN

Democratic Prussia in Weimar Germany, 1919–33

HAGEN SCHULZE
(Translated by PHILIP G. DWYER)

An accurate description of the nature of the Prussian state would take into account several attributes – Prussia was, depending on the standpoint of the observer, a military state or a state based on the rule of law (*Rechtsstaat*), a bureaucratic state or a Junker state. Other descriptions of the Prussian state, however, immediately appear strange if not absurd – Prussia as a parliamentary or a party state? Certainly, Prussian political parties, and with them Prussian parliamentarism, had existed since the Revolution of 1848 even if at first in an embryonic form, but precisely as the fruit of revolution and as such, as long as the monarchy existed, as a concession to the *Zeitgeist* tolerated by those who had state power, constantly under the threat of being overthrown by that state, and domesticated through a monstrously unjust three-tiered electoral system. Another revolution was needed, the November Revolution of 1918, in order to help bring to power what, for old Prussian sensibilities, was such an intrinsically foreign element in the state. The political parties that, on the basis of elections to a Prussian constitutional regional assembly on 26 January 1919, grasped the reigns of power were the Social Democrats, the Catholic Centre Party and the left-wing Liberals. They accordingly brought about the succinct recognition in the lead article of a conservative newspaper, the *Kreuzzeitung*, of 'finis borussiae', that is, the end of Prussia.[1]

This Weimar coalition, consisting of the Social Democratic Party or SPD, the Catholic Centre Party and the German Democrats or DDP, ruled

---

1 *Neue Preußische Zeitung (Kreuzzeitung)*, 91, 21 February 1919.

Prussia under the energetic leadership of the Social Democrat minister-president Otto Braun (1920–1932/33),[2] with few exceptions, right up to 1932 and, legally, even up to 25 March 1933. It demonstrated a stability that was the backdrop to the continual crises of the German Reich government, which struck the contemporary observer and which enabled democratic Prussia to be what, according to the will of the 1848 Liberals, it should have become, and the opposite of what it became in 1871: a support for the continued existence of the state as well as the constitutional order of the Reich. For what was the Reich but nothing more than 'three-thirds of the same thing of which Prussia made up two-thirds'?[3]

Certainly, Golo Mann's aphoristically short description of the relations between Prussia and the Reich needs to be qualified for the period after 1918, not so much, however, because of the diminished constitutional position which Prussia held in the Weimar Constitution in comparison to its Bismarckian predecessor. The Prussian vote in the *Reichsrat* (the parliamentary representation of the German states) was restricted to two-fifths of the overall vote, in spite of the much higher proportion of Prussia's population. What is more, the Prussian vote was split – half its deputies being briefed by the Prussian state ministry and half by the provincial assemblies. Much more crucial was the transfer of the financial autonomy of the states to the Reich. As a result, Prussia became dependent in a number of ways on the establishment of the budget and, in a crisis situation like the one that occurred at the beginning of the 1930s, was effortlessly pacified by the government of the Reich with the help of the financial screw. The most important restriction on Prussia's position in the Reich, however, lay in the complete separation of the government of the Reich from the Prussian state government. Prussia was thereby denied any institutionalized influence, with the exception of the double mandate in the Reichstag and in the Prussian *Landtag* (state parliament) while, on the other hand, the leadership of the Reich not only controlled the situation financially with respect to the *Landtag* but, with the help of the army (Reichswehr) and the full presidential powers according to article 48 of the Weimar Constitution, could also declare a state of emergency. Carl Schmitt's understanding of the situation was right on the nose when he stated that whoever controlled the state of emergency had the last word, and this was shown to be true when, on 20 July 1932, the Papen

---

2   See Hagen Schulze, *Otto Braun oder Preußens demokratische Sendung. Eine Biographie* (Berlin, Frankfurt am Main and Vienna, 1977); Eric D. Kohler, *Otto Braun, Prussia and Democracy, 1871–1955*, Dissertation (Stanford University 1971)
3   Golo Mann, 'Rezension von Otto Braun "Von Weimar zu Hitler"', in Golo Mann, ed., *Geschichte und Geschichten* (Frankfurt am Main 1972), pp. 50f.

government carried out a putsch against the legitimate Prussian government.[4]

On the other hand, however, republican Prussia remained a respectable concentration of power within the Reich as a whole. Above all, there was the existing dominance of the Prussian administration, which included almost two-thirds of the Reich down to the level of the district (*Kreis*), while the Reich, with the exception of a few branches of the administration like the ministry of employment, the post, customs and finance, was simply a figurehead in the shape of ministries and their subordinate departments present in Berlin, but whose domestic policy was incapable of functioning without Prussian co-operation. This was especially the case for the Prussian police, which, besides the Reichswehr, constituted the most important instrument of power in the Weimar Republic. On top of that was the Prussian education administration whose influence dominated the whole German education system. Finally, there was the supervision of the Prussian communes and the Prussian administrative commission in the municipalities (*Gemeinde*), which controlled the largest part of the German communal administration. If Prussia had a disproportionate influence over the material constitutional structure of the Reich on account of its purely territorial predominance, its influence over the legislation of the Reich accordingly far exceeded that of the other states. Despite the limitations that Prussia's position within the *Reichsrat* was subjected to, and despite the reduction in the role of the *Reichsrat* in comparison to the Bismarckian *Bundesrat*, Prussia could counteract the legislature of the Reich with only a few allied votes. Certainly the Reichstag could reject the objections of the *Reichsrat* with a two-thirds majority, but to bring about such a majority was an achievement that became all the more difficult for the government of the Reich as both the extreme right- and left-wing parties became stronger and the fragmentation of political parties became greater. On top of that, no law to change the constitution against Prussia's voice in the *Reichsrat* could come about because here, too, a two-thirds majority was needed.

All of these conditions left Prussia *sui generis* a power in the Weimar Republic far beyond the political influence of the other states. The leader of the Stahlhelm, Franz Seldte, expressed this fact on the occasion of a petition for a referendum for the dissolution of the Prussian state parliament in April 1931 with the formula: 'Whoever controls Prussia controls Germany'.[5] That the parties that made up the republican coalition 'had' Prussia was one of the most important stabilizing factors in the first German democracy; that the Weimar Republic nevertheless survived almost 14 years should to a considerable degree be attributed to the durability of the Prussian

---

4   Carl Schmitt, *Die Diktatur*, 2nd edn (Munich and Leipzig, 1928), p. 17.
5   According to Schulthess's *Europäischer Geschichtskalender* (Munich, 1930), p. 200.

government's coalition. The fall of Prussia preceded the definitive failure of the first German democratic experiment. 'Prussia as Guarantor of the Continued Existence of the German Republic' was the title of an interview the Prussian minister-president Otto Braun gave a French journalist at the beginning of December 1926, and this wording was programmatic.[6] Behind it lay not only the concept of a strong and reliable Prussia that could in times of crisis like 1923 become a solid support to the government of the Reich and through its existence constitute an effective concentration of power (in a strategic sense) for democratic and republican forces, but also, over and above this, lay the vision of a centre from which democratic ideas would radiate and thereby gain a firm footing throughout all of Germany. At the SPD party convention in Kiel in 1927, Rudolf Hilferding, member of the executive committee and leading theorist of the SPD, gave a speech setting out some basic principles for the party in the Republic, and in which he sketched out the current position of the SPD combined with a revised economic theory. He thereby undertook the only serious attempt to re-establish the unity of praxis and theory in German social democracy as a result of which he could refer to Prussia as the shining model of democratic and social democratic governmental organization.[7] In retrospect, Otto Braun also believed at the beginning of 1932 that the paradigmatic task of the new Prussia was almost fulfilled, writing that

> In twelve years Prussia, once the state of the crassest class domination and the political deprivation of working classes, the state of the centuries' old feudal Junker caste hegemony, has been transformed into a republican-people's state. Certainly not everything could be transformed in those twelve years [...] but much was carried out that would have a lasting influence.[8]

The transformation of the pillars of monarchical authority

Certainly, the end result of Prussia's 'domestic policy' was not insignificant, especially in comparison with other German states and not least in

---

6 The German translation of an approximately dated article from the Parisian newspaper, the *Petit Journal*, in Geheimes Staatsarchiv Berlin [GstA], Nachlaß [NL] Braun D/33.
7 *Protokoll des Parteitages der Sozialdemokratischen Partei Deutschlands, abgehalten in Kiel, 11–27 May 1927* (Berlin 1927), pp. 180f.
8 Otto Braun, 'Vor den Entscheidungen!' *Das Reichsbanner*, 8, 20 February 1932.

comparison with the Reich, but it remained very mixed. This was particularly the case in those areas which were considered the central problems of democratic reform policy by the democratic public. The transformation of the pillars of monarchical authority – the civil service, the police and justice – into reliable supports of the new system went painfully slowly ahead. Anyone who rejected out of hand smashing the old state structures – which in a highly differentiated administrative state like Prussia would certainly have led to the collapse of the authority of the state – and instead tackled the changes with the means at the disposal of a state under the rule of law, had to be prepared for a comprehensive process to last at least a generation. This was one more reason to attribute paramount importance to the stability and constancy of the political leadership.

The police

Reforms were most likely to succeed where the least amount of conflicting interest and opinions had to be reconciled and where the executive could act without the aggravating means of an informed parliamentary opinion. This is shown, for example, with the police. Reform of police personnel was comparatively unproblematic because it could essentially be carried out within the domain of the ministry of the interior which, with the exception of a few months in 1921 when the DDP politician, Alexander Dominicus, was head of the ministry, remained in the hands of social democratic ministers. If one adds that the energetic left-wing republican, Wilhelm Abegg, who headed the police department within the ministry of the interior, deliberately filled posts with experts and specialists who belonged to the parties of the coalition government,[9] and that an especially high percentage of the political civil servants in the police administration, the chiefs of police and their representatives were Social Democrats,[10] then the most important prerequisites for a reasonably rapid and thorough personnel reform of the Prussian police were present. Article 129 paragraph 1 of the Weimar Constitution, which guaranteed the 'well acquired rights' of civil servants and which prevented monarchical police officials and officers from

---

9 Grzesinski to Braun, 21 March 1930, Internationales Institut für Sozialgeschichte Amsterdam [IISG], [NL] Grzesinski/204.
10 Of the 30 Prussian Police Presidents as of 1 January 1928, 15 belonged to the SPD, five to the Centre, four to the DDP, three to the DVP, and three were without political affiliation: Grzesinski in Preußentag der Sozialdemokratischen Partei Deutschlands on 14 February 1928 in Berlin, edited by the executive committee of the SPD, typed manuscript, in IISG Amsterdam, p. 18.

being readily removed from office, proved to be a considerable hindrance to reform. Nevertheless, at the beginning of 1928, the interior minister, Albert Grzesinski (1926–1930), could refer to the fact that a quarter of the Prussian police-officer corps consisted of former non-commissioned police officers and that a further 12 per cent over the previous ten years had been promoted in approximately the same percentages from elementary, secondary and grammar schools – that is, the police officer corps possessed a social mobility and permeability that went far beyond the development of the civil service, not to speak of the Reichswehr.[11] Contrary to the recruiting basis of the Reichswehr, the new generation of police was judged not only from the general standpoint of their physical and spiritual suitability, but also according to whether 'their past behaviour offered a guarantee that they would work in a positive sense for the state'.[12] Accordingly, the Prussian police were regarded as a reliable instrument of the new state leadership that, according to Otto Braun, was 'competent and willing' to 'put down any violent attempt' at overthrow.[13]

Nevertheless, question marks still hovered over the police. After all, at the beginning of 1928, 45 per cent of the Prussian police officer corps consisted of former reserve officers in the old army, a considerable number of which were organized into the 'Dillenburger Verband', which was close to right-wing sympathizers.[14] Above all, the influence of these police officers contributed to the relative political neutrality of the police force, which the Prussian government parties often complained about and which, as the Social Democrat deputy Ernst Hamburger once critically remarked, put the 'supporters of the democratic Republic and its opponents' on the same level.[15] Also, towards the end of the 1920s, complaints about the bad relations between police sergeants and the majority of the officers on account of the 'military tone' which dominated the police squads increased (the complaints came from the republican Schrader-Verband in which the majority of lower police civil servants were organized). This led, it was said, to an increase in the number of communist and national-socialist

---

11 Ibid., p. 17f. Cf. the Denkschrift of the Prussian Minister of the Interior 'Wegweiser durch die Polizei' 8 January 1927, in Drucksachen des Preußischen Landtags [PrLT], 2. Wahlperiode, No. 4880.
12 Preußen 1932. Politik in Stichworten. Edited by the Pressestelle des Preußischen Staatsministeriums (Berlin, 1932), p. 96.
13 In an interview with the Berlin representative of the Parisian newspaper, the *Petit Journal*, beginning of December 1926. See n 4.
14 Grzesinski, in Preußentag, pp. 17f; and a written communication from former General Major of the police A.L. Ratcliffe to the author, 8 December 1972.
15 Ernest Hamburger in a letter to author, 12 December 1972.

sympathizers among police officers.[16] As a consequence, one can only speak of a limited 'unreserved' reliability of the Prussian police in a republican-democratic sense. The general radicalization, especially at the beginning of the 1930s, also detrimentally affected part of the Prussian police force and even led the Organization of Prussian Police Officers to protest in 1931 to the minister of the interior against the transfer of a police major for political reasons – he voted in the Stahlhelm's referendum in favour of the dissolution of the Prussian *Landtag* – formally announcing to him that he ran the risk of losing the confidence of the police officer corps.[17] In retrospect, the Social Democratic member of the Prussian *Landtag*, Ernest Hamburger, summed things up when he said: 'The democratisation of the police was not fully achieved before 1932 [...] I would say: If we had had another twenty years, we would have had a fully democratic police force.'[18]

When something as relatively easy as transforming the Prussian police into a reliable instrument of the new state was so difficult to deal with, imagine how difficult it was to republicanize the Prussian bureaucracy! There is no doubt that the Prussian government was not really up to the task.

The civil service

The root of the problem lay in the difficulty the revolutionaries of 1918 faced, on the one hand, in maintaining a functioning administrative apparatus but, on the other, in not having at their disposal an approximately satisfactory replacement for a socially and politically homogeneous higher administrative personnel.[19] As the behaviour of some of the *Oberpräsidenten* and *Regierungspräsidenten* (the presidents of provinces and government districts) who remained in office during the Kapp putsch (a right wing *coup d'état*, 13–17 March 1919) demonstrated, next to technical administrative efficiency, political loyalty, too, was one of the irrefutable requirements which the civil service had to adopt. This was an area that was criminally neglected during the office of the Prussian interior minister, Wolfgang Heine (1919–20), and was dealt with in a manner required by the necessity

---

16 The chairman of the Schrader-Verband to Braun (no date), relative to the election results of the Berlin police of 14 September 1930, with a list of complaints in IISG Amsterdam, NL Braun/301.
17 C. Severing, *Mein Lebensweg*, 2 vols (Cologne, 1950), ii. p. 295.
18 Verbal communication to the author from Ernest Hamburger, 5 October 1972.
19 See W. Runge, *Politik und Beamtentum. Die Demokratisierung der politischen Beamten in Preußen zwischen 1918 und 1933* (Stuttgart, 1965), pp. 44f.

of the moment by the new Social Democratic interior minister, Carl Severing (1921–26, 1930–32). The political positions of the civil service – that is, principally the state secretaries, the state ministers and the presidents of the provinces (*Oberpräsidenten*), government districts (*Regierungspräsidenten*) and the police (*Polizeipräsidenten*) as well as those of the smaller districts or 'circles' (*Landräte*) – were then filled to a greater extent by the representatives of the governmental parties: the 'Severing system' was thus established.[20]

It was in the nature of things that, in this way, a strong party-political element was introduced into the upper levels of the civil service. This was unavoidable because it was a period in which the constitutional, politically reliable top civil servants were part of a civil service whose heart was not close to parliamentary democracy; top civil servants could hardly be recognized other than through their party membership. The drawback to the 'Severing system' was (and even this was unavoidable) that it opened a wide field of official patronage to the government parties, first, because candidates outside the ministry of the interior had overall control, as Severing wrote, over the details of the 'non-official positions' – that is, parties and trade unions – and second, because personnel policy was quickly recognized as an instrument of power by the coalition parties and was intensively pursued so that in practice a part of the competence of the personnel policy of the ministers of the interior and finance came under the influence of party executives.[21] Only the proportional balance between the personal desires of three, sometimes four, governmental coalition parties, which was absolutely necessary for the cohesion of the coalition, prevented an arbitrary, American-style policy of patronage and guaranteed a certain political diversity within the framework of a constitutionally conforming party direction at the top levels of the Prussian administrative machinery.[22]

A decade after the November Revolution, the end result of the republicanization of the Prussian administration was on the whole unbalanced. On the plus side, there was the political understanding which existed between the top levels of the administration and the Prussian state government and its policies. In 1929, of the 540 political civil servants in the Prussian state's general and internal administration, not including the ministries, 107 belonged to the SPD, 112 to the Centre, 95 to the DVP (German People's Party) and 72 to the DDP. The political orientation

---

20 See Schulze, *Otto Braun* pp. 303f.
21 Severing, *Lebensweg*, i. p. 284.
22 E. Pikart, 'Preußische Beamtenpolitik 1918–1933', *Vierteljahreshefte für Zeitgeschichte* 6 (1958), pp. 119f; H. P. Ehni, 'Zum Parteienverhältnis in Preußen 1918–1932' *Archiv für Sozialgeschichte* 11 (1971), pp. 241f.

among the heads of the middle levels of Prussian civil service was even more clear: of 11 presidents of provinces (*Oberpräsidenten*), nine belonged to parties of the Weimar coalition and two to the German People's Party; of the 32 government district presidents (*Regierungspräsidenten*), 21 were members of the SPD, the Centre or the DDP, while nine belonged to the DVP, one was a German National and one partyless.[23] That these far-reaching changes in the structure of the upper strata of the bureaucracy were possible, without impairing the efficiency of the Prussian administration, was a not inconsiderable achievement of Carl Severing and even more his successor, Albert Grzesinski, under whose aegis the politicization of the bureaucracy was energetically pursued from 1926 after it had almost come to a standstill in the last years of Severing's office.[24]

On the minus side of things, there were considerable disadvantages and failings. There were, for example, the accusations of the opposition that the governmental parties were carrying on a sinecure economy in order to provide their members with wages and pensions,[25] a theme that in the course of the years developed into the principal motif of the right-wing criticism of the policies of the Braun government such as that of the German National deputy, Eldor Borck, who before the *Landtag* on 15 October 1930 spoke of: 'The big wigs and the political renegades of the Prussian civil service.'[26] It became an extremely effective means of agitating against the Weimar democracy and found an especially disastrous echo with the middle classes who remained aloof from republican ideas.[27] The expression *Drang zur Futterkrippe* (push to the trough) was malicious and incorrect; in effect, little or no financial gain was to be had from the Prussian public service. Trade union or party functionaries who were called to administrative positions as a rule lost part of their income.[28] The fact that some former Prussian and Reich ministers – Konrad Haenisch, Gustav Noske or Hermann Lüdemann – were considered for the position of regional or governmental president may very well have also been an attempt to guarantee their material well-being, but there were numerous examples of this Prussian administrative tradition from the monarchical era. Moreover, given the modest personnel reservoir, the Republic could hardly afford not to use the technical

---

23 Runge, *Politik*, pp. 200f.
24 Ibid., pp. 143 and 146f.
25 Richter (DVP) in Sitzungsberichte und Drucksachen der Verfassungsgebenden Preußischen Landesversammlung (1919–1921) [PrLVers.], 11 July 1919, Sp.3401.
26 PrLT, 3. Wahlperiode, 15 October 1930, Sp. 14971.
27 K. D. Bracher, *Die Auflösung der Weimarer Republik. Eine Studie zum Problem des Machtverfalls in der Demokratie*, 5th edn (Villingen, 1971), pp. 167f.
28 Runge, *Politik*, pp. 52f.

administrative and political experience of former ministers.[29] But, in the words of Theodor Eschenburg, that 'the interests of a massive, particular patronage system with the goal of obtaining information for party ends and of influencing decisions in the spirit of the party'[30] played an important role in Prussia's personnel policy was obvious and caused ill feeling above all in those circles that were under the illusion that old regime Prussia's civil service was apathetic, something which was never a reality.[31]

However, the resolution of the problem of the modest personnel reservoir of republican forces, just as much as service patronage, would have been only a question of time if a serious failing had not intervened that seemed to suggest that the Prussian coalition parties as well as the state government were perfectly happy with the 'Severing system': a far-reaching structural reform of the civil service, which alone in the long run could have led to a satisfactory solution to the problem, was not only not tackled, but never even taken into consideration. In the long run, a decisive factor in the democratization of the administration was not the filling of the highest administrative positions with republicans, but rather the new entrance requirements to the civil service whose goal it was to open high administrative positions to every social stratum, without the mediation of parties and associations. That meant a thorough education reform was necessary, linked with the removal of the monopoly of the legal profession and a considerable facilitation of the permeability between the different strata of the administrative pyramid. All of these were requirements that were in part recognized by the parties of the Weimar coalition, but whose details brought about such dissent that in the course of time the question of a thorough administrative reform was pushed into the background.[32]

And so the Prussian state government could be assured by means of its consistent personnel policy at the top of the administrative hierarchy that its policies would be carried out, thereby contributing considerably to making Prussia the 'bulwark of the republic'. But the close ties between the political civil servants, the coalition parties and the rest of the bureaucratic apparatus, which remained completely untouched by thorough reform, meant that with every change in government, even an unconstitutional one, the Prussian administration remained readily at the disposal of the new rulers. The conflict between a constitutional politically unreliable civil service

---

29 G. Noske, *Erlebtes aus Aufstieg und Niedergang einer Demokratie* (Offenbach, 1947), p. 181; Severing, *Lebensweg*, i. pp. 307f.
30 Theodor Eschenburg, *Ämterpatronage* (Stuttgart, 1961), p. 44.
31 See the critique by Eckart Kehr, 'Die Diktatur der Bürokratie', in Hans-Ulrich Wehler, ed., *Der Primat der Innenpolitik* (Berlin, 1965), pp. 244f.
32 Pikart, Preußische Beamtenpolitik, pp. 125f.

and a permanently efficient civil service was not reconciled in the Braun era; it needs to be stressed that the attempt to do so was not undertaken.

Justice

A particularly bleak chapter in connection with Prussia's personnel policy appeared in the administration of justice. The reason for this was that from 1919 the ministry of justice was the domain of the centre in addition to being, until March 1927, under the direction of the minister of justice, Hugo am Zehnhoff, under whose aegis, with the exception of a considerably improved pardon system, the Prussian justice system remained a conservative fossil.[33] Am Zehnhoff drew attention to himself in legal circles, which in many ways remained socially blind and aloof from republican ideas, because he was particularly proud of having rejected all attempts at a personnel reform of the administration of justice on the part of his cabinet colleagues,[34] to the extent that the provisional minister of justice and eminent philosopher of law, Gustav Radbruch, who was not exactly a man who came to rash judgements, spoke of a 'state of war between the people and justice'.[35] However, nothing crucial changed when the critically ill Zehnhoff retired from office and was replaced as Prussian minister of justice by a member of the left-wing of the Centre Party and Supreme Court judge, Hermann Schmidt (1927–1932). Schmidt pursued a specific personnel policy in a democratic sense, but he too was faced with a hurdle that he was unable to overcome: the constitutionally established personal and functional independence of the judge.

In the Weimar period, this liberal principle of law and order, which was originally a fundamental institution for protection against the despotism of the ruler, threatened to degenerate into a dogmatic weapon against political, social and legal reform. As long as the judiciary, shaped by the social and political conditions of the Wilhelmine era, unassailable within inherited boundaries, administered a social and politically balanced dispensation of justice, an effective protection of the honour of republican politicians, and a judicial protection of the Republic from the nationalist side was from the outset not guaranteed. The possibilities of making some quick, fundamental changes to the judiciary analogous to the French legislation of 1883, which removed the independence of judges for three months,[36] as some Social Democratic and

---

33 See the criticism of am Zehnhoff's adminstration in E. Hamburger, 'Betrachtungen über Heinrich Brünings Memoiren', *Internationale Wissenschaftliche Korrespondenz* 15 (1972), p. 33.
34 H. Brüning, *Memoiren 1918–1934* (Stuttgart, 1970), p. 60.
35 According to Eugen Schiffer, *Die Deutsche Justiz* (Berlin, 1928), p. 15.

democratic deputies demanded, or like the SPD Erfurt and Görlitz party programmes which laid down the principle of the election of judges, became illusory after the Weimar Constitution came into effect because their realization called for a decisive majority in parliament to bring about a change in the constitution that, in view of the relations between the majority parties, was not about to happen.

So right up to the end of the Weimar period, only partial improvements were made: the fixing of an age limit for judges; disciplinary proceedings against judges carried out by peers and in public, and the increased influence of the minister of justice on the appointment of judges.[37] All in all, not much was gained – the chairman of the senate of the Supreme Court of Berlin estimated that at the end of the Weimar period the proportion of republicans on the bench was around 5 per cent.[38] Even though during the Schmidt ministry Prussian justice reform began to have some notable successes – from the institution of conditional suspension of sentences, to the industrial tribunal legislation and its implementation, to prison reform and the rationalization of the judicial administration, the 'small reform of justice' – the personnel policy of the ministry of justice nevertheless remained a constant bone of contention for the centre coalition parties in Prussia.[39]

Braun himself did not put much effort into the question of the reform of the bureaucracy. Certainly, as minister for agriculture in the Prussian cabinet in 1919, he called for the elimination of the monopoly of justice in the higher civil service, or at least was unsuccessful with this demand,[40] but as minister-president he let the interior and finance ministers have this field and without a second thought accepted the extensive influence of the government parties over executive questions in this matter, which was not at all like him. Obviously, he underestimated the political consequences of this question and considered the 'Severing system' adequate enough to keep the Prussian bureaucracy of the state government firmly in his grasp. However, when he

---

36 Demonstrated in Erich Tigges, *Die Stellung des Richters im modernen Staat* (Berlin 1935), p. 131
37 See H. Christensen, Unabhängigkeit der Richter und Richteranklage im modernen deutschen Verfassungsstaat (PhD thesis, Kiel, 1952), pp. 25f and 97f; G. Jasper, *Der Schutz der Republik. Studien zur staatlichen Sicherung der Demokratie in der Weimarer Republik 1922–1930* (Tübingen, 1963), pp. 196f; T. Eschenburg, *Die improvisierte Demokratie. Gesammelte Aufsätze zur Weimarer Republik* (Munich, 1963), pp. 56f; Thilo Ramm, ed., *Die Justiz in der Weimarer Republik* (Neuwied/Berlin, 1968).
38 Jasper, *Schutz der Republik*, p. 209, n. 73.
39 See the extensive and cutting criticisms made by Ernst Heilmanns on the administration of Prussian justice within the context of his paper to the Prussian convention of the SPD on 14 February 1928, typed manuscript, in IISG Amsterdam, pp. 41f.
40 See Schulze, *Otto Braun*, pp. 244f.

had the impression that the civil service was striving to escape his grasp, he went into action.

The need for reform arose in the autumn of 1929 when the right-wing-led referendum on the Young Plan raised the question to what extent the constitutionally guaranteed fundamental rights of freedom of opinion and freedom to vote were also valid for civil servants. Paragraph 4 of the 'Laws of Freedom' (*Freiheitsgesetze*), put to a vote by the nationalist parties, threatened the minister responsible for signing the Young Plan with treason;[41] whoever voted in the referendum accused the German government, which was determined to sign the Young Plan, and the Prussian cabinet of treasonable behaviour.

On 15 October 1929, Braun made it perfectly clear on the wireless that he expected Prussian civil servants to refuse to sign the petition for the referendum:

> In the people's state, unlike former times, a civil servant certainly has the right to his own opinions and to make extensive use of that right, but he also has certain duties towards the state, more so than other citizens. Where it is a question of the interests of the people and the state, when the authority of the government and its leading statesmen are in doubt, he would offend against his duties as a civil servant if he were to support the referendum.[42]

On the very next day, the German National parties tried to pass a vote of no confidence against the ministry of state in the Prussian *Landtag* on the grounds that Braun's declaration violated the right of civil servants to freedom of expression.[43] Braun made it very clear in the course of the debate that he wanted to use the referendum to bring about a definitive decision about whether civil servants, under the guise of constitutional guarantees, should be allowed to agitate against their government, and reaffirmed his point of view – during tumultuous heckling from the right side of the House – by stating 'that each civil servant had to be clear in the full consciousness of his duty, which he also had towards the state in his private life, that to stand up for the referendum in whatever form would, nonetheless, not be compatible with his duty as a civil servant'.[44]

---

41 Printed in E. R. Huber, ed., *Dokumente zur deutschen Verfassungsgeschichte*, vol. 3, (Stuttgart, 1966), document n. 376, pp. 402f.
42 The text of Braun's speech can be found under the heading 'Volksbegehren und gesunder Menschenverstand' in Wolffs' Telegrafen-Bureau (the official German news agency), 80. Jg., No. 2117, 15 October 1929; IISG Amsterdam, NL Braun/559; GStA Berlin, Rep. 90a, Paket 6, H.126.
43 PrLT, 3. Wahlperiode, 16 October 1929, p. 8414.
44 Ibid., p. 8437.

The German National People's Party (DNVP) immediately lodged a complaint with the constitutional court, which brought down a Solomon-like judgement on 19 December 1929: civil servants should be allowed to vote in a referendum no matter what the content, but they were not allowed to agitate on behalf of a referendum. In such a case, it would be up to the discretion of the civil servant's superior to resort to disciplinary measures.[45] Admittedly, the distinction between voting in a referendum and actively entering into anti-government public agitation was a highly formalistic one; since the referendum was public, voting was already an 'active support'. Braun also had no intention of accepting the judgement of the constitutional court and openly declared before the *Landtag* on 22 May 1930 that its verdict did not have any weight with the Prussian disciplinary courts.[46] The *Wirtschaftspartei* (Economic Party) unsuccessfully moved to bring charges against Braun because he endangered the 'trust in the administration of justice and thereby the authority of the state';[47] and even liberal jurists like Professor Anschütz, a famous commentator on the Weimar Constitution, declared having serious doubts.[48] Despite the hefty reaction, the Prussian state ministry went a step further on 25 May 1930, two days after Braun's judicial scolding before the *Landtag*, and prohibited all Prussian civil servants from being members of the Communist Party (KPD) or the Nazi Party (NSDAP).[49] This was also a demonstrative step, and this time there was a direct correlation between the nomination of a National Socialist minister of the interior in Thuringen and the abrupt infiltration of the Thuringen police and bureaucracy with Nazis.[50] During the preparation of this decree, during the period of Hermann Müller's Reich cabinet (1928–1930), Braun demanded that the government of the Reich pass a corresponding resolution for federal civil servants. The minister of the interior Severing had decided to do so,[51] but the increasing tension within the federal cabinet prevented this topic from even being put on the agenda of a cabinet meeting until Müller's resignation.[52] The Brüning government (1930–1932) did not show the least interest in a general, decisive democratic

---

45 *Vossische Zeitung*, 598, 19 December 1929; and the written explanation in the *Reichsverwaltungsblatt*, 51, 1930, pp. 153f.
46 PrLT, 3. Wahlperiode, 22 May 1930, pp. 141–9f.
47 *Deutsche Tageszeitung*, 279, 17 June 1930.
48 In *Die Justiz*, V (1929/30), pp. 176f.
49 A. Köttgen, 'Die Entwicklung des öffentlichen Rechts in Preußen vom 4. Mai bis zum 1. November 1934', *Jahrbuch des öffentlichen Rechts* 22 (1935), p. 321.
50 Jasper, *Schutz der Republik*, pp. 217f.
51 Reich minister of the interior to all other Reich ministers, 2 January 1930, Bundesarchiv Koblenz, R 43 I/2674.
52 Severing, *Lebensweg*, ii. pp. 233f.

personnel policy with Prussia. Only the 'extreme left-winger' in the Brüning cabinet, Reich minister of the interior Joseph Wirth, let the Prussian interior minister secretly and in the 'greatest confidentiality' know that 'measures of this type' were not to be expected from the Reich cabinet but that he, the Reich minister of the interior, would not consider the Prussian action to be 'an unfriendly act'.[53] That was as much support as Braun could expect from the Reich government on the question of the republicanization of the civil service.

Especially against the background of the Reich, whose constant change of government made a consistent personnel policy impossible from the outset, the Prussian civil service policy with all its serious limitations appears almost enlightened. The specialist in public law, Arnold Köttgen, remarked with unconcealed admiration:

> The hotly disputed decree of the Prussian government on the participation of civil servants in the Nazi Party as well as the Communist Party is in my opinion, without wanting to judge the civil service laws, only an expression of the unity of Prussian politics which, in contrast to the much more hesitant politics of the Reich, is almost in every way equal to the authoritative power, security and certainty of the Kingdom of Prussia.[54]

The demise of the Prussian state

It is one of the ironies of history that it was precisely those parties maintaining a stabilizing function in Prussia that were the most important targets of state discrimination under the Prussian monarchy: the left-liberal, now German Democratic Party (DDP), the Catholic Centre Party and the Social Democrats (SPD). The latter party especially was doing a few things in Prussia, which at the same time it failed to do on the national level, where it all too often and all too easily gave in to the temptation of avoiding political responsibility instead of going into opposition that was more beneficial for maintaining the party organization.

There were several reasons why the skill of the Prussian Social Democrats in entering into coalitions, and keeping a firm hold on them even through difficult and controversial internal party questions, was much more pronounced than the Social Democratic Party committee at the national level. One of them was

---

53 Prussian minister of the interior to the Prussian minister president, 14 June 1930, GStA Berlin, NL Braun B/54 i.
54 Köttgen, 'Entwicklung des öffentlichen Rechts 1926 bis 1930', p. 4, n. 1.

that the Prussian state Social Democratic Party was made up, with very few exceptions, of parliamentarians who entered the *Landtag* only after the fall of the monarchy and who were, therefore, much more receptive to the requirements of a parliamentary democracy than their counterparts in the Reichstag, at least a third of whom, and among them almost all of the top politicians, had been there since the *Kaiserzeit* and who had internalized their former oppositional role. For these old parliamentarians, it was a matter of habit to support and to protect a parliamentary government.

Furthermore, the Prussian Social Democratic parliamentary party was to a large extent its own master, while the national Social Democratic parliamentary party was answerable to a party convention every two years. Not least, however, did the normally underestimated question of personality play a role here. The Social Democratic Party in the Prussian *Landtag* was under the strict leadership of its president, Ernst Heilmann (1921–1933), who not only understood the importance of getting his party to agree in crisis situations to a clear and united course, but beyond that to clarify beforehand with the other party leaders of the Weimar coalition, especially with his colleague in the Centre Party, Joseph Hess (1930–1933), the most important decisions so that the government parties could then regularly act in a unified manner in the plenum. Only on this basis was it possible for Otto Braun to influence the Prussian government's relations in an authoritative, if not an authoritarian, manner over the years. The situation was totally different at the national level where a deeply strife-ridden SPD party only rarely let itself be led by a faceless and colourless collective party executive and which never learnt how to develop a recognizable political line over a long period of time.

In Prussia, unlike at the national level, Social Democracy allowed its ministers to remain in the government through all of these years, with the exception of a short interlude in 1921, and understood moreover how to link the new Prussia with a sympathetic working class. In the course of the 1920s, Prussia became a bulwark of the consciousness of the social democratic and Catholic labour movement much more than the Weimar Republic in general. At a beer evening held by Minister-President Braun for the Prussian parliamentary SPD party, the deputy and editor of the SPD newspaper *Vorwärts*, Erich Kuttner, came out against the left-wing member of the SPD executive committee, Arthur Crispien, who had declared a few years earlier that the worker had no fatherland. Kuttner replied: '[…] Crispien proved himself to be wrong, comrades, we have a fatherland, and it is called Prussia.[55]

---

55 Written communication with the author from Ernest Hamburger, New York, 11 April 1975.

For all these reasons, Prussia offered the traditional picture of severity, concentration and purposefulness while at the national level the Weimar Republic, from the beginning of its creation on, never overcame the crisis. The Prussian government increasingly acted as a crutch for national politics, a democratic nucleus of order for Germany, through its sheer territorial predominance, but essentially through the stability of its exemplary democratic essence on the other German states and on the Reich.

For both sides of the Wilhelmstraße – that is, in the Prussian state ministry as well as the German chancellery – this could only last as long as a common desire for a democratic renewal of Germany existed. Already during the Brüning government, there were increasing periods of friction with the Prussian government because the Prussian state ministry followed with growing mistrust the increasingly blatant illegal attempts to rearm the Reichswehr and, moreover, stood in the way of both Brüning and the Reichswehr coming to an amicable understanding with the National Socialists. Nevertheless, Brüning was, as before, dependent for his policies on the support of the Social Democrats in the Reichstag and he got that only as long as he came to an arrangement with Prussia.

After Brüning's fall at the end of May 1932, the position of interests in the Reich suddenly changed. The new Reich government under the chancellorship of Franz von Papen (June–November 1932) – the 'cabinet of barons' – no longer required the toleration of the Reichstag. The trust of the President of the Reich, von Hindenburg, was enough. Moreover, the Prussian government was now considerably weakened; since the Prussian state elections of 24 April 1932, there was no longer a majority in the *Landtag* and there was only a caretaker government. The minister of the Reichswehr, Kurt von Schleicher, who was the real power behind the new Reich government, had been waiting for just such an eventuality. As early as 1923, he had pleaded for the use of Article 48 in order to eliminate the government in Prussia, and the long struggle between the Prussian government and the Reichswehr ministry had further stirred Schleicher's aversion to the Braun cabinet and had convinced him that a nuisance such as the Prussian executive belonged in the hands of a pro-military Reich government. This view met with the complete agreement of his cabinet colleagues. Reich minister of the interior, Freiherr Wilhelm von Gayl, noted the two most important domestic political tasks in the future:

> The young, ever larger inclusive circles of the Adolf Hitler movement must, in order to make the national powers useful to the reconstruction of the people, free itself from the chains that were laid on it by Brüning and Severing and must be supported in the victorious struggle against international Communism. Second, in order to free the way for the first task

and in order to assert itself against the red/black Prussian government, the contrast between Reich and Prussia must be eliminated once and for all through the removal of the Prussian government.[56]

The view that the Prussian government had previously stood in the way of the 'struggle against international Communism' sparked off roars of laughter in communist circles – it was not for nothing that, in their view, 'Prussian police socialism as presently the most active factor in the fascistisation and preparation for Hugenburg–Hitler'[57] was considered to be the KPD's main battle. But, in principle, the Prussian government, in so far as the increasing influence through the Reich allowed it, had applied the same measure to communist and National Socialist street terror – that was the point that the new Reich interior minister did not like. He and his like-minded friends preferred an alliance with 'the young, ever larger inclusive circles of the Adolf Hitler movement' to the 'red–black November system' – the most serious political misjudgement that Prussian conservatives in a rich history of mistakes were to commit. On 20 July 1932, Prussia's civil servants were relieved of their offices in a coup-like action by the Papen government against the Prussian state government; the duties of the Prussian ministers were taken over by Reich commissioners. It was an irony of history that it was precisely the old Prussian forces that had brought about the demise of the Prussian state.

The failed revolution of 1848–49 once gave birth to a dream – 'Prussia's German and democratic mission' as Friedrich Christoph Dahlmann had called the Frankfurt parliament in the Paulskirche[58] – the transformation of the crumbling German Bund, that was held together only to some extent through legitimate political alliances and economic interests, into a modern, liberal-democratic, constitutional German nation state with the help of the only power that could bring it about, Prussia. Dahlmann's dream could be realized only from 1918 on. The new Prussia in Weimar Germany, as Otto Braun attempted to make it a reality, was a democratic parliamentary state based on strict legal foundations, destined to unite permanently the democratic middle classes and the social democratic working classes, political Catholicism and the left. It was conservative when it came to functioning, democratically suited structures; it was reforming when new

---

56 Freiherr Wilhelm von Gayl: Franz von Papen, unpublished manuscripts in Nachlaß Michael Freund, Bundesarchiv, Koblenz.
57 Decision of the plenum of the Central Committee of the German Communist Party on 12 February 1932 in *Handbuch für den Preußischen Landtag* (Berlin 1932), p. 214.
58 Stenographic report on the negotiations of the German constituted National Assemby at Frankfurt am Main, edited by Franz Wigard, 22 January 1848, vii. p. 4820.

structures had to be created. 'Perhaps never since the era of Freiherr vom Stein', wrote Golo Mann, 'had the Germans been offered such a decent concept of political co-existence.'[59] Democratic Prussia remained an episode, hardly more than a footnote in the all too short history of the German nation state. But when Prussia is spoken of today, one should think of this episode. The democratic Prussia of Otto Braun, Carl Severing and Ernst Heilmann, which is celebrated by no monument, no institution and no street name, to a great extent makes up for the disasters that the heritage of Prussia brought to Germans and their history.

---

59 Mann, 'Rezension von Otto Braun', p. 49.

CHAPTER ELEVEN

Prussia's military legacy in Empire, Republic and Reich, 1871–1945

DENNIS SHOWALTER

This essay focuses on the myths and the realities of the Prussian army in the German nation from 1871 to 1947. As such, it is a study of change and continuity in two spheres: perception and reality. Prussia in the Second Empire, the Weimar Republic and the Third Reich was as much a state of mind as a physical entity. The state that governed two-thirds of Germany's territory and three-quarters of its population bore only a tangential relationship to the world described with the bittersweet nostalgia of Theodor Fontane, or in the reified prose of the general staff histories of Frederick the Great's wars. Since the end of the Third Reich, 'Prussia' has indeed seemed close to becoming a negative abstraction, defined as whatever Nazi Germany was not: simple, honourable, proud, aristocratic.[1]

That pattern of increasing abstraction shaped specifically military images as well. On one hand, 'Prussianism' became – and remains – a synonym for tunnel vision and rote behaviour. Nineteenth-century socialists and contemporary academicians describe soldiers concentrating with blinkered zeal on the narrowest aspects of their craft, developing technical and operational virtuosity at the expense of insight into strategy and policy. Hostile alike to democracy and industrialism, the kaiser's generals remained

---

1 For this process, see Hans Mommsen, 'Preussentum und Nationalsozialismus', in W. Benz, H. Buchheim and H. Mommsen (eds), *Der Nationalsozialismus. Studien zur Ideologie und Herrschaft* (Frankfurt am Main, 1993), pp. 29–41. Of arguably more importance than academic analysis have been the writings of general-audience authors like Marion Donhoff and Sebastian Haffner, whose respective representative works *Namen, die Keiner mehr kennt: Ostpreussischen Menschen*, and *Preussen ohne Legende*, first published in 1962 and 1979, have been repeatedly reprinted and widely translated.

constrained by Prussian paradigms. In the end, rather than risk changing an aristocratic/conservative domestic order, they plunged their country into war in 1914 knowing it might well not be the short conflict that was the only kind of war Germany stood a chance of winning and surviving. For four years, they betrayed the trust of their government and their people.[2] Their successors obscured the truth about Germany's defeat, then brokered Adolf Hitler's rise to power as a desirable alternative to a republic despised not for what it did, but for what it was.

Between 1933 and 1945, according to this model, 'Prussian' generals planned and 'Prussian' soldiers fought in blinkers, refusing to consider either the nature of the regime they served or the nature of the task they faced. Even after the experience of 1917–1918, the High Command greeted Hitler's 1941 declaration of war on the United States with blank surprise, having never seriously considered a second transatlantic conflict and having never collected any data on which to base plans for waging one. From generals downward, however, what rapidly became 'Hitler's army' did participate enthusiastically in the genocidal atrocities of the Eastern Front. It fought until the country it ostensibly existed to protect had been reduced to rubble, with enemy troops occupying anything of any value.[3] Small wonder, in this context, that Konrad Adenauer did not mourn the loss of Germany's eastern lands and the military culture they nurtured. 'Asia', he sourly observed, 'begins at Berlin'.

There is, however, another master story for this period. It, too, focuses on military Prussia as a state of mind. Its narrators, from Theodor Fontane in the nineteenth century to Marion Donhoff in the twentieth, present a structure of values and behaviours as upright as they were limited. In this construction, the Prussian army never disappeared. It offered a sober counterpoint to the tinsel militarism of the Second Reich and its 'men of straw'. It sustained Germany through four years of an unwinnable war, and provided a rallying point in the collapse that followed. It offered a model of public service to its successor institution, the Reichswehr. For all of the soldiers' dislike of the Weimar Republic and its principles, Hitler did not rise to power on the army's bayonets. Political generals like Kurt von Schleicher were disliked and distrusted by their fellows. During the Third Reich, the army provided a refuge to the sons of such incarcerated resisters

---

2 For the most developed statement of this argument, see Stig Foerster, 'Der deutsche Generalstab und die Illusion des kurzen Krieges', *Militaergeschichtliche Mitteilungen* 54 (1995), 61–93.
3 The best brief presentation of this position in English is Jürgen Förster, 'The Dynamics of *Volksgemeinschaft*: The Effectiveness of the German Military Establishment in the Second World War', in A. Millett and W. Murray (eds), *Military Effectiveness*, 3 vols (London, 1988), iii, pp. 180–220.

as Rudolf Pechel. It protected dissident junior officers like Lieutenant Helmuth Schmidt (later Chancellor of West Germany) from the consequences of their outbursts. The army was the heart of the only real attempt to overthrow Hitler. And if the July 20 conspiracy came far too late, if far too many soldiers uncritically served a regime of injustice, then at least they paid full price for their decisions. On meathooks in Ploetzensee Prison, facing SS firing squads, or in the forward lines of a half-dozen fighting fronts, Prussia's soldiers atoned for serving the devil on earth by preparing his quarters in Hell. They died with honour when they could no longer live with honour.[4]

A Prussian army or a German one? The imperial years

To critique either perspective, it must be understood that the Prussian army of a unified Germany was more than a trope, more than a set of symbols. The Second Reich was a federal empire. Psychologically, it is questionable whether a 'German' army existed before 1916. The Prussian army had entered the empire as a 'layered' institution, incorporating *Altpreussen* (Old Prussians) of the post-Napoleonic kingdom and *Muss-Preussen* (Compulsory Prussians) absorbed after 1866. There were significant differences between a grenadier regiment recruited in Brandenburg or Pomerania, heir to the traditions of Frederick the Great and of the units that did not dissolve in 1806, and a regiment drawing its recruits from the former kingdom of Hanover, or the newly-absorbed dwarf states of Thuringia. As time passed, however, the smaller state contingents were more thoroughly absorbed, with only obscure details of custom and uniform to mark their differences. The officer corps became more homogenized, as old Prussians, new Prussians, and non-Prussians mixed cheek by jowl in the increasing number of regiments created in the years before the Great War. Wilhelm Groener expressed a growing conventional wisdom when, in 1911, he argued that senior officers of the Württemberg contingent must be routinely detached to Prussia in order to make a complete career – and shed the certain intellectual clumsiness that characterized the Swabian left too long undisturbed in his native habitat.

---

4 Peter Hoffmann, *Stauffenberg. A Family History, 1905–1944* (Cambridge, 1995), presents this process in a context of value transference. The Stauffenberg brothers; that is; may have been Swabian by heritage, but were German by conviction and 'Prussian' in behaviour.

After 1890, Emperor William II intensively fostered integration. A drill sergeant who described a group of clumsy recruits as 'Oldenburg oxen' found himself in the same hot water under the Supreme Warlord as the American staff officer under General Eisenhower who described his opposite number as 'a British son of a bitch'. In both cases, the adjective, not the noun, was the cause of offence.

Prussia nevertheless was only one of the German Empire's armies. Bavaria's army stubbornly clung to its light blue uniforms, its separate general staff and its autonomous officer corps, stubbornly resisting pressure from Berlin to modify its higher formal educational standards for commissioning. The Saxon army might be numbered in sequence with the rest of the Prussian contingent, but its Saxon identity was plain. Any doubters could listen to its tales of the Battle of St Privat in the Franco-Prussian War, where the Saxons had – by their own account and in the judgement of most observers – pulled the chestnuts of the elite Prussian Guard from French fire in the wake of a failed frontal attack. Nor did regional rivalry disappear from Prussia. When army corps with a history of mutual antagonism collided in the annual autumn manoeuvres, mock battles periodically came to resemble the real thing, with rifle butts and fists supplementing blank rounds fired at point-blank range.

Paradoxically, this incomplete integration fostered increased Prussianization. The military histories of the smaller German states were seldom distinguished enough to establish positive tones – not least because too many of their greatest deeds had been done under French or Austrian command. In 1870, non-Prussian troops had usually been employed on secondary missions. The major exception, the two Bavarian corps, acquired an unsavoury if undeserved reputation as better marauders than fighters. Aside from this, an army that virtually doubled in size between 1870 and 1914 needed traditions. It found them in a 'Prussian' heritage, reinforced by the historical writings of the general staff, the battle paintings of August Roehling, and the public posturings of the kaiser.[5]

Ersatz Prussianism encouraged affirming tradition – even if the traditions were as artificial as the pasts and titles William II enjoyed bestowing on the army's junior regiments. It provided ready-made behaviour patterns for increasing numbers of first- and second-generation officers, serving in an army that became a focal point of national identity by default because other

---

5   Cf. Friedrich-Christian Stahl, 'Preussische Armee und Reichsheer 1871–1914', in O. Hauner (ed.), *Zur Problematik 'Preussen und das Reich'* (Munich, 1984), pp. 181–246; and Hans-Martin Otmer, 'Ursachen und Hintergrunde zur Entwicklung deutscher militaerischer Traditionen vom Ende des 18. Jahrhunderts bis 1914', in Gustav-Adolf Caspar, (ed.), *Tradition in deutschen Streitkräften bis 1914* (Herford, 1986), pp. 67–208.

national symbols remained meagre and shallow. The new empire did not even have a geographic focal point, a Paris or a Muscovy. No one could look at any particular region or province and say that it was more clearly German than any other one. It was, however, possible to become more Prussian – if only by adopting the exaggerated Berlin inflections of the Prussian Guard's officers, the well-known *Jardetoenen*.

Prussia's military legacy influenced the German Empire in another way as well – by maintaining the Frederician approach of seeking decisive battles to resolve limited wars. For 40 years after the Napoleonic Wars, Prussia sought marginal aggrandizement in a stable matrix by a mixture of negotiation and compromise, underwritten by the credible possibility of using force as a final argument. The same approach shaped the Wars of Unification between 1864 and 1871. However revolutionary the results of these mid-century conflicts eventually proved, Prussia's policy goals were nevertheless ultimately negative and ultimately limited. Like the American Revolution, the German Revolution of 1866–70 was more turnout than turnover, involving Austria's expulsion and France's exclusion as much as Prussia's expansion.

The Franco-Prussian War further highlighted the importance of limitation. The defeat of the French Empire was total by any standards. Six weeks after the outbreak of hostilities, one of its field armies was hopelessly besieged in Metz, another had surrendered at Sedan, and the emperor himself was firmly in Prussian hands. But these spectacular victories left France without a government willing and able to conclude peace on terms acceptable to Prussia. Instead, an improvised Third Republic kept the field with armies it seemed able to stamp out of the very soil of France. Guerrillas, the *francs tireurs*, hovered around the invading armies like gnats, destroying rail and telegraph lines, ambushing patrols and convoys, defying suppression by any techniques acceptable to 'civilized' warfare. By the time Prussia's chancellor, Otto von Bismarck, was able to secure French signatures on a cobbled-together set of compromises, European intervention had become a distinct and uncomfortable possibility.

If a war begun under what everyone involved recognized as virtually ideal circumstances generated such difficulties, were there any feasible alternative approaches? Chief of staff Helmuth von Moltke's calls during the conflict's later stages for the complete destruction of France manifested personal frustrations rather than public objectives. After 1871, the empire's geo-strategic position, sandwiched between France and Russia, was a common-sense warning against conceptualizing future wars that ended with the Reich's enemies prostrate at the Reich's feet. Bismarck's Germany was a satiated power; self-interest made it Europe's broker and fulcrum. To cite only the most obvious example, Bismarck's increasing commitment to preserving the balance between Russia and Austria–Hungary was a response to a situation in which any conflict, diplomatic or military, with the potential for becoming overt and protracted was directly contrary to Germany's interests.[6]

The army responded by emphasizing three Prussian virtues: planning, professionalism and paternalism. Moltke the Elder, his contemporaries and his successors saw victory in battle as the sine qua non for maintaining Germany's grand-strategic position without the risk of a general war or a people's war. Either might strain beyond their limits both the Second Reich and the international framework within which it functioned and flourished.

Moltke in particular understood the best practical alternative to the risks of modern war as prophylactic: keeping conflicts short by a combination of victory and negotiation. This principle lay behind his increasing advocacy of preventive war – a concept in Moltke's mind better expressed by the more modern term 'pre-emptive strike'. Moltke did not see such an attack with the eyes of a Tamerlane or a Hitler, as a means of totally destroying an unwary enemy. Instead, he saw it as contributing to the front-loading of warfare in the interests of reaching quick decisions. Moltke's worst-case contingency during the Bismarckian era, his plan for a two-front war against France and Russia, was based not on the sequential annihilation or crippling of Germany's enemies, but rather on the simultaneous bloodying of their noses, thereby establishing favourable conditions for Germany's diplomats.

Exploiting such victories in a military sense involved disproportionate risks. France was too strong, Russia too big, to be taken on cavalierly in a fight to the finish. The Chief of staff's increasing pessimism at the prospects even of preventive war led him by the end of his career to stress what later generations would call deterrence. Any sensible government, Moltke declared in 1891, must hesitate to go to war under existing conditions. The next war could last for seven years or for 30, and 'woe to him who sets Europe ablaze'.[7]

From the perspective of its foremost military expert, then, Germany's most practical national strategy involved avoiding war by military preparation sufficiently massive, and sufficiently systematic, to intimidate potential challengers. In other words, Moltke supported the policy practised for two decades after 1763 by Prussia's Frederick the Great – a policy that did far

---

6   The Prussian strategic heritage is developed in Dennis E. Showalter, 'German Grand Strategy: A Contradiction in Terms?', *Militaergeschichtliche Mitteilungen* 48 (1990), 65–102.
7   See the analysis by Stig Förster in 'Facing People's War: Moltke the Elder and Germany's Military Options after 1871', *Journal of Strategic Studies* 10 (1987), 209–30.

more than the ephemeral battlefield triumphs of the Seven Years' War to confirm Prussia's place among the great powers.

Preparation wore many faces. Decades before the Reich's creation, the Prussian army had accepted and encouraged future orientation as a way to make a career. At a time when troop duty was almost universally understood as the sole legitimate path to military advancement – one only need recall the satiric lyrics of 'When I Was a Lad', from *HMS Pinafore* – the Prussian army sought to assign talented officers to its planning institutions, and treated their work as something beyond pen-pushing. The corresponding improvement of administrative bureaucracies facilitated creating ever-larger armies. The concentration of those forces was made possible by the growth of railway networks. Their successful operational employment depended on adjustment to new battlefield technologies: breechloading rifles, rifled cannon. The Wars of Unification were modern wars, conducted by a military system priding itself on its modernity.

That pride goes far to explain the often-cited 'strategic imbecility' that between 1871 and 1945 allegedly concentrated on war's tactical and operational factors to the exclusion of broader considerations. Policy and strategy demanded quick, decisive victories. Translating that principle to tactical and operational levels proved a daunting challenge. Far from denying the dominance of firepower on the modern battlefield, the German army found the proposition's affirmation in its own casualty lists. Moltke himself consistently affirmed that the best way of minimizing the costs of modern weapons was to take the offensive at the operational level, advance into enemy country, dig in and allow the enemy to break his strength against them, then counter-attack the survivors.

This dialectical 'offensive–defensive–offensive' approach demanded an army itself able to attack without suffering crippling losses. Germany's enemies were not likely to follow Germany's leads blindly, like a trusting dance partner. However skilfully the generals might seek to avoid such a worst-case contingency, at some time and somewhere the infantry would have to go forward and break through. That contingency could be facilitated by preparation. At the strategic level, railroads became so important that the general staff began acquiring a railway's procedural characteristics – continued, reliable, predictable service, with the aim of bringing as many men as possible, as quickly as possible, to the right places. Those places in turn were determined by an operational plan that consciously sacrificed flexibility for the degree of control that implied the ability to get inside an enemy's decision-making loop and win the next war from a standing start.

Tactical doctrine developed increasingly elaborate systems and technologies for directing massed artillery fire and co-ordinating its delivery with infantry movements that emphasized open formations. The machine-guns introduced after the turn of the twentieth century were valued for their ability to support attacks, both directly and by firing on ranged lines, using methods of observation and fire control borrowed from the artillery.

Men, however, were more important than machines and weapons systems. The conscripts who filled the ranks under the Second Empire are usually described as victims of a policy that used military service as a tool of socialization. The values of monarchy and aristocracy, capitalism and Christianity, were hammered into vulnerable youths trapped in an environment demanding 'corpse-like obedience' (*Kadavergehorsamkeit*). In fact, the army's personnel policies reflected Prussian experiences as much as imperial anxieties. Since the days of Frederick the Great, paternalism had been the subtext of the Prussian army's treatment of its rank and file. The cantonists, the rural conscripts who formed around half the strength even in the days of mercenary recruiting, were drawn from the same estates whose owners provided the officers. The distinctions between the *Gutsherr* and the *Herr Hauptmann* tended to erode on both sides of the relationship – particularly when the two men in question might be cousins or brothers.

After 1815, paternalism persisted and prevailed, not least as a counter to the Reform Movement's equating military service with citizenship. In the imperial army, it was no coincidence that the company, the basic building block, was consistently described as a family, with the captain as father, the first sergeant as mother. That some recruits might prefer to be orphans did not change the basic image of an army whose cadres were expected to do more than conduct drills and inspections. Between 1871 and 1914, it became increasingly apparent that under the conditions of modern war, discipline imposed from above might be enough to bring the soldier to battle. It was not sufficient to enable him to function effectively in battle. A German officer should set examples of effectiveness and character. At the same time, he must realize even an optimal military environment was temporary, and not likely to alter established world-views. Instead of investigating what his men read or thought, a company officer should perform his duties so well that even committed socialists might be inspired to emulation. Win the confidence of your men, the subaltern was urged. Participate in their sports and recreations. Bridge the gaps of social class on a human level. A personal attachment to his officers could become a first step to that general commitment to the military system that modern war demanded from the common soldier.

This shift in approaches reflected a growing sophistication of what might be called the army's social psychology. As late as the 1860s, it was a virtual article of faith among the soldiers that a third year of active service was all that was needed to make conscripted civilians into loyal and enthusiastic subjects. Experience had shown instead that the average 20-year-old's 'core values' were established beyond the army's capacity to change them significantly. The growing embourgeoisement of the officer corps meant as well that fewer and fewer lieutenants or captains could tell themselves convincingly they had some kind of genetic ability to give orders. Leadership, however, could be studied, learned and practised just like all the other aspects of modern war. And in that context, there were far worse models than an updated version of the 'Prussian virtue' of paternalism.[8]

The Great War: From spiked helmets to steel helmets

The First World War seemed to mark the end of the Prussian heritage in the German army. Mass national mobilization combined with the exigencies of the wartime replacement system to mix men from all parts of the Reich in the same units. The heavy casualties sustained by the peacetime officer corps – 40 per cent of those serving in 1914 were killed in action – opened the ranks to increasing numbers of men from increasingly divergent backgrounds, even though most belonged to a broadly defined middle class. The conditions of the trenches generated new styles of combat and of leadership. The *Sturmblock*, the small combat team, became the focus of front-line tactics. Consensus became a significant element of effective command. The officer no longer stood above his unit, but functioned as an integral part of it. The elaborately ornamented headgear and the elaborate facial hair styles of the peacetime Reich were increasingly associated with the elderly excellencies who commanded corps and armies from the rear. They offered a stark symbolic contrast to the unadorned steel helmets and simple moustaches of the front-line officers. The intellectuals, the clergymen, the workers, the soldiers, conscript or volunteer – all those who believed the war would bring about renewal in spite of itself – thought not in regional or provincial, but German terms.[9] Field Marshal von

---

8   This position is developed in Dennis E. Showalter, 'Army and Society in Imperial Germany: The Perils of Modernization', *Journal of Contemporary History* 18 (1983), 583–618 ; and 'From Deterrence to Doomsday Machine, 1890–1914: The German Way of War', *Journal of Military History* 64 (2000), 679–710.
9   Wolfgang J. Mommsen, 'German Artists, Writers, and Intellectuals and the Meaning of War, 1914–1918', in J. Horne (ed.), *State, Society, and Mobilization in Europe during the First World War* (Cambridge, 1997), pp. 21–38.

Hindenburg by 1916 symbolized not the Prussia of his birth and youth, but Germany – the mature virility required to bring the country safely through its greatest test.

'Prussian', indeed, increasingly became an all-purpose term of abuse. Before 1914, it had been more descriptive than pejorative: 'with the Prussians' was no more than a way of describing active service. Well before 1918, however, it was being used by Saxons, Bavarians, and just about anyone not born east of the Elbe River and west of the Oder, to describe and explain everything wrong with the army and the war. If an informal trench truce was broken, it was the fault of 'Prussians' who relieved less aggressive soldiers from other contingents. Allied intelligence repeatedly described the morale of Bavarian units in particular as 'good, but quite anti-Prussian'. Even men from Brandenburg or Pomerania used 'Prussian' as a synonym for *Kommiss* – an army system hidebound at best, malevolently unimaginative at worst. Ernst Juenger, anything but a social liberal but an archetype of the emerging front-line techno-warrior, said the 'Prussian' army would regret not giving combat commands to those who could best lead troops in battle, regardless of their peacetime jobs or standing. Non-Prussian officers, from Bavaria's war minister down to regimental levels, deplored their colleagues' blinkered insistence on sustaining such anomalies as Prussia's three-class voting system, or civilian social qualifications for even a wartime reserve officer's commission.

In the front lines, the 'patriarchal/hegemonial' approach of the 'old army', with professional officers and NCOs parenting youthful conscripts and initiating them into adult society, was giving way to a 'collegial/affective' pattern, emphasizing co-operation and consensus in mission performance. Since the days of Frederick the Great, Prussian armies had sought to make their rank and file into soldiers. By 1918, the achievements of the stormtroopers had established the warrior as an alternate archetype. 'Mass man' was a positive danger in the trenches, argued Germany's military futurologists. What was necessary was 'extraordinary man': the combination of fighter and technician who understood combat both as a skilled craft and an inner experience. The Prussian army historically regarded itself as a transmuter of national effort into military effectiveness. The Great War seemed to indicate that the army must become part of a wider synthesis, incorporating and co-ordinating businessmen, politicians and intellectuals in a total enterprise. At general staff levels, the pre-war paradigm of professionalism as focused reason correspondingly changed to incorporate ideological, vitalist and synergistic elements foreign to what was generally understood as the Prussian tradition. Officers like Max Bauer began developing proto-Fascist definitions of national spiritual mobilization, with the *Volk*, the community, replacing both kaiser and state as the focus of loyalty and identity.[10]

Weimar and the Prussian military heritage

The collapse of the Second Reich and the establishment of the Weimar Republic seemed to set the stone on the Prussian army's grave. If the Republic was willing to make what many scholars regard as a devil's bargain with the soldiers for the sake of internal security, the negotiations were conducted not with the 'old army', but rather with the 'new old army'. Generals like Wilhelm Groener and Walther Reinhardt had little use even for the trappings of a system they regarded as having failed Germany in its ultimate test.[11] The state of Prussia survived in the new republican order. The Prussian army, however, disappeared as an entity under a constitution that abolished the separate contingencies and war ministries of Bismarck's empire in favour of a single Reichswehr ministry.

The first responsibility of that institution was to create an army out of the fragments of defeat and the provisions of the Versailles Treaty. Neither of the most obvious post-war tropes, the freebooting exemplified by General Ludwig Maercker nor the 'democratization' allegedly favoured by Reinhardt, shaped the mentality of the emerging Reichswehr. Instead, Hans von Seeckt created a force that was far more *sui generis*, far more a 'thing in itself', than the pre-1914 army, with its broad spectrum of extra-military agendas.

An overlooked, but significant, element of the Reichswehr's restructuring involved the tendency of hard-core adherents of the old ways and the old loyalties to retire rather than change their ways and deny oaths sworn under the empire. There were enough of them, and their position was strong enough, that it greatly reduced tensions when they left of their own accord. The other face of that coin was the fact that those officers who had taken the same oaths, yet chose to serve in the Reichswehr, needed to explain and justify their behaviour – often to themselves above all. One way of doing that involved embracing the future as opposed to looking towards the past. The two major symbols of military Prussia during the Weimar years were living monuments. As field marshal and *Reichspräsident*, Hindenburg stood

---

10 Martin Kitchen, 'Militarism and the Development of Fascist Ideology: The Political Ideas of Colonel Max Bauer, 1916–1918', *Central European History* 8 (1975), 199–220.
11 F. L. Carsten, *The Reichswehr and Politics, 1918 to 1933* (Oxford, 1966).

more for national values and the qualities of stability and calmness than he represented modern ways of war. As for Field Marshal August von Mackensen, with his white moustaches and hussar busby, the old warrior was an icon for veteran's groups, but scarcely a role model for the Reichswehr or its officers.[12]

In selecting a new generation of commanders, Hans von Seeckt began by 'deconstructing' the concept of 'character' that had been so important to pre-war selection processes. No longer was it to be a euphemism for birth or behaviour. What Seeckt demanded was an ability to evaluate circumstances and make judgements based on those circumstances, as opposed to filtering perceptions through a priori world-views. In principle, and to a great degree in practice as well, the officers of Seeckt's Reichswehr were selected and promoted on the basis of their identity with the army and their effectiveness in meeting the army's norms. Concepts of honour based on status had little place in the new army. Now the honour of the officer corps depended on performance.

As much to the point for the new military order, enlisted men, committed to a minimum of 12 years' service, could no longer be expected to regard their time in the army as a rite of passage, with discomfort and disorientation only enhancing the mythic aspect of the transition to adulthood. Reichswehr training methods sought a dialectic between understanding and obedience. There was no room for *Schleiferei* and *Schinderei*, the spectrum of petty and not so petty harassment and abuse that was a staple of so many pre-war conscripts' experience. In the same context, much of the everyday process of developing the Reichswehr as an 'army of leaders' reflected the necessity of preventing the rank and file from stagnating as a consequence of too many years of doing the same things in the same places with the same people.

Operationally, the Reichswehr developed new mouldings for its new metal. Doctrine, tactics and training may not have overtly discarded the Prussian heritage, but all departed from it by fostering comprehensive elitism. The combined-arms mobile battle developed in theory and tested in manoeuvres as early as the 1920s was, in its emphasis on seizing and exploiting opportunities, a far cry from the concept of continuous operation existing under the elder Moltke and his successors – not least because of the extreme demands it placed on officers and men. The new Reichswehr emphasized mobility, manoeuvrability and aggressive response to

---

12 Theo Schwarzmueller, *Zwischen Kaiser und 'Fuehrer:' Generalfeldmarschall August von Mackensen*, 2nd edn (Paderborn, 1996), pp. 172 and *passim*, is an excellent case study of the limits – and the consequences – of this kind of nostalgia.

opportunities. Its striking power was enhanced by technology whenever possible. Trucks originally intended for logistics purposes developed operational missions moving combat troops. The Reichswehr's cavalry, by comparison to its counterparts in other armies, found motor vehicles a promising force multiplier – perhaps because they were deprived of them under the treaty.

This perspective did more than make a virtue of the necessities created by a small professional army. Since the eighteenth century, the Prussian army had stressed the desirability of a high average. The general staff was seen not as a self-referencing corps of experts, but as a leaven and a nervous system for the army as a whole. In operational terms, one regiment, division, or corps was considered in principle as inherently capable as any other. During the Wars of Liberation, the *Landwehr*'s hastily-trained civilians in uniform had been acculturated to the line army. In 1914, reserve corps had been employed in exactly the same way as active formations. Seeckt, however, like many of his counterparts, was in principle hostile to the mass armies of the Great War that had substituted first enthusiasm and then loyalty for military effectiveness. Whatever improvised supplementary units might be raised in case of an emergency were expected to perform no more than secondary missions. The heavy lifting would be up to the men who knew how.[13]

The Reichswehr's way of war was also a preferable alternative to two other distinctively 'Prussian' approaches advocated during the 1920s. One called for reviving the presumed traditions of the Wars of Liberation by pursuing a people's war option. This position foundered on the practical difficulties of getting civilians to take up arms at all, much less carry them into the field against trained adversaries equipped with tanks, aircraft and heavy artillery – all forbidden Germany by the Versailles Treaty. The second approach replicated Prussian behaviour during the Biedermeyer years by advocating close military-political co-operation for the sake of gradual, limited adjustments of the status quo in Germany's favour. It atrophied in a Europe that increasingly regarded diplomacy as the conduct of war by other means, presided over by a France constrained to kill its enemies because it was too weak to flog them.[14]

As the Reichswehr developed new paradigms, it remained aware of a major perceived risk: creating a *Soeldnerheer*, an army of deracinated

---

13 Cf. James S. Corum, *The Roots of Blitzkrieg* (Lawrence, Kans., 1992); and Robert Citino's more narrowly focused *The Path to Blitzkrieg* (Boulder, Colo., 1999).
14 Still the best overview is Michael Geyer, *Aufruestung oder Sicherheit? Reichswehr in der Krise der Machtpolitik, 1924–1933* (Wiesbaden, 1980).

domestic mercenaries. Even before the Reform Movement, Prussia's officers took pride in having significant numbers of native Prussians in their ranks. The nineteenth century had seen the army adopt and internalize a self-definition as 'the school of the nation'. Deprived of that role by a Versailles Treaty forbidding conscription, the Republic's new-era professionals sought alternative ways of keeping the army in touch with its community. Seeckt constantly affirmed the worth of tradition. Institutionally, each company, battery and squadron of the Reichswehr was designated as the successor of specific formations of the imperial army. Other methods were behavioural. Enlisted men still addressed officers in the third person rather than with the less formal '*Sie*'. As late as 1926, junior officers were confronted with a hypothetical social situation. A lieutenant and a civilian accompany a young lady home at night. The civilian invites the other two to come in for a drink. The officer, however, must do all in his power to convince the woman to go straight home, lest her reputation be compromised![15]

In the middle of the Jazz Age, such an admonition might well seem hopelessly old-fashioned. Yet it spoke to Weimar Germany's development as an open, capitalist society. Prior to 1914, these characteristics had been widely regarded as appendages to and departures from a Prussian ideal that emphasized public service and personal honour as opposed to private profit and individual hedonism. Related to this was the post-war challenge posed to a 'Prussian' ethos of a 'modest work culture', stressing the task for the task's own sake, by an efflorescent search for gain, as quickly as possible by any possible means. It was as if the *Gruenderjahren* of the 1870s had come again, and even that era of speculation soon appeared moderate compared to its successor. Diligence, self-denial, self-mastery – were these not liabilities in the post-war order?[16] And yet, at the same time, it was not entirely unpleasant even to committed republicans, in an age when whirl seemed king, to have a Reichswehr that seemed a repository of traditional civic virtue.

Related to what was widely perceived as a tectonic shift in the public ethos was an exponential increase in direct violence after 1918. This phenomenon cannot be entirely ascribed to the Freikorps and their left-wing counterparts, or to the homecoming of a brutalized 'front generation'. German society itself had been coarsened by four years that had removed many of the pre-war restraints on behaviour. Whatever its genesis, the phenomenon was in sharp contrast to a Prussian social contract that historically had in principle

---

15 Adolf Reinicke, *Das Reichsheer 1921–1934* (Osnabrück, 1986), is a mine of useful detail on the army's grass-roots human dynamics. Cf. as well Hans Meier-Welcker, 'Der Weg zum Offizier im Reichsheer der Weimarer Republik' *Militaergeschichtliche Mitteilungen* 19 (1976), 174–181.
16 On this question, see Joan Campbell, *Joy In Work: German Work. The National Debate, 1800–1945* (Princeton, 1989).

offered order in exchange for service, and in practice had been significantly successful in curbing violence by judicious blends of co-option and repression.

Germany, in short, wanted normalcy in the years after 1918, but was unable to achieve it. The gradual turn to Nazism that began in the late 1920s represented a *Flucht nach vorne*, an inability to process the legacy of the Great War, as much as a belief in the Nazis' promises to make things better. In that context, 'Prussian' virtues and traditions seemed increasingly appealing, if only as a stick with which to smite the present.[17] They had far more resonance, indeed, among the general population than in an army well on the way to developing its own traditions through its own behaviours. Anti-republican and anti-democratic these may have been. They were also not Prussian, as that concept was becoming defined.

The Nazi years: Old wine in a new bottle?

Prussianism in its popular forms was also in sharp contrast to the ethos of the National Socialists. The Nazi party has been compared by scholars to almost every possible human organization, even medieval feudalism. It requires only a little stretch of the imagination to see it as a street gang, with leadership based on a constantly-demonstrated combination of charisma and performance. National Socialism also suggests a dysfunctional family with no parents present – only the 'uncle figure' of Adolf Hitler presiding malevolently over ultimately murderous sibling rivalries. But no matter how Nazism is defined, the one adjective that cannot be applied is 'patriarchal'. Hitler's public persona was that of Führer, leader, elder brother, perhaps even erotic symbol, but never a father. Nazi ideology has appropriately been called 'reactionary modernism', but progress was the movement's flywheel. Nostalgia was essentially domestic kitsch; in particular, it had no place in military matters.[18]

In that context, the German Reichswehr and the Nazi *Bewegung* had the common ground of emphasizing a commitment to the future rather than a

---

17 Richard Bessel, *Germany after the First World War* (Oxford, 1993), develops both the multiple levels of violence and the resulting nostalgia for simpler places and times. William L. Patch, *Heinrich Bruening and the Dissolution of the Weimar Republic* (Cambridge, 1998), is a case study of the strengths and limitations of the Prussian tradition in a political context.
18 Jeffrey Herf, *Reactionary Modernism: Technology, Culture, and Politics in Weimar and the Third Reich* (Cambridge, 1984).

vision of the past. Hitler's initially enthusiastic wooing of the soldiers was based on his intention of using them first to consolidate his hold over both the Nazi party and the German people, then as the standard-bearers of territorial and ideological expansion until they could safely be replaced by the SS. The Reichswehr for its part also saw the Nazis as means to an end: increasing the armed forces' human and material resources. By the early 1930s, the German military's view of war had shifted away from the symbiotic models of the Reichswehr's early years. The army's increasing operational/tactical focus drew it away from broad-gauged involvement with industry. The gulf between soldiers and politicians widened as the Republic's crisis deepened. Few officers saw their responsibilities to the state in any but the narrowest terms. The war game of December 1932, with its predictions of domestic disaster should Nazis and communists combine against an overextended, outnumbered and probably outgunned Reichswehr, was presented with a kind of malicious pleasure that reflected more than simple anti-republican sentiment. It suggested instead fundamental detachment from the processes of government in a way alien to a Prussian army with its comprehensive ties to state and society.[19] In the context of later events, one might suggest that even the unhealthier forms of 'Prussianism' provided more appropriate guides than did the Reichswehr legacy of focused professionalism. The soldiers were nevertheless confident that once Germany's young men changed their brown shirts for army *Feldgrau*, their socialization away from any superficial influences of National Socialism would be relatively easy. The relevant virtues the Nazis preached, comradeship, self-sacrifice, courage, community, had been borrowed from the army's ethos. The army knew well how to cultivate them without any outside help. With the reintroduction of conscription in 1935, the new Wehrmacht seemingly continued its movement away from any lingering Prussian heritage. In contrast to its imperial predecessor, which in peacetime had places for only about half those eligible, the German army now drafted virtually every fit man. As a consequence, it was a people's force in ways foreign to Moltke or Frederick II. Its officers were drawn from a broad spectrum of the educated males. It continued as well its de facto elitism. Most of the new divisions were formed by 'waves', each wave with differing scales of equipment and levels of training. In planning for war, the army was correspondingly constrained to develop a hierarchy of reliability, with the peacetime infantry divisions (the 'first wave') and the mobile divisions

---

19 For a more positive view of the breadth of Reichswehr vision, see A. Schildt, *Militaerdiktatur mit Massenbasis? Die Querfrontkonzeption der Reichswehrfuehrung um General von Schleicher am Ende der Weimarer Republik* (Frankfurt, 1981).

created from peacetime formations at the apex. Along similar lines, the limited supply of motor vehicles was concentrated in a relatively few units.[20] In the contexts of a doctrine, developed from the Reichswehr matrix, emphasizing speed and shock as major force multipliers, the army that went to war in 1939 was 'layered' in ways unique in Prussian/German history.

The army of Nazi Germany stressed its 'non-Prussian' identity at the grass roots as well as in tables of organization. A new army had new facilities. Barracks with showers and athletic fields, plenty of windows and ample space between bunks, were a seven days' wonder to fathers and uncles who had worn uniform under the empire. Food was well cooked, and there was a lot of it. Officers were expected to bond with their men, replacing paternalism by fraternalism, leading by example on a daily basis. One anecdote may stand for many experiences. A squad of recruits was at rifle practice. The platoon leader asked who was the best shot among them. When the group reached a consensus, the lieutenant offered a challenge: 'Beat my score and you can have an early furlough.' At the end of three rounds, the private won by a single point – by grace of a lieutenant who knew how to lose without making it obvious.[21] When the wheels came off in a combat situation, such officers seldom had to say 'follow me!' Men would do so of their own wills.

From the beginning, National Socialism's technocratic aspects had appealed to the professionals of the *Truppenamt* and in the rifle companies. As the Wehrmacht expanded and rearmed, however, it tended increasingly to rely on the National Socialist system for the 'populist' features that contributed so much to the new army's effectiveness.[22] The conscripts of the 1930s were motivated, alert and physically fit to degrees inconceivable in all but the best formations of the kaiser's day. Thanks to the 18 months of compulsory labour service required of all 17-year-olds, they required a minimum of socializing into barracks life, and were more than ·casually acquainted with the elements of close-order drill. But they brought more than physical qualities with them.

If the Republic had made a devil's bargain with the soldiers in 1918, 'the

---

20 See R. L. DiNardo, *Mechanized Juggernaut or Military Anachronism? Horses and the German Army of World War II* (Westport, Conn., 1991).
21 The anecdote comes from H. Richardson and D. Showalter (eds), *Sieg Heil! War Letters of Tank Gunner Karl Fuchs, 1937–1941* (Hamden, Conn., 1987) pp. 46–7. Useful as well in this context is Joachim Tautz, *Militaerische Jugendpolitik in der Weimarer Republik: Die Jugendorganizationen des Stahlhelm, Bund der Frontsoldaten: Jungstahlhelm und Scharnhorst, Bund deutscher Jungmannen* (Regensburg, 1998).
22 On this, see Manfred Messerschmidt, 'The Wehrmacht and the *Volksgemeinschaft*', *Journal of Contemporary History* 13 (1983), 719–44.

pike had been turned round' well and truly by 1938. When, during the Czechoslovak crisis, senior officers critical of Hitler's regime discussed a putsch, a major stumbling block involved the willingness not only of the rank and file, but even the regimental officers, to follow their generals against the government. The exact extent of the army's Nazification remains open to debate – but only because the loyalties of Germans in uniform were never put to the proof. By the time the military resistance finally chanced its arm on 20 July 1944, its plans had been developed so as to depend as little as possible on troop units who knew what was happening. Better evidence cannot be offered in proof that even if the army might not have become National Socialist, it was a long way from being Prussian in the sense of being able to expect affirmative obedience as a matter of course.[23]

A similar pattern emerged at the war's sharp end, particularly in the army's defining theatre, the Eastern Front. From the first days of Operation Barbarossa, the German army gave no quarter to commissars and tolerated when it did not accept the hands-on massacre of Jews. Prisoners of war were as a matter of policy deprived of food and medical care. Anything resembling partisan resistance was met with reprisals on scales beyond imagining since the Thirty Years' War. Each and all of these behaviours stood in essential contrast to a Prussian legacy of 'hard war' against armed enemies and 'correctness' towards those who submitted.[24]

Something that defies quantification, but is nevertheless significant, is the level of personal enjoyment a significant proportion of German soldiers seemed to take in that kind of behaviour. Duty under the Prussians significantly often became pleasure under the Nazis.[25] Related to this was the steady 'demodernizing' of the German army in general and the Russian Front in particular. Beginning on 22 June 1941, the army's capacities for high-tech war-making steadily declined. Tanks and half-tracks could at best be replaced one for one, and then usually on a 'surge' basis. Trucks broke down or stalled in the mud. Russian T-34s and KVs defied anti-tank guns so feeble that they were dubbed 'army door-knockers' by disgruntled *Landser*. The immediate response to that particular tactical challenge was the *geballte Ladung*: a bundle of hand grenades placed by hand in a vulnerable spot on

---

23 The best overview of the military resistance is the anthology, BM zur Verteidigung (ed.), *Aufstand des Gewissens* (Herford, 1984).
24 See particularly John Horne and Alan Kramer, 'German "Atrocities" and Franco-German Opinion, 1914: The Evidence of German Soldiers' Diaries', *Journal of Modern History* 66 (1994), 1–33.
25 The most comprehensive overview of this controversial issue, in terms of both analysis and bibliography, is Gerd R. Ueberschar, 'The Ideologically Motivated War in the East', in R-D. Müller and G. Überschar (eds), *Hitler's War in the East 1941–45: A Critical Assessment*, trans. B. Little (Providence, RI, 1997), pp. 208–280.

the tank. Do that enough times and one received a medal – or 'the order of the birch cross', a *Landser* reference to the army's favourite form of grave marker.

These kinds of close encounters had no roots in a Prussian belief that the craftsman requires appropriate tools. They reflected instead a psychological demodernization fostered by technical demodernization. In the absence of artillery, aircraft, and armoured fighting vehicles, will-power and ferocity became desirable, often necessary, platoon-level force multipliers – especially in the 'ordinary' divisions, unfavoured by allocations of new equipment or high priorities for support. Nazi ideology, in turn, came to play a central, albeit instrumental, role by providing explanation and justification for the sacrifices demanded of the ordinary soldier.[26] If the stormtrooper of the First World War had been a prototype of the techno-warrior, the *Ostfrontkaempfer* of 1944–45 was closer to Nietzsche's proto-existentialist 'eternal warrior'. Hard men who neither asked nor gave quarter were welcome when 'Ivan' sent his assault waves forward, and even more welcome when it became a question of escaping encirclement and finding a German front line that might be a hundred miles distant. It was scarcely coincidental that the image of the Waffen SS grew increasingly favourable in a German army that for years had derided the Nazi Party's 'asphalt soldiers'. Nor was it coincidental that within the Waffen SS the Totenkopf Division, originally formed from concentration camp guards and commanded by concentration camp officers, established a combat reputation second to none in a theatre of war that grew ever more congenial to the unit's particular heritage and mentality.[27]

It all seemed light-years away from Prussian concepts that privileged the soldier rather than the killer, that valued structure rather than mêlée, that regarded war instrumentally rather than as an end in itself. Yet at the same time, Hitler's army found the old ways and the old mores coming back 'through door and gate' as the Third Reich progressed. Hitler's army replicated Prussia's in its pursuit of annihilation over attrition and offence over defence. Even as the war entered its end-game stage, German ripostes sought decision, at least at sector levels. Kursk, Mortain, the Ardennes, even the last gasp at Budapest, were not planned or executed as ripostes delaying the inevitable. If Hitler's grandiose strategic visions were seldom shared by his generals, they did retain – or perhaps revive –

---

26 The linkages between demodernization and ideology are particularly emphasized in Omer Bartov, *Hitler's Army: Soldiers, Nazis and War in the Third Reich*, (London, 1991).
27 Charles W. Syndor, *Soldiers of Destruction: The SS Death's Head Division, 1933–1945* (Princeton, 1977).

the Prussian concept of winning a battle as a first step toward winning a war.

The Prussian heritage of concentration on operational aspects of war-making re-emerged as well, in forms more virulent than the original. Intelligence, logistics, administration – these were *Beamtensachen*, the province of paper-shufflers. No army taking intelligence seriously would have retained Reinhard Gehlen as chief of its Russian-front branch in view of his consistent record of miscalculating both Soviet capacities and Soviet intentions.[28] A consistent characteristic of German higher headquarters was their undermanning. This has been described as streamlining by scholars and soldiers who use the German example as a stick with which to beat allegedly bloated American headquarters. The recent work of Geoff Megargee, however, demonstrates that redundancy can be valuable under wartime conditions. Even the OKW staff was so consistently overworked that important issues either slipped through the cracks or were decided ad hoc by tired men. Neither is a long-term recipe for victory.[29]

Weakness in theatre-level combined arms operations was another Prussian pattern that made its way into the Wehrmacht. The Prussian army and its imperial successor had never been able to take maritime operations seriously in any but a financial sense – as a drain on the army's budget. The Reichswehr's shift away from a broader conceptual paradigm has been previously mentioned. 'Jointness' similarly found no place in the Second Reich's military experience. The Norwegian campaign's success in 1940 was a product of ad hoc initiatives at lower command levels, and proved to be a one-off event.[30] The army's plans for Operation Sea Lion treated the English Channel as a wider-than-usual river, projecting almost casually landings of scales and scopes that set D-Day itself in the shade.[31]

When the army considered it important, combined arms became a major force multiplier. The Luftwaffe in particular was increasingly integrated into an early version of 'air-land battle', with the undertow proving strong enough to detach its planners and commanders from their earlier concern for the strategic and theatre level applications of air power.[32] Technology

---

28 Hans Heinrich Wilhelm, *Die Prognosen der Abteilungen Fremde Heere Ost 1942–1945. Zwei Legende aus dem Dritten Reich* (Stuttgart, 1974).
29 Geoffrey Megargee, 'Inside Hitler's High Command' (Lawrence, Kans, 2000).
30 James W. Corum, 'The German Campaign in Norway 1940 as a Joint Operation' *Journal of Strategic Studies* 21 (1998), 50–78.
31 Cf. Egbert Kieser, *Hitler on the Doorstep: Operation Sea Lion: The German Plan to Invade Britain, 1940* (Annapolis, Md., 1997); and Peter Schenck, *Invasion of England, 1940: The Planning of Operation Sea Lion* (London, 1990).
32 James W. Corum, *The Luftwaffe. Creating the Operational Air War, 1918–1940* (Lawrence, Kans., 1997).

faced a similar situation. Where the army thought it was important – small arms, armoured fighting vehicles – German material took pride of place in the world. But there was no systematic effort made to develop the kind of broad-gauged approach that produced DUKWs, jeeps, and all the other semi-martial artefacts that saved lives for the British and Americans – lives that the German army could ill afford to lose.

The Prussian heritage had positive military aspects as well. The German army of the Second World War incorporated the best combination of discipline and initiative at division level and below of any twentieth-century force save Israel's in 1967–73. Underlying specific methods and techniques, the interdependent concepts of mission tactics and personal integrity developed under Frederick the Great and Moltke the Elder endured at the sharp end of war from France in 1940 through Italy in 1943 to the Eastern Front in 1944–45. To cite only one example, the battle groups that were so effective on offence and so staunch in defence were frequently second-best solutions, reflecting overall breakdowns in command and overall shortages of equipment.[33] Nevertheless, no army matched the German in successful improvisation within general frameworks.

These improvisations succeeded in good part because of a Prussian legacy of expecting NCOs and junior officers to be competent. There was no room for the Anglo-American stereotype of the green second lieutenant whose veteran sergeant leads him by the hand until he can stand on his feet. Nor was there cultural space for the hard-drinking, semi-literate non-commissioned brawler whose stripes came off with each pay-day spree, only to be restored by his indulgent superiors. War, particularly its land variant, is essentially an artificial activity, a constructed experience. Assumptions are correspondingly important. Soldiers seek to act as they are expected to act. The parameters may be defined by culture – the Vietnam-era impact of John Wayne has been remarked by many veterans of that war. Or they may be established by history. As the war progressed, the Prussian heritage of leadership at regimental levels was a more reliable, more comprehensive, guide to appropriate behaviour than its relatively rootless, increasingly shrill, Nazi counterpart. Even patriarchs became more welcome as the front-line situation grew more desperate. A father figure, be he in his early twenties, can offer hope in ways closed to an uncle, brother, or comrade.[34]

---

33 Peter Mansoor, *The GI Offensive in Europe: The Triumph of American Infantry Divisions, 1941–1945* (Lawrence, Kans., 1999), pp. 254 and *passim*, is a common-sense critique of the battle-group approach as a second-best solution.
34 Stephen Fritz, *Frontsoldaten: The German Soldier in World War II* (Lexington, Ky., 1995); and Martin van Creveld, *Fighting Power* (Westport, Conn., 1982), for developments of these themes.

Conclusion

Arguably, however, the Prussian military legacy's final significance was mythic. In the Third Reich far more than in Weimar, it came to represent a world lost and values abandoned for the sake of false idols and personal gratification. 'Prussian' stood again for uprightness and honour – concepts ostensibly foreign to the 'new men' of Republic and Reich alike. Wilhelm Groener, Weimar's war minister from 1928 to 1932, was a widower. In 1930, he married a woman some years his junior, who shortly bore him a daughter. Eyebrows were raised when the proud father showed off his new family along Unter den Linden. Tongues wagged when officers – and their wives – counted to nine and concluded that while the baby was on time, the wedding had been somewhat late. While the gossip never escalated into scandal, Groener's critics inside and outside the Reichswehr – especially the Nazis – nevertheless loudly beat the drum of moral decay in high places.[35] Groener's eventual successor, Werner von Blomberg, pushed the envelope even further with his 1938 marriage. That the subsequent scandal was generated by Blomberg's Nazi enemies has obscured the fact that the lady in question did, at the very least, pose for nude photographs of varying levels of explicitness. A rough contemporary equivalent would be a service chief's marrying a minor actress in pornographic films. Even in this permissive age, it is difficult to believe that he would not be expected to resign. Too many of his subordinates would be in a position to see far too much of their commander's bride.

The personal life of Walther von Brauchitsch might have given pause even to those able to dismiss Blomberg's behaviour as proving the truth of the proverb that 'an erection has no brains'. Brauchitsch, Hitler's choice as the army's new commander, was involved in an extramarital affair with the kind of woman who is every first wife's nightmare. Frau von Brauchitsch had consistently refused requests for a divorce – as much, it appears, from anger as from financial considerations. Then Adolf Hitler offered a cash settlement of 800,000 marks from public funds and made a gentle hint that non-compliance might have far less pleasant consequences. The divorce was

---

35 Johannes Huerter, *Wilhelm Groener: Reichswehrminister am Ende der Weimarer Republik* (Oldenbourg, 1993), pp. 263–4, handles the issue with taste and discretion. It is appropriate to make the point that the child's birth may well have been premature. From the military's point of view, the key issue was that mesalliances and sexual misconduct at lower ranks were as much as an officer's commission was worth. The notorious Reinhard Heydrich began his SS career after being dismissed from the navy for compromising a woman's reputation. Rank may have its privileges, sexually as in other areas. Flaunting them is another matter.

immediately forthcoming. Brauchitsch was bought and paid for. And while the exact circumstances of the arrangement were kept secret, officers nevertheless wondered just what had happened to decorum and discretion in the brave new world of the Nazi new order. Certainly, the kaiser's generals had their little affairs, their threatened mesalliances – but never had soiled Prussian linen been washed in such full public view.[36]

Discontent was further exacerbated during the war, as new men succeeded generals discredited by defeat or displaced by Hitler's apparent whims. Many were cut from general staff cloth – Hans Hube, Kurt von Tippleskirch, Hasso von Manteuffel. Others, and the most visible ones, were of the stamp of Walther Model and Georg von Schoenerer – hard men who substituted courage, energy and will-power for the disciplined finesse that was the self-defined proofmark of German military intelligence. As it became increasingly obvious that the war was lost, the 'Prussian soldierly virtues' widely ascribed to Gerd von Rundstedt did more to sustain him in command than his at best dubious operational achievements. Rundstedt's alleged Prussianism really meant his ironic and obvious detachment from the catastrophe breaking over the country and the state he had sworn to serve.[37]

It was a sharp contrast to the behaviour of Prussia's general officers in the aftermath of Jena and Auerstedt. No matter how wrongheaded their particular ideas might have been, these men had at least behaved proactively in an ultimate crisis. Rundstedt's hauteur was more appropriate to an *ancien régime* salon – *après nous la déluge*. But it offered something for lesser men to cling to as the Nazi helmsmen steered the German ship full ahead onto the rocks. It offered as well a way of salvaging something that was called honour from the wreck – even if it would have been unrecognizable by Prussian soldiers of an earlier era.

---

36 Harold C. Deutsch, *Hitler and His Generals* (Minneapolis, 1974). pp. 81ff and 221ff is the best analysis of the two affairs. It should be noted that one of the major reservations among monarchists in the Weimar era to a restoration was the promiscuous private life of Crown Prince William.
37 Charles Messenger, *The Last Prussian: A Biography of Field Marshal Gerd von Rundstedt 1875–1953* (London, 1991).

CHAPTER TWELVE

Prussia, Prussianism and National Socialism, 1933–47

BRENDAN SIMMS

Colonel Rudolf von Gersdorff: 'Perhaps all the Field Marshals should go together to the Führer and hold a gun to his head.'

Field Marshal Erich von Manstein: 'Prussian Field Marshals do not mutiny.'

Gersdorff: 'There are enough examples in Prussian history of senior commanders acting against the will and orders of their monarchs. I remind you only of Seydlitz and Yorck [sic].'[1]

The famous decree of the Allied Control Council of 1947 announcing the dissolution of Prussia was an exorcism, an ideological-historical statement as well as a territorial fiat. It reflected allied – and many German – preoccupations with the allegedly baleful role played by Prussia and Prussianism in the shaping of modern Germany. The rogues' gallery from 'Frederick the Great – to Bismarck – to Hitler' had become a staple of contemporary polemic and historiography and has remained so to this day. 'The path from Roßbach and Leuthen ended', Rudolf Augstein argued in his controversial biography of Frederick the Great, '[...] in Versailles and Stalingrad.'[2] Crude generalizations soon gave way to a more refined view that emphasized Prussian militarism, partial modernization, 'undemocratic thinking', and a host of other 'democratic deficits', but the anti-Prussian

---

1 Cited in Christian Schneider, 'Denkmal Manstein. Psychogramm eines Befehlshabers', in Hannes Heer and Klaus Naumann, eds, *Vernichtungskrieg. Verbrechen der Wehrmacht 1941–1944* (Hamburg, 1995), p. 405.
2 Rudolf Augstein, *Preußens Friedrich und die Deutschen* (new edn, Frankfurt am Main, 1981), p. 256. For a similar view, see Christian Graf von Krockow, *Warnung vor Preußen* (Berlin, 1981).

animus remained. The long-term effects of all this became apparent during the negotiations leading up to German reunification in 1990 when the descendants of those East Elbians expropriated between 1945 and 1949 saw their demands for restitution frustrated. The professed reason was that this had been done at the insistence of the Soviet occupiers; it later emerged that the true motivation was the German state's acute financial need and a joint East German Marxist and western bourgeois fear of a resurrected old Prussian agrarian elite.

This is not to say that Prussia has not had powerful literary and historiographical advocates to defend it from the taint of National Socialism. Hitler, ran a *bon mot* attributed variously to Ernst Niekisch or Karl Kraus, was 'Austria's revenge for Sadowa'. Eberhard Kessel spoke for an older generation of German historians when he wrote that it is 'undeniable that the most sacred Prussian traditions were shamefully betrayed by Hitler and National Socialism'.[3] But even Hans Mommsen, one of the paragons of the 'new' more 'critical' historical schools in the 1960s, asked whether combining National Socialism and Prussianism was not 'squaring the circle': National Socialism was 'as un-Prussian as one could possibly imagine'.[4] More recently, Wolfgang Wippermann, himself no Borussophile apologist, has argued that the relationship between National Socialism and Prussia was impossible to define, since there was not one 'Prussia', but several.[5]

National Socialism and Prussianism

The Nazis themselves laid great stress on their Prussian lineage and affinities. Already in *Mein Kampf* (1925), Hitler, somewhat unusually for somebody of his Austrian background, had stoutly defended Prussia against Bavarian separatism. Prussia was praised as the 'germ-cell of the Empire', the 'most central section of the state structure', whose historic destiny had been to supersede the Habsburgs in the struggle for predominance in Germany. This power-political approval was matched by a spiritual sympathy.

---

3 Eberhard Kessel, 'Adolf Hitler und der Verrat am Preußentum', *Aus Politik und Zeitgeschichte. Beilage zur Wochenzeitung 'Das Parlament'*, 15 November 1961, p. 649.
4 Hans Mommsen, 'Preußentum und Nationalsozialismus', in Wolfgang Benz, Hans Buchheim and Hans Mommsen (eds), *Der Nationalsozialismus. Studien zur Ideologie und Herrschaft* (Frankfurt am Main, 1993), pp. 32, 40.
5 Wolfgang Wippermann, 'Nationalsozialismus und Preußentum', *Aus Politik und Zeitgeschichte. Beilage zur Wochenzeitung 'Das Parlament'*, 26 December 1981, p. 20.

'Prussia, in particular', Hitler argued, 'demonstrates with marvellous sharpness that not material qualities but ideal virtues alone make possible the formation of a state.'[6] It is no surprise that his chief role model was Frederick the Great, to whose determination and defiance of the odds Hitler adverted on many occasions, or that on the night of the Nazi takeover of power on 30 January 1933, the torchlight procession of the SA entered the Wilhelmstraße to the tunes of the 'Fredericus-Marsch'. Ritual exhortations to follow the 'Prussian example' were standard fare in the party newspaper, the *Völkischer Beobachter*, and Nazi electoral material outbid its conservative nationalist rival, the German National People's Party (DNVP), in its emphasis on Prussian themes. In April 1932, Goebbels famously stated that 'National Socialism may justly claim that it is Prussianism [...]. The idea which we carry is Prussian. The hallmarks [*Wahrzeichen*], for which we fight are suffused with the Prussian spirit, and the aims which we are trying to achieve are in rejuvenated form the ideals for which Frederick William I, Frederick the Great and Bismarck strived'.[7]

Cinematic concern with Prussia went back to the mid-Weimar era in the 1920s. But in Nazi Germany, Prussianism was to permeate film and popular literature to an unprecedented degree. The premiere of the *Chorale of Leuthen*, celebrating one of Frederick the Great's most famous victories in the Seven Years' War, was held on the eve of Hitler's takeover of power. As time progressed, these films transcended merely abstract celebration of Prussian virtues and became, to quote Gerhard Schoenberner, part of the process of 'psychological mobilisation and preparation for war'.[8] Sometimes they were directly synchronized with German foreign policy, as in the 1935 film about Major Schill's rebellion against Napoleon – *Der höhere Befehl* – which is anti-French, but sympathetic to Britain; it needs to be seen in the context of the Anglo-German naval agreement of that year. Similarly, *Kadetten*, which deals with a heroic defence against the Russians in the Seven Years' War, was suppressed because of the Hitler–Stalin Pact and only released in 1941.[9] Poignantly, the Third Reich's cinematic engagement with Prussia ended in the ruins of 1945, with *Kolberg*, which was set in the wars

---

6   Adolf Hitler, *Mein Kampf*, trans. Ralph Manheim (Boston, 1943), pp. 558 and *passim*; pp. 154, 512; 152.
7   Manfred Schlenke, 'Das "preußische Beispiel" in Propaganda und Politik des Nationalsozialismus', *Aus Politik und Zeitgeschichte. Beilage zur Wochenzeitung 'Das Parliament'*, 3 July 1968, p. 17.
8   Gerhard Schoenberner, 'Das Preußenbild im deutschen Film. Geschichte und Ideologie', in Axel Marquardt and Heinz Rathsack (eds), *Preußen im Film. Eine Retrospective der Stiftung Deutsche Kinemathek* (Hamburg, 1981), p. 32.
9   See Friedrich P. Kahlenberg, 'Preußen als Filmsujet in der Propagandasprache der NS-Zeit', in Marquardt and Rathsack (eds), *Preußen im Film*, pp. 149, 154–5.

against Napoleon and chronicled the heroic defence of that city against the French.

Nazi enthusiasm for Prussia was, however, very selective. It focused on Frederick the Great; on Queen Louise, who stiffened her husband, Frederick William III's back and acted as a patriotic beacon during the Wars of Liberation against Napoleon; on the Prussian reformers Stein, Gneisenau, and Scharnhorst; on military heroes such as Blücher; and, of course, on Bismarck, the hero of German unification. Very little mention was made of monarchs such as Frederick William II, Frederick William IV, or even of the soldier king, Frederick William I; and any reference to the recent disastrous reign of William II was studiously avoided. Nor, unsurprisingly, did the Nazis show any interest in Frederick the Great's involvement in the French Enlightenment or his friendship with Voltaire. Undoubted Prussian heroes whose 'German-ness' was deemed suspect, such as Stein's erstwhile collaborator and later rival, Baron Hardenberg, were ignored. Needless to say, the Prussian (Jewish) Emancipation Edict of 1812 was never invoked. Cinematic interest was also selective, with nearly all productions devoted to the same classic pantheon.

Perhaps the most striking example of the suggested synthesis between National Socialism and the old Prussia were the ceremonies to mark the opening of the new session of the Reichstag after the elections of March 1933, which have come to be known as the 'Day of Potsdam'. Conceived and executed by Goebbels, this carefully choreographed piece of theatre was captured and reproduced on famous newsreels; parallel events were held all over the country. The venue of the old garrison church at Potsdam was chosen in order to symbolize the old Prussian martial virtues and their roots in traditional religion. The old imperial standards, banished to obscurity in Weimar times, were back on triumphal display; the last emperor's chair remained symbolically vacant. Two of his sons, however, were in attendance, the one in SA uniform, the other in the garb of the old Death's Head Hussars – a symbol which had yet to take on such widespread sinister connotations. Outside the church, the serried ranks of the Reichswehr and the Nazi paramilitary formations paraded with equal enthusiasm, if varying precision.

The Day of Potsdam attempted nothing less than a mystic communion between Prussianism, traditional (both Catholic and Protestant) religion, and the new order.[10] In his opening speech, the President, Field Marshal

---

10 On the liturgical dimension, see Werner Freitag, 'Martin Luther, Friedrich II und Adolf Hitler– der Tag von Potsdam im neuen Licht', in *Preußen und der Nationalsozialismus. Potsdamer Gespräche* edited by the Volkshochschule 'Albert Einstein' (Potsdam, 1992), pp. 15, 23 and *passim*.

Hindenburg, himself a monument to past glories, invoked the 'old spirit of this place of renown'; subsequently Hitler reminded his listeners of the proclamation of the (second) empire in 1871. Later, the historian Friedrich Meinecke was to dismiss the whole exercise as a *Rührkomödie* (a sentimental comedy), but at the time it was an undoubted success. For example, the culturally pessimistic philosopher, Oswald Spengler, though no particular admirer of National Socialism, was persuaded that the spectacle 'was Prussian through and through, just like the mood of 1914'.[11] Similarly, the conservative nationalist historian Gerhard Ritter – much to his later embarrassment – argued in the first edition of his biography of Frederick the Great (1936), that the Day of Potsdam 'was in all senses in the proudest traditions of old Prussian history'.[12] And even such a conservative sceptic as Eberhard Kessel conceded, at 20 years' remove, that the events of that day 'sounded' and in many ways were 'genuinely' Prussian.[13]

The intention behind the Prussian theme was to win over the conservative, often East Elbian, civil and military German elite. To some extent, the Nazis were pushing an open door. The shock of the lost war, the reduction of the old imperial army to 100,000 men, the abolition of remaining noble privileges in the Weimar Constitution of 1919, fear of Bolshevism and economic pressures made many Prussian nobles – and, indeed, other aristocrats – receptive to Hitler's promise of national rejuvenation. Some, such as the Knobelsdorffs, even looked forward to future gains in the east when they observed that the 'rise and fall of the German nobility throughout history has always been linked to the gain or loss of *Lebensraum* in the east'.[14] Those who rejected Nazism from the very beginning – such as Ewald von Kleist-Schmenzin were a minority; so were confirmed National Socialists such as Udo von Woyrsch, who was for a time the supreme SS police chief in Silesia. More typical, perhaps, was Fritz-Dietlof Count von der Schulenburg, later murdered by the Nazis for his involvement in the resistance. He pitted the unifying Prussian myth against the 'divisive' democracy of Weimar. Initially sceptic, especially about the movement's south German roots, he soon came to view National Socialism as a 'new form of Prussianism'; in October 1932, he remarked hopefully that 'It appears as if the North German element is beginning to dominate' in National Socialism.[15]

---

11 Schlenke, "Das-preußische Beispiel", p. 20.
12 Achim von Borries, *Preussen und die Folgen* (Berlin and Bonn, 1981), p. 158.
13 Kessel, 'Adolf Hitler und der Verrat am Preußentum', p. 661.
14 Quoted in Georg H. Kleine, 'Adelsgenossenschaft und Nationalsozialismus', *Vierteljahrshefte für Zeitgeschichte* 26 (1978), 135. In general, see also Shelley Baranowski, *The Sanctity of Rural Life. Nobility, Protestantism, and Nazism in Weimar Prussia* (New York and Oxford, 1995), pp. 144–76.
15 Ulrich Heinemann, *Ein konservativer Rebell. Fritz-Dietlof Graf von der Schulenburg und der 20. Juli* (Berlin, 1990), p. 25.

But there were also considerable tensions that were never satisfactorily resolved. The social disdain with which many East Elbians, and especially President von Hindenburg, regarded the lowly 'Bohemian Corporal', Adolf Hitler, is well known. More particularly, Prussian nobles were worried by point 17 of the NSDAP's party programme, which envisaged the 'expropriation without compensation' of property under certain circumstances. Despite a concerted attempt to win them over to National Socialism, spearheaded by individual sympathisers such as Prince Eulenburg-Hertefeld after 1930, Hitler never really penetrated the reserve with which he was regarded by most Junkers. It is no coincidence, for example, that the former president of the Prussian *Herrenhaus* – the equivalent of the House of Lords – Count Arnim-Boitzenburg, spurned overtures in 1931, on the grounds of religious objections, and reaffirmed his loyalty to the conservative nationalist DNVP.

Nor were these tensions allayed after the Nazi takeover of power. It is true that certain conciliatory gestures were made. A decree dating from 1929 banning serving officers and administrators from membership of the Corporation of German Nobles (*Deutsche Adelsgenossenschaft*, DAG) was rescinded for the army in November 1933. But, much to the disappointment of embattled East Elbian landowners, the *Reichserbhofgesetz* (Reich Entailed Farm Law) of September 1933, designed to protect farms from bankruptcy and partition, only covered smaller and middling holdings. To make matters worse, conservative interest groups such as the veterans' association, Stahlhelm, and the association of estate owners, *Reichslandbund*, very rapidly lost their autonomy to the Nazis in the wave of *Gleichschaltung* after the takeover of power. Equally worrying was the threatened absorption of the Reichswehr into the SA and the dilution of its old Prussian character. For when Ernst Röhm described himself as the 'Scharnhorst of the new army', this was no mere rhetorical flourish, but a direct challenge to the established military elite; the implication that as in the Reform Era, revolutionary elan would replace corporate exclusivity, was not lost on them. Not for the first time, the Prussian heritage showed itself remarkably protean.

A potential sore point was Nazi racial thinking, whose exclusivity in some ways chimed with aristocratic temperament, but whose concrete application by obsessive bureaucrats often grated. Doubtless many Junkers supported or were profoundly indifferent to the introduction of the *Ariernachweis* – documentary proof of Aryan non-Jewish descent by the *Deutsche Adelsgenossenschaft* as part of their self-*Gleichschaltung*. Some, such as Bodo von der Marwitz, an early Nazi sympathiser whose own old Prussian roots and sympathies were beyond dispute, were outraged; he resigned from the DAG in 1935 after ignoring repeated requests to verify his own family tree.

Much more important for the deepening estrangement of large sections of the East Elbian nobility from National Socialism was the question of a Hohenzollern restoration, which Hitler had appeared to encourage in the final stages of the Weimar Republic. Already in 1929, Prince August Wilhelm had made contact with Hitler via the Stahlhelm; contacts with Göring, whose standing within conservative circles was high, had long existed. At this point, the prince claimed to his émigré interrogator after the war, the subject of monarchy 'was not on the agenda.[16] But in 1931 and 1932, Göring made two visits to the former emperor's Dutch exile at Doorn and seems have made restorationist noises. These were echoed in 1932–33 by both Hitler and Göring at the Salon of Viktoria von Dirksen, a Prussian aristocrat whose Berlin home became an important meeting point between Nazis and the conservative establishment. In the immediate aftermath of the takeover of power, there were some signs that monarchist hopes might be fulfilled. Just before the Day of Potsdam, Hitler and Göring had made further restorationist hints to the crown prince at Cäcilienhof in order to win Hohenzollern support for the ceremonies; and when Prince August Wilhelm appeared at the garrison church in SA uniform he did so with the permission of his father. But there was to be a rude awakening. Two days later, on the day of the Enabling Act, Hitler rejected any notion of a Hohenzollern restoration, or indeed of any monarchic experiments in the regions. In February 1934, all specifically monarchic organizations were banned. Very soon, August Wilhelm found himself marginalized, placed under house arrest in 1934 at the time of the Röhm putsch and subsequently issued with a gagging order. At the same time, the state began to pay the Hohenzollerns an annual retainer, which was notionally a compensation for lost property, but in reality a highly successful stratagem to discourage them from political involvement. The resulting disillusionment of some Junkers was epitomized by Count Ewald von Kleist-Wendisch-Tychow, the Landesführer of the *Deutsche Adelsgenossenschaft* in Anterior Pomerania. In January 1937, he announced the dissolution of his provincial section on the grounds that the failure of the new order to deliver a monarchic restoration was 'not compatible with the traditions and honour of the nobility'.[17]

If the Prussian nobility entertained reservations about National Socialism, these were heartily reciprocated by the Nazis themselves, whose relationship with the old Prussian tradition and its contemporary representatives was much more complex than the harmonizing cadences of the Day of Potsdam suggested. Many of the more *völkisch* and socialist members of the

---

16 Robert M. W. Kempner, *Das dritte Reich im Kreuzverhör. Aus den unveröffentlichten Vernehmungsprotokollen des Anklägers* (Munich, 1965) p. 125.
17 Kleine, 'Adelsgenossenschaft und Nationalsozialismus', p. 125.

movement were deeply suspicious of the East Elbian elites and their supposed conversion to the new order. 'Prussian-socialist', the Nazi writer Wilhelm Seddin claimed in 1935, 'is mere code for nationalist reaction.'[18] Particular hostility was shown by the minister for food supply, Walther Darré, the theoretician of 'blood and soil' and a firm advocate of the need for a 'New Nobility' based on achievement rather than birth; this call was echoed by the chief ideologist, Alfred Rosenberg. Darré spoke openly of the 'failure of the nobility' and approvingly quoted Heinrich von Treitschke's attack on the Prussian nobility in his own book: 'The Prussian nobility as a group has achieved only evil over the past three hundred years.'[19] In June 1934, he even told a mass meeting of 30,000 Pomeranian peasants that the sins of the East Elbian nobility should never be forgiven but rather influence the agricultural policy of the new regime. If the reality for the Prussian estate owners turned out to be less bleak than such rhetoric indicated, this was more the result of the need for efficient large-scale food production, than of any inherent sympathy on the part of the regime.[20]

There were other irritations. In many ways, the rational and orderly procedures of the Prussian bureaucracy were anathema to Hitler's polycratic and Bohemian style; he was, to quote Lothar Kettenacker, 'the anti-Prussian *tout court*'.[21] Indeed, Hans Mommsen, himself no apologist for the old Prussia, has argued that Prussian administrators did their best to maintain the rule of law under National Socialism, so much so that the head of the party chancellery, Martin Bormann, increasingly regarded them as a foreign body within the system.[22] As one might expect from an organization eager to distance itself from the more plebeian SA, Heinrich Himmler's SS made strenuous initial attempts to recruit from the nobility, and even the Hohenzollern family, especially after they were withdrawn from front-line service during the Second World War. Yet the affinity was to prove a shallow one. The SS was modelled on the medieval Teutonic knights rather than the classic Prussian tradition. Theoretically, its self-image as 'New Nobility' was fundamentally at variance with any notion of traditional hereditary nobility. It also remains a striking fact that not a single one of the SS divisions was named

---

18 Quoted in Johannes Rogalla von Bieberstein, 'Preußen und Preußentum', *Aus Politik und Zeitgechichte. Beilage zur Wochenzeitung 'Das Parlament'*, 12 January 1980, p. 28.
19 R. Walther Darré, *Neuadel aus Blut und Boden* (Munich, 1934), p. 12.
20 See Joachim Dissow, *Adel im übergang. Ein kritischer Standesgenosse berichtet aus Residenzen und Gutshäusern* (Stuttgart, 1961), pp. 180–1.
21 Lothar Kettenacker, 'Preußen in der alliierten Kriegszielplanung, 1939–1947', in Lothar Kettenacker, Manfred Schlenke and Hellmut Seier (eds), *Studien zur Geschichte Englands und der deutsch-britischen Beziehungen. Festschrift für Paul Kluke* (Munich, 1981), p. 315.
22 Hans Mommsen, *Beamtentum im Dritten Reich. Mit ausgewählten Quellen zur nationalsozialistischen Beamtenpolitik* (Stuttgart, 1966), p. 86.

after a modern Prussian figure or institution.[23] Besides, the SS was particularly preoccupied with racial purity and the fundamental gulf separating it from the traditional corporatism of many Junkers was never bridged; after the failed bomb plot against Hitler in July 1944, this reserve developed into open hostility with full-frontal attacks on the Prussian tradition in the *Schwarzes Korps*, the official organ of the SS.

Hitler's own relationship with Prussia had always been ambiguous and soon deteriorated. In *Mein Kampf*, for example, he portrayed the modern Prussian heritage as merely one of three core German traditions, and explicitly ranked it below the other two, namely the colonization of the 'Ostmark' (Austria) and the medieval settlement of East Elbia.[24] After the takeover of power, he began to develop a strong dislike of the military elite, which he suspected not only of strategic timidity, but also of a lack of inner commitment to the new order. On one occasion, he condemned the General Staff and the Supreme Command of the Wehrmacht (OKW) as a 'Special caste of particularly snobbish empty-headed Junkers and National pests [*Schädlinge*] full of sterile barrenness, lacking in ideas and cowardly'. On another, he announced that 'the General Staff is the last Masonic Order which I have not yet dissolved'.[25] In the end, the Junker presence in the military was not so much dissolved as diluted: already by the mid-1930s, the huge expansion of the Wehrmacht had fundamentally changed the social composition of the officer corps.[26] Under Hitler, the German army became less Prussian, more representative of the population as a whole, and thus more National Socialist.

The National Socialist regime and Prussia

There was more to Prussia than the Junkers and the conservative civil–military elite. Prussia was not just a nebulous historical concept or identity, but also by far the largest of the states making up the Weimar Republic. It contained two-thirds of the Reich's surface area, and three-

---

23 A point made by Bernt Engelmann, *Preußen. Land der unbegrenzten Möglichkeiten* (Munich, 1979), p. 415.
24 Hitler, *Mein Kampf*, pp. 647–8.
25 Cited in Hans Frank, *Im Angesicht des Galgens. Deutung Hitlers und seiner Zeit auf Grund eigener Erlebnisse und Erkenntnisse* (Munich-Gräfeling, 1953), p. 243.
26 See Detlef Bald, *Der deutsche Offizier. Sozial- und Bildungsgeschichte des deutschen Offizierkorps im 20. Jahrhundert* (Munich, 1982), p. 56 and *passim*.

fifths of all Germans lived there. Its political complexion was determined not only by the machinations of a largely aristocratic clique around President Hindenburg, but primarily by the preferences of its diverse electorate, such as East Elbians, Catholic Rhinelanders, Protestant Saxons and Hanoverians, many of whom were Prussians of relatively recent provenance. Unlike the Reich government, the Prussian government was relatively stable: it experienced only seven changes of government; at central level there were 21. Unlike the Reichstag, the Prussian parliament, the *Landtag*, was never dissolved prematurely before 1933.[27] Indeed, by the early 1930s, Social Democratic Prussia under its premier Otto Braun had become a 'bulwark of democracy' against the rising National Socialist tide.

The struggle for control of Prussia, acknowledged by all Weimar parties as the key to Germany itself, was thus at the centre of National Socialist strategy in the final stages of the Weimar Republic. This involved a twin-track approach with a constitutional 'legal' path to power explored by Hitler through electoral success and accommodation with the old elites; at the same time, the paramilitary formations of the SA fought for the streets. But the Nazis never won a majority in Prussia, as indeed they remained a minority in Germany as a whole as late as March 1933. Much of the old Prussian heartland, such as East Prussia, Lower Silesia and Pomerania was strongly National Socialist; the Catholic Rhineland and Upper Silesia, on the other hand, were not. At the same time, the Nazis did well in Protestant areas of south Germany, such as Franconia: confession rather than Prussianism per se appears to have been decisive. Nor did the Nazis succeed in wresting the Prussian *Landtag* from Social Democratic control by conventional electoral means.

In the end, Otto Braun was dislodged by a legally ambiguous coup of questionable legitimacy. For when in mid-1932 a National Socialist victory in the Prussian elections seemed possible, the Social Democratic incumbents changed the order of business concerning the formation of governments. Rather than a relative majority, as previously stipulated, the Nazis now needed an absolute majority to take over. The results of the Prussian elections of April 1932 were thus inconclusive, with 36 per cent for the National Socialists, 6.9 per cent for the DNVP and 12.8 per cent for the Communists; the anti-republican parties had an obstructive but not a constructive majority. This meant that Braun could remain as acting prime minister for so long as the Nazis were unable to muster a majority within the

---

27 Horst Möller, 'Das Ende Preußens', in Wolfgang Böhme (ed.), *Preußen – eine Herausforderung* (Karlsruhe, 1981), p. 108.

Landtag to support a candidate of their own. But in July, von Papen at the head of the imperial government, fully supported by President Hindenburg and the old Prussian elites, unilaterally deposed Braun and installed his own acting government, claiming under article 48 of the Constitution that the existing situation was both a threat to order and a threat towards Prussia's obligations to the Reich; this became known as the *Preussenschlag*. The lawful Prussian government appealed to the Constitutional Court (*Staatsgerichtshof*): the resulting Solomonic judgement absolved Braun of the charge of defaulting on his federal responsibilities, but upheld the right of the central government to transfer competencies to Reich ministries.

The old Prussia had thus conspired with the Reich and the Nazis to bring down the new democratic Prussia. But the subsequent behaviour of some of the old elites was to have more far-reaching consequences still. For the sequence of events which led to the appointment of Adolf Hitler as German chancellor was triggered by Chancellor Heinrich Brüning's plan to alleviate economic hardship by settling several hundred thousand unemployed on confiscated bankrupt East Elbian estates. Not since the short-lived 'socialization' debate after the Revolution of 1918 or the days of the Prussian Reform Movement had the Prussian Junkers faced such a profound threat to their property and privilege. They condemned the *Ostsiedlungsprogramm* (the programme for the colonization of eastern Europe) as 'agrarian Bolshevism' and prevailed upon President Hindenburg to sack Brüning and replace him by Franz von Papen. His new government, the 'cabinet of barons', was dominated by Prussians of the old school, such as Freiherr Wilhelm von Gayl, the DNVP minister of the interior, General von Schleicher, as minister of the Reichswehr, Magnus Freiherr von Braun, DNVP, as minister for food supply and agriculture. The *Preussenschlag* of July 1932 was thus something of a latent intra-Prussian civil war during which Reichswehr units under Gerd von Rundstedt, later the prototypical 'Prussian' Second World War general, were instructed to maintain order in Berlin and Brandenburg with armed force if necessary.

At the same time, the imperial government began a process of rapprochement with the National Socialists, especially after they became the largest party at the July 1932 elections; as a conciliatory gesture the banning of the uniformed SA was reversed. But very soon Papen was replaced by Schleicher, who in desperation with the worsening economic situation revived the *Ostsiedlungsprogramm*. Once again Hindenburg, under heavy East Elbian pressure, stepped in and sacked his chancellor. The new man was Adolf Hitler, whom the clique around the president vainly supposed they could manipulate. At one level, therefore, the Nazi takeover of power was the direct result of an essentially 'Prussian' intrigue, carried out by 'old'

Prussians, on behalf of a rather narrow conception of Prussian interests. But it is also true that the revival of *Ostsiedlungsprogramm* was championed by Schleicher, himself a Prussian aristocrat, albeit of relatively recent provenance; the man who led the intrigue against him was Franz von Papen, a Catholic grandee from Westphalia, a Prussian by territorial affiliation only. Furthermore, the rapprochement between the conservative German nationalist DNVP and Hitler was speeded by the de-Prussianization of the party with the replacement of Kuno Count Westarp, an old Junker relic from Wilhelmine times, by Alfred Hugenberg. Moreover, the key figure in all of this, *Reichspräsident* Hindenburg, may have been a quintessentially Prussian figure, but his re-election in 1932 had been as the candidate of the pro-Weimar Centre, SPD, and liberal parties against the conservative nationalist Duesterberg, the Communist Ernst Thälmann and, of course, Hitler. Paradoxically, the Junker who helped to bury the Republic was elected by Catholic and socialist votes.

The old elites hoped to retain direct control of Prussia even under Hitler. On 30 January 1933, Papen was made imperial commissar for Prussia with the extensive powers inherited from the *Preussenschlag*; his task was to keep the Nazis out. He failed, partly because the totality of the Nazi takeover at imperial level rendered him irrelevant, partly because Göring was installed as acting Prussian minister of the interior, and partly because many Nazis themselves were determined to eliminate all regional – as opposed to party – autonomy in the new Germany. At the symbolic level, the Prussian state eagle acquired a Swastika and Göring re-established the historic Prussian *Staatsrat* (State Council), but the reality was that of a takeover, not a merger. The Prussian *Landtag* elections of 1933 once again failed to yield an absolute Nazi majority; it was dissolved to the protests of its Rhenish Catholic president, the Centre Party politician Konrad Adenauer. In February 1933, Hitler introduced the *Reichsstatthaltergesetz* (Reich Commissar Law), which gave him the power to take over the individual regional governments. However, uniquely among all the German territories in the Third Reich, Prussia was never formally dissolved, but rather progressively emasculated. Hitler himself became imperial commissar – *Reichsstatthalter* – of Prussia: Papen was edged out, and Göring became prime minister. At the same time, Prussia was attacked from below by the regional party leaders – the Gauleiters – striving for greater independence from the centre, and from above by Wilhelm Frick's imperial ministry of the interior. Once Göring had lost interest in it as a power base, Prussia had no strong advocates. In January 1934, the *Gesetz über den Neuaufbau des Reiches* (Law on the Reorganization of the Reich) subjected regional governments and the new imperial commissars to the ministry of the interior; 'Germany', Frick announced, 'has been transformed from a federal into a unitary state'.[28] Eventually, all the Prussian ministries were merged with their imperial equivalents, save, for purely technical reasons, the finance ministry. Plans to divide Prussia into its component provinces were well advanced. To all intents and purposes, the Prussia which dominated the united Germany since 1871 had ceased to exist.

The Nazis saw no contradiction between all this and their proclaimed spiritual affinity with Prussianism. Hitler had always stressed that the National Socialist movement was not the conservator of the *Länder* of the past, but rather their liquidator for the benefit of the future Reich.[29] It was this dynamic and synthetic conception of Prussia that Göring expounded to the *Staatsrat* in June 1934:

> It is clear that the concept of the Prussian state has been subsumed into the Reich [...]. What remains is the eternal spirit of Prussianism [...]. Prussia has thereby fulfilled its final task. Now the new Reich, the Third Reich, which is no longer the Reich of the Prussians, Bavarians, or Württembergers, but the new Reich of the Germans, takes the place of the old and Prussia happily passes on its tradition and its mission into these hands [...]. [The] question of a reform of the Reich is in the first instance a Prussian question. The other regions already have more or less the dimensions and the borders of the future *Reichsgaue*. But Prussia will have to split up into a number of *Gaue*.[30]

This view was echoed in 1939 by Ernst Rudolf Huber, next to Carl Schmitt the most prominent Nazi jurist, when he wrote that:

> According to the present legal situation, Prussia remains the *Hausmacht* [patrimonium] of the Reich [...]. Even if, as the imperial minister of the interior [Frick] has repeatedly announced, there will soon be a new organization of the Reich, the power of Prussia as a state will not disappear. Prussia and Prussianism are unlosable basic concepts of the German conception and organization of the state (*Staatsgesinnung und Staatsgestaltung*). [...] even after Prussia has ceased to be a unit of state organization in the conventional sense.[31]

In short, the synthesis between National Socialism and Prussianism

---

28 Kettenacker, 'Preußen in der alliierten Kriegszielplanung', p. 315.
29 Sabine Höner, *Der nationalsozialistische Zugriff auf Preußen. Preußischer Staat und nationalsozialistische Machteroberungsstrategie, 1928–1934* (Bochum, 1984), p. 482.
30 'Aus der Rede des Ministerpräsidenten Göring vor dem Preußischen *Staatsrat* vom 18. Juni 1934 über Preußen und die Reichseinheit', in Herbert Michaelis and Ernst Schraepler (eds), *Ursachen und Folgen. Vom deutschen Zusammenbruch 1918 und 1945 bis zur staatlichen Neuordnung Deutschlands in der Gegenwart*. Vol. 9: *Das dritte Reich. Die Zertrümerung des Parteienestaates und die Grundlegung der Diktatur* (Berlin, 1958), pp. 122–3.
31 Cited in Borries, *Preußen und die Folgen*, p. 172.

proclaimed at the Day of Potsdam was limited to the spiritual sphere and was in no sense incompatible with an anti-Prussian territorial animus. The only reason why the planned dissolution of Prussia never actually took place was that Hitler hesitated to strengthen the bureaucrats of the interior ministry against his faithful Gauleiter, who had moved into the vacuum at regional level.

Prussia, Prussianism, resistance and the Allies

It is therefore ironic that so much of the outside world should have taken the Nazis at their word and regarded the Third Reich as Prussia revived. Already in 1933, the British popular press foresaw the return of Wilhelm II from Holland in triumph; this expectation was reinforced by the spectacle of Potsdam and pictures of the crown prince in SA uniform. The following month, the British statesman Austen Chamberlain launched a fierce attack on the 'New Prussianism' of the Third Reich in the House of Commons, ascribing to it 'The worst of the all-Prussian imperialism [...] with an added savagery, a racial pride, an exclusiveness'.[32] In 1938, some members of the House of Lords held that National Socialist policies were in a long line of continuity stretching back to the Prussia of Frederick the Great;[33] and during the outbreak of war, the foreign secretary, Anthony Eden, was to declare that 'Hitler is not a phenomenon; he is a symptom; he is the Prussian spirit of military domination come up again'.[34] Similar views prevailed in the Soviet Union for most of the 1930s, and of course in France and Poland.

These allied perceptions were to have grave consequences. During and immediately after the war, Prussia acted as a focus for Germanophobia; for many German émigrés, eager to establish their democratic credentials, it functioned as a kind of lightning conductor. There was also the very real question of what to do with Germany once Hitler had been defeated, and how to guard against a revival of its expansionist ambitions. At one conference, Stalin recommended – only half in jest – that some 50,000 German officers be shot to eliminate the 'Prussian' core of the Wehrmacht. But even the less drastic solutions aimed at the emasculation and

---

32 Rolf Kieser, *Englands Appeasementpolitik und der Aufstieg des Dritten Reiches im Spiegel der britischen Presse (1933–1939). Ein Beitrag zur Vorgeschichte des Zweiten Weltkrieges* (Winterthur, 1964), pp. 15–18.
33 Bernd-Jürgen Wendt, *München 1938. England zwischen Hitler und Preußen* (Frankfurt, 1965), p. 44.
34 Kettenacker, 'Preußen in der alliierten Kriegszielplanung', p. 319.

democratization of Germany through the dismemberment of Prussia. The British view was summed up by the chief diplomatic adviser to the government, Sir Robert Vansittart, in 1940: 'Don't break up Germany; break up Prussia, and do it good and proper.'[35] Just like generations of German administrators and regionalists, the Allies – expertly advised by German refugees – wrestled with the problem of how to reconcile the federal system with Prussian dominance. 'It would be essential', Sir Orme Sargent argued in September 1944, 'that *inter se* the federal states should be more or less equal in strength so that no single state should be able to dominate the central government. For this purpose Prussia, which is after all an entirely artificial creation of the 19th century would have to be broken up into its component parts [...]. If we cannot dismember Germany as a whole we certainly can and should dismember Prussia.'[36] The echoes of Weimar and even Nazi Reich reformers are striking.

The allied argument that Hitler represented the worst traditions of Prussian militarism and expansionism had something to be said for it. Even such stalwarts of old East Elbia as the men of famous Infantry Regiment 9 in Potsdam – the amalgamated Prussian guards regiments – were mostly initially well-disposed towards Hitler, whom they undertook to serve as faithfully as they had generations of Hohenzollern monarchs; in retrospect, they were lucky that Hitler refused the suggestion that he become honorary chief of the regiment. There are also parallels in the field of foreign policy, which Hitler himself never tired of invoking. In November 1939, for example, he told his generals: 'I have to choose between victory and annihilation. [A] great historic decision, which can be compared with that of Frederick the Great before the First Silesian War.'[37] It is certainly undeniable that Hitler shared some of his hero's characteristics, that same recklessness and contempt for his advisers. There is a seductive symmetry between the young Frederick, who published his *Antimachiavell* on the eve of invading Silesia, and Hitler's proclamation of 'no further claims' shortly before plunging Europe into all-out war.

In most ways, however, Prussian diplomatic and military traditions were fundamentally at odds with the National Socialists. This was as true of style as of content: the gulf that separates Hitler's limitless racially-based annihilatory expansionism from the careful *Realpolitik* of the Hohenzollerns could not be greater. It must be remembered that Frederick the Great and Bismarck developed from being the pariahs of the international system to

---

35 Kettenacker, 'Preußen in der alliierten Kriegszielplanung', p. 319.
36 Kettenacker, 'Preußen in der alliierten Kriegszielplanung', p. 332.
37 Cited in Mommsen, 'Preußentum und Nationalsozialismus', p. 36.

'satiated' statesmen later on; for Hitler this progression would have been inconceivable. More concretely, National Socialist anti-Soviet foreign policy was seen at the time as a break from the more collaborative tendencies of the Weimar Republic and the early Second Empire. Indeed, it is strange to relate that in 1933 the Polish dictator, Marshal Pilsudski, saw Hitler initially as the chance of a 'fresh start' in Polish-German relations, which would transcend the traditional Russophilia of the old 'Prussian' foreign office. Nor was the true Prussian military tradition limited to unconditional subservience, what critics have called *Kadavergehorsam*, the 'obedience of corpses'. 'True Prussianism', the Prussian resister Henning von Tresckow said, 'cannot be separated from the concept of freedom. True Prussianism means a synthesis between freedom and obligation.'[38] A shining example of this in past times had been Lieutenant Colonel Johann Friedrich Adolph von der Marwitz, who had refused for ethical reasons to burn the Saxon elector's palace at Hubertusburg during the Seven Years' War. Another was the Prussian justice minister, of Hanoverian descent, Ernst von Münchhausen, who was invoked by Bishop von Galen of Münster in his sermon against the Gestapo in July 1941:

> Take as your example and model that Prussian justice minister of a bygone age [...] whom Frederick the Great once instructed to bend a legally valid judgment to the will of the monarch. Whereupon that true nobleman [...] gave the splendid answer: 'My head is at the disposal of your majesty but not my conscience'. [...] Has this sort of nobleman [...] this sort of Prussian bureaucrat died out?[39]

Perhaps the most resonant figure in the Prussian political-military tradition was that of General York von Wartenburg, hero of the Wars of Liberation against Napoleon. His army corps had been assigned to protect the northern flank of the Grande Armée retreating from Moscow in 1812. In December of that year, without the knowledge of his monarch, Frederick William III in Berlin, and entirely against the grain of Prussian foreign policy, which was still aligned with France, York came to terms with the advancing Russians and neutralized his corps in the famous Convention of Tauroggen. He was never forgiven by the king, but went on to become one of the heroes of the Wars of Liberation. Oddly enough, the Nazis were blind to the subversive potential of the Yorkist tradition. In one film in 1936, York was celebrated in the following terms: 'It is the will to freedom which sustains a man who has engaged in a profound struggle between realisation

---

38 Cited Bieberstein, 'Preußen und Preußentum', p. 38.
39 Bieberstein, 'Preußen und Preußentum', p. 28.

(*Erkenntnis*) and duty in order to steel himself for an act of world-historical importance: Yorck [sic].'[40] They did not foresee that his name would later become the rallying cry for opposition. For example, when SS-General Karl Wolff concluded his separate peace with the Allies in Italy, it was the 'spirit of York [sic]' which he invoked.[41] But perhaps the most striking instance of the protean Prussian tradition at work was the exchange between the resister Rudolf von Gersdorff and Field Marshal von Manstein during the Russian campaign cited at the start of this chapter. When the latter claimed that Prussian field marshals did not mutiny, Gersdorff reminded him of York.

It thus comes as no surprise to find Prussians well represented among the German opposition to Hitler, which included the Silesian estate-owner Hellmuth James von Moltke, head of the Kreisauer Kreis, Carl Goerdeler, the head of the civilian resistance, Count Peter Hans York von Wartenburg, a direct descendant of the hero of Tauroggen, all of whom perished in the aftermath of the 20 July bomb plot. Among them were also numerous officers of Infantry Regiment 9, whose swearing-in ceremony at the old garrison church at Potsdam famously eschewed Nazi themes such as the otherwise obligatory singing of the *Horst Wessel* song after the national anthem. Many resisters justified themselves with specific reference to traditional Prussian virtues of 'Prussian cleanliness and simplicity', as General Beck, the middle-class elective Prussian former chief of the general staff, and later a prominent victim of the failed bomb plot, put it in 1938.[42] Two-thirds of the conspirators of 1944 came from the 'Prussian milieu'. Their motives and aims were very mixed. Some such as Ewald von Kleist-Schmenzin had deep-seated religious reservations. Others, such as Tresckow, were disgusted by what they had witnessed of the extermination of the Jews. Some, including Kleist-Schmenzin and Victor von Koerber were monarchists seeking a restoration. Others, however, such as Moltke's Kreisau Circle, rejected a Hohenzollern solution; indeed, together with figures such as Johannes Popitz, the former Prussian finance minister, and Carl Goerdeler, they favoured the dissolution of Prussia into smaller administrative units. Nearly all of them were to some degree influenced by fear of Germany losing the war, and most of them wanted to retain the bulk of Germany's territorial gains, at least up to 1939.

---

40 Cited in Kahlenberg, 'Preußen als Filmsujet', p. 137.
41 'Vernehmung des Karl Wolff durch Mr Barr', 1 December 1947, Institute für Zeitgeschichte 317 IV, fo. 2. See also Brendan Simms, 'Karl Wolff – Der Schlichter', in Enrico Syring and Ronald Smelser (eds), *Die braune Elite*. Bd. IV: Die SS (Berlin, 1999).
42 Manfred Schlenke, 'Nationalsozialismus und Preußen/Preußentum. Bericht über ein Forschungsprojekt', in Otto Büsch (ed.), *Das Preussenbild in der Geschichte. Protokoll eines Symposions* (Berlin and New York, 1981), p. 263.

The Prussian character of the German resisters did them no favours with the Western Allies. Already before the war, Neville Chamberlain had dismissed the plotters as 'Jacobites'; very little co-operation was extended during the war, and the persecution of the conspirators after 20 July was the occasion of much *Schadenfreude* on the British side. They were handicapped by their own misconceptions about the relationship between Prussianism and National Socialism. Exiled advocates of a reconstructed democratic Prussia, such as Otto Braun, its last legal prime minister, found themselves sidelined: he complained in 1942 that his 'labours and struggles for a new peaceful and free Prussia had been so completely ignored'.[43] He vainly tried to persuade his hosts that 'what I understood as the Prussian spirit is sobriety, hard work, incorruptibility and the rule of law'.[44] Other refugees saw the approaching German defeat as the chance to implement a reform of the Reich and subdivide Prussia into smaller territories, thus reinforcing Anglo-American prejudices.

It was the Russians who were the most sensitive to the tensions between National Socialism and Prussian traditions. The Soviet media, unlike its Western counterpart, praised the men of 20 July as 'realistic generals of the Seeckt school', a phrase hinting at the fruitful co-operation between the Reichswehr and the Red Army in Weimar times.[45] More concretely, Soviet propaganda played the Prussian card in setting up the *Nationalkomittee Freies Deutschland* – National Committee for a Free Germany – in 1943 composed of disillusioned captured German officers, such as General von Seydlitz and Field Marshal Paulus. Its manifesto appealed explicitly to the traditions of Stein and Clausewitz, who had joined the Tsar after the defeat of Prussia in 1807, and of course York; when Seydlitz returned to his prison camp, it was to calls of 'Tauroggen, Tauroggen'. The Soviets – much to the chagrin of German communist émigrés – even allowed these officers to display the old imperial and Prussian colours, rather than the liberal-democratic red, black and mustard. The *Nationalkomitee* was much less successful than its sponsors hoped, but it was an imaginative attempt to harness the Prussian heritage for anti-Nazi purposes. At the same time, the Soviets employed the Prussian card in their diplomatic strategy. Contrary to what one might expect, the move to the anti-Prussian and pro-Polish policy that led ultimately to the territorial dismemberment of Eastern Germany was no foregone conclusion

---

43 See 'Rückblick auf Weimar. Ein Briefwechsel zwischen Otto Braun und Joseph Wirth im Exil'. Dokumentation von Hagen Schulze', *Vierteljahrshefte für Zeitgeschichte* 26 (1978), 145.
44 Cited in Hagen Schulze, *Otto Braun, oder Preußens demokratische Sendung. Eine Biographie* (Berlin, Frankfurt am Main and Vienna, 1977), p. 807.
45 Martin Schulze-Wessel, *Rußlands Blick auf Preußen. Die polnische Frage in der Diplomatie und der politischen öffentlichkeit des Zarenreiches und des Sowjetstates 1697–1947* (Stuttgart, 1995), p. 345.

after 1941; 'de-Prussianization' was not yet a Soviet demand. Stalin's anti-Prussian broadside at the Teheran conference and his support for partitionist policies was not immediately reflected in Soviet policy after capitulation, which was in no immediate hurry to effect a formal dissolution of Prussia. The reason for this was that Stalin planned somewhat optimistically to use the Prussian bait to win over bourgeois elements within his own zone of occupation, which would then function as a springboard for the takeover of the whole of Germany.

In the end, none of this saved Prussia. In the Soviet-occupied zone, the resurgent German communists – fearful of being sacrificed once again to the dictates of Stalin's foreign policy – pressed for an irrevocable rapid 'socialist transformation'. In August 1945, the Central Committee of the KPD announced that 'The feudal estate-owners and the Junker caste have always been the bearers of militarism and chauvinism. Under Nazism, their reactionary ideology developed into an extreme form of war ideology [...]. Removing the socio-economic power of the Junkers and large estate-owners is therefore the most important precondition for the extirpation of Prussian militarism'.[46] A month later, the *Bodenreform*, the Orwellian title given to the expropriation of the large estates, was introduced with the following justification:

> A democratic land reform is a national, economic and social necessity which cannot be delayed any longer. The land reform must lead to the liquidation of the feudal-Junker large estates and put an end to the dominance of the Junkers and large estate owners, because this dominance has always been a bastion of reaction and of fascism in our country and was one of the main sources of aggression and wars of conquest against other peoples.[47]

This measure was fundamentally more anti-Prussian than anti-Nazi: Prussian aristocratic resisters were pointedly not exempted; the estates of the executed Count Schwerin von Schwanenfeld were among those confiscated. Indeed, only 4 per cent of the land seized was on the basis of Nazi sympathies or war crimes.[48]

---

46 Cited in Arnd Bauerkämper, 'Der verlorene Antifaschismus. Die Enteignung der Gutsbesitzer und der Umgang mit dem 20 Juli 1944 bei der Bodenreform in der Sowjetischen Besatzungszone' *Zeitschrift für Geschichtswissenschaft* 42 (1994), 627. See also Arnd Bauerkämper, ed., *'Junkerland in Bauernhand?' Durchführung, Auswirkungen und Stellenwert der Bodenreform in der Sowjetischen Besatzungszone* (Stuttgart, 1996).
47 Jesko Count von Dohna, 'Die kommunistische Bodenreform in der Sowjetischen Besatzungszone (1945–1949)', in Christoph Rechberg (ed.), *Restitutionsverbot. Die 'Boden reform' 1945 als Finanzierungsinstrument für die Wiedervereinigung Deutschlands 1990, Eine Dokumentation* (Munich, 1996), p. 14.
48 Dohna, 'Die kommunistische Bodenreform', p. 20.

Two years later, the Allies applied the *coup de grâce*. In its famous decree no. 46, the Allied Control Council pronounced that 'the state of Prussia, which has always been a bearer of militarism and reaction in Germany', was now 'dissolved'.[49] Few tears were shed in the communist eastern zone, where the German communists were now busy dismantling not only the legacy of old Prussia, but everything else deemed incompatible with the dictatorship of the proletariat. Many in the capitalist-democratic western zones, soon to be merged into the Federal Republic of Germany, were equally unconcerned. The death of Prussia seemed to them a guarantee for the recreation of a democratic political culture and the development of a Western orientation. 'We in the west', the first prime minister of the later *Bundesrepublik*, Konrad Adenauer, said in 1946, 'reject much of what is widely termed the Prussian spirit' and warned against the creation of a 'new Prussia'.[50] De-Prussianization was carried a stage further by the Poles and Soviets. Virtually the entire population of Silesia, Pomerania, West and East Prussia was deported, whether or not it had collaborated with National Socialism; tens of thousands were murdered in the process. It was left to old stalwarts of democratic Prussia like Otto Braun to lament the passing of a state that had left them homeless twice-over: once, because his East Prussian home had been partitioned between Poland and Russia and its population expelled; and again with the destruction of the territorial unit which had shaped his political horizons throughout his career. 'One can merely plead', he wrote in January 1947, 'for a just and factual historical assessment of Prussia.'[51]

The relationship between Prussia, Prussianism and National Socialism was thus complex and in many ways contradictory. Ironically, the one area that most Nazis, resisters, German émigrés and Western statesmen could agree on was the need to split Prussia up into its regional components. Everything else was furiously contested. There is no doubting that the Nazis felt a genuine spiritual affinity with Prussian military and expansionist traditions; at the same time, their suspicion of the old East Elbian elite and its exclusivity was unmistakable. Many Junkers and Prussian bureaucrats supported the Nazis, particularly in the final days of Weimar and the early years of the Third Reich; it is also undeniable that the most vibrant strand of the conservative opposition was 'Prussian', rather than south German. For the imperatives of the Prussian legacy were deeply ambiguous. Who was the more Prussian: men like Seydlitz who embraced the Yorkist heritage

---

49 Michaelis and Schraepler (eds), *Ursachen und Folgen*. Vol. 23: *Das dritte Reich. Der militärische Zusammenbruch und das Ende des dritten Reiches* (Berlin, 1958), p. 372.
50 Bieberstein, 'Preußen und Preußentum', p. 26.
51 Cited in Schulze, *Otto Braun*, p. 837.

and defected to the Russians? Those who plotted to kill the man they had sworn to obey in the broader interests of state and people? Or those countless men who 'did their duty' to the bitter end in the service of a genocidal dictatorship? The protean Prussian legacy was surely no more and no less responsible for National Socialism than many other German traditions.

Perhaps one should leave the last word to Hermann Pünder, a prominent Catholic Rhinelander, colleague of Konrad Adenauer, and yet a Prussian. This is what he wrote in 1968:

> And is it to be Prussia, in spite of everything? I answer [...] with a wholehearted yes! [...] The Prussia which I remember with affection does not depend on its borders after 1866, it is by no means only the Prussia of the *Pickelhaube* and certainly not that of the be-monocled Lieutenant of the Guards. The unique greatness of Prussia manifested itself in other characteristics and events [...]. Prussia was destroyed once again by the allies in Spring 1947 as a result of the Second World War. But its spirit is not dead yet [...] [indeed] the apparently dead Prussia could in future become the link between west and east and thus an important cornerstone in the [new] Europe. The capital of this state construction on German soil would then have to be our old and yet ever youthful Berlin.[52]

---

52 Hermann Pünder, *Von Preussen nach Europa. Lebenserinnerungen* (Stuttgart, 1968), p. 549.

SUGGESTIONS FOR FURTHER READING

Wherever possible, prominence is given to works in English, though foreign-language books and articles are cited when they are of particular importance or where no titles in English can be given.

1. Prussia in history and historiography from the nineteenth to the twentieth centuries

Heinrich von Sybel tried to explain his own perception of the meaning of German unification to a British audience in 1871. His article allows a good glimpse of the aspirations and self-understanding of the Protestant-Prussian mainstream among German historians. See Heinrich von Sybel, 'The German Empire' in *Fortnightly Review*, January 1871. On the perception of the old Prussia in historiography and journalism from the Kaiserreich to the two Germanies after 1945, see Jürgen Mirow, *Das alte Preußen im deutschen Geschichtsbild seit der Reichsgründung* (Berlin, 1981). Specifically on the impact of Otto Hintze, see Otto Büsch and Michael Erbe (eds), *Otto Hintze und die moderne Geschichtswissenschaft* (Berlin, 1983). For British historiography on Prussia-Germany and its influence on British policy making, see Donald Cameron Watt, 'Perceptions of German History among the British Policy-Making Elite, 1930–1965, and the Role of British and German Emigré Historiography in its Formation', in Henning Köhler (ed.), *Deutschland und der Westen* (Berlin, 1984), pp. 140–58. Tinged by the anti-Prussianism of the Allies in the Second World War is S. D. Stirk, *The Prussian Spirit: A Survey of German Literature and Politics, 1914–1940* (London, 1941). The seminal work on *Ostforschung* is Michael Burleigh, *Germany Turns Eastwards: A Study of Ostforschung in the Third Reich* (Cambridge, 1988). On the early GDR historiography on Prussia, see Andreas Dorpalen, 'Post-Mortem on Prussia: The East German Position', *Central European History* 4 (1971), 322–45. See also Georg Iggers, 'New Directions in Historical Studies in the German Democratic Republic', *History and Theory* 28 (1989), 59–77. Some of the best examples of GDR social history, including pieces on Prussian history, are collected in Georg G. Iggers (ed.), *Marxist Historiography in Transformation. East German Social History in the 1980s* (Oxford, 1991). On the state of research on Prussia in the 1980s (mainly considering West Germany and the impact of the 'Bielefeld school'), see T. C. W. Blanning, 'The Death and Transfiguration of Prussia', *Historical Journal* 29 (1986), 433–59. See also, from a Polish perspective, Gerard Labuda, 'The History of Prussia in the Opinions of German and Non-German Historiographers', *Polish Western Affairs* 27 (1986), 3–30. An excellent survey and comment of the *Historikerstreit* of the 1980s is provided by Charles Maier, *The Unmasterable Past. History, Holocaust and German National Identity* (Cambridge, Mass., 1988). On efforts to revive Prussianism in the context of the renationalization of German historiography after 1989, see Stefan Berger, *The Search for Normality. National Identity and Historical Consciousness in Germany Since 1800* (Oxford, 1997).

2. Restoration Prussia, 1786–1848

Germans have not made up their minds yet if they prefer to use the noun *Konservatismus* or *Konservativismus*, as a result of which readers may come across both versions. The student of conservatism in the years between Frederick the Great and the Revolutions of 1848 should start with Robert Berdahl's *The Politics of the Prussian Nobility* (Princeton, 1988). Its subtitle – *The Development of a Conservative Ideology* – links conservatism to the material interests of a well-defined class, although no vulgar concept of materialism is to be found here.

For a better understanding of the position that conservatism had among the different ideologies springing up in the late eighteenth century, one should still consult the earlier works of Fritz Valjavec, *Die Entstehung der politischen Strömungen in Deutschland 1770–1815* (Munich, 1951) and Klaus Epstein, *The Origins of Conservatism in Germany* (1966), although their conclusions are not in complete harmony with Berdahl's. The classic work on conservatism is Karl Mannheim's *Conservatism: A Contribution to the Sociology of Knowledge* (London, 1986) taken partly from unpublished manuscripts dating back to the years between the world wars, and now also available in an English translation. In Germany, Panaiotis Kondylis contributed much to the theory of conservatism in his book *Konservatismus* (Stuttgart, 1986). A brilliant intellectual, Kondylis is a conservative himself, although he claims that no conservatism like that of Marwitz and Haller has survived to the present day, and that most contemporary conservative parties in Western Europe are in fact organizations of cautious liberals. On Adam Müller, one may read Benedikt Koehler, *Ästhetik der Politik: Adam Müller und die politische Romantik* (Stuttgart, 1980).

The intrigues against Stein are described painstakingly in R. C. Raack's *The Fall of Stein* (Cambridge, Mass. 1965). A modern biography of Hardenberg is missing, as well as a satisfying book on Metternich. Hardenberg's diaries (Munich, 1999) may serve as a substitute, especially since the sections from the years 1810–22 are the most detailed. Heinrich von Srbik's *Metternich. Der Staatsmann und der Mensch*, 3 vols (Munich, 1925–54), suffers from a heavy anti-democratic bias. Ironically, Viktor Bibl's *Metternich, der Dämon Österreichs* (Leipzig, 1936) is much better, although its author later turned into an ardent supporter of Hitler's *Anschluss*.

Considerable research on the inter-state level of counter-revolutionary cooperation has been done by Harald Müller, *Im Widerstreit von Interventionsstrategie und Anpassungszwang: die Aussenpolitik Österreichs und Preussens zwischen dem WienerKongress 1814/15 und der Februarrevolution 1848*, 2 vols (Berlin, 1990). Theodore Hamerow's *Restoration, Revolution, Reaction: Economics and Politics in Germany 1815–1871* (1958) is somewhat simplistic. From the 90 pages reserved for the period up to 1848, pp. 56–74 deal with 'the ideological conflict'. Two German dissertations of the last decade, however, dealing with more special aspects of the period, are worthwhile: Eckhard Trox's *Militärischer Konservativismus: Kriegervereine und 'Militärpartei' in Preußen zwischen 1815 und 1848/49* (Stuttgart, 1990), and Lothar Dittmer, *Beamtenkonservativismus und Modernisierung. Untersuchungen zur Vorgeschichte der Konservativen Parte: in Preußen in 1810– 1848/49*. Studien zur modernen Geschichte, 44 (Stuttgart, 1992). There is a thoroughly researched book forthcoming by Monika Wienforth on *Patrimonialgerichtsbarkeit* (the jurisdiction of the landlord over the inhabitants of his district) and the attempts to professionalize it or to abolish it altogether up to 1848.

3. Revolution and counter-revolution in Prussia, 1840–50

Although an enormous amount has been written about the European revolutions of 1848, relatively little material is available in English about events in Prussia, and most of that literature is now rather old. As a result, serious students of the revolution in Prussia must be able to read German. The most up-to-date survey in English is Jonathan Sperber, *The European Revolutions, 1848–1851* (Cambridge, 1994), although, as its title suggests, it is not limited to Prussia or Germany. Recent English-language surveys of nineteenth-century German history include James J. Sheehan, *German History 1770–1866* (Oxford, 1989); Eric Dorn Brose, *German History 1789–1871: From the Holy Roman Empire to the Bismarckian Reich* (Providence and Oxford, 1997); and David Blackbourn,

The Fontana History of Germany 1780–1918: The Long Nineteenth Century (London, 1997). The classic account of the revolutions in Germany is Veit Valentin, *Geschichte der deutschen Revolution von 1848–1849*, 2 vols (Cologne, 1977; orig. 1931–32). An unsatisfactory English-language abridgement was published some years ago under the title *1848: Chapters of German History*, trans. Ethel Talbot Scheffauer (London, 1940). English-speaking students should also consult Theodore S. Hamerow, *Restoration, Revolution, Reaction: Economics and Politics in Germany, 1815–1871* (Princeton, 1958), although it is now seriously dated. By far the best one-volume treatment of the German revolutions is Wolfram Siemann, *Die deutsche Revolution von 1848/49* (Frankfurt am Main, 1985), a book that deserves to be translated into English. The most up-to-date analysis of the Prussian revolutions of 1848–50 can be found in Ilja Mieck, 'Preußen von 1807 bis 1850. Reformen, Restauration und Revolution', in Otto Büsch (ed.), *Handbuch der preußischen Geschichte*, Vol. 2: *Das 19. Jahrhundert und Große Themen der Geschichte Preußens* (Berlin, 1992), pp. 198–286. General or comparative analyses of the revolutions are, of course, quite numerous. But see especially the still-indispensable account by Valentin, and the more recent analyses by Siemann, *Die deutsche Revolution*, and Sperber, *The European Revolutions*. For the preceding, see David E. Barclay, *Frederick William IV and the Prussian Monarchy 1840–1861* (Oxford, 1995), pp. 52–5.

Among various first-hand accounts, see the report of Flügeladjutant August von Schöler, 18 March 1848, in Karl Haenchen (ed.), *Revolutionsbriefe 1848. Ungedrucktes aus dem Nachlaß König Friedrich Wilhelms IV. von Preußen* (Leipzig, 1930), pp. 49–52; Adolf Wolff, *Berliner Revolutions-Chronik. Darstellung der Berliner Bewegungen im Jahre 1848 nach politischen, socialen und literarischen Beziehungen*, 3 vols (Berlin, 1851–54, repr. Vaduz, 1979), i. pp. 125–40; Karl Ludwig von Prittwitz, *Berlin 1848. Das Erinnerungswerk des Generalleutnants Karl Ludwig von Prittwitz und andere Quellen zur Berliner Märzrevolution und zer Geschichte Preußens um die Mitte des 19. Jahrhunderts*, ed. Gerd Iteinrich (Berlin, 1985), pp. 130–48. Among innumerable secondary accounts, see Adolf Streckfuß, *500 Jahre Berliner Geschichte: Vom Fischerdorf zur Weltstadt. Geschichte und Sage*, 4th edn (Berlin, 1886), ii. pp. 972–6; Felix Rachfahl, *Deutschland, König Friedrich Wilhelm IV. und die Berliner Märzrevolution* (Halle, 1901), pp. 139–44; Valentin, *Revolution*, i. pp. 426–30; Günter Richter, 'Zwischen Revolution und Reichsgründung (1848–1870)', in W. Ribbe (ed.), *Geschichte Berlins* (Munich, 1997), ii, pp. 614–15; and, most thoroughly and recently, Rüdiger Hachtmann, *Berlin 1848. Eine Politik- und Gesellschaftsgeschichte der Revolution* (Bonn, 1997), pp. 157–202.

For popular movements during the revolutionary era, see Manfred Gailus, *Straße und Brot. Sozialer Protest in den deutschen Staaten unter besonderer Berücksichtigung Preußens, 1847–1849* (Göttingen, 1990). By far the most thorough account of the revolution in Berlin can be found in the massive study by Hachtmann,

Berlin 1848; his analysis is summarized in his article 'Berlin' in Christof Dipper and Ulrich Speck (eds), *1848. Revolution in Deutschland* (Frankfurt am Main, 1998), pp. 82–98. For Cologne, see Jürgen Herres, 'Köln' in Dipper and Speck, pp. 113–29. On the democratic movement in Rhenish Prussia, see the pioneering study by Jonathan Sperber, *Rhineland Radicals: The Democratic Movement and the Revolution of 1848–1849* (Princeton, 1991). Mary Lee Townsend, *Forbidden Laughter: Popular Humor and the Limits of Repression in Nineteenth-Century Prussia* (Ann Arbor, 1992), is a fine study of subversive popular humour and official censorship. For liberalism, see James J. Sheehan, *German Liberalism in the Nineteenth Century* (Chicago, 1978); Dieter Langewiesche, *Liberalismus in Deutschland* (Frankfurt am Main, 1988); and, for the connections between liberals and business interests, James M. Brophy, *Capitalism, Politics, and Railroads in Prussia, 1830–1870* (Columbus, Ohio, 1998). For conservatism, see Robert M. Berdahl, *The Politics of the Prussian Nobility: The Development of a Conservative Ideology 1770–1848* (Princeton, 1988); and Hans-Christof Kraus, *Ernst Ludwig von Gerlach, Politisches Denken und Handeln eines preußischen Altkonservativen*, 2 vols (Göttingen, 1994). Hermann Beck, *The Origins of the Authoritarian Welfare State in Prussia: Conservatives, Bureaucracy and the Social Question, 1815–70* (Ann Arbor, 1995), is an important analysis of conservative and bureaucratic efforts to confront the problem of poverty. For biographical material, see Sabine Freitag (ed.), *Die Achtundvierziger. Lebensbilder aus der deutschen Revolution 1848/49* (Munich, 1998). For parliamentary and constitutional developments, see Herbert Obenaus, *Anfänge des Parlamentarismus in Preußen bis 1848* (Düsseldorf, 1984); Manfred Botzenhart, *Deutscher Parlamentarismus in der Revolutionszeit 1848–1850* (Düsseldorf, 1977); Günther Grünthal, *Parlamentarismus in Preußen 1848/49–1857/58: Preußischer Konstitutionalismus – Parlament und Regierung in der Reaktionsära* (Düsseldorf, 1982). Theodor Fontane, *Von Zwanzig bis Dreißig*, ed. Walter Keitel (Frankfurt am Main, Berlin and Vienna, 1980), is a brilliant 'literary' memoir of the revolution in Berlin, comparable to Gustave Flaubert's descriptions of Paris in *Une éducation sentimentale*.

4. The changing concerns of Prussian conservatism, 1830–1914

Before 1945, the history of Prussian conservatism, conservative thought, individual conservative figures and the social conservative tradition was a prominent topic of research, since a sizeable part of the German historical profession identified itself with Prussia's conservative heritage and interpreted it as a prehistory to their own present (for specific references on the literature, see Hermann Beck 'Die Rolle des Sozialkonservatismus in der preussisch-deutscen Geschichte als Forschungsproblem' *Jahrbuch für die Geschichte Mittel- und Ostdeutschlands* 43 (1995), pp. 59–92). After the Second World War, when the Allied Control Council decreed Prussia, as 'the stronghold of militarism and reaction in Germany', out of existence, the history of Prussian conservatism tended to be interpreted as a 'historical problem'; it is only in the last two decades that conservatism has been fully rediscovered as a field of research.

The more recent publications in English that cover the first period up to the 1860s include Robert Berdahl's *The Politics of the Prussian Nobility: The Development of a Conservative Ideology, 1770–1848* (Princeton, 1988), David Barclay's *Frederick William IV and the Prussian Monarchy, 1840–1861* (Oxford, 1995) and Hermann Beck's *The Origins of the Authoritarian Welfare State in Prussia: Conservatives, Bureaucracy and the Social Question, 1815–1870* (Ann Arbor, 1995). The most reliable guides through the middle period (1866–76) are Robert Berdahl's 'The Transformation of the Prussian Conservative Party, 1866–1876' (PhD University of Minnesota, 1965) and Hans-Christoph Kraus's two-volume biography, *Ernst-Ludwig Gerlach: Politisches Denken und Handeln eines preussischen Altkonservativen* (Göttingen, 1994). The best comprehensive studies covering the period after 1876 are James Retallack's *Notables on the Right: The Conservative Party and Political Mobilization in Germany, 1876–1918* (Boston, 1988) and, on nationalist pressure groups, Geoff Eley's *Reshaping the German Right: Radical Nationalism and Political Change after Bismarck*, 2nd edn (Ann Arbor, 1991). Valuable texts that cover large segments of the history of Prussian conservatism include Larry E. Jones and James Retallack (eds), *Between Reform, Reaction and Resistance: Studies in the History of German Conservatism from 1789 to 1945* (Providence and Oxford, 1993), Hans-Christoph Kraus (ed.), *Konservative Politiker in Deutschland: Eine Auswahl biographischer Porträts aus zwei Jahrhunderten* (Berlin, 1995) and Thomas Nipperdey's *Deutsche Geschichte, 1866–1918. Machtstaat oder Demokratie* (Munich, 1992).

5. The Prussian *Zollverein* and the bid for economic superiority

The best starting point for further reading is William Henderson's *The Zollverein* (London, 1984). The wider context of German economic development is described in Henderson's *The Rise of German Industrial Power* (London, 1975). An elegant summary of Rolf Dumke's innovative work is his contribution 'Tariffs and Market Structure: The German Zollverein as a Model for Economic Integration,' in R. Lee (ed.), *German Industry and Industrialisation* (London, 1991), pp. 77–113. P. Krugman and M. Obstfeld's chapter on tariffs and customs unions in *International Economics: Theory and Policy* (New York, 1997), pp. 227–49, provides a good introduction to the main economic issues. J. Viner's classic study *The Zollverein Issue* (New York, 1950), now appears dated as a result of further research, but it is still useful as an elegant and concise summary of the main economic arguments.

6. The Prussian labour movement, 1871–1914

There are few specific studies of Prussian labour in English, though national and local accounts obviously include a great deal about Germany's largest state. There is a reasonable survey of the general history of the German labour movement: Helga Grebing, *History of the German Labour Movement* (London, 1966). A controversial overview is offered by Dick Geary, 'The German Labour Movement, 1848–1919' *European Studies Review* 3 (1976), 297–330; and Dick Geary, 'Socialism and the German Labour Movement', in Dick Geary (ed.), *Labour and Socialist Movements in Europe before the First World War* (Oxford, 1989), pp. 92–119.

The development of unions is covered in Michael Schneider, *A Brief History of German Trade Unions* (Bonn, 1989); and Wolfgang J. Mommsen and Hans-Gerhard Husung, *The Development of Trade Unionism in Britain and Germany* (London, 1985). Gary Marks, *Trade Unions and Politics* (Princeton, 1989) contains many useful comparative insights. There are numerous studies of the SPD before 1914. The early history of the movement is examined with great subtlety in John Breuilly, *Labour and Liberalism in Nineteenth-Century Europe* (Manchester, 1992). The standard work on the anti-socialist law is Vernon L. Lidtke, *The Outlawed Party* (Princeton, 1966). On the classic period (1890–1914) Carl E. Schorske, *German Social Democracy* (Cambridge Mass., 1955) remains outstanding, as does W. L. Guttsman, *The German Social Democratic Party* (London, 1981). Roger Fletcher (ed.), *From Bernstein to Brandt* (London, 1984) contains several useful articles. Guenther Roth, *Social Democrats in Imperial Germany* (Totowa, NJ, 1963) develops the classic 'negative integration' argument and makes some telling points about social democratic culture. Cultural questions are also discussed in Gerhard A. Ritter (ed.), *Working-Class Culture in Imperial Germany* (special issue of the *Journal of Contemporary History* 13 (1978)); and in the excellent Vernon L. Lidtke, *The Alternative Culture* (New York, 1985). An important local study of

Düsseldorf has appeared: Mary Nolan, *Social Democracy and Society* (Cambridge, 1981).

Interesting debates about the nature of both the organized and the unorganized German working class appear in Richard J. Evans (ed.), *The German Working Class* (London, 1982) and Richard J. Evans, *Proletarians and Politics* (London, 1990). David Crew, *Town in the Ruhr* (New York, 1979) analyses social relations in Bochum; whilst Stephen Hickey, *Workers in Imperial Germany* (Oxford, 1985) portrays an image of non-radical miners in the same area. Polish workers feature in Richard Charles Murphy, *Guestworkers in the German Reich* (Boulder, 1983), which arguably overstates their integration; and in John H. Kulczycki, *The Foreign Worker and the German Labour Movement* (Oxford, 1994), which probably does the opposite. On Catholic workers and confession more generally, see Eric Dorn Brose, *Christian Labour and the Politics of Frustration* (Washington DC, 1985); Michael Schneider, 'Religion and Labour Organization: the Christian Trade Unions in the Wilhelmine Germany', *European Studies Review* 12 (1982), 345–68; Richard J. Evans, 'Religion and Society in Modern Germany', *European Studies Review* 12 (1982), 249–88; Hugh McLeod, 'Protestantism and the Working Class in Imperial Germany', *European Studies Review* 12 (1982), pp. 323–44.

The issue of gender is becoming increasingly central to studies of German labour. See, for example, Kathleen Canning, 'Gender and the Politics of Class Formation: Rethinking German Labour History', *American Historical Review* 97 (1992), 736–68; Eve Rosenhaft, 'Women, Gender and the Limits of Political History', in Larry E. Jones and James Retallack (eds), *Elections, Mass Politics and Social Change in Modern Germany* (Cambridge, 1992); Eve Rosenhaft, 'Women in Modern Germany', in G. Martel (ed.), *Modern Germany Reconsidered* (London, 1992), pp. 149–73. On women and the SPD, see Jean Quataert, *Reluctant Feminists* (Princeton, 1979); Werner Thonesson, *The Emancipation of Women* (London, 1969); Ute Frevert, 'Women Workers, Workers' Wives and Social Democracy in Imperial Germany', in Fletcher (ed.), *From Bernstein to Brandt*, pp. 34–44; Richard J. Evans, 'Socialist Women and Political Radicalism', in Evans, *Proletarians and Politics*, pp. 93–123. On women and work, see Jean H. Quataert, 'Social Insurance and Family Work of Oberlausitz Home Weavers', in John C. Fout (ed.), *German Women in the Nineteenth Century* (New York, 1984), pp. 270–94; Jean H. Quataert, 'Teamwork in Saxon Homeweaving', in R. B. Joeres and M. J. Maynes, *German Women in the Eighteenth and Nineteenth Centuries* (Bloomington, 1986), pp. 3–23; Robyn Dasey, 'Women's Work and the Family', in Richard J. Evans and W. R. Lee (eds), *The German Family* (London, 1981), pp. 221–5; Babara Franzoi, *Women and German Industrialization 1871–1914* (Westport, Conn., 1988). Kathleen Canning, *Languages of Labour and Gender* (Ithaca, NJ, 1996) identifies female workers for whom the factory was a centre of culture and identity.

Labour's changing role in the First World War is examined in Gerald D. Feldman, *Army, Industry and Labour 1914–1918* (Princeton, 1966); and more recently in the chapters by Ullrich, Eley and Daniel in Fletcher (ed.), *From Bernstein to Brandt*, pp. 54–95. Jürgen Kocka, *Facing Total War* (Leamington Spa, 1986) argues that class polarization was a central feature of the home front. A straightforward account of the German revolution is provided by A. J. Ryder, *The German Revolution of 1918* (Cambridge, 1968); whilst F. L. Carsten, *Revolution in Central Europe* (London, 1972) concentrates on the role of the workers' councils. David W. Morgan, *The Socialist Left and the German Revolution* (Ithaca, NJ, 1975) examines the emergence of the USPD and is excellent in its treatment of regional variations. Wolfgang Mommsen, 'The German Revolution', in Richard Bessel and E. J. Feuchtwanger (eds), *Social Change and Political Development in Weimar Germany* (London and Toronto, NJ, 1981), pp. 21–54, takes a sceptical look at the potential for fundamental social change.

For labour in the Weimar Republic, see G. Braunthal, *Socialist and Labour Politics in the Weimar Republic* (New York, 1978); Dick Geary, 'Employers, Workers and the Collapse of the Weimar Republic', in Ian Kershaw (ed.), *Weimar: The Failure of German Democracy* (London, 1990), pp. 92–119 ; Dick Geary, 'The Failure of German Labour in the Weimar Republic', in Michael Dobkowski and Isidor Wallimann, *Towards the Holocaust* (Westport, Conn., 1983), pp. 177–96. On unions, see Klaus Schönhoven, 'The Socialist Trade Unions in the Weimar Republic', in Fletcher (ed.), *From Bernstein to Brandt*, pp. 123–33. On the SPD, see again Guttsman, *Social Democratic Party*; Richard N. Hunt, *German Social Democracy 1918–1933* (Princeton, 1966); Richard Breitmann, *German Socialism and Weimar Democracy* (Chapel Hill, 1981); Detlef Lehnert, 'The SPD in German Politics and Society', in Fletcher (ed.), *From Bernstein to Brandt*, pp. 115–23; William Harvey Maehl, *The German Socialist Party* (Philadelphia, 1986). As far as the Communist Party is concerned, Werner Angress, *Stillborn Revolution* (Princeton, 1963) deals with the attempted communist insurrections in the early years of the Weimar Republic. Ben Fowkes, *Communism in the Weimar Republic* (London, 1983) deals with much the same period, albeit more sympathetically. Eve Rosenhaft, *Beating the Fascists?* (Cambridge, 1983) is a fascinating study of the relationship between Berlin youth gangs and communist paramilitary politics; whilst her 'Communism and Communities', *Historical Journal* (1983), 229ff, examines the quandaries of social democratic councillors in the Depression. Quite outstanding is Eric D. Weitz, *Creating German Communism, 1890–1990* (Princeton, 1997), which takes seriously gender and community politics and destroys old views of a Moscow-dominated, ossified KPD.

The impact of the world economic crisis on German labour is analysed in Peter D. Stachura (ed.), *Unemployment and the Great Depression in Weimar Germany*

(London, 1986); Richard J. Evans and Dick Geary (eds), *The German Unemployed* (London, 1987); and Peter D. Stachura, *The Younger Proletariat and the Weimar Republic* (London, 1989). The relationship between workers and the rise of Nazism has been the subject of much debate. See Conan Fischer, *The Rise of Nazism and the Working Classes in Weimar Germany* (Oxford, 1996) and for a critique thereof, Dick Geary, 'Who voted for the Nazis?', *History Today* 48 (October 1998), pp. 8–14.

7. Agrarian transformation and right radicalism: Economics and politics in rural Prussia, 1830–1947

For those with a reading knowledge of German, the footnotes contain references to major works in that language, including Hans-Ulrich Wehler's *Deutsche Gesellschaftsgeschichte*, now in three volumes (Munich, 1994). Based on extensive research in primary sources and a magisterial command of the scholarship, Wehler's synthesis offers a wealth of detail on economic and political trends in German agriculture as a whole. This bibliographical survey contains works in English that should deepen readers' understanding of the transformations in Prussian agriculture and their political implications from the Napoleonic wars to the end of the Third Reich.

For economic developments and labour relations beginning with the literature on the nineteenth century, see J. A. Perkins, 'The Agricultural Revolution in Germany, 1815–1914', *Journal of European Economic History* 10 (1981), 287–306, and 'The German Agricultural Worker, 1815–1914', *Journal of Peasant Studies* 11 (1984), 3–27, as well as Steven B. Webb, 'Agricultural Protection in Wilhelmian Germany: Forging an Empire with Pork and Rye', *Journal of Economic History* 42 (1982), 309–26, Frieda Wunderlich, *Farm Labour in Germany 1810–1945. Its Historical Development within the Framework of Agricultural and Social Policy* (Princeton, 1961), and Ulrich Herbert, *A History of Foreign Labour in Germany, 1880–1980. Seasonal Workers/Forced Labourers/Guest Workers*, trans. William Templer (Ann Arbor, 1990). Herbert is, *passim* especially sensitive to the ways in which securing labour for the large estates provided precedents for the use of foreign labour generally. Consult as well Max Weber's classic discussion of the formation of an agricultural labouring class in this translation, 'Developmental Tendencies in the Situation of East Elbian Rural Labourers', *Economy and Society* 8 (1979), 175–205. For the Weimar period, see the detailed discussions of agrarian difficulties from varying political perspectives in David Abraham, *The Collapse of the Weimar Republic. Political Economy and Crisis*, 2nd ed (New York, 1986), pp. 42–105, Gerald Feldman, *The Great Disorder. Politics, Economics, and Society in the German Inflation 1914–1924* (New

York and Oxford, 1996), *passim*, Dieter Gessner, 'The Dilemma of German Agriculture during the Weimar Republic', in Richard J. Bessel and E. J. Feuchtwanger (eds), *Social Change and Political Development in Weimar Germany* (London and Totowa, NJ, 1981), pp. 134–54, and Harold James, *The German Slump. Politics and Economics 1924–1936* (Oxford, 1986), pp. 246–82. Richard Bessel's article, 'Eastern Germany as a Structural Problem in the Weimar Republic', *Social History* 3 (1978), 199–218, discusses the specific problems of East Elbia. For the Nazi period, see Gustavo Corni, *Hitler and the Peasants. Agrarian Policy of the Third Reich*, trans. David Kerr (New York, Oxford and Munich, 1990) and John E. Farquharson, *Plow and Swastika. The NSDAP and Agriculture in Germany 1928–45* (London and Beverly Hills, 1976). Both underscore the contradictions between the Nazi regime's agrarian romanticism and its rapid rearmament.

The debate regarding the influence of estate owners versus the self assertion of peasants, which Gerschenkron initiated, has generated a wealth of scholarship. Works in English that emphasize the adaptability and resourcefulness of Junkers and other estate owners include Robert Berdahl, *The Politics of the Prussian Nobility. The Development of a Conservative Ideology* (Princeton, 1988); Shearer Bowman's comparative perspective, *Masters and Lords. Mid-19th Century U.S. Planters and Prussian Junkers* (New York and Oxford, 1993); Shelley Baranowski, *The Sanctity of Rural Life. Nobility, Protestantism, and Nazism in Weimar Prussia* (New York and Oxford, 1995); Francis L. Carsten, *A History of the Prussian Junkers* (Aldershot, 1989); and Gregory Pedlow, *The Survival of the Hessian Nobility 1770–1870* (Princeton, 1988). Studies that emphasize the rationality and autonomy of peasants, also at least partially applicable to Prussia, include Robert G. Moeller's excellent book, *German Peasants and Agrarian Politics 1914–1924* (Chapel Hill and London, 1986), which deals with the peasantry and Catholic politics in the Rhineland and Westphalia; Jonathan Osmond's *Rural Protest in the Weimar Republic. The Free Peasantry in the Rhineland and Bavaria* (New York, 1993); and the collection of essays in Richard J. Evans and W. R. Lee (eds), *The German Peasantry. Conflict and Community in Rural Society from the Eighteenth to the Twentieth Centuries* (New York, 1986). Pay special attention in that volume to William W. Hagen's essay, 'The Junkers' Faithless Servants: Peasant Insubordination and the Breakdown of Serfdom in Brandenburg-Prussia, 1763–1811', pp. 71–101, for Hagen has been especially critical of scholarship that in his view overstates the political and economic weight of estate owners. Robert Moeller has also edited a collection of essays, *Peasants and Lords in Modern Germany. Recent Studies in Agricultural History* (Boston, London, Sydney, 1986), which juxtaposes scholarly positions. In addition to containing strong articles on the peasantry, it includes essays from Hans-Jürgen Puhle on the Junkers, 'Lords and Peasants in the Kaiserreich', pp. 81–109, and Hanna

Schissler, 'The Junkers: Notes on the Social and Historical Significance of the Agrarian Elite in Prussia', pp. 24–51.

A number of the essays in Larry Eugene Jones and James N. Retallack's edited collection, *Between Reform, Reaction, and Resistance. Essays in the History of German Conservatism from 1789 to 1945* (Providence and Oxford, 1993), address the political implications of Prussian agriculture. Consult especially the editors' introduction, as well as Geoff Eley's and George Vascik's articles already cited in the footnotes of this essay. The latter two pieces challenge Puhle's of the Agrarian League, and they represent good examples of the critique of the 'Bielefeld School', especially Wehler and Puhle, which came to fruition in the 1980s. Retallack's monograph, *Notables of the Right. The Conservative Party and Political Mobilization in Germany 1876–1918* (Boston, 1988), highlights the degree to which that party became mortgaged to the Agrarian League with its troublesome implications for the post-First World War period. Finally, an excellent starting point for understanding the Nazi penetration of the countryside is Rudolf Heberle's now-classic study, *From Democracy to Nazism* (Baton Rouge, 1945).

8. Religious conflicts and German national identity in Prussia, 1866–1914

A deeper appreciation of the importance of religious confession and the *Kulturkampf* in the social and political history of nineteenth-century Prussia has emerged from the writings of many historians in recent times. Stimulating historical interpretations of the links between the popular religious piety, sociability, and political behaviour of German Catholics are presented in Jonathan Sperber, *Popular Catholicism in Nineteenth Century Germany* (Princeton, 1984) and David Blackbourn, *Populists and Patricians: Essays in Modern Germany History* (London, 1987). David Blackbourn provides a 'thick description' of the Catholic religious revival in the diocese of Trier and the responses of the Prussian state authorities in *Marpingen: Apparitions of the Virgin Mary in Bismarckian Germany* (New York, 1994).

Bismarck's reasons for launching the state's attack on the Catholic Church are analysed with acuteness and depth in Otto Pflanze, *Bismarck and the Development of Germany*, vol. 2 (Princeton, 1990). Margaret Lavinia Anderson's outstanding study of the Centre Party's foremost leader, *Windthorst: A Political Biography* (Oxford, 1981), contains an extensive discussion of the Catholics' resistance to the *Kulturkampf*. Lech Trzeciakowski, *The Kulturkampf in Prussian Poland* (New York, 1990) documents the severity of the persecution of the Catholic Church in the Polish-speaking areas, whereas Ronald Ross's argument questions the effectiveness of the execution of the antichurch measures in 'Enforcing the *Kulturkampf* in the Bismarckian State and the Limits of Coercion in Imperial Germany', *Journal of Modern History* 56 (1984), pp. 456–82. Geoff Eley, 'State Formation, Nationalism and Political Culture in Nineteenth-Century Germany', in Eley, *From Unification to Nazism: Reinterpreting the German Past* (Boston, 1986), pp. 61–84, and Helmut Walser Smith, *German Nationalism and Religious Conflict: Culture, Ideology, Politics, 1870–1914* (Princeton, 1995) offer many valuable insights by placing the *Kulturkampf* in the historical context of the Protestant elite's attempts to consolidate a national high culture in the aftermath of German unification. Smith's work also contains an account of the founding and anti-Catholic agitation of the Evangelical League. Using extensive archival evidence, Marjorie Lamberti, *State, Society, and the Elementary School in Imperial Germany* (New York, 1989) discusses the influence of religious confession in public elementary education and school politics in Prussia and the attempts to carry out school reforms during the *Kulturkampf*. Michael Gross analyses the motives of the liberals in the Prussian state parliament and the *Reichstag* in passing the antichurch legislation in '*Kulturkampf* and Unification: German Liberalism and the War Against the Jesuits', *Central European History* 30 (1997), 545–66. Thomas Mergel, 'Ultramontanism, Liberalism, Moderation: Political Mentalities and Political Behavior of the German Catholic *Bürgertum*, 1848–1914', *Central European History* 29 (1996), 151–74, examines how the *Kulturkampf* altered the political alignment of middle-class Catholics.

Useful analyses of the solidarity and politics of the Catholic and Protestant milieus can be found in Ellen Lovell Evans, *The German Center Party 1870–1933: A Study in Political Catholicism* (Carbondale, IU, 1981); Ronald Ross, *Beleaguered Tower: the Dilemma of Political Catholicism in Wilhelmine Germany* (Notre Dame, 1976), and Stanley Suval, *Electoral Politics in Wilhelmine Germany* (Chapel Hill, 1985). Catholic and Protestant responses to industrialization and the 'social question' are examined in John Groh, *Nineteenth-Century German Protestantism* (Washington, DC, 1982), Harry Liebersohn, *Religion and Industrial Society: the Protestant Social Congress in Wilhelmine Germany* (Philadelphia, 1986), and W. R. Ward, *Theology, Sociology, and Politics: The German Protestant Social Conscience, 1890–1933* (Berne and Frankfurt am Main, 1979). Eric Dorn Brose, *Christian Labour and the Politics of Frustration* (Washington, DC, 1985) is a valuable study of the attempts of Christian labour leaders to organize industrial workers in western Prussia outside the socialist trade union movement. Hugh McLeod, 'Protestantism and the Working Class in Imperial Germany', *European Studies Review* 3 (1982), 323–44, and Wilfried Spohn, 'Religion and Working-Class Formation in Imperial Germany, 1871–1914', *Politics and Society* 19 (1991), 109–32, provide a differentiated picture of the attitudes of industrial workers towards religion and the church. Many thought-provoking, comparative insights can be found in two works by Hugh McLeod, *Religion and the People of Western Europe, 1789–1989* 2nd edn (Oxford, 1997) and *Piety and Poverty: Working-Class Religion in Berlin, London, and New York, 1870–1914* (New York, 1996), and in Ellen Lovell Evans, 'Catholic Political Movements in Germany, Switzerland, and the Netherlands: Notes for a Comparative Approach', *Central European History* 17 (1984), 91–119.

Readers without a knowledge of German will find a crisp and provocative critical commentary on recent works published in Germany by Wilfried Loth, Thomas Nipperdey, Christoph Weber, and other historians in the review articles of Margaret Lavinia Anderson, 'Piety and Politics: Recent Work on German Catholicism', *Journal of Modern History* 63 (1991), 681–716, and Eric Yonke, 'The Catholic Subculture in Modern Germany: Recent Work in the Social History of Religion', *Catholic Historical Review* 80 (1994), 534–45.

9. Prussian Protestantism

Serious work needs to be done now on the social and economic history of the Lutheran, Reformed and United churches. An up-to-date German re-evaluation in paperback can be found in J. C. Kaiser *et al.* (eds), *Konfession und Gesellschaft* (Stuttgart, 1988), and G. Besier, *Kirche, Politik und Gesellschaft im 19. Jahrhundert* in *Die Enzyklopädie deutscher Geschichte* 48 (Munich, 1998), and *Kirche, Politik und Gesellschaft im 20. Jahrhundert*, in ibid, 56 (Munich, 2000).

Many key topics such as church association political and social, Protestantism and socialism, religious education in school and university, clergy and the pastoral care, prayer and spirituality, the liturgy, church music, and church architecture cannot be treated here. An attempt is made in Nicholas Hope's recent book *German and Scandinavian Protestantism 1700–1918* (Oxford, 1995). It contains a critical bibliography chapter by chapter divided theme by theme; Part II covers this period. A comparative German account which includes 'theology' and runs to *c.*1950 is K. Nowak, *Geschichte des Christentums in Deutschland: Religion, Politik und Gesellschaft vom Ende der Aufklärung bis zur Mitte des 20. Jahrhunderts* (Munich, 1995).

Biography is at last back in German fashion, but new critical studies of twentieth-century Protestant churchmen are needed. A few recent titles are listed below.

The following Protestant encyclopaedias contain excellent biographical and subject entries with comprehensive bibliographies: *Evangelisches Kirchenlexikon*, *Realencyclopädie für protestantische Theologie und Kirche*, 3rd edn

(1890–1913), *Die Religion in Geschichte und Gegenwart* 3rd edn (1957–65), *Theologische Realencyclopädie* (1977–); complementary *Geschichtliche Grundbegriffe*, and *Die Musik in Geschichte und Gegenwart*. Articles in earlier editions should not be overlooked such as 'Deutschland: IIA. Die evangelische Kirche in der Gegenwart' (1927), or Erich Foerster's 'Preußen' (1930) in *Die Religion in Geschichte und Gegenwart* 2nd edn (1927–32). Essential is the *Jahrbuch für Berlin-Brandenburgische Kirchengeschichte*.

General surveys can be found in the suggestive introduction and essays by Manfred Richter (ed.), *Kirche in Preußen: Gestalten und Geschichte* (Stuttgart, 1983), a re-evaluation prompted by the 1981 Prussia exhibition in West Berlin. J. F. Gerhard Goeters and Joachim Rogge *et al.* (eds), *Die Geschichte der Evangelischen Kirche der Union: Ein Handbuch 1817–1850*, Vol. 1 (Leipzig, 1992); Vol. 2, *1850–1918* (Leipzig, 1994); Vol. 3, *1918–1960* (Leipzig, 1998), is now basic. Good maps are included.

After 1918, two excellent comprehensive studies in English are D. R. Borg, *The Old-Prussian Church and the Weimar Republic: A Study in Political Adjustment, 1917–1927* (Hanover and London, 1984) and, as a comparison, D. J. Diephouse, *Pastors and Pluralism in Württemberg 1918–1933* (Princeton, NJ, 1987). The English translation of K. Scholder's pioneering *The Churches and the Third Reich*, 2 vols, (London, 1987–88), contains much on Prussia, as does H. McLeod, *Piety and Poverty: Working-Class Religion in Berlin, London and New York 1870–1914* (New York and London, 1996).

On the provincial churches, see W. Friedensburg, *Die Provinz Sachsen, ihre Entstehung und Entwicklung* (Halle, 1919); H. Heyden, *Kirchengeschichte Pommerns*, 2nd edn (Cologne, 1957); W. Hubatsch, *Geschichte der evangelischen Kirche Ostpreussens* 3 vols (Göttingen, 1968); H. Neumeyer, *Kirchengeschichte von Danzig und Westpreußen in evangelischer Sicht* (Leer, 1977), Vol. 2; M. Schian, *Schlesien* (Tübingen, 1903); on Berlin, see the religious section in H. Herzfeld (ed.), *Berlin und die Provinz Brandenburg im 19. Jahrhundert* (Berlin, 1968); McLeod, *Piety and Poverty*; W. Wendland, *700 Jahre Kirchengeschichte Berlins* (Berlin, 1930); on the Rhineland and Westphalia there are useful chapters in vols 2 and 3 in W. Kohl *et al.* (eds), *Westfälische Geschichte* (Düsseldorf, 1983–84), and F. Petri and G. Droege (eds), *Rheinische Geschichte* (1976–79).

For documents on church and state there are a number of basic texts: E. R. Huber and W. Huber (eds), *Staat und Kirche im 19. und 20. Jahrhundert* (Berlin, 1973), 4 vols until 1933. Modern constitutional language of church organization given here should be compared with that in pre-contractual Reformation church orders: E. Sehling (ed.), *Die evangelischen Kirchenordnungen des XVI Jahrhunderts* (Leipzig, 1902–), 18 vols so far and still incomplete; Brandenburg and Silesia are treated in vol. 3; the Duchy of Prussia and Polish-speaking Prussia in vol. 4; Brandenburg-Nuremberg in vol. 11. On the reformed church orders, see W. Niesel, *Bekenntnisschriften und Kirchenordnungen der nach Gottes Wort reformierten Kirche*, 3rd edn (Zurich, 1938); W. Göbell (ed.), *Die Rhein-Westphälische Kirchenordnung vom 5.März 1835*, 2 vols (Duisburg and Düsseldorf, 1948–54).

On Prussian kings and the United Church, see R. Bigler, *The Politics of German Protestantism: The Rise of the Protestant Church Elite in Prussia 1815–1847* (Berkeley, Calif., 1972). E. Foerster, *Die Entstehung der preussischen Landeskirche unter der Regierung König Friedrich Wilhelm III*, 2 vols (Tübingen, 1905–7), is basic; and two short studies, by W. Wendland, *Die Religiösität und die kirchenpolitischen Grundsätze Friedrich Wilhelms des Dritten in ihrer Bedeutung für die Geschichte der kirchlichen Restauration* (Giessen, 1909), and L. Dehio, *Friedrich Wilhelm IV. von Preußen: Ein Baukünstler der Romantik* (Munich, 1961). They can be supplemented by Chris Clark, 'Confessional Policy and the Limits of State Action: Frederick William III and the Prussian Church Union 1817–40', *Historical Journal* 39 (1996), pp. 985–1004; and J. Mehlhausen, 'Friedrich Wilhlem IV. Ein Laientheologe auf dem preußischen Königsthron', in H. Schröer and G. Müller (eds), *Vom Amt des Laien in Kirche und Theologie* (Berlin, New York, 1982), pp. 182–214. Wilhelm II and Prussian Protestantism is best approached now through Bernd Andresen's excellent, *Ernst von Dryander: Eine biographische Studie* (Berlin, New York, 1995).

For Protestant Prussia and 1871, see G. Besier, *Preussische Kirchenpolitik in der Bismarckära* (Berlin, 1980), as well as the long essay by E. Bammel, *Die Reichsgründung und der deutsche Protestantismus* (Erlangen, 1973). Two Prussian coronations (1701 and 1861) only are compared in P. E. Schramm, *Sphaira, Globus, Reichsapfel: Wanderung und Wandluung eines Herrschaftszeichens* (Stuttgart, 1958) including (figure 142) Adolph Menzel's sketch of the 18 October 1861 Königsberg coronation ceremony.

For Prussia in the German nation state, see Hans Goldschmidt, *Das Reich und Preußen im Kampf um die Führung: Von Bismarck bis 1918* (Berlin, 1931); R. von Thadden, *Fragen an Preußen. Zur Geschichte eines aufgehobenen Staates* (Munich, 1981) and 'Wie Protestantisch war Preußen? Gedanken zur evangelischen Kirchengeschichte Preußens', in Richter (ed.), *Kirche in Preußen*, pp. 126–39. On the modern German Protestant controversial ecclesiology of the *Volkskirche*, the 'people's church', to which one belonged by birth and parental beliefs, see A. Adam, *Nationalkirche und Volkskirche im deutschen Protestantismus* (Göttingen, 1938) which, despite its publication date, is very useful in a Prussian context. After loss of the monarchy in 1918, see the brief survey by K. Meier, *Volkskirche 1918–1945. Ekklesiologie und Zeitgeschichte* (Munich, 1982).

On the *Kulturkampf* and Protestant Prussia, see Margaret Anderson, '"The Kulturkampf" and the course of German history', *Central European History* 19 (1986), 82–115; G. Besier compares its European setting in '*Kulturkampf*', *Theologische Realencyclopädie* (1977–). There is now a handy paperback edited by the authoritative R. Lill, *Der Kulturkampf* (Paderborn, 1997).

On the clergy, patronage, and church tax, see Hope, *German and Scandinavian Protestantism*, chs 18–20; O. Janz, *Bürger besonderer Art: Evangelische Pfarrer in Preußen 1850–1914* (Berlin, New York, 1994); J. Niedner, *Die Ausgaben des preußischen Staats für die evangelische Kirche der älteren Provinzen* (Stuttgart, 1904) and *Die Entwicklung des städtischen Patronats in der Mark Brandenburg: Ein Beitrag zur Geschichte der kirchlichen Lokalverwaltung* (Stuttgart, 1911); and G. Arndt, 'Die kirchliche Baulast in der Mark Brandenburg', *Jahrbuch für Berlin-Brandenburgische Kirchengeschichte* 13 (1915), 119–81; 14 (1916), 1–66; 15 (1917), 1–22.

On social action, see W. O. Shanahan, *German Protestants Face the Social Question: The Conservative Phase 1815–1871* (Indiana, 1954), only Vol. 1 published; C. Sachße and F. Tennstedt, *Geschichte der Armenpflege in Deutschland vom Spätmittealter bis zum Ersten Weltkrieg* (Stuttgart, 1980) and *Fürsorge und Wohlfahrtspflege 1871–1929* (Stuttgart, 1988). An excellent comparative guide can be found in K. Elm and H. D. Loock (eds), *Seelsorge und Diakonie in Berlin: Beiträge zum Verhältnis von Kirche und Gesellschaft im 19. und beginnenden 20.Jahrhundert* (Berlin, 1990); W. R. Ward, *Theology, Sociology and Politics: The German Protestant Social Conscience 1890–1933* (Berne and Frankfurt am Main, 1979).

On the First World War, see Hope, *German and Scandinavian Protestantism*, epilogue. M. Schian, *Die deutsche evangelische Kirche im Weltkriege*, 2 vols (Berlin, 1921–25), is basic. For the American and European context, G. Besier, *Krieg-Frieden-Abrüstung* (Göttingen, 1982).

On the question of East Prussia, see W. W. Hagen, *Germans, Poles, and Jews. The Nationality Conflict in the Prussian East, 1772–1914* (Chicago, 1980); Goeters and Rogge *et al.* (eds), *Geschichte der Evangelischen Kirche der Union*, iii.; the chapter by Shelley Baranowski in this volume; and R. Bessel, 'Eastern Germany as a structural problem in the Weimar Republic', *Social History* 3 (1978), 199–218.

On National Socialism and the end of the Old-Prussian Church, a basic survey of research so far can be found in J. Mehlhausen, 'Nationalsozialismus und Kirchen' in *Theologische Realencyclopädie* (1994); and J. S. Conway, *The Nazi Persecution of the Churches 1933–1945* (London, 1968). On Prussian Protestant opposition during the Nazi period, an excellent survey in English is V. Barnett, *For the Soul of the People: Protestant Protest Against Hitler* (Oxford, 1992). One can also consult J. Bentley, *Martin Niemöller* (Oxford, 1984), and E. Bethge, *Dietrich Bonhoeffer: Theologian, Christian, Contemporary* (London, 1970). British assessments of this opposition, and the issue of guilt can be found in N. Hope, 'Zum heutigen Verständnis des protestantischen und katholischen Widerstandes in Großbritannien', in J. Kuropka (ed.), *Clemens August Graf von Galen: Menschenrechte, Widerstand, Euthanasie, Neubeginn* (Münster, 1998), pp. 149–61; and W. R. Ward, 'Guilt and

Innocence: The German Churches in the Twentieth Century', *Journal of Modern History* 68 (1996), pp. 398–426.

10. Democratic Prussia in Weimar Germany, 1919–33

Prussia in Weimar Germany has only attracted peripheral attention from historians although certainly in English there is the excellent work in two volumes by Dietrich Orlow, *Weimar Prussia, 1918–1925: The Unlikely Rock of Democracy* (Pittsburgh, 1986), and *Weimar Prussia, 1925–1933: The Illusion of Strength* (Pittsburgh, 1991). Orlow clearly analyses the history of Prussia as the bulwark of democracy first and foremost from the perspective of the parties, the constitution and the complicated relations between the Reich and Prussia. Helpful are a number of general surveys of the Weimar Republic, especially Eberhard Kolb, *The Weimar Republic* (London, 1988) and Detlev Peukert, *The Weimar Republic: The Crisis of Classical Modernity* (New York, 1992). The work by Kolb is especially worth emphasizing because it contains an extensive portrayal of the state of research, the historical controversies and the lacunas, while Peukert's book stands out above all because of its cultural history. The role of social democracy, especially important for Prussia's development, is examined by Richard Breitman, *German Socialism and Weimar Democracy* (Chapel Hill, 1981). The social democratic dilemma in the defence of Prussia in the last years of the Republic is examined by Heinrich August Winkler, 'The Lesser Evil: The German Social Democrats and the Fall of the Weimar Republic' *Journal of Contemporary History* 25 (1990), pp. 205–27. On the second largest party in the Prussian coalition government during the Weimar era, see Eric D. Kohler, 'The Successful German Center-Left: Joseph Hess and the Prussian Center Party, 1908–1932' *Central European History* 23 (1990), pp. 313–48.

11. Prussia's military legacy in Empire, Republic and Reich, 1871–1945

This section focuses on English-language sources that are particularly useful for developing the Prussian/German theme of the text. Material for the period of the Second Empire is somewhat limited. Dennis E. Showalter, 'German Grand Strategy: A Contradiction in Terms?', *Militaergeschichtliche Mitteilungen* 48 (1990); and 'Army and Society in Imperial Germany: The Perils of Modernization', *Journal of Contemporary History* 17 (1983) remain useful. Arden Bucholz, *Moltke, Schlieffen, and Prussian War Planning* (Providence, RI, 1991); and Terence Zuber, 'The Schlieffen Plan Reconsidered', *War In History* 6 (1999) combine to show the erosion of Prussian approaches to planning. There is no good monographic overview of the German army of the First World War in English, though Holger Herwig, *The First World War: Germany and Austria–Hungary, 1914–1918* (London, 1997), is brilliant on the military aspects. Wilhelm Deist, 'The Military Collapse of the German Empire: the Reality Behind the Stab-in-the-Back Myth', *War In History* 3 (1996) is excellent for the army's last two years. Thomas Nevin, 'Ernst Juenger: German Stormtrooper Chronicler', and Hew Strachan, 'The Morale of the German Army, 1917–1918', in H. Cecil and P. Liddle (eds), *Facing Armageddon* (London, 1996), are fine case studies. Much, however, remains to be done with the army's social and personal dynamics during wartime.

For the Weimar era, James Corum, *The Roots of Blitzkrieg* (Lawrence, Kans., 1992); David Spires, *Image and Reality: The Making of a German Officer, 1921–1933* (Westport, Conn., 1984); and Robert Citino, *The Evolution of Blitzkrieg Tactics* (Westport, Conn., 1987) combine for a good overview of the nuts and bolts. Azar Gat's two-part 'British Influence and the Evolution of the Panzer Arm: Myth or Reality?', *War In History* 4 (1997), is a study in institutional adaptability. The two dozen essays in Klaus-Juergen Mueller (ed.), *The Military in Politics and Society in France and Germany in the Twentieth Century* (Oxford, 1995); and W. Deist (ed.), *The German Military in the Age of Total War* (Leaming-ton Spa, 1985), offer insight into the army's increasingly conflicted mentality.

For the Third Reich, Stephen Fritz, *Frontsoldaten: The German Soldier in World War II* (Lexington, Ky., 1995); and Omer Bartov, *Hitler's Army: Soldiers, Nazis and War in the Third Reich* (New York, 1991), are starting points for the grass roots. Geoffrey Megargee, *Inside Hitler's High Command* (Lawrence, Kans., 2000), does the same for the upper levels. The contributions to C. Barnett (ed.), *Hitler's Generals* (London, 1989), are uneven in quality, but clearly indicate the tensions and synergies between Prussian and Nazi values in the Wehrmacht. Martin van Creveld, *Fighting Power* (Westport, Conn., 1982) is the most frequently cited tribute to the German army as an operational military instrument. Juergen E. Förster, 'The Dynamics of *Volksgemeinschaft*: The Effectiveness of the German Military Establishment in the Second World War', in A. Millett and W. Murray (eds), *Military Effectiveness* (London, 1988), vol. 3, is more balanced and comprehensive.

12. Prussia, Prussianism and National Socialism, 1933–47

There is no full-length study of the relationship between Prussia, Prussianism and National Socialism. Useful shorter treatments are Hans Mommsen, 'Preußentum und Nationalsozialismus', in Wolfgang Benz, Hans Buchheim and Hans Mommsen (eds), *Der Nationalsozialismus. Studien zur Ideologie und Herrschaft* (Frankfurt am Main, 1993), pp. 29–41; Wolfgang Wippermann, 'Nationalsozialismus und Preußentum', *Aus Politik und Zeitgeschichte. Beilage zur Wochenzeitung 'Das Parlament'*, 26 December 1981; Manfred Schlenke, 'Nationalsozialismus und Preußen/Preußentum. Bericht über ein Forschungsprojekt', in Otto Büsch (ed.), *Das Preussenbild in der Geschichte. Protokoll eines Symposions* (Berlin and New York, 1981), pp. 247–63. *Preußen und der Nationalsozialismus. Potsdamer Gespräche* edited by the Volkshochschule 'Albert Einstein' (Potsdam, 1992) is more promising than the provenance suggests and deals with individual themes such as 'The Day of Potsdam', resistance, the Prussian nobility and National Socialism.

The relationship between National Socialism, the NSDAP and Prussia during the Weimar Republic is covered in Horst Müller, 'Das Ende Preußens', in Wolfgang Böhme (ed.), *Preußen – eine Herausforderung* (Karlsruhe, 1981) pp. 100–114; Shelley Baranowski, *The Sanctity of Rural Life. Nobility, Protestantism, and Nazism in Weimar Prussia* (New York and Oxford, 1995); Wolfgang Zollitsch, 'Adel und adlige Machteliten in der Endphase der Weimarer Republik. Standespolitik und agrarische Interessen', in Heinrich August Winkler (ed.), *Die deutsche Staatskrise 1930–1933* (Munich, 1992), pp. 239–56; and the eyewitness account of Arnold Brecht, 'Warum in den Abgrund? (1932–1933)' in Dirk Blasius (ed.), *Preussen in der Deutschen Geschichte* (Königsstein/Taunus, 1980), pp. 335–48. For a Marxist view of the relationship between Nazism and Prussian Junkers leading up to the Nazi takeover of power, see Kurt Gossweiler and Alfred Schlicht, 'Dokumentation: Junker und NSDAP 1931–32', *Zeitschrift für Geschichtswissenschaft* 15 (1967), 644–62.

The role of Prussian themes in the Third Reich is covered by Friedrich P. Kahlenberg, 'Preußen als Filmsujet in der Propagandasprache der NS-Zeit', in Axel Marquardt and Heinz Rathsack (eds), *Preußen im Film. Eine Retrospective der Stiftung Deutsche Kinemathek* (Hamburg, 1981), pp. 135–63; and Konrad Barthel, 'Friedrich der Große' in *Hitlers Geschichtsbild* (Wiesbaden, 1977). See also the rather bleak view of S. D. Stirk, *The Prussian Spirit. A Survey of German Literature and Politics 1914–1940* (London, 1941).

The question of a monarchic restoration and Hohenzollern relations with Nazism are treated somewhat apologetically in Friedrich Wilhelm Prinz von

Preußen, *Das Haus Hohenzollern 1918–1945* (Munich and Vienna, 1985), especially pp. 59–90.

There is no single volume dealing with Prussia and the resistance, but some of the complexities are dealt with by Ekkehard Klausa, 'Preußische Soldatentradition und Widerstand. Das Potsdamer Infanterieregiment 9 zwischen dem "Tag von Potsdam" und dem 20. Juli 1944' Jürgen Schmaedke and Peter Steinbach (eds), *Der Widerstand gegen des nationalsozialismus. Die deutsche Gesellschaft und der Widerstand gegen Hitler* (Munich and Zurich, 1985) pp. 533–45. On Prussian themes in the Soviet-sponsored resistance among captured German officers, see Bodo Scheurig, *Freies Deutschland. Das Nationalkomitee und der Bund Deutscher Offiziere in der Sowjetunion 1943–1945* (Munich, 1960).

Allied attitudes towards Prussia and Prussianism are surprisingly well covered. In general, see Lothar Kettenacker, 'Preußen in der alliierten Kriegszielplanung, 1939–1947', in Lothar Kettenacker, Manfred Schlenke and Hellmut Seier (eds), *Studien zur Geschichte Englands und der deutsch-britischen Beziehungen. Festschrift für Paul Kluke* (Munich, 1981), pp. 312–40. For British attitudes before the war, see Bernd-Jürgen Wendt, *München 1938. England zwischen Hitler und Preußen* (Frankfurt, 1965), especially pp. 17–45. I was unable to consult Lothar Kettenacker, 'Preußen-Deutschland als britisches Feindbild', in Bernd-Jürgen Wendt (ed.), *Das britische Deutschlandbild im Wandel des 19. und 20. Jahrhunderts* (Bochum, 1984), pp. 145–68. For Soviet attitudes, see Martin Schulze-Wessel, *Rußlands Blick auf Preußen. Die polnische Frage in der Diplomatie und der politischen öffentlichkeit des Zarenreiches und des Sowjetstates 1697–1947* (Stuttgart, 1995), especially pp. 279–380. For France, see Henning Köhler, *Das Ende Preussens in französischer Sicht* (Berlin and New York, 1982). For Poland, see Andreas Lavaty, *Das Ende Preussens in polnischer Sicht. Zur Kontinuität negativer Wirkungen der preußische Geschichte auf die deutsch-polnischen Beziehungen* (Berlin and New York, 1986). See also Arnold Brecht, *Federalism and Regionalism in Germany. The Division of Prussia* (New York, Toronto and Oxford, 1945). Brecht had been a senior civil servant in the final days of democratic Prussia.

The vexed question of aristocratic property rights and the role which anti-Prussian resentments played in denying demands for restitution from Junkers expropriated by the Nazis and the Soviets is tackled by Christoph Rechberg (ed.), *Restitutionsverbot. Die 'Bodenreform' 1945 als Finanzierungsinstrument für die Wiedervereinigung Deutschlands 1990. Eine Dokumentation* (Munich, 1996).

FURTHER RESEARCH POSSIBILITIES

The ideas for further research possibilities compiled below are the result of suggestions made by the contributors.

1. Prussia in history and historiography from the nineteenth to the twentieth centuries

The fruitfulness of methods and ideas connected with the 'linguistic turn' in the field of Prussian history could well be explored further. So far, for example, we lack entirely any studies on the gender of history-writing in Prussia along the lines of Bonnie Smith's work on French historiography.

Post-1871, in the unified German nation state, it became increasingly difficult to delineate a distinct 'Prussian' historiography from its 'German' counterpart. While we know a lot about 'Prussianism', it would be interesting to explore in greater detail the impact of geographical location on individual historians and their writings. Some of the most well-known Prussians, for example August von Sybel and Georg von Below, spent long periods of their careers outside Prussia. We also find occasional references, for example in the works of Friedrich Meinecke and Max Weber, about the alleged impact of their respective stays outside Prussia on their views of Prussia. Yet we lack any systematic exploration of this issue.

Furthermore, the relationship between Prussian historians and non-German historians needs to be analysed in greater detail. Historical texts were not produced in regional/national isolation. While the nineteenth century witnessed a massive nationalisation of historiography, historians at the same time began to feel part of a greater cosmopolitan scholarly community. Historiographical connections were established that were part of a wider cultural transfer between nationally-organized societies. Any further exploration of such cultural transfers will reveal that hardly any area of historical investigation, including that of historiography, can be properly understood unless we take into account the hybrid nature of European nation states.

During the last decade, much attention has been focused on the impact of *Volksgeschichte* on German historiography post-1918. While there is a perception that in Prussian historiography the traditional political and state-centred history continued to prevail, there are no systematic investiga-tions on the impact of *Volksgeschichte* on the perception of Prussian history.

For the inter-war period, the construction of diverse regional identities and pasts by Polish and German historiography respectively needs to be deconstructed further. Too much history-writing about Prussia remains informed by the historical myths produced in the struggle over the historical legitimacy of ruling over particular territories.

Prussian history was exploited by National Socialism with great aplomb to legitimate its own regime. This might have contributed to the Allies' decision to dissolve Prussia after 1945, but it did not lead to any significant long-term crisis in the historiography of Prussia. While we are relatively well informed about the perceptions of Prussia in GDR historio-graphy, the transmutations of Prussian historiography in West Germany need yet to be explored in detail. A more self-critical analysis of its own traditions has certainly begun in the 1990s and this must be a hopeful sign for the future of Prussian historiography in the twenty-first century.

2. Restoration Prussia, 1786–1848

While church histories of the period exist, no thorough study of the Awakening in Pomerania and other parts of Prussia has been done. It would be helpful, however, only if the social setting of the meetings and the social background of the protagonists were included. Was the Awakening a movement of the Junkers, of the peasants or of town artisans? A monograph on one of the prominent Pomeranian families of the time – the Thadden, the Puttkamer or the Krockow – would also be a welcome addition. The invasion of the Red Army, the pillage of the manor houses, the expulsion of the German inhabitants from the area east of the River Oder have destroyed many sources. However, the regional archives in Poland and East Germany may contain many hidden treasures.

The economic theory of the Romantics and the anti-capitalism of the political right deserve more attention, as does the police repression during the *Demagogenverfolgung*. There is no detailed survey of the police actions, and no prosopography of the victims. As with the files of East German *Staatssicherheit*, many of the records of the political police and the Mainz *Zentral-Untersuchungskommission* seem to have been destroyed by their authors in the revolutionary spring of 1848, although some still survive.

3. Revolution and counter-revolution in Prussia, 1840–50

Although the revolutions of 1848–50 have often been studied, there is still a great deal of research that remains to be done on this crucial period of Prussian history. With the end of the Cold War and the unification of Germany, vast quantities of unpublished, archival material have now become readily accessible to scholars, both in Germany and in the former Prussian territories in Poland. As a result, in-depth regional studies, of the sort that have long enriched our understanding of French history, have become increasingly feasible (and necessary) for scholars of Prussian history. A great deal of work still needs to be done on local urban revolutions as well as on the revolutions in the countryside; studies of Silesia, the Mark Brandenburg, Prussian Saxony, Pomerania and East Prussia would be especially helpful in this regard. We also need analyses of social relationships on East Elbian estates as well as in-depth analyses of proto-industry in the countryside. Although East German historians like Hartmut Harnisch undertook some important investigations on these matters in the 1970s and 1980s, research has tended to languish in recent years. Cultural histories of East Elbia, informed by recent developments in cultural studies, would also be quite illuminating.

In addition to regional and cultural studies, we still need a great deal of work on topics in gender history and religious history in the context of the revolutions of 1848. Women's involvement in the political and cultural history of those years remains underinvestigated, even at the level of high politics. We still know very little about women at the powerful Prussian court, or about the important political activities of people like Queen Elisabeth or the Princess of Prussia.

In fact, 'high' politics in general have been unfortunately downplayed in much recent scholarship. Up-to-date analyses of Prussian foreign policy in the 1840s and 1850s, grounded in solid archival scholarship, are badly needed. These would include a modern history of the Schleswig-Holstein issue, with appropriate attention to the domestic sources of foreign policy in Denmark and in the German states.

4. The changing concerns of Prussian conservatism, 1830–1914

The areas not sufficiently covered by historical research since 1945 include the following: the politics, background and influence of the different conservative *Fraktionen* in the Prussian *Landtag* before 1858. While we have a detailed study on associations during the 1848 Revolution in Wolfgang Schwentker's *Konservative Vereine und Revolution in Preußen 1848/49. Die Konstituierung des Konservativismus als Partei* (Düsseldorf, 1988), there are only very general accounts that deal with the 1850s, such as Günther Grünthal's *Parlamentarismus in Preußen 1848/49–1857/58* (Düsseldorf, 1982). For the 1850s, even a basic institutional history of the structure of Prussian conservatism is missing.

The history of the Conservative Party between 1858 and 1866 could well become the subject of a monograph, for the literature on the topic is largely outdated. The best monograph is still Gerhard Ritter's first book, *Die preussischen Konservativen und Bismarcks deutsche Politik* (Heidelberg, 1913).

The multi-faceted history of conservatism between 1866 and 1876 has not been sufficiently explored; the best account on the period is still Robert Berdahl's dissertation from the mid-1960s. 'The Transformation of the Prussian Conservative Party, 1866–1876'.

Prominent events in the history of conservatism during the 1880s and 1890s, such as Wilhelm von Hammerstein and the *Kreuzzeitungspartei* – the most detailed study is still Heinrich Heffter's *Die Kreuzzeitungspartei und die Kartellpolitik Bismarcks* (Leipzig, 1927) – should be analysed from a new perspective. The articles in Larry E. Jones and James Retallack (eds), *Between Reform, Reaction and Resistance: Studies in the History of German Conservatism from 1789 to 1945* (Providence and Oxford, 1993) did much to elucidate the history of conservatism during the empire and can be used as a foundation for further studies.

5. The Prussian Zollverein and the bid for economic superiority

The Zollverein issue points to two fundamental gaps in the economic history of nineteenth-century Germany. First, there is an urgent need to replicate the breakthroughs achieved in historical statistics in the British case (Crafts, Feinstein, Deane and Cole). Most debates concerning the Gerschenkron hypothesis, the impact of the Zollverein or the effects of state interventionism will be resolved only if the now very dated material used by Hoffmann is re-analysed properly, employing many of the methodological insights that are now commonplace in Anglo-Saxon countries. Also, these time series need to be extended backwards. Only quinquennial (or best, annual) output series for the main Zollverein states will enable us to say with certainty if it made any difference at all. Compiling satisfactory time series of output, prices and wages before 1850 remains a tantalizingly obvious quantum leap that nobody appears to tackle in earnest.

The second embarrassing gap concerns demographic history. While some excellent micro-level studies exist (notably by Knodel), there is still no organized effort to replicate the Wrigley/Schofield approach in the German case. The data in many areas would be sufficiently good, and it betrays the insular nature of German economic and social history that this project is not given the highest priority. Since the size of the population was the largest single determinant of living standards in the pre-industrial world, this would also enable us to assess the relative positions of Zollverein ins and outs much better.

6. The Prussian labour movement, 1871–1914

There is now a large volume of work on the history of both trade unions and the SPD at a national level and some at a regional and local level. However, we have few local studies of trade union mobilization in non-craft sectors of the labour force, and next to nothing on either socialist or union recruitment in the countryside. This applies in particular to the agrarian east. Studies of rural labour, labour–landlord and urban–rural relations would be most welcome in this area, especially where they also attempt to address questions of German-Polish relations in an everyday rather than simply high-political context.

Despite some notable advances in recent years, female labour remains largely unknown. The history of domestic servants and female agricultural labour remains almost completely unexplored, for example.

Though there are many good histories of labour in localities where the SPD was strong, this is less true of towns where the party was weak. Here there exists a substantial counter-factual potential and also the possibility of rediscovering the 'lost' working class, which was far from exclusively female. What is also needed is investigation of the dynamic of inter-class relations in a local setting. A knowledge of precisely how workers and bourgeois encountered one another in work or leisure (i.e. the history of class relations as distinct from that of an isolated working class) might also lead to a significant revision of stereotypes.

The study of the Weimar Republic has tended again to concentrate on national developments and social democrat/communist relations. What social democratic government actually meant for workers both regionally and locally requires far more investigation, as does the social history of the Ruhr occupation and of the Depression.

7. Agrarian transformation and right radicalism: Economics and politics in rural Prussia, 1830–1947

The collapse of the Soviet Bloc and the unification of the two post-war Germanies has provided an opportunity to address the most serious gap in the literature on Prussian agriculture, the lack of detailed research on the rural regions of the eastern provinces. There exists an impressive corpus of scholarship on the Rhineland and Westphalia, yet until recently the seeming unavailability of archival sources in the former German territories of Poland and the administrative restrictions associated with archival research in the German Democratic Republic discouraged Western scholars from undertaking comparable work on the Prussian east. The result was a distorted relationship between the significance that historians have assigned to Prussian agriculture and the East Elbian landed elite and our relatively meagre understanding of how agricultural villages in the eastern provinces of Prussia actually worked. Fortunately, new scholarship is now emerging on the social composition and economic practices of the East Elbian landed elite that makes use of previously inaccessible sources, but we are in need of more history from below – that is, local studies on eastern Prussian agricultural villages, the long-term development of their social structures and relationships, economic behaviour and cultural practices. Cross regional comparisons between and among villages, especially between the eastern and western provinces, would be especially valuable.

8. Religious conflicts and German national identity in Prussia, 1866–1914

This is an exciting time to do research on the history of religion and the confessional divide in German society in the nineteenth century. The simple model of the secularization of modern industrial society no longer informs historical scholarship on this subject, and historians are now more sensitive to new forms of church adherence and religious piety in the nineteenth century and to the important role that religion and confessional issues continued to play in the political, social and cultural life of the German people. Although recent works have made an important contribution to historical scholarship by presenting a more differentiated picture of the Catholic and Protestant communities and by linking religious piety, sociability and political behaviour, the tendency to study each church or confession separately persists. We cannot understand the social history of either confession in isolation. Sorely needed is a social and cultural history of religion in modern Germany, which looks across the confessional divide, examines the ways in which the Catholic and Protestant confessions perceived each other and interacted in civic life, and compares their attitudes towards the Jewish minority. Confessional conflicts loomed very large in national politics after 1870. Studies of the confessional divide in cities such as Breslau, Düsseldorf or Frankfurt am Main would enable us to see how far these tensions were played out in the local community and daily life. In comparison with the rich and growing body of historical literature on the Catholic religious revival connected with ultramontanism, the Centre Party, and the network of associations of the Catholic subculture, Protestant religiosity and political Protestantism have received surprisingly far less attention. Recent studies on the Evangelical League and the Protestant clergy during the First World War provide a penetrating view of national Protestantism. We know much less about the other religious and cultural milieus within Protestantism and the political camps that corresponded to them – orthodox Lutheranism, liberal Protestantism, and Protestant socialism. Our understanding of how Protestants adapted to the challenges of industrial mass society would certainly be enhanced by further study of the *Evangelisch-sozialer Kongress* (Protestant Social Congress), founded by conservative Protestants shortly after the expiration of the anti-socialist legislation in 1890, and the *Nationalsozialer Verein* (National Social Association), founded by Friedrich Naumann and other Christian Socialists in 1896. The 'resacralization' of religious life in nineteenth-century Germany has been studied extensively in relation to the Catholic religious revival promoted by parish priests and Jesuit evangelists. Protestant religiosity, on the other hand, is far more open for new historical research, as Lucian Hölscher points out in 'Secularization and Urbanization in the Nineteenth Century. An Interpretative Model', in Hugh McLeod (ed.), *European Religion in the Age of Great Cities* (London, 1995), pp. 263–85. Studies of the Centre Party have illuminated the heterogeneity of the social constituency of political Catholicism and, in doing so, have raised questions that deserve further investigation: how united was political Catholicism? To what extent was the Centre Party dominated by the ultramontane clergy? Finally, a social history of the Catholic priesthood and Protestant pastors in nineteenth-century Germany would fulfil a big need in this field. Further investigations would deepen our understanding of the causes and context of the changing nature of the clergy after 1850.

9. Prussian Protestantism

The opening paragraphs to this section in Suggestions for further reading (page 287) point already to future research topics ranging from new biographies (twentieth-century Protestant churchmen especially) to gender (the women both in the pew and at home or in the vicarage are largely neglected), and up-to-date surveys of the economic and social history of the Lutheran, Reformed, and United Churches. Modern IT database work might help here very much in collating data on the church life of the extremely diverse church provinces described in this chapter.

Above all, English-speaking readers have little idea of what it was like in the Protestant Prussian parish and the parish church both in town and country in this period, or earlier for that matter. The relationship with other religious denominations – the Catholic church in particular, and with an eye to the twentieth century, Judaism and other religious minorities – is often not treated sufficiently well in previous Protestant church histories.

The field is still wide open on the following topics: the economic and social topography of the parish in town and country (particularly the impact of urbanization and industrialization in this period); religious education at school and university (continuity and change); the clergy and pastoral care; prayer, devotional literature and spirituality; and what parish worship was like (the sermon, liturgy and church music) for the man or woman in the pew. A black hole, too, is still the experience both at home and at the front during the two world wars. Apart from Martin Schian's official coverage of the First World War mentioned in Suggestions for further reading, we have hardly begun to exploit such evidence as war diaries or letters home, or tried to assess, with the exception perhaps of coverage on war sermons, the experience of Prussian or German Protestantism in wartime. One could compare First World War and Second World War sermons.

And turning to contemporary church history themes, John Conway's very informative recent survey in 'Coming to terms with the past: interpreting the German Church Struggles, 1933–1990' *German History* 16 (1998) 372–96 might act as a starting point on what needs to be done. Above all, Conways's call for 'a new approach which will attempt to rethink the complex relationship between church and society' adopting the techniques of the social historians 'so that a more collaborative relationship with secular historians can be found' is urgently required.

10. Democratic Prussia in Weimar Germany, 1919–33

Few historians have so far been interested in the history of Prussia during the Weimar period. Prussia was no longer a sovereign state and the question that has interested most historians above all else, the collapse of the Weimar state and the rise of Hitler, seems much more approachable at a national rather than at a state level. Moreover, the reasons why the heavily burdened Weimar Republic nevertheless survived 14 years seems to have been lost from view. In this connection, Prussia appears in the foreground as the bulwark of democracy. How was it possible that democracy was so sickly in the Weimar Republic and yet so healthy in the state of Prussia?

Answers to this question may be found in comparative studies: why were the democratic parties in Prussia committed to the parliamentary process while the Reich parties were not? Why was the democratization of the police in Prussia possible and not in the Reich? Why was it easier for the Prussian government to combat National Socialism than the Reich government? Many other questions remain unanswered.

Another greatly neglected area is comparative studies between German states. Above all, the contrast between conservative Bavaria and republican Prussia would be worth studying as well as their contrasting relations with the Reich. In this respect, not only questions of political, but also cultural, history and mentalities would be worth examining – how was the change from Prussia as a state dominated by the agrarian nobility to an industrial republican community made possible? Bavaria, on the other hand, which was a stronghold of reaction during the Weimar period, was in the nineteenth century a state with one of the earliest German constitutions with a profound liberal tradition. What had changed in Berlin and Munich?

Finally, detailed studies are lacking on the opposition of the democrats and the penetration of National Socialism at a local and regional level. We hardly know anything about the 1920s in East Prussia, Pomerania and the Ruhr. Broader fields of study are waiting to be opened by future research which will undoubtedly lead to new, more sophisticated findings.

11. Prussia's military legacy in Empire, Republic and Reich, 1871–1945

Dennis Showalter's essay is as much a study of mentalities as realities, and offers correspondingly fruitful ground for post-structuralists. The relationships of the armies of the lesser states of the Second Empire to the Prussian hegemon remains largely unexplored, as do the processes of homogenization during the First World War. The Reichswehr's place in Germany's post-1918 search for 'normalcy' remains undeveloped, as does the Wehrmacht's ambivalent attitude to its Prussian heritage. The extent to which 'Prussianism' was a conscious construction after 1933 merits inquiry. The recent emphasis on the army's Nazification opens doors for study of its 'Prussification' on lines suggested in his essay. Finally, it is worth investigating the accuracy in a military context of Ralf Dahrendorf's familiar claim that Prussia as a concept disappeared with the Third Reich.

12. Prussia, Prussiansim and National Socialism, 1933–1947

There is no systematic in-depth single-volume study on Prussia, Prussianism and National Socialism in any language. Some individual aspects – such as Prussia and the resistance, the churches, Prussian themes in Nazi literature and film, and Prussia and the Allies – have been relatively well covered, but much remains to be done on other topics. Thus, although there are a number of – usually rather uncritical – family histories, there is no overarching account of the experience of the Prussian nobility after 1933; the prominent role of some in the SS, for example, might repay closer scrutiny. The role of Prussia in reform plans of Wilhelm Frick, the imperial minister of the interior, needs further elucidation, as do the various polycratic conflicts between the Prussian Gauleiter, the imperial administration and others. Another fruitful topic would be the ambivalent treatment of Prussia in Nazi historiography. Furthermore, the progressive 'de-Prussianization' of the German army in the Second World War, although touched upon in the existing literature, needs more attention. Finally, it is worth noting that, unlike the first 40 years or so after 1945, would-be researchers now have the benefit of free access to archives in central Germany, and – albeit more restrictedly – to material in the former Soviet Union.

MAPS

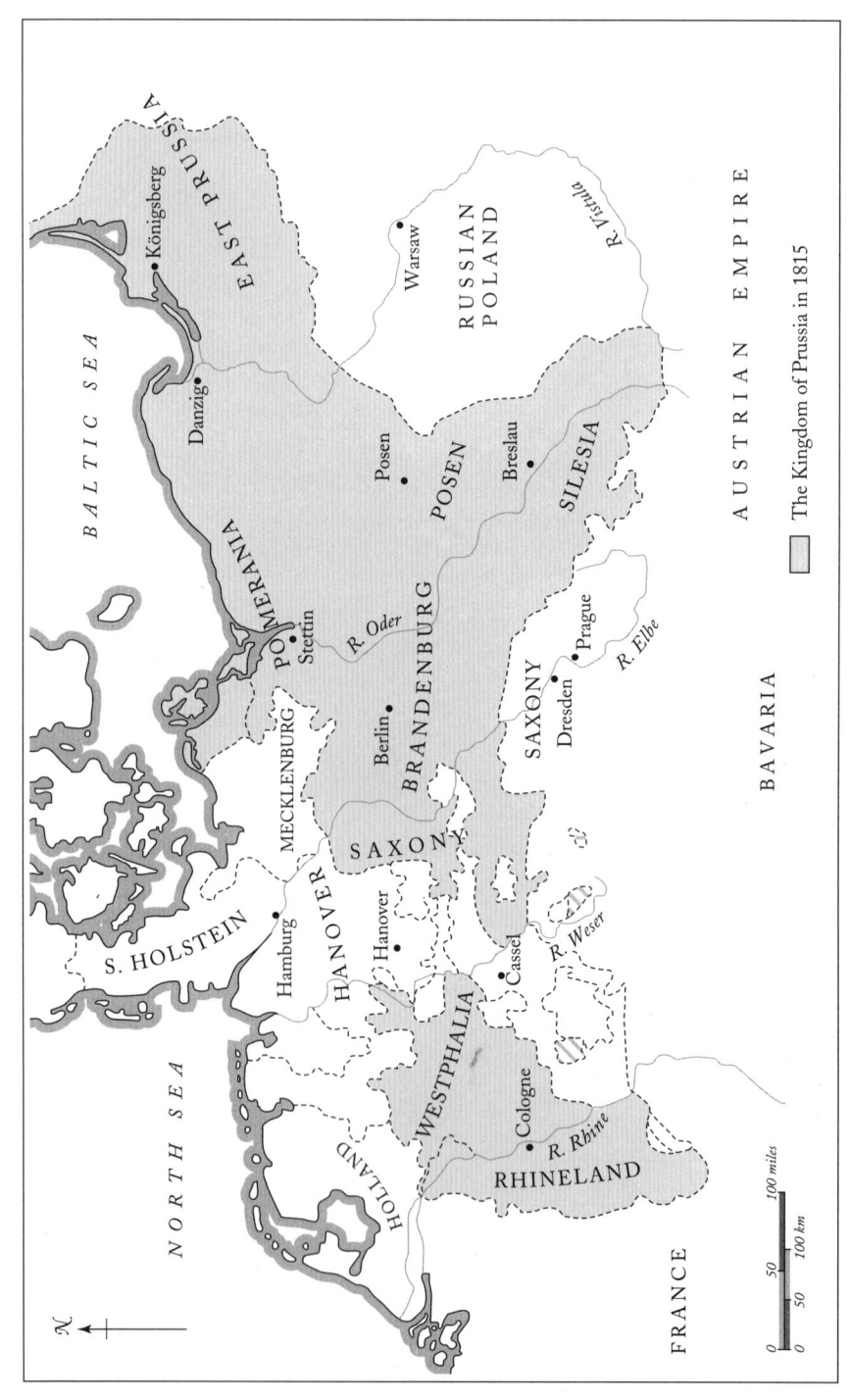

1. The Kingdom of Prussia in 1815

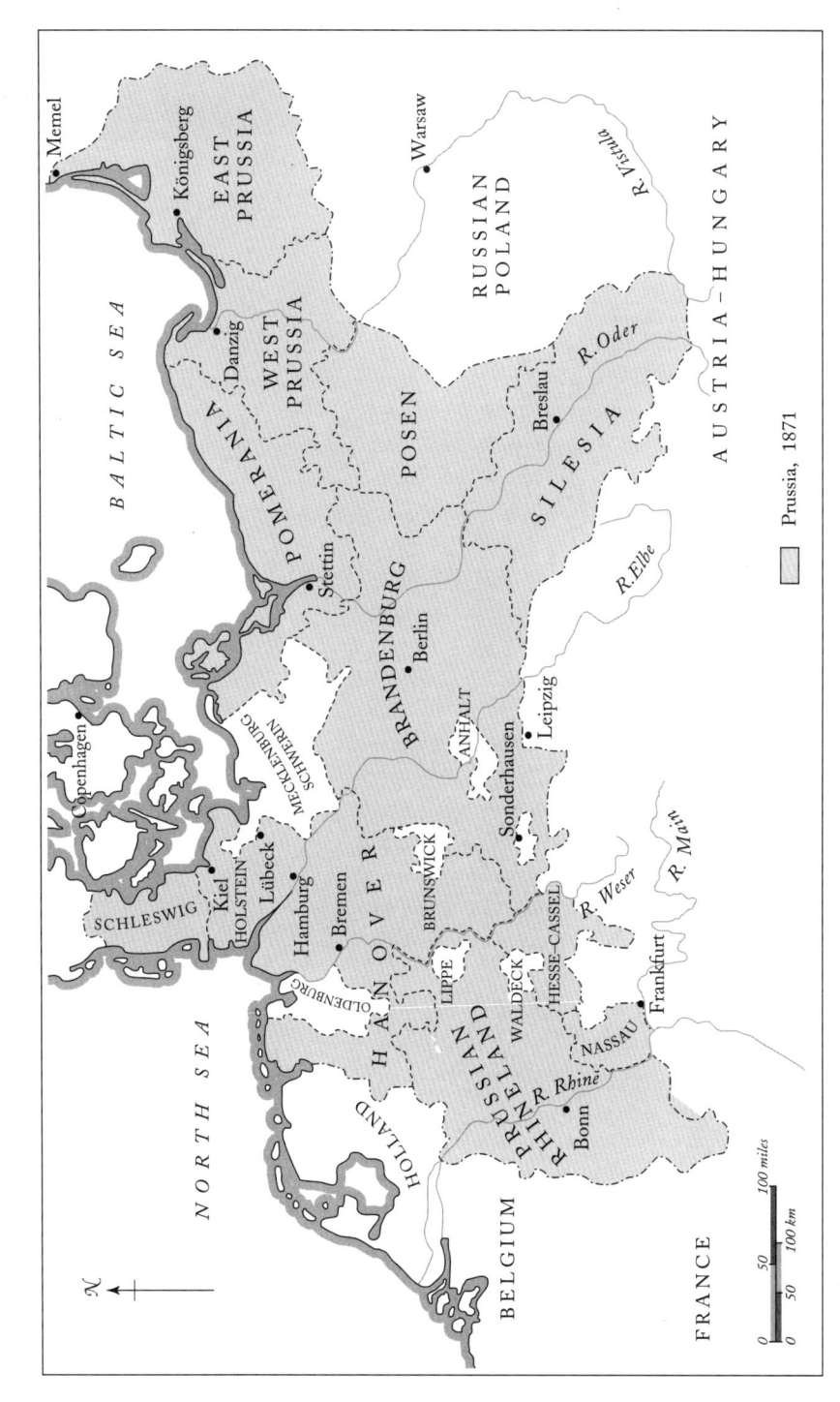

2. Prussia, 1871

INDEX

Aachen, 131, 139–40, 204
  congress of (1818), 57
Adenauer, Konrad, 231, 264, 272–3
Agrarian League, 8, 11, 103, 146, 153–5, 158
Alexander I of Russia, 56
Altenstein, Karl von, 91–2
Ancillon, Johann Peter Friedrich, 56
Arnim-Boitzenburg, Count Adolf Heinrich von, 74–5, 92, 258
Arnim-Wiepersdorf, Ludwig Achim von, 55–6
August Wilhelm, Prince, 259
Austria, 3, 9, 14, 44, 50, 56–7, 84–5, 102, 114, 116, 118–19, 122, 124, 153, 170–1, 254
  and Seven Weeks' War (1866), 119, 121
Austria-Hungary, 156, 234

Baden, 15, 83–4, 97, 114, 122, 132, 134, 192
Barth, Karl, 189, 207
Bavaria, 14, 83, 97, 119, 134, 169, 199, 233, 239, 303
Bavaria-Württemberg, 114, 119
Bebel, August, 126
Beck, General, 269
Belgium, 102, 115–16
Benedict XV, Pope, 200
Berlin, 4, 11, 30, 36, 38, 60, 68, 70, 74–5, 77–8, 81, 100, 129–31, 134–7, 141, 143, 145, 170, 190–1, 193–4, 196–8, 204, 206, 263, 303
  population of, 8, 10, 69, 130, 202
Bethmann-Hollweg, August von, 93
Bethmann-Hollweg, Theobald von, 87
Beyme, Carl Friedrich von, 62
Beyschlag, Willibald, 181, 184
Bischoffwerder, Hans Rudolf von, 49
Bismarck, Bernhard von, 96
Bismarck, Prince Otto von, 3, 7–8, 13–14, 16, 20, 31, 35–7, 66, 87–8, 92–7, 100–2, 119, 124, 153–4, 171–5, 177–8, 181, 193, 195, 199, 234, 253, 268
Blankenburg, Moritz von, 94
Blomberg, General Werner von, 251
Blücher, Gebhard Leberecht von, 20, 256
Bodelschwingh, Ernst von, 74
Bonaparte, Jérôme, 45
Borck, Eldor, 219
Border Mark (*Grenzmark*), 204, 206
Bormann, Martin, 260
Boyen, Hermann von, 51, 61
Brandenburg, 38, 76, 79, 81, 90, 97, 152, 190–1, 202, 204–6, 232, 239, 263, 297
Brandenburg, Count Friedrich Wilhelm von, 71, 77, 81–2, 84
Brauchitsch, Walther von, 251–2
Braun, Otto, 202, 212, 214, 216, 219, 222–9, 262–3, 270, 272
Breslau, 128, 130, 134–5, 139, 170, 177, 193, 204, 301
Brüning, Heinrich, 18, 162, 224–5, 227, 263
Bülow, Prince Bernhard von, 102, 104–5, 185
Bülow-Cummerow, Ernst von, 58–9

Camphausen, Ludolf, 75–6, 78, 81
Caprivi, Count Georg Leo von, 102–3, 154, 184–5
Catholic Centre Party (*Zentrum*), 15, 97, 100, 137, 140, 153, 156, 159–60, 162, 173–4, 176–7, 180–7, 202, 204, 211, 219, 221, 225–6, 264, 301
Catholicism, 3, 10, 13–15, 21, 60, 70, 100, 131, 136–7, 140, 143, 148, 153–4, 158–60, 162, 169–87, 193, 202, 204, 256, 262, 264, 301
Chamberlain, Austen, 266
Chamberlain, Neville, 270
Christian VII of Denmark, 49
Christian Miners Union, 137, 140
Christian National People's Party, 160
Christian Social Party (CSP), 100–3

INDEX

Christian Textile Workers Union, 139
Christian Trade Union, 15
Clausewitz, Karl von, 31
Cobden-Chevalier, Treaty of, 114, 119
Cologne, 70, 77–8, 131, 139, 177, 185, 193
Colonial Society, 105
Communism, 34–5, 227–8
Communist Party of Germany (KPD), 144–5, 224–5, 228, 245, 264, 271
Conservatism, 4–8, 16, 34, 55, 60, 72, 78–80, 86–105, 156, 162, 298
Corporation of German Nobles, 258
Crimean War, 93
Czechoslovakia, 247

Danzig, 25, 204
Darré, Richard Walther, 163–4, 260
Denmark, 80, 171, 195, 297
Dibelius, Otto, 189, 200–1, 206–7
Dresden, 131
  uprising in (1849), 84
Düsseldorf, 77, 129, 301

East Elbia, 5, 66, 77, 90, 100, 102–3, 147–8, 150–1, 154–5, 162, 165, 254, 257, 259–63, 267, 272, 297, 300
East Prussia, 16, 26, 53, 76, 79, 97, 158, 190, 200, 202, 204, 206, 262, 272, 297, 303
Ebert, Friedrich, 36
Economic Party (*Wirtschaftspartei*), 224
Eden, Anthony, 266
Eisenhower, Dwight, 233
Elbe river, 103–4, 146, 239
Elisabeth, Queen, 75, 297
Engels, Friedrich, 21, 29, 75
Eulenburg-Hertefled, Prince, 258
Evangelical League, 178, 181–2, 184–6, 301
Eyelert, Rulemann Friedrich, 59–60

Falk, Adalbert, 177
Fernando VII of Spain, 43
Fichte, Johann Gottlieb, 50
Fouqué, Baron Friedrich de la Motte, 55–6
France, 14, 21, 35, 43–4, 49–51, 56, 61, 73, 76, 114–16, 122, 171, 234–5, 250, 266

and Franco-Prussian war (1870–71), 121, 233–4
Francis II of Austria, 44, 57
Frankfurt am Main, 3, 76, 97, 114, 193, 301
  National Assembly of, 80–3, 195
Frederick I of Prussia, 28
Frederick II (the Great) of Prussia, 13, 20, 23, 29, 31–2, 35, 50, 55, 199, 230, 232, 235, 237, 239, 245, 250, 253, 255–6, 266–8
Frederick William, Elector of Brandenburg (The Great Elector), 45
Frederick William I of Prussia, 28, 255–6
Frederick William II of Prussia, 12–13, 48–9, 64, 256
Frederick William III of Prussia, 44, 50, 53–4, 56–8, 62–4, 190–1, 256, 268
Frederick William IV of Prussia, 6, 14, 63–4, 67–8, 71–5, 78–85, 88, 190–1, 194, 256
  'Camarilla' of, 67, 80–4
Free Conservative Party (FKP), 8, 87, 93, 98–9, 102, 182
Free Miners Union, 140
Free Textile Union, 142
Free Union of Factory Workers, 141
Freikorps, 158, 243
French Revolution, 5, 44, 47–50, 53–4, 70, 89
Frick, Wilhelm, 264, 304

Gayl, Freiherr Wilhelm von, 227, 263
General Union of German Workers, 126, 129, 133
Gentz, Friedrich, 54, 58
Gerlach, Ernst Ludwig von, 6, 34, 55, 60, 64, 71, 79, 86–8, 91–2, 94–6
Gerlach, Leopold Ludwig von, 6, 34, 71, 79–81, 87–8, 95
German Conservative Party (DKP), 8, 87, 97–102, 104–5, 177, 298
German Democratic Party (DDP), 16, 202, 211, 215, 218–19, 225
German Farm Labour Union, 158
German National People's Party (DNVP), 8, 11, 102, 105, 159–62, 200, 202, 204–5, 224, 255, 258, 262, 264

INDEX

German People's Party (DVP), 218–19
German Social Democratic Party (SPD), 10–11, 15–17, 21, 87, 98, 100–1, 126–8, 130–45, 157–9, 163, 186–7, 197, 202, 204, 211–12, 214–15, 218, 222, 227, 264, 299
   activities in Prussia, 225–6, 262
Germany
   agriculture, 146–65
   army, 18, 19–20, 158, 200, 212, 216, 227, 230–52, 261, 303–4
   civil service, 17, 158, 216–21
   economic development, 114–18, 124–5, 157–9
   empire, 95–6, 105, 153–4, 172
   foreign policy, 1, 131, 255, 267–8
   historiography, 21–9, 295–6
   industrialisation, 103, 110, 128–9, 147
   Luftwaffe, 249
   militarism, 2, 230–52
   nationalism, 14, 38–40, 181–2
   navy, 104, 110
   population, 109, 128
   'Prussianism' of, 4, 18, 21, 22–40, 230–54, 304
   Reichsrat, 212–13
   Reichstag, 8, 15, 97–9, 103–4, 129, 131–3, 140, 157, 161–2, 171, 173–5, 177, 182–5, 212, 227, 262
   reunification of (1990–91), 38–40, 254
   revolution in (1918), 144, 211, 218, 263
   unification of (1871), 9, 14, 32, 35, 109, 113, 121, 124, 234–6
   urbanisation, 128
   'war guilt', 25–6, 36;
Germany (West), 22, 29, 34–9, 272
   historiography, 33–8
Germany (East), 21, 29–32, 37, 38, 165, 254, 271–2, 300
   historiography, 29–33, 296
   militarism of, 31–2
Gersdorff, Colonel Rudolf von, 253, 269
Gneisenau, August von, 256
Goebbels, Joseph, 29, 255–6
Goerdeler, Carl, 269
Göring, Hermann, 259, 264–5

Great Britain, 2, 24, 35, 52, 84, 111–12, 114–16, 118, 122, 129, 148, 154, 255, 266
   Royal Navy of, 110
Great Depression, the, 144–5, 152, 300
Groener, General Wilhelm, 232, 240, 251
Grzesinski, Albert, 216, 219

Haller, Karl Ludwig von, 43, 65
Hamburg, 98, 131, 143
Hamburger, Ernest, 216–17
Hammerstein, Wilhelm von, 100–2
Hanover, 3, 95, 97, 104, 131, 153, 170, 193, 195, 232
Hansemann, David, 73, 75–6, 78, 81
Harburg, 135, 141
Hardenberg, Karl August von, 5, 45–6, 52–4, 56, 58, 62–3, 109, 256
Heilmann, Ernst, 226, 229
Heine, Heinrich, 70
Heine, Wolfgang, 217
Helldorf-Bedra, Otto von, 100–1
Hesse-Nassau, 3, 95, 153, 193, 195
Hessen-Cassel, 3, 153
Hessen-Darmstadt, 114, 134
Heydebrand und der Lasa, Ernst von, 86, 104
Himmler, Heinrich, 163, 260
Hindenburg, Paul von, 162, 201, 206, 227, 239–40, 257, 263–4
Hitler, Adolf, 11, 18–20, 27, 29–30, 34–5, 37, 146, 161–3, 165, 194, 205, 206, 227–8, 231–2, 235, 244–5, 247, 251, 253–5, 257–68, 303
Hohenzollern, House of, 2–3, 16, 32, 90, 153, 174, 191, 259–60, 266–7
Holy Roman Empire, 14, 83
Huber, Viktor A., 90, 92
Hugenberg, Alfred, 161–2, 228, 264
Huguenots, 56, 191
Humboldt, Alexander von, 68
Humboldt, Wilhelm von, 62

Imperial League, 178
Independent Social Democratic Party of Germany (USPD), 144, 157–8

INDEX

Italy, 57, 102, 250, 269

Jena-Auerstadt, battle of (1806), 45, 51, 109, 252
Jews, 52, 55, 101, 131, 136, 155, 247, 256, 301–2
  anti-Semitism, 100–2, 155
  Jewish historians, 27, 34
Junkers, 5, 11, 18, 30, 37, 101, 146–8, 153, 155, 161–3, 165, 211, 214, 258–61, 263–4, 271–2, 296

Kapp putsch (1919), 217
Karlsbad Decrees, 45, 58–9
Kautsky, Karl Johann, 130
Kleist, Heinrich von, 54
Kleist-Schmenzin, Ewald von, 162, 257, 269
Kleist-Wendisch-Tychow, Count Ewald von, 259
Köckritz, General Karl Leopold von, 51
Koerber, Victor von, 269
Königgrätz, battle of (1866), 9, 119, 121
Königsberg, 25, 27, 77, 129, 191, 207
Kottwitz, Baron Hans Ernst von, 63
Kotzebue, August von, 57, 60
'Kreisau Circle', 269
Kulturkampf, 7, 14–16, 153, 169, 173–83, 186–7, 193, 195, 200
Kurmark, 51, 189

Lassalle, Ferdinand, 94–5, 126, 129
Leipzig, 128, 131
  battle of (1813), 57
Leo XIII, Pope, 178
Leopold II of Austria, 44, 49
liberalism, 16, 54, 65, 72, 75, 79–80, 90–1, 94–5, 170–5, 187, 211
List, Friedrich, 110
Louis XVI of France, 43
Louis XVIII of France, 43–5
Louise, Queen (wife of Frederick William III), 51, 54, 56, 256
Lüdemann, Hermann, 219
Ludendorff, General Erich, 201
Lutheranism, 12, 60, 190–4

Magdeburg, 71, 79, 131
Malmö, treaty of, 80
Manstein, Field Marshal Erich von, 253, 269
Manteuffel, Edwin von, 80
Manteuffel, Hasso von, 252
Manteuffel, Otto von, 81–2, 84–5, 92
Mark, 79, 297
Marwitz, Friedrich August Ludwig von der, 52, 54
Marwitz, Johann Friedrich Adolph von der, 268
Marx, Karl, 21, 29, 75, 78, 94
Marxism, 125–6, 134, 157, 161–2
Mecklenburg-Schwerin, 3, 97, 152, 156, 158
Metternich, Prince Clemens von, 44–5, 55–8, 83, 114
Moltke, Count Helmuth Karl von, 121, 234–6, 241, 245, 250
Mönchen-Gladbach, 140, 180
Möser, Justus, 48
Müller, Adam, 54–5
Munich, 128, 130, 303
Münster, 193, 268

Napoleon I, 5, 43–4, 51, 56, 63, 70, 109, 200, 255, 256, 268
National Liberal Party, 98, 100, 102, 136, 139, 155, 172–3, 176–8, 182–5
National Rural League, 158, 160–1
National Union of Commercial Employees, 143
Navy League, 8, 105, 178, 186
Nazi Party (National Socialist German Workers Party) (NSDAP), 2, 16, 20, 27–9, 34–5, 37, 144–7, 155, 163–5, 205, 224–5, 227–8, 244–50, 303
  army and, 244–50, 261, 303–4
  'Prussianism' of, 20, 253–73, 304
  propaganda, 29
  racial policies, 188, 258, 267
  religion and, 189, 192, 201, 205–8
  rise of, 11–12, 18–19, 161–2
Nicholas I of Russia, 84
Niemöller, Martin, 199, 207

INDEX

North Atlantic Treaty Organisation (NATO), 35
North German Confederation, 94
Noske, Gustav, 219

Oder river, 150, 239

Paderborn, 177, 193, 204
Pan-German League, 105, 178
Papen, Franz von, 18, 162, 202, 212–13, 227–8, 263–4
Paris, 53, 69
  revolution in (1830), 88
Paulus, Field Marshal, 270
Pechel, Rudolf, 232
People's Association for Catholic Germany, 15, 180
Pfuel, Ernst von, 81
Philip II of Spain, 59
Pietism, 12, 49, 60
Pillnitz, Declaration of, 49–50
Pilsach, Baron Ernst Senfft von, 71
Pilsudski, Marshal, 268
Pius IX, Pope, 172
Poland, 2–3, 11, 13, 26, 35–6, 137, 139, 185, 201, 266, 268, 272, 297, 300
  division of, 32, 192
  German occupation of, 33
  historiography, 32–3
  'Polish Corridor', 204
  Polish immigration to Germany, 151–2
  Prussian rule of, 3
  universities of, 32
Pomerania, 16, 33, 58, 76, 79, 97, 150, 152, 157–8, 161–2, 193, 202, 204–6, 232, 239, 259–60, 272, 296–7, 303
Posen, 16, 140, 158, 193, 204
Potsdam, 33, 75, 80, 132, 201, 256, 267
Preuss, Hugo, 16
Prittwitz, General Karl Ludwig von, 74
Progressive Party of Prussia, 93, 172, 176, 187
Protestantism, 3–4, 10–15, 23, 70–1, 100–1, 128, 131, 135–7, 140–1, 145, 148, 153–5, 159–63, 169–87, 188–208, 256, 262, 301–2

'synodal' church order, 195–9
Prussia
  agriculture, 122–3, 146–65
  army, 5, 19–20, 44, 51, 61–2, 67, 81–2, 113, 121, 171, 194, 230–52, 303–4
  civil service, 217–21, 225, 228
  dissolution of, 1–2, 253, 266–7, 272
  dominance of Germany, 16–17, 22–40, 121, 211–29
  economy, 120–4
  historiography, 21–38, 295–6
  industrialization, 8, 69, 113, 123
  justice system, 221–25
  labour movement, 9–11, 126–45, 299
  Landtag, 7, 86–7, 92–3, 97–8, 103–4, 132, 134, 140, 175, 184, 212, 217, 219, 223–4, 226–7, 262, 264, 298
  Landwehr, 61–2, 242
  militarism, 23, 30, 34, 230–54
  National Assembly of, 76, 78, 81–2
  and Nazism, 253–73, 304
  nobility, 5, 7, 19–20, 90, 165
  peasantry, 11, 146–50, 158
  police, 213, 215–17
  political influence, 17
  population, 10, 69, 169
  Reform Movement, 5, 45–6, 89, 109, 237, 242, 263
  religion, 13–15, 169–208, 300–2
  'restoration party', 43–65
  revolutions (1848–50), 6, 45, 66–85, 89, 92, 297
  rural areas, 12
  trade policies, 115–18
  universities, 58
  urbanisation, 8–9, 69
  virtues, 2, 34
  and Weimar Republic, 17–18, 211–29

Quitzow, House of, 90

Radowitz, Joseph Maria von, 6, 70–1, 84, 87–8, 90–1, 94
Ranke, Leopold von, 50, 73
Reinhardt, General Walther, 240

INDEX

Rhine, river, 103
Rhineland, 10, 13–14, 70, 76, 83, 90, 137, 140, 142, 147, 153, 170–1, 173, 176, 182–3, 185, 190–4, 201–2, 207, 262, 300
Röhm, Ernst, 258–9
Romania, 102
Romanticism, 53–6, 64
Roon, Prince Albrecht von, 62
Rosenberg, Alfred, 260
Ruhr, 8, 10, 98, 133, 135–9, 141, 159, 180, 197, 300, 303
Rundstedt, Gerd von, 252, 263
Rural League, 11, 159
Rural People Movement, 160–1
Rural People's Party, 160
Russia (Soviet Union), 24, 27, 93, 102, 152, 165, 200, 234–5, 248–9, 254, 266, 270–2

Saarbrücken, 129
Saar, 131, 140
Savigny, Friedrich Carl von, 55
Saxony, 83, 90, 97–8, 113, 126, 138, 141, 149, 151, 193, 197, 199, 202, 206, 233, 239, 297
Sayn-Wittgenstein-Hohenstein, Prince Ludwig von, 57, 62–3
Scharf, Kurt, 205, 207
Scharnhorst, Gerhard von, 31, 256
Schilden, Baron, 51, 56
Schleicher, Kurt von, 18, 162, 227, 231, 263–4
Schleswig-Holstein, 3, 49, 80, 153, 160, 193, 297
Schmidt, Helmuth, 232
Schmidt, Hermann, 221–2
Schmitt, Carl, 212, 265
Schutzstaffel (SS), 245, 248, 260–1
Seeckt, Hans von, 240–1
Serbia, 102, 156
Severing, Carl, 218–20, 222, 229
Seydlitz, General von, 270, 273
Silesia, 10, 13, 33, 73, 76–7, 83, 90, 131, 135, 137, 139, 153, 158, 170, 191–2, 194, 202, 204, 206, 262, 267, 272

Simon, Saint, 94
Smith, Adam, 55
Society for the Eastern Marches, 105
Society of Jesus (Jesuits), 175, 184–5, 301
Söderblom, Nathan, 188–9, 200
Solingen, 129, 135
Spartacists, 158
Spengler, Oswald, 257
Stalin, Josef, 255, 266, 271
Stauffenberg, Count Claus von, 36
Stein, Baron Karl Freiherr vom-und-zum, 43, 46, 51–2, 63, 109, 229, 256, 270
Stockholm, 189, 201
Stoecker, Adolf, 100–2, 198
Stolberg, Count Friedrich von, 49
St Petersburg, 69
Strelitz, 3, 152, 156, 158
Stresemann, Gustav, 36
Sturmabteilung (SA), 206, 255–6, 259, 262, 266
Stuttgart, 138, 143
Sweden, 188–9
Switzerland, 84, 102
Sybel, Heinrich von, 21

Talleyrand, Charles-Maurice de, 44
Teplitz Agreement (1819), 45
Thälmann, Ernst, 264
Tilsit, Peace of (1807), 51
Treitschke, Heinrich von, 68, 172, 260
Tresckow, Henning von, 268–9
Trier, 177

United States of America, 84, 115–16, 129, 152, 186, 231

Vansittart, Sir Robert, 267
Versailles, Treaty of (1919), 11, 13, 28, 192, 201, 204–5, 240, 242–3
Vienna, Congress of, 70

Wagener, Hermann, 7, 79, 87–8, 91, 94–5, 99
Waldeck, Benedikt, 76, 81
Wartenburg, Count Peter Hans York von, 269

INDEX

Wartenburg, General York von, 268
Waterloo, battle of (1815), 20
Weimar Republic, 11, 16–18, 24–7, 144–5, 157–61, 163–4, 189, 192, 198, 202–3, 230–1, 251, 255–7, 259, 262, 268, 272, 299, 303
  historiography, 24–7
West Prussia, 16, 26, 140, 158, 193, 204, 272
Westphalia, 13, 83, 118, 121, 136, 147, 153–4, 162, 170–1, 173, 176, 182–3, 185, 190–4, 201–2, 206–7, 264, 300
Wilhelm I, King of Prussia and Emperor of Germany, 3, 7, 50, 61–2, 73–4, 84, 93, 171, 177
Wilhelm II, Emperor of Germany, 4, 23, 101, 105, 184–6, 190, 233, 256, 266
  abdication of, 13, 16

Windthorst, Ludwig, 3, 173
Woellner, Johann Christof von, 49
Wolff, SS-General Karl, 269
World War I, 11, 15–16, 24–6, 30, 86–8, 121, 129, 131, 138, 140, 142–3, 151–2, 156–7, 163, 232, 238–40, 242, 301–2
World War II, 2, 19, 21, 27–9, 146, 164–5, 190, 208, 267–73, 302
Wrangel, General Friedrich von, 81
Württemberg, 114, 119, 122, 199, 232

Yalta, conference of, 33
Young Plan, 161–2, 223

Zollverein (Prussian Customs Union), 9, 109–25, 298–9